Judgments of Love in Criminal Justice

Farhad Malekian

Judgments of Love in Criminal Justice

Springer

Farhad Malekian
Institute of International Criminal Law
Uppsala, Sweden

ISBN 978-3-319-46899-0 ISBN 978-3-319-46900-3 (eBook)
DOI 10.1007/978-3-319-46900-3

Library of Congress Control Number: 2016958570

Printed on acid-free paper

This Springer imprint is published by Springer Nature
The registered company is Springer International Publishing AG
The registered company address is: Gewerbestrasse 11, 6330 Cham, Switzerland

To my mother the blind Lady Justice
To my father the Gavel of Justice
And my tribute to the dearly beloved
perpetual bouquet
0214 and our buds 0912, 0623, 0604, 0308
Kapca

Preface

I initiate and end almost all of my lectures and examination questions with the phrase "with love and respect". This phrase brings all students close together and encapsulates the *raison d'être* that the lectures highlighted a *tangible award for the understanding of law*. I most often received a standing ovation from the students as I stood in front of them with the globe of love.

While teaching law courses to inmates incarcerated in one of the notorious Swedish prisons, the *Anstalten Kumla*, I decided on one occasion to deliver a lecture face-to-face. One of the head guards drove me to the prison and asked me if he could give me some information about my students and the crimes for which they had been convicted. 'No thanks', I replied. He repeated his question again. My answer was the same. He ultimately decided to tell me, even though I did not have any curiosity to know. I succeeded in not hearing his words with a variety of tricks. While driving me back in the evening, the guard wished to confess about our meeting in the morning: "if you would really like to know my heart's feelings, I would like to open all those gates, take down the whole of the barbed wire, and free all those *poor boys*. What we are doing against them all is much more unrealistic than what they did against us. *The period in the prison will not serve to teach them love, but hate*."

My late father was and is my true academic campus. It was he who irrevocably tutored me not to lose "self-restraint." *My ethical philosophy in a nutshell is* that the spirit of the law has to be good; the metaphysical elements of justice have to be rational; the basis of morality has to be to serve *without expectations* of gain; faith in humanity has to rise from the chambers of a compassionate heart; and the purity of loving brotherhood/sisterhood/family unity is under no circumstances for sale. Using any form of power for personal advantage not only falls short of the spirit of the rule of law but humiliates the integrity of the dead and the victims. Regrettably, a number of lawyers in the field are not only millionaires, but even multimillionaires—the innocent victims and 'human rights law' itself have become the cargo of incomes. Nietzsche correctly says, "Of all that is written, I love only what a person has written with his own blood."

I have suffered far too much and far too long for the voice of justice and love in one of the most well-known democratic countries in the world. *My irrevocable decision is that justice is not for sale*. Nelson Mandela, a lawyer by profession, aptly asserts, "The greatest glory in living lies not in never falling, but in rising every time we fall." The American lawyer, Martin Luther King, the composer of songs of spiritual love and the originator of *I have a dream* reflects that "life's most persisting and urgent question is: What are you doing for others?" Similarly, the Indian lawyer, Mahatma Gandhi, correctly puts "you must not lose faith in humanity. Humanity is like an ocean; if a few drops of the ocean are dirty, the ocean does not become dirty." And, ultimately, Professor Mohammed Mossadegh, a Persian father of democracy and human rights, a friend of my own father, thoughtfully demanded of himself, "If I sit silently, I have sinned." Those who love justice with truth have to suffer.

There cannot be words adequate enough to communicate my heartfelt appreciation to my four sisters who have devoted all their love in order that I survive after a sequence of undeserved tragedies in my life.

I am deeply thankful to Professor Albin Eser, the former head of the Max Planck Institute of Foreign and International Criminal law (MPI) and a former judge at the ICTY, for his comments and his valuable time. It is important for me to state here that he is not only an established positivist but also, having substantive knowledge of naturalism and righteousness in his writings, a wholly trustworthy person. *I would also like* to extend my sincerest personal *thanks* and admiration to the brilliant philosophical knowledge of Professor David A.J. Richards from the Faculty of Law, University of New York. Richards is the pioneer of a faculty of love against injustice. However, responsibilities for errors remain mine alone.

I also wish to extend *face-to-face* my *sincere* thanks to Dr. Johanna Rinceanu, who I may call 'the MPI *angel*'—a woman of great intellectual substance, integrity of knowledge in criminal law, as well as being at once gentle like soft water and vivacious like a waterfall. Her Italian husband must be proud to have her at the centre of their family unit. For the friendly discussions of law, I thank the professors of criminal law in the Departament de Dret Penal, Facultate de Dret Universitat de Valencia. They are Professors Emiliano Borja Jiménez, Asunción Colás Turégano, Dra Elena Górriz Royo, Ricardo Juan Sanchez, Juan Carlos Carbonell Mateu, and Alberto Alonso.

Many other professors of criminal law and researchers all over the world have encouraged me that writing this book constitutes a duty for the treatment of the ill body of our criminal justice. They have my full thanks. I am also deeply thankful to Anke Seyfried, the law editor at Springer, for her efforts and cooperation in the publication of this volume. Thanks also to the very positive cooperation of the librarians at the MPI, particularly Mrs. Elisabeth Martin.

The Islamic political philosopher and jurist Al-Farabi, who is known in the West as Alpharabius (872–951), concludes that "a just city should favour justice and the just, hate tyranny and injustice, and give them both their just deserts." Alexander Pope, the English poet (1688–1744), expresses the same sentiment in his proclamation, "*curse on all laws but those which love has made*."

Farhad Malekian
Accomplished in the Institute of International
Criminal Law, Uppsala, Sweden
Departament de Dret Penal, Facultate
de Dret Universitat de Valencia, Spain
Max Planck Institute of Foreign and
International Criminal law, Fribourg, Germany
February 14 and July 23, 2017

Introduction

Most national, regional, or international conflicts, in which millions of people in the world lose their lives, are the result of the misapprehension and misinterpretation of the law and the absence in the rule of law of love for human beings, for justice, and for real democracy.[1] This is the truth: justice and love. What separates us from the strength that allows us to love humanity, and instead leads to the enforcement of the system of international criminal law, is the ideological use of force, which saps the power of love and trust between groups, nations, and states and leads to ever-increasing conflict between nations.[2] This means we ignore the moral obligations, whether integrated into our culture or natural law, which we ought to perform.[3]

It is at such moments that we have to teach law with love in order that the future generation of lawyers and judges will realise that peace with justice can never be achieved as long as the concept of law is not performed and interpreted with love. They have to promulgate these principles to convince the population of the world that alienable rights, law, and love are an integral part of one another, and the science of law is incapable of adequately describing any of them in the absence of the others. Although we understand that love is not equivalent to law, it has a particular sense within the human mind that orients the role of objective justice towards achieving the protection of our essential humanity. That is why the appropriate Islamic law says, 'if they kill, this does not require that you kill. The spiritual gratification, which exists in forgiveness, does not exist in revenge.' One may compare the institution of forgiveness in the relevant law with the institution of non-trial justice, truth and reconciliation commissions, amnesty, and restorative justice. "Humanity is not saved by ideological manifestos, but by the 'acts/of kindness and of *love*.'"[4]

---

[1]Mohammad Taghi Malekian, *The Voice of Zanjan* (the Newspaper published by my father in Persian language – the chief editor, 1952–1953).

[2]Ibid.

[3]Ibid.

[4]Ward (2001), p. 941 at 946 (citing Wordsworth 1977). *Cf.* Ruiz (1999). Consult *also* Lessa and Payne (2012).

The United Nations' educational system therefore has a leadership responsibility for teaching law with an attitude of love in all angles of its remit. The objective is to make the people of the world conscious of the horrendous consequences of violations, aggressions, or resorting to the use of force against them. As Bertrand Russell aptly puts it, "*The good life is one inspired by love and guided by knowledge*." Here Russell means surely, *inter alia*, that even if we have the freedom of expression to hate one another, it is our duty, in the first instance, to obtain knowledge.

Although Shakespeare did not study law, his discussions of the law show a profound knowledge of legal terminology and a sympathy with the universal principles underlying the rule of law, whether in Europe, the United States, or in the Islamic world. "*The first thing we do, let's kill all the lawyers*," that is, if they do not express love for the pure philosophy of reasonable justice. "*When law can do no right, let it be lawful that law bar no wrong: Law cannot give my child his kingdom here, for he that holds his kingdom holds the law*." This passage highlights two significant questions for our discussion: what are the reasons behind the use of force by administrators of public international law? In addition, why is the system of law concerning the identification of the use of force monopolised by the legal provisions of the United Nations and the ICC? The answer to both questions may simply be that what is really missing in the process of justice is love of law for the sake of human dignity and the truth.

In addition, the new generation of lawyers *ought* to be educated to realise that the canon of real love for humanity in the world does not come from International Human Rights Law, the International Humanitarian Law covering armed conflicts, genocide, torture, and apartheid or discrimination treaties. Neither does it arise from the regulations within the Statutes of the International Criminal Courts or tribunals, or the provisions of other criminal laws but by the prevention of violations from the very infancy of their existence with the strength of love of justice for one another. Therefore, this work introduces the norm of love as the most significant norm of law, criminal law, and criminal justice. Following this approach, we will advance towards real justice, develop our knowledge, and secure the future generations of humankind from the consequences of criminal activities. Personal interests have to be accounted for nil if justice with love is going to survive for all of us.

References

Lessa, F., & Payne, L. A. (2012). *Amnesty in the age of human rights accountability: Comparative and international perspectives*. Cambridge: Cambridge University Press.

Ruiz, D. M. (1999). *The mastery of love*.

Ward, I. (2001). Universal jurisprudence and the case for legal humanism. *Alberta Law Review, 38*, 941

Wordsworth, W. (1977). Lines composed a few miles above Tintern Abbey. In J. O. Hayden (Ed.), *1 POEMS*

Contents

Part I
The Corpus of Love in the Chambers of Criminal justice

It may sound like a departure from the traditional process of legal reasoning to lecture about the philosophy of love in connection with criminal rules, principles, and justice. Many will react against this very strongly. A considerable number of international lawyers may believe that the inspiration of love is merely hypothetical, and that, in addition, it is not possible to formulate a lucid theory on the concept of law.[1] The notion of law relies heavily on its multilingualism as an interpretation strategy in contemporary international relations.[2] In reality, not every lawyer in the world speaks an identical language of law or has a similar interpretation of the rule of law. The same is true in the case of the choice of terminologies. Not everyone uses the same expression. However, the word 'love' should be the final description of the guiding principle behind the dialect of the language of any law.[3] If the law is written and interpreted with love for human beings, the position on the use of any form of force in any system of law will be significantly modified and will concede its place to the primacy of the rule of law, guided by love, in the peaceful settlement of national, regional, or international disputes. Augustinian scholarship on the theological or naturalism theory also assures us of human capacities for loyalty, belief, perseverance, and love, and defines human nature as the *imago dei*, which means one who has the capacity for loving rightly and "the only way of hearing God's voice."[4] As Charles Dickens says:

> A wonderful fact to reflect upon, that every human creature is constituted to be that profound secret and mystery to every other. A solemn consideration, when I enter a great city by night, that every one of those darkly clustered houses encloses its own secret; that every room in every one of them encloses its own secret; that every beating heart in the hundreds of thousands of breasts there, is, in some of its imaginings, a secret to the heart nearest it! Something of the awfulness, even of Death itself, is preferable to this. No more

---

[1]Schaumburg-Müller (2009), pp. 11–12. Zahle (2005).

[2]Zahle (2005), p. 285.

[3]See Atwell (2008), p. 495. Available at http://digitalcommons.pace.edu/cgi/viewcontent.cgi?article=1548&context=lawfaculty (Accessed September 12, 2015).

[4]Richards (2016), p. 110. See *also* Elshtain (2006), p. 154.

> can I turn the leaves of this dear book that I loved, and vainly hope in time to read it all. No more can I look into the depths of this unfathomable water, wherein, as momentary lights glanced into it, I have had glimpses of buried treasure and other things submerged. It was appointed that the book should shut with a spring, forever and forever, when I had read but a page. . . . My friend is dead, my neighbour is dead, my love, the darling of my soul, is dead; it is the inexorable consolidation and perpetuation of the secret that was always in that individuality, and which I shall carry in mine to my life's end.[5]

By the term 'love' we do not mean holistic love of God, nor romantic love, but the love which exists as a powerful tool to achieve justice or the most powerful energy that exists in human nature.[6] Its purpose is to attain the good of man by all means, the good of our neighbours, and the rightful norms of justice. Part I deals with several concepts of criminal law and the anatomy of the significant positive influence of love in the system of criminal law. It provides the first primary definition of the concept of the norm of love in the criminal justice system and its role in the theory of rule of law and the rule of love. In other words, this part addresses theories of legality, morality, and love.

Most of Part I therefore focuses on the norm of love as a powerful norm in the system of criminal law and public international law. The norm exists in the structure of international human rights law, European Union law, the Arab Charter on human rights law, the African Charter of Human and Peoples' Rights, the American Convention on Human Rights, and many other bodies of law in the world. It sometimes overlaps with moral obligations, meaning the duties which one owes to a set of values and authentic justice. This part supports not only positivist views, but also moralist views, with the reservation that there is also an implicit third view on the enforcement of legal positivism and moral legalism. This latter view is the existence of the norm of love as the strongest feature of the implementation of the principle of justice when the international criminal justice system no longer functions for the enforcement of its intentions. We will analyse different theories as to their understanding of the position of the norm of love in our international legal system. A comprehensive philosophical account of Western and non-Western theories will be our focus, and the intention is to make it clear that the similarities between different legal systems should take priority with the purpose of reducing international violations.

The chapters in this part conclude that the norm of love is a norm which concerns all states, and states are under international obligations to follow certain principles that are significant for all states and should not violate those principles. These principles concern all states, Western and non-Western. Consequently, we will

---

[5]The Night Shadows in Charles Dickens, A Tale of Two Cities A Story of the French Revolution (1859).

[6]The term "love" is a complex theory. According to one writer, there are "four kinds of love in Western tradition. One is sex, or what we call lust, libido. The second is Eros, the drive of love to procreate or create--the urge, as the Greeks put it, toward higher forms of being and relationship. A third is philia, or friendship, brotherly love. The fourth is agape or caritas as the Latin's called it, the love which is devoted to the welfare of the other, the prototype of which is the love of God for man." May (1969), p. 37.

examine the discussions on the prerequisite for the existence of the norm of love present in most bodies of law, such as criminal law, criminal justice, Jewish law, Islamic law, European law, Scandinavian law, United States law, international criminal law, international humanitarian law, and the system of international criminal justice. This part stresses the fact that criminal justice has to follow the principle of love for justice if it is going to be secured and trusted by an increasing proportion of the population of the world.

References

Atwell, B. L. (2008). The Jurisprudence of Love. *University of Detroit Mercy Law Review, 85*, 495.

Elshtain, J. B. (2006). Concrete levels of being and their political implications. In D. Browning (Ed.), *Universalism vs. Relativism: Making moral judgments in a changing, pluralistic, and threatening world*. England: Rowman and Littlefield Publishers.

May, R. (1969). *Love and will*. W W Norton.

Richards, D. A. J. (2016). *Why love leads to justice: Love across the boundaries*. New York: Cambridge University Press.

Schaumburg-Müller, S. (2009). *Fem Retsfilosofiske Tester*. Jurist- og Økonomforbund forlag.

Zahle, H. (2005). *Praktisk restfilosofi*. Christian Ejlers' Forlag.

Chapter 1
Surveillance of the Norm of Love in Criminal Law

1.1 Criminal Law

We will come back time and again to a few key terms in this volume. They are "crime", "legal", "moral", "criminal justice", and "love". The alarm clocks of the terms "crime", "legal", and "moral" are ringing, but it seems that no one is truly listening. Almost in parallel, one can refer to the term "criminal justice" as constituting the most miserable institution. The unjust nature of criminal justice in practice and its impact on natural law justice is like Hitler and Stalin's cruel marching music colliding with Édith Piaf's harmonious voice—*non, je ne regrette rien*. Natural law justice works for the *reestablishment of vanished rights for the sake of justice*.[1] The last but the most honourable term is *"love"*—let me echo her name again—the *norm love*. This is the most rational term that has to be established and integrated, with certain measures, into the terms "criminal law" and "criminal justice," if justice is to be trusted and not misused by those with power. One of the world's most romantic voices, Tom Jones, sang about "*sex bomb*"—I will demonstrate the necessity of the completion of our criminal law with a *love bomb*.

Allow me here to advocate the sincere words of Darius the Great (549–486 BCE), ruler of the Achaemenid Empire, who foreigners called "the lawgiver": "*What is right I love and what is not right I hate*."[2] He goes further and declares that "it is not my pleasure, that the lower one suffers injustice because of the higher one, nor is it my pleasure, that the higher one suffers injustice because of the lower

[1]Let us to say, the "ethical judgment of our inadequate responses to political injustice." Richards (2016), p. 120; See *also* https://www.youtube.com/watch?v=Q3Kvu6Kgp88; https://www.youtube.com/watch?v=vwe3CzWZ4Bg; https://www.youtube.com/watch?v=iEMggo5o0FM; https://www.youtube.com/watch?v=6-CA8jp6yoY; https://www.youtube.com/watch?v=ToB0Gez3Hdw (Accessed May 31 and June 1, 2015). See *also* Haveman et al. (2013).

[2]Drapkin (1989), p. 95; Starr (1965), p. 280; Olmstead (1948), p. 125.

F. Malekian, *Judgments of Love in Criminal Justice*,
DOI 10.1007/978-3-319-46900-3_1

one. What is right, that is my pleasure."[3] He therefore condemns the "man who lies."[4] "*Strong words from the king of the World.*"[5] These words, which are inscribed in the Naqsh-Rustem in Persia, are based on the Ahura-Mazda lectures on an ethical faith centred on the God of light and truth. According to him, human beings must support the good by their deeds in order to overcome the spirits of darkness and witness a good last judgment on their relations. Love for the truth, purity, and perseverance in good deeds constitutes love for the soul of the dignity of justice.

The Persian Emperor, Cyrus the Great (576–530 BC) expressed similar opinion before Darius. This is the King whose 'just empire' and loves for justice confirmed by Thomas Jefferson and Benjamin Franklin (the American founding fathers of independence) to Julius Caesar, Alexander the Great and the Italian philosopher Niccolò Machiavelli (1469–1527). For Cyrus, love was a norm in the service of humanity, justice and peace. He ordered the *Ancient* Declaration of Human Rights Law which is known *Cyrus Cylinder* and gave freedom with full love and respect to the Jews or the Babylonian captivity. He clearly maintains that "Whenever you can, act as a liberator. Freedom, dignity, wealth–these three together constitute the greatest happiness of humanity. If you bequeath all three to your people, their love for you will never die."

Criminalisation of conduct has become our duty, and pursuing our duties has contributed to criminalisation. We have not considered in any depth that upholding justice and humanity while reducing violations does not fit with the wide-ranging replacement of the standards of morality and our social habits by this criminalisation or with sincerely expressing the norm of love without fearing the consequences which may occur. In speaking about real justice with love, one is always living under threat, whether from those who are in power or from those who are the servants of the power through the action of law. Criminal law has therefore been labelled as "the pathology of civilisation."[6] From another view, it consists mainly of "la philosophie, l' étude historique, la sociologie du droit et l'épistémologie."[7]

It cannot be denied that at first glance criminal law is one of the concrete arenas of law for the restoration of justice.[8] It is described as being "dogmatic law."[9] That is law creating for the state the right of punishment.[10] On a second glance, one may require a substantial amount of time to understand why the offender committed the criminal conduct. One may debate many motives. At third glance, we ought to apprehend one day the reality that our criminal laws are the most treacherous

[3]Voegelin and Franz (2000), pp. 207–208.

[4]Thornton (2011), p. 18.

[5]Walton (2008), p. 50.

[6]Cohen (1949), p. 1025.

[7]Raoult (2011), p. 26.

[8]Andernaes (1974), p. 1.

[9]Maeland (2013), p. 29.

[10]Skeie (1937), p. 1; consult *also* Eser (2007). www.freidok.uni-freiburg.de/volltexte/6198.

offenders against human civilisation. What tool is more dangerous than criminal law itself? The chief question here is what constitutes the substance of criminal law. A satisfactory discussion on criminal law deals with all ethical issues of the law. These include the principle of equality, the principle of adjustment of conflicting interests between different parties and their moral presentation of the law, and the principle of social responsibility as well as the significant question of solidarity in connection with personality.[11]

One may state that criminal law is a body of norms, rules, regulations, principles, legislations, statutes or cases, which suggests which conduct, behaviour, or omissions constitute a violation or violations of the body of criminal law. The part of criminal law, which deals with the definitions of crime and punishment, is substantive criminal law.[12] That fragment of the law, which concerns the way in which we apply the entire system of criminal law from the initiation of discovering a wrongful conduct to the judgment of the court, embodies the procedural aspects of criminal law.[13] *In other words, this part of criminal law* deals with the set of rules leading to a considerable number of proceedings by which the government's juridical machinery implements substantive *criminal law*. Thus, criminal law may present certain norms that symbolise the substantive and procedural language of criminal law. Both parts are an integral part of one another, and one cannot function without the existence of the other. One may liken this to the structure of a car: the criminal law is the whole body of the car, and the wheels constitute the cause of its movement. These wheels are together the procedural aspects of criminal law. If one of the wheels does not function, the entire system of criminal law may crash and may not be possible to apply.

From the time of its establishment, the first purpose of criminal law has been to identify criminals and bring them before certain courts for the prosecution and punishment of wrongful conduct. That purpose was and still is one of the chief aims of criminal law in the world despite struggles to modify the intentions of criminal law. Notable operational amendments within the framework of criminal law are the abolition of capital punishment, prohibition of torture, and the settlement of the principle of *ne bis in idem*.[14] A further development is the recognition that keeping a person in slavery or a condition of servitude is a serious criminal offence. All three offences, which were previously officially permitted in the law and the practice of hegemonic states, such as in the United Kingdom's colonies, constitute serious crimes in the structure and processes of criminal law today.

However, the world's systems of criminal law have not properly implemented any one of these three leading principles of criminal law. Capital punishment is still widely practised throughout much of the world, although the European Union

[11]Cohen (1949), p. 990.

[12]For instance, see the Danish criminal law Langsted et al. (2011), p. 18.

[13]*Id.*

[14]Schabas (2002), pp. 1–3.

member states have abolished it.[15] As yet, the function of the principle of *ne bis in idem* is not entirely settled among European states. Above all, the use of life imprisonment serves as the highest level of our morality in the policy of our criminal law and typically replaces the death penalty. Equally, the institution of slavery has been camouflaged with modern modus operandi but the same is true of torture. Meanwhile, trafficking in persons, including the trafficking of women and children across national borders with the intention of prostitution, has actually increased.

In spite of these facts, international criminal law is developing rapidly, as the escalating number of cross border crimes means that these borders will soon be almost impossible to protect. Clear examples are the development of cybercrimes that are becoming impracticable to control and new methods of armed conflict that have created unexpected heights of sophistication with the use of cyberspace as a theatre for hostilities. The boundaries of application of the traditional territoriality principle in criminal law are not so useful, because the computerization of systems of international relations has created the possibility of committing various crimes in different territories. Crimes committed in Bangladesh may affect the American legal order, and crimes committed in China may affect the criminal system of the United Kingdom or *vice versa* in both examples. The only alternative, which is itself a conundrum, is more and more criminalisation of new acts, since offences are not limiting themselves to a particular scope of criminality and they are increasing with the development of technology. One of the reasons for this may be that the enforcement of ethical, cultural, and moral obligations is decreasing rapidly. This is due to the fact that most individuals are motivated solely by economic gain, and the great majority of serious crimes have economic roots.

1.2 Criminal Responsibility

We should pay particular attention to the dissimilarities between, on the one hand, the notion of international crimes and their inhumane and unjust nature, and on the other hand, crimes committed under national criminal law as well as international human rights law. However, all of these criminal conducts or infractions may overlap in nature. The language of the Pre-Trial Chamber of the ICC illustrates the demarcations between these crimes. It says that:

> There are, in law and in the existing systems of criminal justice in the world, essentially two different categories of crimes which are crucial in the present case. There are, on the one side, *international crimes of concern to the international community as a whole,* in particular genocide, crimes against humanity, and war crimes pursuant to articles 6, 7 and 8 of the Statute. There are, on the other side, common crimes, albeit of a serious nature, prosecuted by national criminal justice systems... (a) demarcation line must be drawn between international crimes and human rights infractions; between international crimes

[15] Consult Morrow (2002); see *also* Novak (2014), pp. 31–32, 73–74, 125–126.

> and ordinary crimes, between those crimes subject to international jurisdiction and those punishable under domestic penal legislation.[16]

The system of international criminal law has long struggled to bring the perpetrators of international crimes under its purview for prosecution and punishment.[17] States have enforced the system nationally and internationally.[18] This is particularly evident in the case of individual criminal responsibility.[19] The laws of both the international criminal tribunals conducted after the Second World War, namely Nuremberg and Tokyo, were drafted and implemented for the prosecution or accountability of individuals who were guilty of violations of crimes against humanity, war crimes, and crimes against peace. The system of international criminal law has even enlarged the concepts of these crimes into other internationally criminally wrongful conducts such as genocide, aggression, apartheid, and torture.[20] However, the nature of these crimes may overlap and may frequently be impossible to separate. For all these, one can refer to the judgments of courts dealing with the clarification of different categories of international crimes.[21]

Neither these courts nor the international criminal tribunals established in recent decades, such as the ICTY, ICTR, or SCSL, could bring the question of state criminality inside their courtrooms.[22] The idea was and still is taboo. This policy of the courts does not, however, mean that the concept of the international criminal responsibility of states does not exist. The idea is as old as the history of wars itself. In the historical development of the system of international law, when a state or states waged war against another, the idea of punishing a state for failing to fulfil its obligations was always behind the conflict.[23]

The question of the criminal responsibility of states and their governments is more controversial when it comes to the jurisdiction of the permanent International Criminal Court. The ICC in fact has no jurisdiction on state crimes.[24] Although the

---

[16]Pre-Trial Chamber II, "Decision Pursuant to Article 15 of the Rome Statute on the Authorization of an Investigation into the Situation in the Republic of Kenya, ICC-01/09-19-Corr, p. 87, para 8 and 65. Italics added.

[17]Cryer et al. (2010), p. 109.

[18]Eskeland (2000), pp. 162–169. See also Rinceanu (2011a), pp. 281–296. Also Rinceanu (2011b), pp. 227–238.

[19]Hirst (2003), pp. 236–281. Eskeland (2000), pp. 162–169; see *also* Eser (2008), pp. 863–893. www.freidok.uni-freiburg.de/volltexte/6318.

[20]Consult several relevant articles on Darcy and Powderly (2010).

[21]Robert Cryer, 'The Ad Hoc Tribunals and the Law of Command Responsibility: Aquite Earthquake' in Darcy and Powderly (2010), pp. 159–183.

[22]The reference has solely been on joint criminal responsibility; see Mohamed Shahabudeen, 'Judicial Creativity and Joint Criminal Enterprise' in Darcy and Powderly (2010), pp. 184–203.

[23]In the conclusion of my first book on international criminal law (1985), I drafted the concept of international criminality of states in seven articles in order to facilitate the future development of the concept (pp. 195–197). For the concept of international criminal responsibility of states see Malekian (1985).

[24]*Id.*

International Law Commission discussed the notion of the international criminal responsibility of states, the notion in its Article 19 has mostly a symbolic rather than practical significance.[25] This means that the development of the concept of the criminal responsibility of states has settled in the draft proposals of the Commission and not in the international criminal courts.[26] The theory is very simple: states are not prepared to admit the concept of their criminal responsibility.[27]

In any event, by the concept of international criminal responsibility of states, we are talking about the cumulative responsibility of certain organs of the state in question that have prepared, participated in, and committed criminal conduct.[28] By collective responsibility, I am not referring to the traditional concept but a concept under which states' individuals have *jointly* participated in the decisions of the state and their implementation.[29] As the Appeal Chamber of the ICTY asserts, "A State can act in international law directly through governmental authorities and officials, or indirectly through individuals or organisations who, while not being official agents of the government, receive from it some power or assignment to perform acts on its behalf such that they become de facto agents."[30] This means that, with the concept of the criminal responsibility of states, the complete international legal personality of the state is under question and under investigation within the philosophy of criminal law.[31]

What is significant for the question of refusing to acknowledge the criminal responsibility of certain states, for instance the non-criminalisation of possession of atomic bombs by some states and prohibition in other states, is that there is not yet sufficient understanding of the fact that force or threat of force cannot create love for justice.[32] The heart of justice—I repeat it again and again—the heart of justice is lost. We must recognise that the norm of love for true justice is absent in the system of international criminal law, and the legal body of justice is fundamentally mistreated.[33] Here, with the norm of love as an integral norm of international criminal law, we censure state criminal conducts at an international level.[34] Therefore, the norm of love means a norm which is mediated solely via justice, and criminal justice cannot be trusted in its absence or survive long without its presence.[35]

---

[25]For entities criminal liability see Rinceanu (2016), pp. 407–418.

[26]*Id.*

[27]Farhad Malekian, International Criminal Responsibility in Bassiouni (1999), pp. 192–221.

[28]*Id.*

[29]*Id.*

[30]Often quoted from the Appeals Chamber in the *Tadi* jurisdiction. Majority Opinion para. 8. ICTY, *Prosecutor v. Zlatko Aleksovski*, Case No.: IT-95-14/1-A (24 March 2000). Available at http://www.icty.org/x/cases/aleksovski/acjug/en/ale-asj000324e.pdf (Accessed April 4, 2015).

[31]*Id.*

[32]Malekian (2015a), pp. 591–628; Shah-Kazemi (2014), pp. 73–101; Fouladvand (2012).

[33]*Id.*, pp. 593–594.

[34]*Id.*, p. 603.

[35]*Id.*, p. 601.

1.3 Types of Criminal Laws

To speak of the norm of love in the system of criminal law or criminal justice is not only 'unconventional' but also as strange as it may sound. It is even more troublesome when one puts the word 'love' into actual practice for criminal lawyers. For the rule of law, one has to learn to identify criminal offences from other provisions by referring to their particular characteristics and see what the norm of love can do concerning certain criminal offences. This task is not only difficult but also very elusive, based on the fact that criminal law still constitutes a basic plethora of laws in most societies and has far to go to become uniform as one law all over the world. That is why the number of offences is very high within most disciplines and varies from one region to another and from one country to another. Having considered this, I have distinguished three types of criminal law. They are *normative* criminal law, *political* criminal law, and *detective* criminal law. At first sight, it seems that all three concepts of criminal law are the same. However, this is not true, and there is a clear distinction between these three concepts, although they are panoptical but not identical.

1.3.1 Normative Criminal Law

The *normative criminal law* is the criminal law forum which deals with the traditional standard of criminal law and criminal justice. This criminal law is legalised and applied under different legislations by different states. The concept of criminal responsibility constitutes its core. This body of normative criminal law is the collection of legal cases or legal statutes describing the various concepts of criminal offences as applied by the courts. Its boundaries come from the traditions of common law or civil law systems. They are known as adversarial or inquisitorial systems. However, the degree of criminal responsibility is not solely shaped by the normative concept but also by an evaluative assessment of the moral character displaced in criminal conduct. The procedural aspect of the normative criminal law varies from country to country; however, there is a clear tendency among the member states of the European Union to create a comprehensive procedural criminal system. This is, however, quite different in other countries in the world.

Generally speaking, a legal system must respect many principles of criminal jurisdiction in the implementation of criminal proceedings. These are such principles as accusation on authentic evidence, arrest based on proper and impartial order, and the time limit under which a person may be kept in custody. In any event, the legal authorities must conduct the first hearing without any unnecessary delay. A number of criminal jurisdictions impose a twenty-four-hour limit on initial detention before a hearing. However, a prosecutor may extend this limit if there are certain unclear answers to questions or arrest is carried out on a day before a holiday. Nevertheless, the length of arrest has to follow certain regulations of the given jurisdiction and should not violate international regulations however it is done.

It is a basic principle of all criminal proceedings that the accused shall enjoy the right to a speedy and public trial by an impartial prosecutor and judge. Authorities should inform the accused of the nature and cause of the accusation. The accused has the right to cross-examine the witnesses testifying against her/him. In addition to this, the legal authorities should give the accused the right to obtain witnesses in her/his favour. In all criminal proceedings, the legal authorities of criminal jurisdiction should provide the accused the assistance of counsel for her/his defence. As I have stated above, criminal proceeding forms the wheels of substantive criminal law, and these are essential for the implementation of an unbiased outcome.

1.3.2 Political Criminal Law

Political criminal law should not be confused with political crime, although both may have some shared roots. Political criminal law was historically the act of the monopolisation of the definition of criminal law by central power.[36] In other words, political power demonstrates its monopoly of law by underlining "which crimes are permitted."[37] Political criminal law is the same as normative criminal law, but its boundaries of application are sometimes much stronger than those of normative criminal law. This is because the latter is based on the concept of different norms that are created under different processes, whether by legislators or by case law, whilst the former is the forum in which the political parties see the notion of criminal law and liability for criminal offences. For instance, English criminal law is traditionally "not product of any principled inquiry or consistent application of certain criteria, but largely dependent on the fortunes of successive governments, on campaigns in the mass media, on the activities of various pressure groups."[38] Governments like "control over punishment policy" with the assumption that "the severity of punishment will be effective—because it is within their power to increase punishment levels and it sounds good."[39] Further:

> There is little sense that the decision to introduce a new offence should only be made after certain conditions have been satisfied, little sense that making conduct criminal is a step of considerable social significance. It is this unprincipled and chaotic construction of the criminal law that prompts the question whether it is a lost cause. From the point of governments, it is clearly not a lost cause... But from any principled viewpoint there are

[36]Sundin (1992), p. 13.

[37]Alexius (1997), p. 15.

[38]Ashworth (2013), p. 2.

[39]Ashworth (2006), p. 68.

> important issues – of how the criminal law ought to be shaped, of what its social significance should be, of when it should be used and when not- which are simply not being addressed in the majority of instances.[40]

Political criminal law may sometimes negate normative criminal law and may sometimes aggravate its concept. Several groups of politicians in the world are influential in the national or international criminal justice system. This means that the jurisdiction and procedure of criminal law may come under the criminal control of politicians according to their individual or collective interests. Here, the term "jurisdiction" consists of four requirements. These are subject matter (ratione materiae), which refers to the jurisdiction of the court over the nature of the case; temporal (ratione temporis), which refers to the prescribed time limitations; personal (ratione personae), referring to the jurisdiction of the court over the person involved; and territorial (ratione loci), referring to the place involved. However, the last two requirements are sometimes interchangeable.

The most undesirable form of political criminal law is when outdated religious codes are interwoven into criminal codes. This means that the leaders of the government control the criminal justice system.[41] Clear examples of this are the systems of criminal justice in the Islamic Republics of Afghanistan and Iran and the Kingdom of Saudi Arabia. We must remember that, in many countries of the world, acts are not criminal "because they are harmful, but because they are deemed harmful, by those who make or interpret the law."[42] This means, in turn, the "acts deemed criminal at a given time in a given community often turn out to be of the greatest value for human life."[43] Therefore, the nature of political criminal law implies the power of politicians, authorities, or the leaders of a country to criminalise certain acts within the decisions of parliament or legislation. After a certain given time, the government authorities may invalidate or aggravate this power. This includes rebellions, riots, or insurgences, which finally end in a revolution and become either a reason to defeat the revolutionaries or a victory for the new political movement.

1.3.3 Detective Criminal Law

The third type of criminal law is *detective criminal law*. Although this type of criminal law has characteristics of both of the other branches of criminal law, it serves as a separate branch of criminal law with its own distinct attributes. The function of detective criminal law is to search and examine the problem of both normative and political criminal law and to suggest the way out of all the serious

---

[40] Ashworth (2013), p. 1.

[41] Ashworth (2006), p. 68.

[42] Cohen (1949), p. 996.

[43] *Id.*

conundrums of humanity in its quest for global justice. Detective criminal law is in fact the presentation of what it is, and what it should be, including critical analysis of the violations of fundamental principles of criminal law under the given legal systems. It also concerns the questions of *de lege ferenda*. The difference between these three characteristic criminal laws is as follows: the first is a separate institution; the second interferes in the first system's position, and the third integrates both systems inside its own legal theory for further development, requires strict liability for commission of national or international crimes, and requires application of justice for all and abolition of the unjustified practice of impunity. The third looks for purity and a freedom from impurity.

All three forms of criminal law are the subject of this work, although I emphasise the importance of the third type of criminal law for the prevention of injustice under the first two categories. *The detective criminal law reopens the wounds of the criminal law, victims, and criminal justice and raises the question of why the commission of a number of national or international crimes is ignored under the first two categories. The detective criminal law seeks the authentic implementation of justice and the prevention of impunity. It is a presentation of a system, which seeks justice, not from the personal or group point of view but from the aspect of justice for the sake of the dignity of human beings constituting a part of their substantive rights.* Here, I am dealing not with the concept of detective criminal law focusing on the common notion of a private or a public *detective* and her/his function in a *criminal* investigation as was and is exercised in the United Kingdom. Instead, my purpose is to address the fact that we are forced by the requirements of love for justice, of morality, of conscience, and by the force of justice for all to investigate the systems of our criminal laws and international criminal law to perceive whether they are applied on equal footings. In other words, the purpose is to see whether we have created a decent criminal justice system.

Are our systems of justice healthy for the attribution of the concept of criminality or do they function solely against a particular class of individuals, groups, or states? Here, we are not only bound by the legal obligations of criminal law but also by the moral obligations of the law to determine the sphere of ethical rationality of criminal law and its first principle of justice, i.e. the same law with the same power of recognition, application, and implementation of sanctions.

1.4 The Anatomy of Love without Witnesses

One of the most famous examples of true love is set out in the *Judgment of King Solomon of Israel* in the Hebrew Bible. His judgment implies that the concept of love is one of the most significant norms of legal discipline in order to find the truth. It also concerns the true love for our children when it comes to a fight between persons. In this episode, two women lived with two baby sons in the same house. One baby died and both came to Solomon claiming that the living child was hers. Solomon ordered a soldier to cut the remaining child into two equal parts. In response to this brutal verdict, the compassion for her son burned within the true mother's heart, she cried out, 'Please, my lord, give her the living boy; certainly do not kill him!' However, the other woman said, 'He shall be neither mine nor yours; divide him.' The King rendered his judgment as follows: 'Give the first woman the living boy; do not kill him. She is his mother.' Here, the lack of witnesses in a court following the true norm of love did not create an intractable judicial deadlock.

Delivering authentic judgment and confidence in justice does not need witnesses but wisdom. This wisdom should exist in every single judge and in every lawyer. A legal representative who fights for the rights of her/his client without using her/his intuition for true and wise justice is not true to the soul of justice but a person blind to fairness. Parallel versions of this narrative can be found in other literature of the world, *inter alid*, in Chinese and Indian. The moral is that *a substantive love cannot be divided into two parts* and that, in such a case, you should instead give your rights to the parts to another plaintiff if, and only if, you truly love your children, respect the rights of victims, care for justice and humanity. It also indicates that justice may not be fair, *but* all decisions taken for the sake of one you love are fair. A person, who beyond doubt loves her/his children, may sacrifice her/his life in order never to use such proprietary language, e.g. in a divorce court, the effect of which may be seriously to harm the best interests of the children or grandchildren in the future. Such compassion and devotion manifests perpetual parental sentiments for her/his children and shows that true love is the basic principle of judgment.

Although the concept of the word 'love' in law is different from the notion of romantic love, both have some basic affinities.[44] As Charles Dickens justly wrote, the establishment of justice and the incorporation of the power of the unity of man need love. "A loving heart is the truest wisdom."

> It was the best of times,
> it was the worst of times,
> it was the age of wisdom,
> it was the age of foolishness,
> it was the epoch of belief,
> it was the epoch of incredulity,
> it was the season of Light,
> it was the season of Darkness,
> it was the spring of hope,
> it was the winter of despair,
> we had everything before us,
> we had nothing before us,
> we were all going direct to Heaven,
> we were all going direct the other way—in short, the period was so far like the present period, that some of its noisiest authorities insisted on its being received, for good or for evil, in the superlative degree of comparison only.[45]

---

[44]Fromm (1956). Available at https://archive.org/stream/TheArtOfLoving/43799393-The-Art-of-Loving-Erich-Fromm#page/n15/mode/2up (Accessed June 4, 2016).

[45]Dickens (1859); See also Richards (2016).

A concrete example is when we start to build our own four-floor building with our own hands in order to avoid huge charges. We must arrive at a central energy, or a magnetic field, which can help us to tolerate the heavy period of building while caring for four newly-born children. This can only be solved with one idea, i.e. *we will make love present in each single corner of the house with the oxytocin of love as the glue of family unity*. The French playwright Jean Racine aptly writes: "*The quarrels of lovers are the renewal of love*." As Fromm puts it: "One neglects to see an important factor in erotic love, that of *will*. To love somebody is not just a strong feeling—it is a decision, it is a judgment, it is a promise. If love were only a feeling, there would be no basis for the promise to love each other forever. A feeling comes and it may go. How can I judge that it will stay forever, when my act does not involve judgment and decision?"[46] I round off his words here with those of a Japanese lecturer after I had married for the third time with the same lady. "It was a fantastic time with you in Japan; especially I was very impressed to witness what you are with Kerstin. Japanese men should learn from the behaviour of you in love."[47]

Love is what Hegel, the German Philosopher calls the genuine universality of substantial unity. He points out that love is the most significant norm, which makes me, and I am part of we. He therefore concludes that:

> Love means in general terms the consciousness of my unity with another, so that I am not in selfish isolation but win my self-consciousness only as the renunciation of my independence and through knowing myself as the unity of myself with another and of the other with me. Love, however, is feeling, i.e. ethical life in the form of something natural. In the state, feeling disappears; there we are conscious of unity as law; there the content must be rational and known to us. The first moment in love is that I do not wish to be a self-subsistent and independent person and that, if I were, then I would feel defective and incomplete. The second moment is that I find myself in another person, that I count for something in the other, while the other in turn comes to count for something in me. Love, therefore, is the most tremendous contradiction; the Understanding cannot resolve it since there is nothing more stubborn than this point (*Punktualität*) of self-consciousness which is negated and which nevertheless I ought to possess as affirmative. Love is at once the propounding and the resolving of this contradiction. As the resolving of it, love is unity of an ethical type.[48]

In order to work towards resolving the conflicts between the ideologies, cultures, and laws of the various regions of the world, one may refer not only to the law and rights but also to the law in its connection to the wonderful power of love. By this, I mean the will to protect and support the fundamental moral intentions of international human rights laws with a determined will and clear objectives. As it has been

---

[46]Fromm (1956), p. 56.

[47]An email message from Miss Dr. Narumi (2013-11-15-14:18).

[48]PhR, Para.158A. Quoted in Westphal (1984), pp.77–92, at 87.

rightly put, 'The hunger for love is much more difficult to remove than the hunger for bread.'[49] That is why the theme of extending love to human beings, as well as to the natural environment and its flora and fauna, is recognised as an integral part of most literatures[50] and is also encouraged in public international law.[51]

However, to understand the relationship between love and law requires a sophisticated analysis of the whole body of international human rights law.[52] The reason for this is that we are used to referring to our rights within the relevant provisions of the law rather than analysing them with the term 'love'. We should remember that the Universal Declaration of Human Rights is based on a resolution of the General Assembly of the United Nations and, therefore, its content is not based on 'law-making' treaties. Despite this fact, the Declaration constitutes not only a part of customary international law and the general principles of law but is also an integral part of the international law of *jus cogens*. This means that the moral obligations of the declaration have become a significant part of the international obligations of individuals, groups, and states. We should not modify or nullify the obligations of the Declaration contrary to its intentions. These obligations confirm our sincere love and our firm commitment to respect one another's human integrity.[53] They have also developed into the system of international criminal law and, for this reason, we have recognised several categories of international crimes.

1.5 Efficiency of Love in Criminal Justice

The major difficulty in writing is not how to put into writing our theories but how to adopt the writing within our mind and how to be fair and not contravene the principles of morality, love, and justice in the theory of law. The central elements of these principles are not obvious for any writer, but they should be a manifestation and amalgamation of many things, including our own thoughts, the thoughts surrounding our social unity, and, most necessarily, the peaceful respect for our neighbours' thoughts. One may register these thoughts in a different order, i.e. morality is the manifestation of our neighbours' thoughts, the presentation of thoughts in our social environment, and the expression of our own thoughts. Here

---

[49]Mother Teresa.

[50]Richards (2016), pp. 231–232; Malekian (2015b), pp. 889–892. For instance, the use of force against the natural environment or its destruction is clearly prohibited.

[51]See Atwell (2008), p. 495; Gray (1995).

[52]For a useful analysis of international human rights law, see Shelton (2014).

[53]As it is stated "The human race, says Suárez, though it is divided into different peoples, possesses unity, not only as a species, but also a kind of political and moral unity. We know that that is so because there is a precept of natural law which enjoins us to love and to be charitable to all, even to strangers of every nation. Hence, though each single state is a perfect community, yet in relation to the human race states are none the less also in a sense members of a universal whole" Brierly (1948). Francisco Suárez was a Spanish philosopher and lawyer (1548–1617).

we are approaching the same matter of interest but with different priorities and classifications.

One view may put the heaviest weight on our own wishes whilst putting less weight on the wishes of the furthest nations in the world. This means that we may attain the norm of love for each other from different angles and both perspectives may represent two sides of the same coin. The disparity is that the first view begins by searching for the objectivity of morality as the method of learning of other views or learning the advantages of their inner visions, and the other begins with the promotion of ones owns choices.

It was not easy to choose a title for this chapter. Different titles were weighed against each other and different reasons won out over others. The title is thus a juxtaposition of several titles such as *the Oxytocin of Love in Criminal Justice and Peace*, *the Philosophy of Love in Justice*, *the Similarities between the Jurisprudence of Laws*, *the Norm of Love on the Aquarium of Criminal Justice*, and *Lecturing on the Norm of Love in Criminal Law*. The intention is to bring into focus that love, justice, peace, humanity, union, universality, sisterhood, brotherhood, criminal law, and understanding are all the same, but with the difference that we are accustomed to using different terms which are more familiar from our own culture. That is to say that to describe African law or Islamic law as European Union Law, or European Union Law as African Law, is really, one can believe, all one and the same.[54] The whole idea is to find suitable humane provisions for our different laws, including the machinery of criminal justice. The following words properly express the position:

> As the product of the criminal machinery is not a suitable witness to justice, we have turned to the process of manufacturing the product and have found that it can quite reliably be so convinced as to satisfy criteria of (procedural) justice. To a large extent it can be kept under control by the manufactures, and it can, and even must, be visible to those who want to see. The criminal process has the function, *inter alia*, of demonstrating that justice is done, and how it is done.[55]

I am here referring to the fact that all proper laws have the same roots, the same ambitions, the same intentions for their objects, and aim to present a fair picture of justice. A law cannot be a law if it does not consist of good justice. With the term "justice", I shall verify that justice has to bring love to its audience, and this love has to secure justice if it is competent. This is a particularly necessary corollary in criminal justice. The well-known Italian criminal lawyer Beccaria, who is known for his opinions against torture and capital punishment and on the protection of robust justice, asserted this almost 300 years ago. According to him:

> how odious so ever is the empire of force over the opinions of mankind, from whom it only obtains dissimulation followed by contempt; and although it may seem contrary to the spirit of humanity and brotherly love, commanded us by reason, and authority, which we more respect, it is nevertheless necessary and indispensable. We are to believe, that all these

[54]Malekian (2015b). For the development of the European Law consult. Weiler and Wind (2003).

[55]Trechsel (1997), pp. 101–105.

paradoxes are resolved beyond a doubt, and are conformable to the true interest of mankind, if practiced by a lawful authority.[56]

Obviously, Beccaria had a great love for the implementation of apposite love for justice and truth.[57] We shall see that these two institutions—justice and love—*are* indispensable for humanity, human integrity, equality, and all those principles that we have integrated into the system of human rights law in order to prevent criminal violations against mankind.[58] The difference between these two is that justice consists of legal norms, morals, love, and sometimes of political norms, and the entire picture of justice is abstract and cannot be seen, as long as it is not complete. However, the norm of love in law is not an abstract norm; it is the main duty of law, lawyers, judges, prosecutors, and the whole machinery of the court to respect the principle of purity in legal terms for the right and fair application of justice in their judgments. For instance, lawyers, should make sure that their clients are conscious of the moral requirements of the case, and they should not ignore the requirements of truth and faithfulness. "Lawyers need to be able to engage their clients in a moral dialogue, which requires some familiarity with, and sensitivity to, moral reasoning." The lawyers evidently do not need to determine the solution for moral requirements of the case for their clients. However, they should help the client to find the correct answer with pure love for justice concerning these moral questions.[59]

1.6 Preliminary Definition of the Norm of Love

When one speaks about the character of these three types of criminal law and the existence of the norm of love in all of the legal systems mentioned above (normative, political, and detective criminal law), the position becomes not only unconventional, but lawyers, judges, and politicians also become defensive. Therefore, the ethic of 'love' as a method of argumentation is not welcomed, in particular, when one asserts that it is the equal of legal and moral principles in law or even that it is significantly stronger than the other principles. Love constitutes not only a principle in law but has also a high value in deepening our understanding of law for the maintenance of justice and keeping away the maladies of law such as hidden discriminations in law, the interpretation of law against the freedom of individuals, the notion of non-impartiality of jurisdiction, the non-objectivity of judges, and non-neutrality of prosecutors. Above all, the love norm creates trust in the system of jurisdiction of the state in question.

What? This is the first antiphon, which is levelled by a lawyer against the term 'love' in law. "Yet love is at the heart of . . . a decent society.. Love I shall argue, is

[56]di Beccaria (1872), pp. 143–144; http://oll.libertyfund.org/titles/beccaria-an-essay-on-crimes-and-punishments (Accessed April 27, 2015).

[57]Venturi (1972), pp. 106–109.

[58]Cohen (1949), pp. 1014–1018.

[59]Martin Luther King. See also Vischer (2014), p. 6.

what gives respect for humanity its life, making it more than a shell."[60] However, I shall admit the fact that the word 'love' is the strongest expression of criminal justice, and it should be recognised as the most rational explanation of the philosophy of law in general and the philosophy of international criminal law in particular.[61] This love exists within the inner structure of our society and "with that love of society, implanted in man, by nature, and improved by neighbourhood and alliance, at length furnished out a civil state."[62] *However, I am also fully aware of the fact that most of us, including the layman, lawyers, prosecutors, judges, and students of law, when coming across the word love, consider it to be the depiction of romantic love. The love which is expressed by us to the one that we adore, that we may sacrifice our lives for, with whom we may share our innermost sexuality, our feelings of isolation and collectivism. I also believe that most buildings, dwellings, rooms, walls, doors, and windows are constructed to keep private our sensual feelings exchanged with the one with whom we like to share our physical movements, amorous experiences, and love. Nonetheless, with love here we do not mean any of these but justice within the naked judgment of law.*

Consequently, one may initially define the word love as a mandatory norm incorporated into law, as is the case for established legal and moral norms. Like all norms, the love norm's goal is to create relations, but normative, positive ones which are actually against the impurity that may otherwise exist in the construction of legal or moral norms because of the influence of "certain invisible powers". A love norm indicates the conditions of its effectiveness by demonstrating its reasons of existence for justice with power of fairness, impartiality, and absolute security of justice. "Power at its best is love implementing the demands of justice, and justice at its best is power correcting everything that stands against love".[63]

A love norm is against peace in the absence of justice, for instance, the existence of an unequal treaty. It demands an automatic sanction for the failure to perform a legal or moral duty integrated into the rule of law. Love norms are not directly adopted by authorised state entities but are the strength and spirit of the philosophy of positive and even natural law, law has to be positive or fruitful.

> He who knows nothing, loves nothing. He who can do nothing understands nothing. He who understands nothing is worthless. But he who understands also loves, notices, sees ... The more knowledge is inherent in a thing, the greater the love.... Anyone who imagines that all fruits ripen at the same time as the strawberries knows nothing about grapes.[64]

---

[60]Nussbaum (2013), p. 15.

[61]Consult also Souryal (2015).

[62]Pufendorf (1717), p. 457. Available at http://find.galegroup.com/mome/quickSearch.do?now=1427655629859&inPS=true&prodId=MOME&userGroupName=mpi_vb (Accessed March 29, 2015).

[63]Luther King (1967), p. 247. See *also* http://mlk-kpp01.stanford.edu/index.php/encyclopedia/documentsentry/where_do_we_go_from_here_delivered_at_the_11th_annual_sclc_convention/ (Accessed May 25, 2015).

[64]Paracelsus (1493–1541).

If the law is not positive, it is not law but a cover for the use of force behind the law. The application of certain measures of coercion by a state to enforce the law may not be recognized violations of the norm of love as long as the relevant measures are in accordance with the standard of international human rights law which are integrated into the body of the international law of *jus cogens*. A norm of love, like a legal norm in law, has a hypothetical character which implies the conditions under which a person should be treated and directed by the given norms of human rights law. It also indicates the nature of the rights and duties of the subjects, entities, and states in the performance of legal obligations. This resembles the function of substantive and procedural rules applicable in the European Court of Human Rights.[65] The norm of love also has sanctions with the aim of the implementation of the essence of secure justice. It obliges conflicting parties to solve their differences by moral and legal means: negotiations, arbitrations, mediations, and international court options, including the pure philosophy of love for justice.

1.7 Triangulating the Normative Power of Love

Criminal justice is one of the first institutions to have been founded in primitive societies.[66] It has always been very conservative in its scope of application. It has been not only a tool of the relevant society to bring criminal wrongdoers within its jurisdiction but also to underline which actions are criminal according to the ruling authorities in order to maintain their hold on power. For instance, Church, Canon, and Roman law had significant comportment in its consolidation of severity.[67] This was and is the same for the interpretation of Islamic law. Thus, the apparatus of criminal justice has not always been seeking the truth but has instead applied its power in order to hide the truth.

Consequently, by the term "pure", we do not only mean norms that are inherent in and developed by the operations of reason but also those principles that are revealed through processes of universally available experience based on truth. Here we are not searching for a supreme principle of morality, as many philosophers arguably look for a form of *conceptual* analysis, but a norm, the extreme violation of which *seeks* to reconcile a certain account of *theoretical* examination through *philosophical* understanding of human nature within any set of moral principles, even by the hypothesis of "love of one's country". A clear example is the monstrous criminality of Hitler's state against its victims and the few Germans who rose against such criminality. In these circumstances, the concept of "love of one's

[65]Wägenbaur (2013), p. 1.

[66]McAuley and McCutcheon (2000), pp. 2–3.

[67]*Id.*, pp. 4–6.

country" appeared revolting and could no longer have any valid place in moral reasoning for those Germans.[68]

In some aspects, the criteria of morality exercised by one society may be quite different from those of another. However, one may draft several other questions in the consideration of the role of morality and its influence on the law and the decision of a court. According to one opinion, there is a serious "dilemma" in the case of the question of morality, since one's moral perception is to some extent not only personal and free but also bound to judicial tradition and the conditions of the values of a specific case based presented in a court. Thus, a decision of a court may bear both legal and moral concepts of the law.[69]

However, we can already see that there will still be similar, overlapping attitudes of decency or a common context for moral principles. *I will argue in this work that this is the very essence of human authority; the constitutional nature of human law; the value protecting the common principles of the human race; the existing synchronization of the basic regulations of our organic body; and, not least of all, all these aspects are the expression of similar norms requiring love for mankind.* This means we should place a sufficiently heavy emphasis on similarity. We have to find the central key of morality, integrity, or triangulation for the formative power of love, which is more or less acceptable to all human beings in order to prevent the use of force or international criminal violations. Searching for similar principles among different moral forums may reduce the frequency of armed confrontations between states.

Moral reasoning has a long history and deep philosophical foundations. The German philosopher Kant developed a hybrid view of law, morality, and love. It is therefore sometimes very difficult to separate his views from *legal moralism* or *legal positivism*. The former is the philosophy of law, which maintains that laws may be employed to prohibit or permit certain behaviour that seems right or wrong based on majority judgement. This arises from the moral attitude of the given society. The latter view or 'legalism' is the extension of and the respect for the former when we adopt or formulate the will of society into a legislation or constitution. This legislation is enforceable. One may assert that Kant was a moral realist or value realist in stark contrast to a representative of Neo-Darwinian materialism.

Kant tried to avoid any damage to moral autonomy; a position which followed inevitably from value realism. Accordingly, there are things that constitute moral facts and do not cause illusion. That is the nature of moral judgment. This is a judgment, which is capable of distinguishing between true or false regarding such facts. Actually, Kant agrees to a divine command view of moral obligations. He therefore tries to connect the good ordered by divine law and the good for the

[68] Al-Hussein (2009), p. 653. Available at http://www.auilr.org/; http://digitalcommons.wcl.american.edu/cgi/viewcontent.cgi?article=1098&context=auilr (Accessed October 20, 2014). See also the next sub-section.

[69] Zahle (2005), pp. 317–319.

autonomy of moral obligations. Since divine laws are not in themselves enforceable, he places them within the moral agent itself rather than in God's theory. Thus, according to this philosophy, good has to be a part of the principle of morality. In other words, morality has to be good; this is also the nature of morality under the command of God. The good is itself the rejection of bad intentions and the presentation of love for humanity. This notion of good in morality also has to be seen in our international conventions, in our interpretations, and it must be a part of the rule of law as well. Morality is a positive action in opposition to evil or immoral action. In addition, good morality does not apply solely to practical motive but also to the substance of our wills.

Some philosophers may therefore regard the motives of a person as the essential factors for the evaluation of good or bad morality. Although such evaluations may be significant, there are other factors for the understanding of good morality. A better morality has to be pure and its intention should not harm the common understanding of human beings for justice. Thus, as Ross indicates, our actions should keep the balance between what is good and bad. In other words, we must be aware of the fact that many actions are morally bad, even though the law permits their intentions and recognises them as right. He further states that "to say we ought to act from love is to say that we ought to think that a certain act would promote someone's welfare, that we ought to desire his welfare, and that we ought to do the act on that account."[70]

We should not be blind to the fact that there are, as always, serious problems with the interpretation of most international criminal conventions. In analogy with Roman law, interpretation could have two features: grammatical and logical. If an interpretation of the letter of the law was concerned, it was considered 'grammatical'. It was a logical interpretation if it contributed to the meaning by reference to the context as well as the origin and object of the rule of law.[71] If states acted in good faith, rather than merely preaching, they would ratify a treaty for the complete elimination of nuclear weapons and total global disarmament, which contains a logical interpretation by "means of a true perception of its actual conditions and effects."[72]

---

[70]Ross (1939), pp. 325–326. David Ross clarifies that a clear distinction between the morally good and the morally right 'will do much to remove some of the perplexities of our moral thought.' Ross (1930), p. 7. See *also* Stern (2012).

[71]Sohm (1935), pp. 28–29.

[72]*Id.*, p. 29.

1.8 Pure Theory of Love in Criminal Justice

The term *pure theory of love in criminal justice* has a different definition. By this term, we mean that love is an invisible, unreadable, and intangible *norm* integrated into the common principles of human nature and the general principles of customary law requiring empathy for one another. Love underlies the strong human drive for justice and fairness. It is the animating spirit of international humanitarian conventional criminal law in preventing flagrant violations of human integrity. It also is the basis of the norm of understanding for unanimous consent in the General Assembly of the United Nations resolutions. In addition, it gives us the power to prevent irrational actions and underlies the very well established norm, allowing and requiring the international community of human beings to respond against grave breaches committed by powerful states when nothing else is effective. All of these factors rely on the final purity of understanding of the norm of love that has to be implemented by the use of devoted love for justice. Such are the motives behind the creation of the ICTY, ICTR, and the Special Court for Sierra Leone.

Another clear example is the inhuman attacks against the *norm of love* in Gaza by the Israeli and the United States military coalition and the earth-shattering protest against it by the population of the world in 2014. Thus, love is, or has to be, an integral norm of any relevant law for the prevention of the use of criminal force and a deeper understanding of our essential similarities beyond any differences.

With the term *pure theory of love in criminal justice*, we also mean that love exists and has to exist in the legal body of criminal law. The principle of purity demands that criminal jurisdiction, criminal courts, criminal lawyers, criminal judges, and criminal proceedings should have clarity of understanding of the norms of criminal law for the application of accurate justice and not solely the application of the rule of law. Even though the rules of law are narrow, the judge has the discretion to exercise good judgment.[73] Most laws are the manifestation of what is good for our collective national or international life and should therefore convey good moral obligations. By this, we mean obligations which are virtuous, of a good nature, and good for the welfare of human beings. They should present the pure theory of love; that is to say, we ought to pay attention to good results, the promotion of social welfare, and should not destroy for others in one part of the world and build for ourselves in another part of the world.

Let us now examine what the pure theory of law is. Kelsen, the most well-known writer on the concept of pure theory of law defines it as follows:

> The pure theory of law is a theory of positive law; a general theory of law, not a presentation or interpretation of a special legal order. From a comparison of all the phenomena which go under the name of law, it seeks to discover the nature of law itself, to determine its structure and its typical forms, independent of the changing content which exhibits in different times and among different peoples. In this manner, it drives the

[73]Bentzon and Agersnap (2005), p. 8.

> fundamental principles by means of which any legal order can be comprehended. As a theory, its sole purpose is to know its subjects. It answers the question of what the law is, not what it ought to be. The latter question is one of the politics, while the pure theory of law is science. It is called "pure" because it seeks to preclude from the cognition of positive law all elements foreign thereto. The limits of this subject and its cognition must be clearly fixed in two directions: the specific science of law, the discipline usually called jurisprudence, must be distinguished from the philosophy of justice, on the one hand, and from sociology, or cognition of social reality, on the other.[74]

Kelsen uses the term 'pure' for the theory of positive law. It means a law which is written within the legislation and is independent from natural law. With this in mind, he recognises the subjects of the law. Thus, pure theory of law orders its subjects to respect the rule of law. Pure theory of love in law does the same, with the difference that it encourages its subjects to love justice and not to bind themselves to a law which is unjust and degrades human dignity, undermines equality before the law with demarcation, and applies sanctions to the weak and not to the strong. This means, with reference to the bulk of bodies of national, regional, and international, legal instruments, including the jurisprudence of law, not only to have norms to be positive but they should also not create phrases that may have a negative effect at the time of interpretation or implementation. They have to keep and respect the good of human beings.

Unlike the pure theory of law, the function of the pure theory of love is not to demonstrate what the law is, but what law ought to be. It questions the substance, essence, and core function of the law. It imparts to politicians, legislators, lawyers, prosecutors, and judges, including the implementers of the law, that they have a natural and positive responsibility (maintained by the bulk of legal documents and orders) to question what they do, so they should not violate the purity of love for justice. This is also based on the fact that the sole intention of the basic instruments of law cannot be a degradation of human beings, cannot create prejudice between man and man, cannot violate the principles of human rights law, and should not contradict the moral obligations of norms.

No law is logically valid if its implementation goes against those basic natural rights of man. With this, I do not mean divine law but the natural law, the nature of which is even beyond divine law. This is a law which belongs to all human beings and nature to the same degree and at the same level. This manmade law has to produce good for all and that has to be the nature of the law. A law that goes against the commonly accepted standard of morality, i.e. the respect for human nature, human security, and human integrity, is not the law but the formulation of orders. In addition, the law of nature obliges us by the norms of human rights law, and by the genetic law of love, not to enact a law that goes against the fundamental principles of natural law or international human rights law. This means our laws should also not violate the rights of the population of a neighbouring country. By 'neighbour', I do not just mean 'our neighbours', but the neighbours of neighbours and so forth.

[74]Kelsen (1941), p. 44.

Here, I am arguing for the yielding of all laws to the natural rights of all men. This is the law of love.

The pure theory of love in law is free of all types of intrigue and ought to be the substance of the law. I call it 'pure' since it aims to preclude from the cognition of jurisprudence of law all provisions that are harmful to the principle of good and love. For instance, any mental process of acquiring permission to use the bulk of instruments of the law for personal, group, or governmental advantages is invalid. The intention of the law has to be good, pure, and motivated by love for justice. Again, any law which permits killing, torture, or capital punishment by the use of various reasoning should not only be avoided by prosecutors and judges but also by the implementers. This is because the pure philosophy of law should not permit the degradation of human beings, whether ordered by the content of law or by authorities. Such orders should be foreign to the pure philosophy of fairness, to humanity, and to justice.

If the basic norm of a legal system is good and derives its reasons from the implementation of love for justice, the entire machinery of the same system has to create love for justice. We cannot have a legal system, the constitution of which is based on respecting human rights principles but the legislators of which create norms, which is against the basic idea of the constitution. The legal validity of the basic norm therefore has to be seen within other norms. I am referring here to the norms of law that are not only integrated into national legal systems but also the international legal system. If the Constitution of the United Nations demands justice for all, such justice should also be formulated into all international treaties. This means that we cannot create treaties in contradiction to the core intention of the UN Charter. Love for justice has to be seen within all legal systems. The basis of this philosophy is that the provisions of the Charter shelter all members of the United Nations, and therefore their constitutions and actions have to follow the structure of the organisation. We are all obliged to respect the good norm or the good intention of any law, and the contrary cannot be a fact but a political reality. Any interpretation of the Charter based on radical evil will surely end in radical terror.

Better put, the rule of law, which does not look upon any given decision with the power of love for justice, cannot be the rule of law but instead the rule of order and criminal discipline. *Although a criminal lawyer is bound by criminal statute to apply criminal provisions, she/he has to keep in mind that the criminal rules cannot be valid if justice for the victims, fairness to the witness, and impartiality towards the convicted person are not met with due regard to her/his circumstances. A criminal judge is therefore duty bound by moral, legal, and love norms to examine her/his decision under power of reason of judgment and the strength of the quintessence of the law to arrive at the essence of justice under consideration of all motives.*

A rule of law that permits cutting of members or parts of the body as its penal sanction is not law but a terrible statement, and a judge who applies such law is not a judge but a butcher of humanity and justice. A law which permits marriage of a nine-year-old girl in its legal provisions is obviously not a law but a misunderstanding of culture and therefore unjust. A professor of criminal law or criminologist who teaches such a law as a part of his lecture, with the reasoning that he has no alternative and is forced by rules to follow legislation, is not a tutor of justice but a servant of the relevant legal system. Even if her/his motivation is not to lose his job or position. As a whole, one who works for any reason within the criminal justice system of such legislation or society is the violator of the rules of ethics of morality, justice, and philosophy and of the dignity of human beings.

A law ought to have a good intention and this good is not based on the criteria of what the authorities claim it to be but on the substance or the nature of law. It is not a matter of choice but a question of principle. A positive law should not violate the natural rights of man, by asserting that natural law is not law or law has to be codified. This is the most injudicious argument that can be presented by a lawyer today. We should not violate the consolidated natural rights of people and claim that we are applying the power of law. No provision of positive law is in reality permitted to violate the integrity of a human being by referring to its source of inspiration, e.g. a constitution. The validity of a law, which is given authority solely in its positive aspect as a written law, has to be recognised as very low and as an insult to human morality. It follows that, if we accept that any law is a proper law and authoritative, then we admit the fact that any totalitarian command is law because the political power in force is constitutionally a valid legal authority.

Evidently, the law which was enforced in the United States before Martin Luther King's movement for civil rights was far from appropriate as a positive law; the law straight forwardly violated the natural rights of the black population of the United States. That is to say, not everything labelled 'law' is a proper law. If a dictator's command tends to be obeyed by the majority of the population of the respective state, as was the case in Germany before and during the Second World War, this does not necessarily give it the validity of proper law because it is not a positive law. An appropriate positive law is a law, which does not in any degree, diminish the standard of natural law or moral obligations for the recognition of the equal dignity of human beings. Civil liberty, freedom of opinions, equal application of the law, right to life, non-application of capital punishment or torture, and respect for well-known *jus cogens* principles are some of the virtues of a good positive law. In other words, immoral aspects of a law cannot give it the power of validity. When we are speaking about the validity of law, we are not talking about whether it is a positive law but whether its legal characterisation respects the essence of human nature.

One should remember that moral obligations are not a matter of what the legal authorities or political parties select for their given community. There is no such rule in the essence of law that can empower the breach of law, morality, and ethics. A law has to be good. This has to be the pure philosophy of regulating rules. All those aspects of law that are dictated by those who have the words of the law under their control and interpretation are far from being called morality and even law. In fact, most of the serious and uncontrolled violations within national or international legal systems occur because of the moral obligations of the positivists. Clear examples of this were the laws under the control of Stalin, the Nazis, and the United States government in Vietnam. All violations and killings were carried out under the guise of a pervasive positivist mentality. This is a mentality which insists on the enforcement of the terms of the law, regardless of whether those terms contradict with human beings' fundamental natural rights. All terms, such as legal values, moral values, or justified rules, are imperfect as long as their character is used against the best value of man. This is the value which can only create equal rights and duties without violation of each other's rights.

Luther King rightly formulates that one has a moral responsibility to disobey unjust law, replicating the legal phraseology of Saint Augustine that *lex iniusta non est lex* or *unjust law is not law whether it is manmade law, religious rules, or natural law*. As Robert Henryson (1460–1500) puts in his *The Tail of the Wolf, and the Lamb*:

> The poor folk, then, this Lamb may signify,
> Like cottars, pedlars, and such labouring men;
> Their life is half a purgatory aye,
> Even with honest work, as we well ken.
> The Wolf stands for extortioners, who then
> Oppress such poor folk, as we often see,
> By violence, or by guile and subtlety.
> There are three Wolves which in this world now reign:
> The first are those preventers of the Law,
> Who, by their weasel words, their powers maintain,
> And swear it's nothing but the truth on show;
> But, for a bribe, the poor they'll overthrow,
> Suppressing right, helping the wrong succeed;
> Hell's fire awaits all such when they are dead...
> The second breed of Wolves so ravenous,
> Are mighty men who need no more to gain,
> But are so greedy and so covetous,
> That, for small debt, they'll tenants press with pain,
> Driving them out into the wind and rain
> To beg their bread. To some, it seems fair game
> To dispossess them, and their farm to claim...
> The third Wolf is a lord by heritage,...

Therefore, the concept of criminal justice has to be pure, naked, and decent - free of wolves. By this, we mean that criminal justice has to deal with the fundamental questions causing the commission of crimes and not hide the truth, the reality, the facts, and the genuine evidence by various excuses.[75] Consequently, investigating phenomena to understand why events occur and cultivating the principle of non-impunity constitute some of the most significant principles of justice. The concept of purity and nakedness in international criminal justice must be regarded as the first principle of fairness, equality, truth, presentation of evidence, and love for justice. This means that if we want to decrease violations, we should also be pure in our own conduct and not hide the truth. A theory of justice that is not pure and constitutes intrigue is a dangerous game which soon or later leads to genocide,

[75]For the concept of reliability of evidence, see Roberts and Redmayne (2009), pp. 1–18. See also the new examination of evidence by Daniele (2015a), pp. 179–194.

crimes against humanity, torture, war crimes, mass rape, and, ultimately, the emergence of organisations such as ISIS. In other words, pure love for justice has to be vigilant and free from lapdogs. Love leads us to ethical resistance and to reject the division into class, gender, Western, and non-Western nations, Muslim and non-Muslim, Christian and non-Christian, Jewish and non-Jewish, and even into nationality. Love, as the principle of law, resists accepting cases which are not based on truth and are calculated to take national resources from one part of the world and deliver them to another part.

1.9 Similarities of Policies

The presentation of differing systems of jurisprudential logic should not negate the many similarities between the policies of the pure jurisprudence of laws of different nations or pure European law. Whether Europeans, Muslims, Africans or Australians, politicians, lawyers, judges or prosecutors, all must realise the significant purpose of this fact and reality, but those who do not agree with the philosophy of love for justice should also become conscious, in a given situation, of the fact that our laws and needs are greatly similar. We have to respect the essence of one another's law and we have to fight for the love of justice for the entire human race. Rawls states that there is a qualitative connection between the concepts of justice and love. He formulates it as follows:

> We must... distinguish between the love of mankind and the sense of justice. The difference is not that they are guided by different principles, since both include a desire to give justice. Rather, the former is manifested by the greater intensity and pervasiveness of this desire, and in the readiness to fulfill all the natural duties in addition to that of justice, and even to go beyond their requirements. The love of mankind is more comprehensive than the sense of justice and prompts to acts of supererogation, whereas the latter does not....Although justice as fairness begins by taking the persons in the original position as individuals, or more accurately as continuing strands, this is no obstacle to explicating the higher order moral sentiments that serve to bind a community of persons together.[76]

As Rawls says, "the sense of justice is continuous with the love of mankind."[77] Still, love goes beyond the moral requirements of justice. "Yet clearly the objects of these two sentiments are closely related, being defined in large part by the same conception of justice."[78] This means there are very deep similarities between our natures. Love of justice aims at the safety of core principles shared by human beings. In addition, "it supports those arrangements that enable everyone to express his common nature. Indeed, without a common and overlapping sense of justice

[76]Rawls (1971), pp. 191–192.

[77]Rawls (1971), p. 172.

[78]*Id.*

civic friendships cannot exist."[79] We shall learn by the end of this volume that what the law wants and what "law is about is much the same world over."[80]

Nothing can harm our knowledge of happiness, freedom, liberty, privacy, and language, if and only if, we describe the followers of European law as also followers of the African law, Armenian customs, Australian law, the Mohammedan system, Jewish tradition and vice versa. However, there may be opposition to this opinion from those who are absolute legalists and see the law as the law and separate it from its soul, i.e. the morality principle. Therefore, for them, preaching the principle of morality on the law as an integral part of the law is solely an "illusion."[81] The question is what happened when England followed Lutheranism and Scotland the doctrines of John Calvin. Europe had to experience these theories before placing the moral rights system, in its broader political and social contexts, into European Union law.[82]

Happiness does not come through invitation and theories, or through accusation, self-revision, self-judgment, assassination, self-scarification for religious or metaphysical theories, nor is it generated by self-protection, self-seeking tactics, self-defence, or the use of force or beheadings. However, happiness is not a Christmas present wrapped with red paper or the legislation of a considerable number of international human rights conventions. Happiness may constitute the way that we understand the pure theory of love, reality, and truth and that the intention of all human beings is to live in peace and justice. Yet, according to John Stuart Mill, people should learn to identify general happiness with their own happiness, but since we are not at that stage, he believes a person may sacrifice individual happiness for the general happiness. "Though it is only in a very imperfect state of the world's arrangements that anyone can best serve the happiness of others by the absolute sacrifice of his own, yet so long as the world is in that imperfect state, I fully acknowledge that the readiness to make such a sacrifice is the highest virtue which can be found in man."[83]

If there are those who struggle for differences or those who do not want to perceive the similarities, we have to be patient. We should be sure that the norm of love *has* to come to our union, to our family of humankind, to the children of the globe, to the right hands of this generation of human beings, and to the union of our grandchildren within the jurisdiction of love. If we cannot solve the minor differences of our regulations, provisions, principles, norms, rules, or conflicts with the existing similarities between them, how can we expect our future children to be

---

[79]*Id.*

[80]Derrett (1968), p. vii.

[81]Ross (1958), p. 29. Thus, the writer strongly attacks the opinion of Bentham and the doctrine of morality, pp. 290–292.

[82]White and Willock (2007), p. 22.

[83]Mill (1863), available at https://www.marxists.org/reference/archive/mill-john-stuart/1863/utility/ch02.htm (Accessed June 10, 2015).

talented enough to resolve these invalid, preposterous, and pathetic differences without atomic bombs?

Therefore, I suggest that the principle of love has to be recognised as the first principle of human law, human norm, human sense, human will, and not least the human union of love in order to decrease criminal violations. Any description of law has to be wise enough to balance out these various interpretations of law side-by-side with the love norm. The norm of love has to be the norm of justice, jurisprudence, and the norm that each government has to recognise within all its decisions for building, rebuilding, and destruction.[84] If the norm of love cannot be evaluated and respected by the most civilised nations in the world and prevent various criminal as well as political conspiracies, how can we expect it to be respected by others and expect not to see the bloodshed of human suffering?

We plan for the possession of the wealth of other nations by the force of armed conflicts and resolutions, by creating different fanatical groups, and by means of our secret intelligence agencies. Such plans inject political illness into the Security Council of the United Nations through our political manoeuvring. How can we insist that our justice is good and that other nations of the world who are the target of our own political decisions—motivated as they are by love of wealth, love of power, and love of superiority—should respect it?

1.10 Decriminalisation by the Norm of Love

Many institutions in Europe, among others, are working towards the settlement of law, settlement of peace, and the settlement of their own or other governmental organisation's views. The reality is that these institutions knowingly or unknowingly are developing differences in law, differences in ideologies, differences in cultures, and differences that are directly or indirectly guided by the politics of the most powerful states. The term 'human rights law' has become a byword for more funding, recommendations behind doors, corruption with money, and manipulation with wine.[85]

Although the purposes and objects of human rights may be correct and demanding, individual rights may still be in danger.[86] "There is every reason to yell that the

[84]Love is principle that most governments do not give any attention to. As has rightly been formulated "It's the human principle of contact. It was my experience in dealing with people in soup kitchens and in our AIDS shelter that they were thirsting for someone to know them by name, to care about their life story, to care if they woke up the next morning, simple things like that. And government can't do that. President Bush says this all the time, 'Government cannot love.' It's very hard for government to be a neighbour." *Crisis Interview with Jim Towey*, CRISIS, June 2002, at 40, 43 (defining subsidiary). Quoted in Czarnetzky and Rychlak (2003), p. 121.

[85]Shelton (2014), pp. 294–295.

[86]Ashworth (2008), p. 11.

ravening wolves are here. And it is no comfort that they are in sheep's clothing."[87] *An institution, which delivers the message of peace, human rights law, and justice, cannot be a true and rightful institution as long as it does not see the reality that peace does not come from the slogans of peace lectures. It also does not come by the waging of fights against terrorists or counter-terrorist movements; by resumption and encouragement of formulation of new conventions, regulations, and protocols; by strengthening of peace through the unwanted politicians of different political parties; by settling criminal justice for criminal behaviour or criminal punishments; and by competing with other institutions through their blogs*. All these elements also mean that criminal organisations are simultaneously increasing all over the world.[88]

The duties of criminal justice, criminal policy, and criminal regulations should not solely be the application of criminal regulations via criminal proceedings, but also the decriminalisation of the criminal justice system by encouraging the norm of love for justice. We argue that the criminalisation of various conducts no longer aspires to prevent the commission of grave crimes at the international level and, actually, it never has. By this, we also mean that the historical evolution of various civilizations in the world demonstrates the fact that the commission of grave crimes under the international criminal system have not only decreased but also have dramatically increased. The question is how we evaluate the policy of criminal justice.[89] The increase in crime results from two basic facts.

Firstly, we have armed the world so extensively and dangerously that every human being on the globe can be killed at least 40–50 times over by the use of these weapons. Secondly, the gravest violations of the system of law and morality in the history of civilizations of the world occurred after the creation of legal unions such as the League of Nations, the United Nations, the North Atlantic Treaty Organisation (NATO), the European Union, the Arab Charter, the Organisation of African Unity, and many Latin American intergovernmental organisations. *This means that there must be some misunderstanding of the law, misinterpretation of morality, disorientation of our thought and interests, derelictions of political roles, mistreatment of our natures, and denigrations of our cultural norms by one another's conduct. Above all, there must be a misunderstanding of equality, including democracy.*[90]

It may then be high time for the United Nations to examine the problem, not from the view of law or morality but also from the perspective of what is actually erroneous in the policy of all the treaties that are supposed to prevent national, regional, or international criminal violations. It should also examine what is wrong with the policies of the Security Council and the General Assembly of the United Nations and with the extensive overlapping norms of international human rights law, international humanitarian law of armed conflict, and statutes of international criminal justice. One could certainly believe that the transformative policy of the

[87]Greve (2005), p. 532.

[88]Fashing and Gottschalk (2008), p. 11.

[89]Greve (2005), p. 515.

[90]*Id.*

norms of law and morality into international conventions or organisations must not be accurate. Otherwise, why has the average number of violations increased? Why have the elements of peace brought us solely elements of injustice? In addition, why has the contemporary human historical evolutionary context resulted in us being armed more heavily than ever before?

1.11 Discretion of Criminal Justice

In 1660, Pufendorf, the classical theorist of international law, rightly emphasised the potential function of similarities and the *rule of law with love* in human relations. For him, the norms of legality, morality, and love can overlap one another, and their separation may sometimes be impossible. Accordingly, our rightful or wrongful conduct gives us the following value:

> Now as for the further objection: 'If man loved man in the course of nature, that is, as man, no reason could be given why each single individual should not love each other single individual, as being equally a man, or why he should the rather frequent those in whose society honour and advantage are accorded him beyond others.' To meet this it should be known that all men, indeed, have been brought together by the similarity of their nature towards one another, so that in actual fact that general friendship resulting from a common nature ought also to be common to all, unless someone, perchance, has by his crimes made himself unworthy of it. Now, in truth, a number of circumstances are added to that common nature which are responsible for one loving this one more than that one; suppose, for example, that there was between them a greater congruence of dispositions in regard to special inclinations, or else that their birthplaces were not far apart. But then and only then could no reason be given, if all men had grown up out of the earth together like fungi, without any relationship to one another, or if they had among one another a similarity of dispositions at every point.[91]

We need to work with a dynamic understanding of the terms 'similarities', 'love' and 'justice' and their functions within the inner structure of international law and international human rights law, including the reason of natural existence. Obviously, as Pufendorf suggests, we are not fungi. Herewith, we have to find out whether the word love is a visible or invisible norm of human rights law or the rule of law in general and whether this norm constitutes a part of national or international criminal justice. Thus, it may be necessary first to speak about what a norm is and what its functions are. This definition may be useful for comparison of false forms with the norm of law and the norm of love, too.

A norm of law constitutes a provision or a principle within the law, which contains certain obligations or duties of the subjects of the law. It is a mandatory rule of social behaviour establishing certain evidence for the recognition of certain conduct. A law may consist of a number of norms that cannot be isolated or treated

[91]von Pufendorf (1931), p. 319. Available at http://oll.libertyfund.org/titles/2220 (Accessed March 29, 2015).

separately. Such norms are integrated into the structure of most international human rights instruments that not only have an independent character but also complement one another's function. The norm of love in criminal justice does not seek association with false evidence, nor does it accept false witnesses or coincide with the use of force by its components, but it tolerates poverty in order to keep humanity, division of love, and the integrity of trust for the future of good judgment as well as justice.[92] However, keeping to the theory of proper evidence and protecting its integrity for use in the process of prosecution in an international criminal court is so indispensable and important that it has become a part of the duties of private and public bodies today.[93]

For instance, in order to prevent submission of false evidence, international tribunals increasingly underline that the public distribution of views and information entails risks and serious consequences for the machinery of justice.[94] In one of the judgments of the ICTR, the Tribunal clarifies that "the power of the media to create and destroy fundamental human values comes with great responsibility. Those who control such media are accountable for the consequences."[95] Here, although the Tribunal has restricted the exercise of the right of freedom of expression for a certain time, it has done so solely with the obvious intention of love for justice and the necessary protection of important evidence.[96] The Tribunal also intends that the use of other values against the machinery of criminal jurisdiction must not violate the basic values for human beings.[97]

1.12 Radical Love Versus Radical Evil

Immanuel Kant did not speak directly about the norm of love for the prevention of criminal behaviour or a better implementation of criminal justice, but he suggested that people must be made aware of their bad habits. Consequently, in his essay *Religion within the Bounds of Bare Reason*, he argues that bad habits are a universal concept in the human mind, and degrading treatment of others is sociologically a part of human nature. He called this phenomenon "propensity to radical evil." Therefore, he believed that "Given this description, you'll recognise the person who can be reverenced as the founder of the first true church; but not of the religion which, free from every dogma, is engraved in all men's hearts, because that wasn't

[92]For false evidence, see Roberts and Redmayne (2009), p. 17.

[93]Daniele (2015b), pp. 179–194, 181; Malekian (1992). Cited in Gray, note 58, at p. 12.

[94]Roberts and Redmayne (2009), p. 17.

[95]*Prosecutor v. Nahimana, Barayagawiza and Negeza* Case ICTR-99-52, Judgment and Sentence p. 945 (December 3, 2003).

[96]*Id.*, at para. 46.

[97]*Id.*

chosen by anyone and therefore doesn't have a founder."[98] Participation of people in the right church could help to develop good ethics in an individual's mind in order to increase social morality and decrease bad habits or criminal actions. Kant goes further and concludes that:

> One oughtn't to venture anything that risks being wrong — that is a moral principle that needs no proof. Hence, the consciousness that an action that I intend to perform is right is an unconditional duty. Whether an action is over-all right or wrong is judged by the understanding, not by conscience. And it's not absolutely necessary to know, concerning all possible actions, whether they are right or wrong. But concerning the action that I am planning to perform I must not only judge and form an opinion that it is not wrong but be certain of this; and this requirement is a postulate of conscience, to which is opposed probabilism, i.e. the principle that the mere opinion that an action may well be right is a good enough reason for performing it. So conscience could also be defined as follows: Conscience is the moral faculty of judgment.[99]

Kant emphasises the value of the moral faculty of judgment with the term "conscience." This means that he is referring to moral obligations. This concept of morality is so important and essential that it comes from the inner sense of what is right and wrong in man's conduct. Conscience is therefore our intuition or judgment regarding certain matters with moral reasoning, moral argumentation, and sometimes a superior moral justification for selfishness. This is a synonym for evil. Consequently, it is not a matter of choice but a matter of what is just and what is unjust for humanity.

Kant obviously deduced this view of radical love and radical evil from the theological concept of Christianity, since it addresses the ultimate questions of metaphysics and morality. Kant analysed that the universal moral law does not entirely rely on the question of the existence of God but rather upon reason. That is why he does not separate the source of morality from the concept of God. This can be seen in his *Groundwork of the Metaphysics of Morals* and *Religion within the Bounds of Bare Reason* by emphasising that morality "inevitably leads to religion." According to Kant, the concept of radical evil is located in human nature.[100] This evil can be a genuine moral alternative for human beings and can be authoritative.

Radical love has to reform the concept of radical evil. This is because we may unfortunately apply the moral law according to our personal interests and advantages. This means we can become radically evil and not realise that our morality has already violated moral law by modifying the moral sense into more limited goods. The consequence is that radical evil occurs with and without our appropriate personal knowledge. We devote love to objects which would be worthy of the love for each other and less interest to other objects, causing harm to the victims. As, for instance, we may support our government's criminal actions for economic interests without realising that its activities are seriously harming other nations and

[98]Kant (1793), p. 87. Launched by Jonathan Bennett, available at http://www.earlymoderntexts.com/pdfs/kant1793part4.pdf (Accessed April 12, 2015).

[99]*Id.*

[100]Bernstein (2002), pp. 11–14.

creating great suffering to the victims. The clearest examples are the present wars in Iraq and Syria. However, Kant still considers that radical evil may slowly grow into good morals if a gradual change in our habits occurs.

In order to control our bad habits, we express our obedience to the letter of the law. A norm of law may have two particular well-settled functions, namely a legal and a moral function.[101] Yet a norm may have both these objectives at the same time depending on the intention of the legislators. Most human rights norms and the international humanitarian law of armed conflict have such discipline. Normally, the authorities of states adopt the norms of law, but norms can also have a customary nature. This means a customary law may consist of customary norms of law or conventional norms that have become a part of customary law over time. All these norms, whether conventional, customary, or legislative, constitute the law in force.

Almost all norms of law present conditions, provisions, or principles that are crucial for their purpose, but this does not necessarily mean that the norm does not enjoy or have any requirements of the principle of morality. What the requirements of the principle of morality are are simply such matters as good faith, good action, good interpretation, good result, and good achievement. I am, however, aware that these aims should also be a part of a legal norm. In other words, it is almost impossible to separate these requirements from the body of legal or moral norms, or even to separate legal, moral, and love norms from one another's discipline in the body of criminal law. This is not only the case for good law, but it should also be true for the body of bad law. One cannot properly present the content of norms of legality without the putative norms of morality.

In criminal matters, judges should decide whether they are delivering a judgment under the discretion of law or discretion of love for justice. It is for this reason that a judge should have a wide range of knowledge regarding other legal systems of law and should know how their courts work and solve national or regional issues. For instance, the substantive and procedural parts applicable in European courts are the legacy of the French system and are to some degree influenced by German administrative law, i.e. Continental law. The Common Law legal tradition found in the United Kingdom and Ireland also has some effect on the function and legal reasoning of the European courts.[102] In fact, the *Court of Justice of the European Union* is the name of the overall European Union institution comprising three judicial instances. These are the Court of Justice, the General Court, and the Civil Service Tribunal, the judges of which must be familiar with the basic principles of legal justice in Europe in order to judge failures to comply with all norms.[103]

[101] Bondeson (2006), pp. 3–5.
[102] Wägenbaur (2013), p. 1.
[103] *Id.*, pp. 2–3.

1.13 The Invisibility of Love in Criminal Justice

The body of legal norms in a given society constitutes its law. Thus, when we say that norms of law are visible, this means that one can see what the relevant obligation or law requires, wants, and performs. The visibility of norms of law does not, however, mean that the relevant norms do not have any inherent tendency that denotes their invisible nature. Otherwise, the theory of Kant must be invalid, the development of society may slow down automatically, and interpretation of the law will be reduced. In other words, we may soon consider all acts within society to be criminal acts and punishable based on the fact that obedience to the law is the first primary requirement of the law. Therefore, it may be proper to rethink the following:

> It is well to remember that Moses murdered an Egyptian and left the country, that Socrates was, by a majority of his fellow citizens that voted, found guilty of a crime, and that George Washington and others would have been treated as criminals if the American Revolution had been as unsuccessful as was the Scotch rebellion under William Wallace. Those who, like Kant, regard obedience to the law as an absolute duty, must logically deny the moral right of any revolution. But this cannot be carried out consistently, since most, if not all, established governments, even the constitution of the United States, have arisen out of revolutions and military conquest. Some dim, uncomfortable perception of this may be responsible for Kant's remarkable prohibition of any inquiry as to how the existing government acquired its authority.[104]

In the above case, George Washington would have been recognised as a criminal if he had not succeeded, and his love for justice would have been treated as unfavourably as possible. He could have been brought before a criminal court by the rule of criminal law of the given time and probably would have been sent to prison because of his strong views against the prevailing system of justice. We can express the same opinion about the Khomeini regime. If he and his supporters had lost in their revolutionary struggle, one could have brought them to criminal court for prosecution and punishment. Of course, one should not put aside the fact that winning a case does not necessarily mean winning the identification of future criminality of a criminal political group. According to George Washington, love is the only apparatus which reaches the heart of man and justice. He states that:

> Anything will give up its secrets if you love it enough. Not only have I found that when I talk to the little flower or to the little peanut they will give up their secrets, but I have found that when I silently commune with people they give up their secrets also – if you love them enough.

What all this adds up to is that the rule of criminal law is mostly the presentation of the habit or morality which we have codified in a certain given time by a certain given political power. Another illustrative example is the case of independence leader Patrice Lumumba of Congo. He was one of the great men in the history of civilization and the first democratically elected prime minister of the Democratic

[104] Cohen (1949), pp. 989–990.

Republic of Congo in 1960. Although rebel forces ostensibly tortured and killed Lumumba, his killing was organised by the Belgian government with assistance received from the CIA. An apology from the Belgian government came 42 years later, long after the crimes against the Congolese population and Lumumba had been committed. By this, we mean that the criminal conduct did not fall under the definition of the codified rules of criminal law, neither in Belgium, nor in Congo, nor in Europe. In addition, the most important principles of legality and morality in justice were not only violated by the system of criminal law itself but also by the politicians of Europe.

If the norm of love for pure justice and the prevention of impunity had real value, we would bring the Belgium government before a criminal court for prosecution and punishment. However, this did not occur and, ironically, the problem was solved with a simple apology for the crime committed against true democracy and love of justice. This means that a radical evil retained its evil nature. Morality was valued as very low as was the concept of good moral obligations, and replacement of true radical love with radical evil did not take place with purity. This is the mentality of political criminal law as we have seen it elsewhere. A political party or legal authority is the owner of criminal law and its interpretation, including application of sanctions. It is here that we enter into normative and political criminal law in order to evaluate to what extent they violate the concept of good moral obligations and its requirements. In other words, the love norm in criminal law not only has the function of recognition of legal validity of the provisions of the law and its applicability but has also an investigative function to bring the occurrence of the crimes to an end and apply just sanctions.

1.14 Criminal Violations of Moral Standard

A healthy norm of law is intended to create not only the norm, but also justice based on morality, non-volatile behaviour, equal division of the balance of power, and also the inner satisfaction of the substance or intention of the law. A good norm of international law, international criminal law, international human rights law, international humanitarian law, and international criminal justice ought not to insist on differences according to the pluralism or bijuralism theory but instead focus on the similarities that are essential in finding the way to the unity of human beings.

In the beginning, there were many differences in the inner structures of the European state civil law, family law, criminal law, and economic law. However, all states had a strong tendency to adopt and enforce the norms of the Union's law. If the chief intention of the European Union's law was to divide Europe into disagreements, the Union could never achieve its positive goals. That is why the member states of the European Union are moving towards removing their differences in order to create a united law. This means that the tendency has been to formulate similarities and not differences and at the same time to attain the high value of individual rights.[105]

The question is, therefore, very simple: is the purpose of law to solve, reduce, and apply equal norms of law for a peaceful and reasonable international society or is it to depart from the central shared principles of humanity that can also easily be understood by a layman? Great democratic leaders, such as Martin Luther King, cultivated positive sanctions with the full intention of doing good for the spirit of justice by sowing the seeds of love. They guide society towards love norms but by peaceful methods. Can we achieve a decent international society, one that offers justice and equal rights of humanity for all human beings based on the power of love? According to Martha Nussbaum, this is feasible. A decent international human society can approach its intention by use of different resources inherent in human psychology in order to prevent violations.[106]

When we speak about the philosophy of the prohibition of genocide, we not only mean that such breaches of norms or rules of relevant law are criminal behaviours but also that they are crimes against the moral standard of law, the moral level of custom, and also the moral limit on violations. These concern all states or each human being as a whole. In other words, the concept of international criminal law or a country's penal law "reflects more clearly the conditions of its society and its prevailing moral precepts than most other areas of law."[107]

The same is true when we examine the provisions of other international conventions such as torture, discrimination against women, or the international conventions governing the rights of workers.[108] For all these, we mean that a norm not only has a legal function by virtue of being drafted and accepted as a legal norm, but also that the norm has a moral function of a legal norm of the law or *vice versa*. The norm of the law therefore carries out the rule of the law, which consists of two attributes. These are the visible attribute of legality and the invisible attribute of morality. One can scarcely deny the fact that most international criminal conventions also contain the strong essence of the principle of morality. Here, morality means the limit at which the law no longer tolerates or can permit the occurrence of, for example, acts of genocide, acts of torture, acts of crimes against humanity, rape, infanticide, war crimes, aggression, and grave violations of the system of international criminal law.

I am not opposed to the fact that a norm of law is strict and does not necessarily need to join the principle of morality. However, I intend, at the same time, to voice some doubts, which I have long held. It is not easy to pin down what the purpose of legality or morality really is. We have enacted many rules of law in international criminal law with the obvious influence of the principle of morality and, if this is not the case, then we have a law not because we want to preserve the standard of our

[105] Ashworth (2008), pp. 13–15.

[106] Nussbaum (2013), pp. 2–4. See *also* Weiler (1999).

[107] Andenaes (1965), p. 4.

[108] Comprés (2009), p. 1027.

cultural norms but the standard of legalisation for our decisions. At the same time, I very much doubt that the prohibition of sexual slavery, forced sexual penetration, sexual labour or rape at a time of armed conflict is the manifestation solely of the norm of legality. There must be love for justice and love for the maintenance of women's dignity and thus we have enacted certain rules. This is the whole purpose of the criminalisation of non-consensual sexual behaviour against men or women.

References

Alexius, K. (1997). Politisk Yttrandefrihet: *En Studie i Lagstiftning och Praxis under Demkratins Genombrottstid*. Lund.

Al-Hussein, Z. (2009). For love of country and international criminal law. *American University International Law Review, 24*(4), 647–664.

Andenaes, J. (1965). *The general part of criminal law of Norway*. London: Sweet & Maxwell Limited.

Andernaes, J. (1974). *Alminnelig Strafferett*. Oslo: Universitertsforlaget.

Ashworth, A. (2013). *Positive obligations in criminal law*. Oxford: Hart Publishing.

Ashworth, A. (2006). Four threats to presumption of innocence. *South African Journal*, 63–97.

Ashworth, A. (2008). Criminal procedure, human rights and 'balance': Towards the dark night sea? In *Ikke Kun Straf: Festskrift til Vagen Greve* (pp. 11–20). Jurist- og Økonomforbunds forlag.

Atwell, B. L. (2008). The jurisprudence of love. *University of Detroit Mercy Law Review, 85*, 495.

Bassiouni, M. C. (1999). *International criminal law: Crimes* (2nd ed.). New York: Transnational Publishers, Inc. Ardsley.

Bentzon, A. W., & Agersnap, T. (2005). Retssikkerhed, Legitimitet og Tillid i et Aendringssmfund med Kulturelfoldighet. In C. Damgaard, C. Henrichsen, & H. Peterson (Eds.), *Ret & Usikkerhed* (pp. 5–20). Jurist- og Økonomforbunds forlag.

Bernstein, R. J. (2002). *Radical evil: A philosophical interrogation*. Cambridge: Blackwell Publishing.

Bondeson, U. V. (2006). Theory of law and morality. In U. V. Bondeson (Ed.), *Law and morality* (pp. 3–16). Forlaget Thomson.

Brierly, J. L. (1948). Suárez's vision of a world community. *An address delivered before the University of Granada*.

Cohen, M. (1949). Moral aspects of the criminal law. *Yale Law Journal, 49*, 987–1026.

Comprés, T. (2009). Labour of love: Using international labour law to achieve human rights for women sex workers in the Dominican Republic. *Georgetown Journal of International Law, 40*, 1027.

Cryer, R., Friman, H., Robinson, D., & Wilmshurst, E. (2010). *An introduction to international criminal law and procedure* (2nd ed.). Cambridge: Cambridge University Press.

Czarnetzky, J. M., & Rychlak, R. J. (2003). An empire of law: Legalism and the international criminal court. *Notre Dame Law review, 79*, 55–126.

Daniele, M. (2015a). Evidence gathering in the realm of the European investigation order from nations rules to global principles. *New Journal of European Criminal Law, 6*(2), 179–194.

Daniele, M. (2015). Evidence gathering in the realm of the European investigation order from nations rules to global principles. *New Journal of European Criminal Law, 6*(2), 179–194, 181.

Darcy, S., & Powderly, J. (2010). *Judicial creativity at the international criminal tribunals*. Oxford: Oxford University Press.

Derrett, J. D. M. (1968). *An introduction to legal system*.

di Beccaria, C. B. (1872). *An essay on crimes and punishments* [1764]. De Voltaire.

Dickens, C. (1859). *A tale of two cities a story of the French revolution.*
Drapkin, I. (1989). *Crime and punishment in the ancient world.* Toronto: Lexington Books.
Eser, A. (2007). The nature and rationale of punishment. *Cardozo Law Review, 28*, 2427–2436.
Eser, A. (2008). Article 31: 'Grounds for Excluding Criminal Responsibility'. In O. Triffterer (Ed.), *Commentary on the Rome Statute of the International Criminal Court. Observers' Notes Article by Article* (2nd ed.). C.H. Beck, München et al.
Eskeland, S. (2000). *Strafferett.* Oslo: Cappelen Akademisk Forlag.
Fashing, I. A., & Gottschalk, P. (2008). *Kriminelle Organisasjoner: Hvordan forstp organisert kiminalitet.* Fagbokforlaget.
Fouladvand, S. (2012). *Complementarity and cultural sensitivity: Decision-making by the International Criminal Court (ICC) Prosecutor in Relation to the Situations in the Darfur Region of the Sudan and the Democratic Republic of Congo (DRC).* Sussex.
Fromm, E. (1956). *The art of loving.* Harper & Row.
Gray, M.A. (1995). The International Crime of Ecocide. *California Western International Journal, 26*(2), 215–271. http://scholarlycommons.law.cwsl.edu/cgi/viewcontent.cgi?article=1335&context=cwilj. Accessed 25 Aug 2016.
Greve, V. (2005). Sheep or wolves. *European Journal of Crime, Criminal Law and Criminal Justice, 4*, 515–532.
Haveman, R., Kavran, O., & Nicholls, J. (2013). *Supranational criminal law: A system sui generis.* Intersentia.
Hirst, M. (2003). *Jurisdiction and the ambit of the criminal law.* Oxford: Oxford University Press.
Kant, I. (1793). *Religion within the Limits of Bare Reason.*
Kelsen, H. (1941). The pure theory of law and analytical jurisprudence. *Harvard Law Review, 55* (1), 44–70.
Langsted, L. B., Greve, V., & Garde, P. (2011). *Criminal law in Denmark.* London: Kluwer Law International.
Luther King, M., Jr. (1967). *Where do we go from here: Chaos or community?*
Maeland, H. J. (2013). *Norsk Alminnelig Strafferett.* Bergen: Grafisk Formidling AS.
Malekian, F. (1985). *International criminal responsibility of states.* Stockholm: Almqvist & Wiksell International.
Malekian, F. (1992). The principal function of an international criminal tribunal, delivered at U.N. Int'l Inst. of Higher Studies in Criminal Sciences. In *World Conference on the Establishment of an International Criminal Court to Enforce International Criminal Law and Human Rights*, Siracusa, Italy, 2–5 December 1992.
Malekian, F. (2015a). The Canon of love against the use of force in Islamic and public international law: Part I: The chamber of love within legal discipline. *International Criminal Law Review, 15*(4), 591–628.
Malekian, F. (2015b). The Canon of love against the use of force in Islamic and Public International Law: Part II: The anatomy of love against violations. *International Criminal Law Review, 15*, 861–895.
McAuley, F., & McCutcheon, J. P. (2000). *Criminal liability.* Round Hall, Seet & Maxwell.
Mill, J. S. (1863). *Utilitarianism: What unitarianism is?*
Morrow, A. (2002). *Killing in the name of love: Genocide of a nation.* Rising Sun Publications.
Novak, A. (2014). *The global decline of the mandatory death penalty: Constitutional jurisprudence and legislative reform in Africa, Asia and the Caribbean.* Surrey: Ashgate.
Nussbaum, M. C. (2013). *Political emotions: Why love matters for justice.* Harvard University Press.
Olmstead, A. T. (1948). *History of Persian Empire.* Chicago: University of Chicago Press.
Pufendorf, B. (1717). *Of the law of nature and nations.* Eight books (translated by Basil Kennet).
Raoult, S. (2011). *La theorisation de l'évolution pénale.* Presses Universitaires D'Aix-Marseille.
Rawls, J. (1971). *A theory of justice.*
Richards, D. A. J. (2016). *Why love leads to justice: Love across the boundaries.* New York: Cambridge University Press.

Rinceanu, J. (2011a). Extraterritorial jurisdiction – The applicability of domestic criminal law to activities committed abroad in Romania. In U. Sieber, S. Forster, & K. Jarvers (Eds.), *National criminal law in a comparative legal context*. Volume 2(1): *Max-Planck-Institute für ausländisches und internationals Strafrecht* (pp. 281–296). Berlin: Duncker & Humblot.

Rinceanu, J. (2011b). Objective aspects of the offense in Romania. In U. Sieber, S. Forster, & K. Jarvers (Eds.), *National criminal law in a comparative legal context*. Volume 3(1): *Max-Planck-Institute für ausländisches und internationals Strafrecht* (pp. 227–238). Berlin: Duncker & Humblot.

Rinceanu, J. (2016). *Criminal liability of legal persons in Romania in Riccardo Borsari, Responsabilità da reato deli enti* (pp. 407–418). Padova: Padova University Press.

Roberts, P., & Redmayne, M. (2009). Introduction: Teaching evidence scholarship. In P. Roberts & M. Redmayne (Eds.), *Innovations in evidence and proof*. Oxford: Hart Publishing.

Ross, W. D. (1939). *Foundations of ethics*. Oxford: Clarendon.

Ross, W. D. (1930). *The right and the good*. Oxford: Clarendon.

Ross, A. (1958). *On law and justice*. London: Stevens & Sons Limited.

Schabas, W. A. (2002). *The abolition of the death penalty in international law* (3rd ed.). Cambridge: Cambridge University Press.

Shah-Kazemi, R. (2014). The metaphysics of oneness and sanctifying love in Islamic mysticism. In S.T. Hidden (Ed.), *Jewish, Christian, and Islamic mystical perspectives on the Love of God* (pp. 73–101). Springer.

Shelton, D. L. (2014). *Advanced introduction to international human rights law*. USA: Edward Elgar Publishing.

Skeie, J. (1937). *Den Norske Strafferett*. Oslo: Olaf Norlis Forlag.

Sohm, R. (1935). *A textbook of the history and system of Roman private law* (J. C. Ledlie, Trans.). Oxford: Oxford University Press.

Souryal, S. S. (2015). *Ethics in criminal justice: In search of the truth* (6th ed.). New York: Routledge.

Starr, C. G. (1965). *A history of the ancient world*. Oxford: University Press.

Stern, R. (2012). *Understanding moral obligation: Kant, Hegel, Kierkegaard*. Cambridge: Cambridge University Press.

Sundin, J. (1992). För Gud, Staten, Folket: *Brott och Rättskipning I Sverige*. Lund.

Thornton, B. (2011). *The Book of Ancient Bastards: 101 of the Worst Miscreants and Misdeeds from the Ancient Sumer to the English Tenement*. USA: Adams Media.

Trechsel, S. (1997). Why must trials be fair. *Israel Law Review, 31*, 94–119.

Venturi, F. (1972). *Italy and enlightenment: Studies in a cosmopolitan century*. New York: New York University Press.

Vischer, R. K. (2014). *Martin Luther King Jr. and the morality of legal practice: lessons in love and justice*. Cambridge: Cambridge University Press.

Voegelin, E., & Franz, M. (2000). *Order and history* (Vol. 4). University of Missouri Press.

von Pufendorf, S. (1931). *Two books of the elements of universal jurisprudence* (1660) (W. Abbott, Oldfather, Trans.).

Wägenbaur, B. (2013). *Court of the European Union*. C.H.Beck. Hart. Nomos.

Walton, W. S. (2008). *The Demos at Dawn*. US: Author House.

Weiler, J. H. H., & Wind, M. (2003). *European Union law consult European constitutionalism beyond the state*. Cambridge, UK; New York, NY: Cambridge University Press.

Weiler, J. H. H. (1999). *The Constitution of Europe: "Do the New Clothes have an Emperor?" and other Essays on European Integration*. Cambridge; New York: Cambridge University Press.

Westphal, M. (1984). Hegel's radical idealism: Family and state as ethical communities. In Z. A. Pelczynski (Ed.), *The state and civil society: Studies in Hegel's political philosophy*. Cambridge: Cambridge University Press.

White, R. M., & Willock, I. D. (2007). *The Scottish legal system* (4th ed.). Glasgow: Tottel Publishing.

Zahle, H. (2005). *Praktisk restfilosofi*. Christian Ejlers' Forlag.

Chapter 2
The Oxytocin of Love in the Context of Medical Science

2.1 Significance of Love in Law

'What else is the help of medicine than love?'[1] Pure love constitutes not only the *de facto* but also the *de jure* criterion of the intention not to depart from the legal discipline which is the foundation of human rights norms, such as the abolition of the death penalty.[2] Medical practices old and new have also confirmed the significant role of love, namely in the evaluation of proposed treatments and therapies, as well as in reducing uncertainty. As such, love undoubtedly plays a prominent role in the health and well-being of human society. The celebrated Persian polymath, Avicenna (A.D. 980–1037), writes about the significant function of love in human physiology in his five-volume work, The Canon of Medicine. "A cachectic patient was brought to me with a plethora of chronic and debilitating diseases and prolonged fever, all of which were related to the love disorder. By reaching his sweetheart, I was amazed at how quickly he became reenergized. So, it became clear to me that human health is obedient to and under the control of mind."[3] One

---

[1]Paracelsus (1493–1541).

[2]Schabas (2002), p. 2.

[3]http://ajp.psychiatryonline.org/data/Journals/AJP/3798/07aj0228.PDF (Accessed October 15, 2014). In addition, the 1959 Declaration of the Rights of the Child recognises the significant function of love in the life of a child. Principle 6 of the Declaration reads: "The child, for the full and harmonious development of his personality needs love and understanding" Similarly, the Convention on the Rights of the Child refers in its preamble to the important role of love for children: "Recognizing that the child, for the full and harmonious development of his or her personality, should grow up in a family environment, in an atmosphere of happiness, love and understanding." The Convention was adopted and opened for signature, ratification, and accession by General Assembly resolution 44/25 of 20 November 1989. It entered into force on 2 September 1990, in accordance with Article 49. Further, the 1990 African Charter on the Rights and Welfare of the Child recognizes that "the child occupies a unique and privileged position in the African society and that for the full and harmonious development of his personality. The child should grow

F. Malekian, *Judgments of Love in Criminal Justice*,
DOI 10.1007/978-3-319-46900-3_2

may also see the unique metaphysical philosophy of Avicenna in the letters of the Austrian writer, Erich Fried:

> What it is
> It is madness, says reason.
> It is what it is, says love.
> It is disaster, says logic.
> It is nothing but pain, according to fear.
> It is hopeless, says insight.
> It is what it is, says love.
> It is ridiculous, so says pride.
> It is reckless, says prudence.
> It is impossible, says experience.
> It is what it is, says love.

The French philosopher and moralist Jean de La Bruyère vividly echoes the discovery by Avicenna with the epigram "the sweetest of all sounds is that of the voice of the woman we love." It is this spirit of love that constitutes the key to building a more conscientious, responsible, and dynamic international human society.

Even the state-of-the-art methods of medical science confirm that love has a great practical function and value in preventing aggression and generating peace for each individual in our national, regional, and international communities. This is also true in the case of children who are in particular need of love and understanding. Similarly, the spirit of love also constitutes the key to building a more conscientious, responsible, and dynamic international human society. All of these different arenas in which humans need and express love have a close connection with the oxytocin hormone. According to medical science, "Healthy Real Love is a powerful, vital, natural process of highly valuing, desiring for, often acting for, and taking pleasure in the well-being of the loved."[4]

Each one of the terms used here to describe love has a particular definition and all of them are necessary for the recognition of a healthy love. Pseudo-love lacks one or several of these principles. The description 'high valuing' refers, *inter alia*, to respect, appreciation, admiration, and assessment as important, excellent, superior, uniquely fitting, incomparable, and special. The statement that love is 'powerful' denotes that it is vigorous, indomitable, potent, forceful, influential, effective, dynamic, and ascendant. The term 'vital' implies the importance of certain matters of life and the processes which allow it and its cardinal processes to continue. Healthy, real love constitutes a vital force for the healthy continuation of life. The term 'natural' indicates that love is essential for existence, which thrives naturally and through which the virtue of love can be realised. The word 'process' indicates that it is possible for the feeling of love to grow. The principles of desiring, acting,

---

up in a family environment in an atmosphere of happiness, love and understanding." See *also* Lewis et al. (2000, 2001, 2007); Erich (1956, 2006).

[4]Dr. J. Richard Cookerly, How Do we Succeed at Healthy Real Love, available at http://whatislovedrcookerly.com/97/the-definition-of-love/ (Accessed February 14, 2015).

and taking pleasure in the well-being of the beloved refers to wishing well and behaving for the protection and the happiness of our love.

The absence of those who love therefore causes unnecessary suffering for human beings.[5] All of these qualities are relevant to the matter of recovering love.[6] The following expresses a more precise definition of the term 'love' as recognised in medical science. It is a

> natural process which functions to (1.) personally and profoundly connect us (with others and internally), (2.) provide effective, balanced safeguarding of the loved, (3.) endeavour for the development and improvement of the loved in multiple, healthful ways, (4.) bring about healing and maximize recovery from sickness and injury of the loved, (5.) reward and reinforce us for behaving from and with love via the many joys of love.[7]

2.2 The Hormone of Love in Law

In medical science, oxytocin constitutes a hormone produced in the brain, in the hypothalamus, which is conveyed to, and concealed by, the pituitary gland, situated at the base of the brain. The pituitary is one of the most important glands in the human body and is thus called "the master gland." Oxytocin is, among other names, called the "love hormone." The *love hormone* acts as a neurotransmitter in the *brain*. Its function is to control many other hormones such as adrenals and those of the thyroid gland.[8] Although opinions vary, medical science is of the view that the hormone has a significant function in the emotional, cognitive, and social behaviour of man:

> Traditionally, it has been artists, poets, and playwrights who have made the greatest progress in humanity's understanding of love. However, recently endocrinologists, who were never considered very romantic, have challenged this notion, and now rather have a lot to say about how and *why people love each other*. Research is also shedding light on some of the more extreme forms of sexual behaviour. And, controversially, some endocrine scientists see hormonal manipulation as the doorway to a future where *love is guaranteed*, because it will be provided chemically, or even genetically engineered from conception.[9]

The significant function of oxytocin has also been associated with several other phenomena, such as that oxytocin increases trust in humans, oxytocin increases generosity in humans,[10] and the search for autism treatments has even turned to this 'trust hormone'.[11] It could be said that oxytocin is what makes us human beings

---

[5] *Id.*

[6] Cookerly (2001).

[7] http://whatislovedrcookerly.com/340/a-more-ample-definition-of-love/ (Accessed July 20, 2015).

[8] http://www.medicalnewstoday.com/articles/275795.php (Accessed July 20, 2015).

[9] Magon and Kalra (2011).

[10] Zak et al. (2007). Available at http://www.ncbi.nlm.nih.gov/pmc/articles/PMC2040517/ (Accessed July 20, 2015).

[11] Opar (2008). Available at http://www.ncbi.nlm.nih.gov/pubmed/18391923. (Accessed July 20, 2015).

able to love: neuroscience reveals all,[12] and oxytocin is the great facilitator of life.[13] The role of oxytocin can thus be summarized as follows:

> The story of oxytocin begins right before pregnancy, continues during birth and later, travels from the brain to the heart and throughout the entire body, triggering, or modulating a full range of physiological functions and emotions: happiness, attraction, love, affection, and hatred after stress. These are all governed directly or indirectly, at least in part, by oxytocin.[14]

As has been demonstrated above, oxytocin has a definite function in the human body, and the virtuous effects of this hormone can be blocked, reduced, affected, and eliminated by stress, social inequality and by the use of force. The power of law, the law of force, the law of war, the law of retaliation, and the law of murder may harm and replace the significant function of the norm of love—this in order to have the authority and power to control the love of man by the power of the gun.

Encompassing all this in this work, I mean that the norm of love is the necessary condition of all laws if they are going to be healthy and practical. It has to be a duty of our social structure and social services to give high value to the distribution of the norm of love in law in order to increase the institution of morality for the prevention of violent behaviour.[15] This means a clear understanding of one another in the constant awareness of love for justice and obedience to the moral requirements of law such as human rights law, laws concerning protection of women's integrity, or laws relating to the protection of children and the family as a whole.[16] The norm of love has to be cultivated in our national and international criminal justice systems if crimes against national or international legislations are to decrease.[17] This has been recognised by the philosopher of social ethics, Martha Nussbaum, who encourages the necessity of the cultivation of love in social relations.[18]

2.3 The Vision of Love in Law

Medical science tells us how we can use the norm of love in the human body as a master of generosity, facilitation, big-heartedness, kindness, assistance, aid, support, relief, vision, morality, ethics and, ultimately, accredits the power of love to

[12]Young (2009). http://www.ncbi.nlm.nih.gov/pubmed/19129828. (Accessed July 20, 2015).

[13]Lee et al. (2009). Available at http://www.ncbi.nlm.nih.gov/pmc/articles/PMC2689929/. (Accessed July 20, 2015).

[14]Magon and Kalra (2011). Available at http://www.ncbi.nlm.nih.gov/pmc/articles/PMC3183515/. (Accessed July 20, 2015).

[15]Nussbaum (2013), pp. 46–47.

[16]Malekian (2015), pp. 569–593.

[17]Malekian (2005).

[18]Nussbaum (2013), pp. 4–5.

hinder the catastrophic result of injustices created through war. However, I am *aware* that medical science is not law and does not constitute a body of legislation. Nevertheless, most jurisdictions, at least in European courts of justice, are bound, due to the requirement of certain provisions, to use medical science for various purposes, if not love. The intention is to determine the physical and psychological health of the accused. A clear example of this is the case of the Norwegian murderer who killed at least 77 people in the government buildings and summer camp on the island of Utøya in 2011. Yet, we must also be well *aware* of the fact that all manmade laws are the product of our physical bodies.

Justice and law, justice and peace, justice and victims, justice and criminals, justice and lawyers, justice and courts, justice and prosecutors, justice and the United Nations members, as well as justice and the permanent members of the Security Council are encouraged and urged to use this potential validation of human love. They should exploit oxytocin as a norm of understanding and ad the basic key to the resolution of various conflicts. With the norm of love, we do not mean the legislation of new norms but the norm, which exists in our nature, in the spirit of our international human rights instruments, in the course of international movements for the prosecution and punishment of international crimes, in international criminal courts, and in the general principles of all laws, whether American, British, Chinese, Indian, Egyptian, Israeli, Palestinian, or in the Nordic countries.

There are already a large number of national, regional, and international provisions within the law of different nations that may be classified under the term "pure theory of love." They are the provisions of different laws, whether Western or Muslim, which influenced each other, and one may speak of them under the terms "similar provisions," "similar wills," "similar intentions," "similar interests," "similar cognisant," and also "similar juxtaposition of life principles." All these principles and terms, as we will see later, guide and encourage us towards human unity. We have to realise that the principle of unity or unity of love between Westerners and Muslims is not an impossible norm but a fact and reality that exists in the philosophy of the development of law, not to mention the development of various philosophies of European classical lawyers. These include Kant, Kelsen, Bertrand Russell as well as the well-established, prominent international lawyers of the United States, such as Martin Luther King. Kant describes this unity and human universality as follows:

> Everywhere around us we observe a chain of causes and effects, of means and ends, of death and birth; and, as nothing has entered of itself into the condition in which we find it, we are constantly referred to some other thing, which itself suggests the same inquiry regarding its cause, and thus the universe must sink into the abyss of nothingness, unless we admit that, besides this infinite chain of contingencies, there exists something that is primal and self-subsistent—something which, as the cause of this phenomenal world, secures its continuance and preservation...This argument always deserves to be mentioned with respect. It is the oldest, the clearest, and that most in conformity with the common reason of humanity. It animates the study of nature, as it itself derives its existence and draws ever new strength from that source. It introduces aims and ends into a sphere in which our observation could not of itself have discovered them, and extends our knowledge of nature, by directing our attention to a unity, the principle of which lies beyond nature. This

knowledge of nature again reacts upon this idea—its cause; and thus our belief in a divine author of the universe rises to the power of an irresistible conviction.[19]

2.4 The Disappearance of Love from the Law

The norm of love constitutes the most important norm of legal discipline. Here again by 'the norm of love' we mean all law in the body of international human rights law or international criminal law which has been formulated for the prevention of serious violations against humanity. All of these regulations show how much human beings have in common concerning certain matters in their life on earth, their existence on their continent, their subjectivity in their relevant country, their membership in different organisations, and their fundamental membership in their family unit. All of these areas express the strong relations of law with love. If international human rights law or rules of law relating to human rights do not constitute the norm of love for human beings, then they are not law but 'strict regulations'. The definition of 'strict regulations' amounts to hard discipline and hard discipline assimilates to the law of despotism, totalitarianism, autocracy, and tyranny. The purpose of human rights law is certainly not to be strict disciplinary law but a body which requires the understanding of its norms by the human heart: the power of love, justice of love, love for justice and not love of power. However, the existence of the norm of love in the philosophy of human rights law demands love but does not dictate love.

It is here that the *bona fide* nature of love changes and in its place appears love of opinion, love of one's own society's norms, love of cultural habits, love of oneself over others, love of economic gain, and the empty pretence of practising human rights law with love, as is the case in many European Union states' politics. Thus, the three principles within the inner structure of the philosophy of the rule of love are mistreated. They are the legal principle, the moral principle, and the principle of love, all of which are an integral part of human philosophy and ethics. These violations cause conflict and conflict brings into concrete reality stories of war and, in turn, the latter becomes genocide, crimes against humanity, war crimes, aggression, torture, rape, and grave violations of every system of penal law in the world, including those of both Islamic and Western law. This means that we have humiliated and mutilated the principle of legality and that we focus on our differences rather than our similarities.

Some examples of the leading criminal propensity of the human mind to favour the use of force over love, which is confirmed in medical science, motivated by political, military, and above all with economic objectives and mutual detestation between both Muslim and non-Muslim nations, are internationally dishonourable. These are, for instance, the Somali Civil Wars (1986–1981 and 1993), the 1991

[19]Kant, p. 360. Available at http://www2.hn.psu.edu/faculty/jmanis/kant/critique-pure-reason6x9.pdf. (Accessed December 27, 2014).

Gulf Crisis in Iraq, the 1993 Yugoslavian war, the Rwanda Genocide (April 7 to July 15, 1994), the South African apartheid system (1948–1994), the Albanian Civil War (1997), the genocide of the Kurds (1998), and the Indonesian invasion of East Timor (1999). Other examples are the Angola Civil War of Independence (1961–1974 and 1975–2002), the Sierra Leonean Civil War (1991–2002), the Liberian Civil Wars (1989–1996 and 1999–2003), the Congolese Civil Wars (1996–1997 and 1998–2003), the Burundian Civil War (2003–2005), the Sudanese Civil Wars (1955–1972 and 1983–2005), and the recent civil war and subsequent internationalisation of the conflict in Syria. Almost 20 % of the population of Rwanda, approximately 1,000,000 innocent human beings were slaughtered in just 100 days in 1994. Another clear example of the disappearance of love and its replacement with the power of will and the pursuit of interests is the conflict that came into reality in South Sudan in December 2013. It resulted in the killing and fleeing of thousands of homeless people. This implies the fact that oxytocin has been used for its negative function rather than its positive one.

The norm of love in criminal law and international criminal law encourages the prevention of impunity and the empowerment of justice for the purpose of prosecution and punishment of criminals.[20] It creates a legal norm according to which all societies are bound by the duty to take all reasonable measures to bring criminals to justice before national, regional, or international criminal courts. One of the advantages of the norm is that it encourages the criminal justice system to call for the criminal accountability of those who are the main cause of the commission of crimes. Whilst all of these statements are facts and seem rational, I must acknowledge that none of the norms of legality, morality, and love is a practical answer for the actual conduct of states or the crimes of governments.

The love norm was seriously infringed in each of the conflicts mentioned above. The conflicting parties violated the basic elements of public international law, Islamic international law, human rights law, the international humanitarian law of armed conflicts, the African states' human rights laws, European Union law, the Charter of Fundamental Rights, and, above all, the general principles of love for human integrity governing the prevention of resort to the use of force. This means the disappearance of love in the preservation of the health of humanity. What was really missing in these conflicts was the basic understanding of each other as human beings, as integral members of their national or international societies, as valuable subjects having human rights coupled with the failure to adhere to the spiritual paths of morality, philosophy, humanitarian ethics, and the acknowledgement of the permanent existence of love for justice in natural law in all situations.

[20] Eser (2012), pp. 621–663; Eser (2011a), pp. 108–148. www.freidok.uni-freiburg.de/volltexte/9713; see *also* Eser (2011b). www.freidok.uni-freiburg.de/volltexte/9742.

2.5 The Core Intention of Love in Law

The sole intention of medical science should naturally be to nurture our capacity to love, to preserve the hormone of love in the human body rather than to destroy it. Most systems of law, such as Hammurabi's Code, the Cyrus Charter of the Human Rights Cylinder, Canon Law, Roman Law, Common Law, European Union Law, Jewish law, Islamic Law, and all other human rights instruments have certain historical similarities. These are, namely, the ambition to ensure the application of the principles of equality, justice, peace, and respect for human integrity through the provisions of their legislation. This means that, with the enforcement of the sole purposes of different systems, one does not only necessarily place emphasis on the application of the power of the law but also, as much as possible, the power of the implementation of equal human rights law principles, which can approach the heart of the needs of the international community as a whole. As Jeremy Gans has rightly stated, "human rights law is a standard for judging other laws."[21] Giving privileges to one body of rules, regulations, principles, and norms of law over another, or condemning one or another of them on different grounds, diminishes the standards of law and justice and incites political opposition to the application of an objective philosophy over and above regional sentiment:

> We are hopeful that, by establishing contact with one another and by a policy of negotiation, nations will come to a better recognition of the natural ties that bind them together as men. We are hopeful, too, that they will come to a fairer realization of one of the cardinal duties deriving from our common nature: namely, that love, not fear, must dominate the relationships between individuals and between nations. It is principally characteristic of love that it draws men together in all sorts of ways, sincerely united in the bonds of mind and matter; and this is a union from which countless blessings can flow.[22]

As far as the people of the world are concerned, it is not the name of the law that is crucial but rather its content, substance, essence, and whether it fulfills the requirements of the international community of human beings within its given practical framework. This is what might be termed 'the main purpose of the law', whether it is called 'Islamic law', 'Jewish law', 'the European Union's framework of law', 'Common Law', 'Latin American law', etc. It is not the name or cultural origins of a body of law, which gives it its sense but the underlying philosophy, in the absence of the monopolization of its real nature by those who exercise legal or political power over the law.[23] A communist ideology, an interpretation of the spirit of indigenous law, a Christian religious rule, a Jewish ceremony of norms, a common law principle, a European Union legal condition, or a United Nations

[21]Gans (2012), p. 40.

[22]*On Establishing Universal Peace in Truth, Justice, Charity and Liberty*. http://www.vatican.va/holy_father/john_xxiii/encyclicals/documents/hf_j-xxiii_enc_11041963_pacem_en.html, article 129.

[23]Malekian (2015).

provision may all have elements of both bad and good laws, depending on the policies and the hidden intentions of those who apply them.

Bearing this in mind, we can see that the norm of love exists within all legal systems to different degrees. In all legal systems, when a situation or political development seriously violates legal and moral principles, the principle of love becomes visible. This means that the invisibility of the principle of love that we have repeatedly described throughout this work becomes impossible because the combined power of the people to stop violations or injustice transforms itself into the collective form of love for justice. This can come from any law or by the cooperation of all these laws together in order to stop serious human rights violations in the world, such as genocide. One can see clearly that the differences between different laws not only disappear, but that these different legal systems also become the foundation upon which to combine the power of their similarities to struggle against unjust criminal behaviour. This means a collective expression of oxytocin, the hormone of love, in the service of love.

Consequently, Islamic law becomes Jewish law and Jewish law becomes Islamic law, European Union law becomes the concept of the jihadist struggle for justice and the jihadist struggle becomes the philosophy preventing all criminal violations. Here, I would like to suggest that Jewish law is the most important facet of European law, and that Islamic law is present in some of the most fundamental principles of Jewish law. Equally, the philosophy of Kant loses its concept of 'Kantianism' and becomes like the philosophy of Marxism, and Marxist philosophy becomes akin to the philosophy of Islamic law, and the latter akin to the philosophy of the Constitution of the United States as a whole, and so forth. This interconnectedness between all laws of humanity is what we have to look for.

References

Cookerly, J. (2001). *Recovering love: Co-dependency to co-recovery.*

Erich, F. (1956). *The art of loving*. Harper & Row.

Erich, F. (2006). *The art of loving*. Harper & Row.

Eser, A. (2011a). Procedural structure and features of international criminal justice: Lessons from the ICTY. In B. Swart, A. Zahar, & G. Sluiter (Eds.), *The legacy of the international criminal tribunal for the former Yugoslavia* (1st ed., pp. 108–148). Oxford University Press.

Eser, A. (2011b). *Transnationales Strafrecht/Transnational Criminal Law*. Ausgewählte Beiträge/ Collected Publications. Compiled and edited by G. Heine, B. Burkhardt, W. Gropp. Berliner Wissenschaftsverlag.

Eser, A. (2012). Transnational measures against the impunity of international crimes. *Journal of International Criminal Justice, 10*(3), 621–663 (Oxford University Press).

Gans, J. (2012). *Modern criminal law of Australia*. Cambridge: Cambridge University Press.

Kant, I. *The critique of pure reason* (J. M. D. Meiklejohn, Trans.). An Electronic Classical Series Publication.

Lee, H., Macbeth, A., Pagani, J., & Young, W. R. (2009). Oxytocin: The great facilitator of life. *Progress in Neurobiology, 88*, 127–151.

Lewis, T., Amini, F., & Lannon, R. (2000). *A general theory of love*. Random House.

Lewis, T., Amini, F., & Lannon, R. (2001). *A general theory of love*. Vintage Books.

Lewis, T., Amini, F., & Lannon, R. (2007). *A general theory of love*. Vintage Books.
Magon, N., & Kalra, S. (2011). *Indian Journal of Endocrinology and Metabolism, 15*(Suppl. 3), S156–S161. doi:10.4103/2230-8210.84851. http://www.ncbi.nlm.nih.gov/pmc/articles/PMC3183515/.
Malekian, F. (2005). Emasculating the philosophy of international criminal justice in the Iraqi special tribunal. *Cornell International Law Journal, 38*(3), 673–723.
Malekian, F. (2015). The canon of love against the use of force in Islamic and public international law: Part II: The anatomy of love against violations. *International Criminal Law Review*, 861–889.
Nussbaum, M. C. (2013). *Political emotions: Why love matters for justice*. Harvard University Press.
Opar, A. (2008). Search for potential autism treatments turns to 'trust hormone'. *Nature Medicine, 14*, 353.
Schabas, W. A. (2002). *The abolition of the death penalty in international law* (3rd ed.). Cambridge: Cambridge University Press.
Young, L. (2009). Being human: Love: Neuroscience reveals all. *Nature, 457*, 148.
Zak, P., Stanton, A., & Ahmadi, S. (2007). Oxytocin increases generosity in humans. *PLoS One, 2*, e1128.

Chapter 3
The Rule of Love for the Interrogation of Criminal Justice

3.1 The Norm of Love Beyond All Norms

The ignorance in the mind of the human body as to the nature of law and its provisions may be counteracted by the strength of love. This moves us to assist one another in confronting bad law, threatening habits, serious violations, and grave offences against human integrity. In other words, the philosophy of love in legal theory is not to say that love has to be the first touchstone of human justice, human morality, human action, human will, human interests, and human rules; rather, my intention is to show that love is a norm beyond all norms of law when the other norms are wholly incapable of performing their function. It is again here that, over and above the law of all nations,' Jewish and non-Jewish, European Union and non-European Union states, American organization and non-American organization, United States or non-United States legislation, there is a norm that signifies the fact that all these laws, regulations, and concepts are free from naturalist and legal positivist opinion. This is when the focus is solely on humanity and protecting human beings from unnecessary suffering. This concept constitutes a norm for the existence of unity without relying on the concept of any religion or any other theory at all. *It is not only free from religious ties, religious monopolization, fanatical religious expressions but also from dictatorial laws, false human rights law, inconsistent morality, and any political ties, whether from the sanctions of the Security Council of the United Nations or the law ordered by a Jewish or Islamic state.*

The fact is that the disappearance of love in a human society which has entered into armed conflict calls upon the profound need of that society for the empowering norm of love in law. As Rousseau Jean-Jacques expresses it, "Wherever men love their country, they respect the laws."[1] This norm of law has to function for the reconstruction of society and for the understanding of similarity and stagnation of

[1] Rousseau (1761), p. 270. Available at http://oll.libertyfund.org/titles/638 (Accessed April 13, 15).

F. Malekian, *Judgments of Love in Criminal Justice*,
DOI 10.1007/978-3-319-46900-3_3

pluralism. The same opinion of Rousseau is also applicable to international societies when there are excessive violations, particularly terrorist activities of any kind. The international legal and political community must realise that the path to peace and justice cannot be solved by accusations against Muslims, Jews, or any other peoples behind closed doors. They have to comprehend what the reasons behind the violations are.

If the Austrian Parliament drafts the Reform Law of Islam and the law becomes a model for the whole of Europe[2] and also comes into place in other parts of the world, even if the United Nations integrates the law into its Charter, it will still not be effective and prevent violations. This is because, if the real love for justice and humanity in the inner structure of Austria's policy and polity is not cultivated, the law cannot function properly.

By 'cultivation', we mean that the people of the world who are protesting against laws, politics, or the economy have something to say about which law we have to value and take notice of. The law cannot be respected if there is no trust in the law, if there is no love for the law, and if—as Schwarzenberger argues—the smaller nations do not cease participating in and conspiring with the policies of larger nations. A Persian maxim rightly states that if you are seeking justice, you cannot lament with the shepherds for the loss of a sheep and at the same time eat a meal of the sheep with the wolves. If Jesus was the shepherd of God, he did not have a meal with the Romans. If we are looking for the pure philosophy of justice and the establishment of an international society free from violations, we are forced by the power of love to pursue the respect of human dignity by adhering to truth and rejecting lies. Love is in fact a gate towards the harmonisation of what is to be avoided and what is to be encouraged, even if love ends in our suffering. As St. Augustine points out "God had one son on earth without sin, but never one without suffering."

In the former Yugoslavian conflict between different ethnic groups, it became obvious that none of the conflicting parties could acknowledge the fact that their divergences were not working for peace and justice and that law could not be respected by force, violations, or without love. Divergences were not only destructive of culture and civilisation but were also militating against the balance that had been achieved between their ethnic differences and similarities and threatened their very existence. All parties were therefore violators of national, regional, and international criminal law, and all were losers in this long divisive conflict. War could not bring justice for them; war could not prevent killings, and war could not stop 60,000 instances of rape. The war was against all human morality, the principles of ethics, the principle of the prevention of genocide, the elements of crimes against humanity, the norms of warfare, the United Nations Charter, the European Union's laws, and the Islamic concept of lawful defence.

[2]Schmid (2014).

Although many Serbian leaders have been brought before the jurisdiction of international criminal tribunals, their prosecution and punishment does not amend in the slightest the injustices that have occurred. If certain permanent members of the UN Security Council were searching for true equality, and if the similarities between states had been taken into account from the beginning, war would not have been waged, and the criminal law would not have been violated so barbarously. It is always differences that make a part of a nation arm itself against its own nation. Yet, we should recognise that most wars have occurred between two or several states, and that many states have made other nations the target of armed attacks solely for economic reasons. A clear example is Afghanistan, which suffered from heavily armed attacks by two superpowers, namely the Soviet Socialist Republic and the United States, with the latter conflict including the involvement of two other permanent members of the Security Council, the United Kingdom and France.

What these powers were committing was surely neither the law of the UN Charter, nor the provisions of other laws, nor the ethic of European Law, nor the resolutions of a healthy political and legal philosophy. The politically powerful parties had evidently replaced norms of love with the norms of love of force, love of power, love of wealth, and love of gaining new territories.[3] All of these denote false forms of love, false forms of norms, false forms of morality, and false forms of the implementation of justice. The application of love for justice should not be a conundrum for humanity if the intention of legislators, the purpose of judges, the aim of governments, the objective of the United Nations Security Council, and the goal of a given stronger democratic power is justice and not law, and beyond even justice, the investment of love.[4]

We could discuss in similar terms the case of many other wars, both those of an international and those of a civil nature. In all of these wars as well, *it is the disappearance of understanding of our similarities and the replacement of love for justice with love for injustice that make the most grave violations of the system of international criminal law possible.* As one of the classical writers of international law asserts:

> . . .the very injustice of all offences ought to be a general motive with men, to restrain them from the commission of them. For at present we are not considering sins of any kind, but those, which extend their consequences beyond the offender himself, and affect others. And injustice is the more heinous and criminal in proportion to the greatness of the injury, which it inflicts.[5]

---

[3]George Washington also speaks about love of power. He expresses that "A just estimate of that love of power, and proneness to abuse it, which predominates in the human heart is sufficient to satisfy us of the truth of this position." Allen (1988), p. 521. Available at http://oll.libertyfund.org/titles/washington-george-washington-a-collection#lf0026_mnt485 (Accessed April 5, 2015). See *also* Bentham (2016), p. 62.

[4]Nussbaum (2013), p. 123.

[5]Grotius (1625), p. 241; http://oll.libertyfund.org/titles/grotius-the-rights-of-war-and-peace-1901-ed (Accessed April 27, 2015).

It bears repeating again that the concept of international crimes is not based solely on the concept of international criminal conventions or international criminal customary law. The criteria for the recognition of international crimes also borrows from the basic concept of national criminal law.[6] I am not talking here about the Kelsen concept of *grundnorm* but instead the reality of the fact that many basic principles of international criminal law have a long history of existence within national criminal laws. Again, I am not saying that national criminal law is the same as international criminal law or *vice versa,* but the fact is that they complete one another's intentions. Both systems infer from the concept of positivist theory that law is the expression of certain norms that are to be followed and respected in national or international social relations.

In addition, within the law, there is a norm which is above all norms in order to keep justice secure and unharmed. This is what I have repeatedly called "the norm of love." It is the norm of pure substance, the norm of justice, and the norm which brings different systems, such as dualism and monism, very close to each other. The reality is that whatever we do and whatever we desire, the concept of the pure unity of law cannot be changed. This means, for example, that whether or not we accept national and international law as two different legal systems, the result is the same. We do not necessarily need to transmit the norm of love in law into national or international legal systems. The norm has incorporated itself into the substance of all law. If it has not, then it is not law, but merely the presentation of unequal norms. For instance, all international human rights conventions have to have a positive substance rather than a negative one.

In other words, we fully understand that the ratification of laws has a highly significant function in the implementation of an international convention, but this does not mean necessarily that the act of non-ratification subverts the positive substance of the relevant law, its intention, its goodwill, its purity, and its love for human beings. That is why, in some states, a judge is permitted to declare a national rule invalid if it contradicts with international obligations. For instance, Germany considers treaties an integral part of its domestic legislation. This is the effect of the principle of *lex posterior,* which is a principle of treaty interpretation due to the provisions of Article 32 of the 1969 Vienna Convention on the Law of Treaties.[7] It means a treaty's provisions may take precedence over enacted provisions of national legislation prior to its ratification. Without doubt, an international convention invalidates national provisions which are against its basic substance. However, none of these situations has any effect on the substance of law and the maintenance of the purity of the law which has to be sound and to serve love for justice. The pure goodness of the law constitutes the love norm. We have to love the law and the law has to love us if our provisions and the law's provisions are going to be watchful of the heart of real justice and indicate an objective standard.

[6]Consult Bozbayindir (2013), pp. 148–153.

[7]*1155 U.N.T.S. 331.*

Yet, it has to be acknowledged that there are a number of states which do not incorporate international conventions into their laws immediately. Even they have already ratified the applicable agreements—they have to adopt them into their legislations by particular acts of their governments or parliaments. Although this should not necessarily be interpreted as implying that the subject matter of the conventions are invalid, the policy in practice creates a substantial amount of legal and impractical issues that have to be drafted and resolved by the government in question, or under the European Union's judicial system when the relevant state is a member of the Union. For instance, several of these issues have been brought against Sweden for non-incorporation of its international obligations, such as the provisions of the Convention on the Rights of the Child. Although Sweden has been flexible regarding European Human Rights decisions, its own decisions have been very slow.[8]

Without doubt, laws cannot be durable if they do not adhere to justice, and justice cannot be secured if love for its purity does not exist among legal and political authorities. *"Make men, therefore, if you would command men: if you would have them obedient to the laws, make them love the laws, and then they will need only to know what is their duty to do it."*[9] The philosophy on the norm of love does not refer to the preference for national or international law one over the other.

As we have stated elsewhere, our philosophy does not look for divergences between different laws, different rules, different political ideologies, the statutes of various criminal jurisdictions, or the various implementations of the laws. It instead looks for the establishment of a principle which already exists within most laws and which has to be the master key for purity of justice, whether it has a national, regional, or international character.[10] The philosophy of love therefore takes into consideration the main duty of man to man, the leading responsibility of state to state, and the core obligation of the law to obey the philosophy of love for justice. *This is not to say merely that the norm of love is beyond criminal law but instead amplifies the fact that the norm of love is not only beyond the criminal law but also has to be the entire system of law, justice, morality, judgment, prosecution, punishment, and jurisdiction. That is, if the law is to be respected by everyone and if the system of punishment, prosecution, imprisonment, and violation is to be utilised only minimally.*

---

[8]On 17 occasions, Sweden came under the lens of the European Commission and the European Court of Justice in 2014. Available at http://www.eu-upplysningen.se/Sverige-i-EU/EU-lagar-galler-framfor-svenska-lagar/Sverige-i-EU-domstolen/ (Accessed September 24, 2015); See *also* http://www.dagensjuridik.se/2013/10/skatteverkets-vrakningar-kan-ga-emot-fns-barnkonvention-fragan-provas-av-hd (Accessed September 24, 2015).

[9]Rousseau (1761), p. 260. Available at http://oll.libertyfund.org/titles/638 (Accessed April 13, 2015).

[10]This is what is called different methods of approach to basic rights. Shelton (2014), pp. 103–106.

3.2 The Nature of Norm of Love

Turning back to the query which may be raised by some international lawyers concerning the nature of love in law, I must also add the following: the law is not solely what we see or what we read. More than this, a law actually relies on the historical evolution of its existence. Such is the case concerning the laws which came into effect after the American Civil War and French Revolution. They brought and aimed for love for justice. Thus, because of the circumstances, laws possess certain characteristics and they possess them by their substantive nature as law. This makes them universal which means they imbibe certain values that can be seen within the civilization of most nations because of their essence. Therefore, the complex characterisation of the law and its intentions give rise to serious challenges for and against the personality of laws. An attempt to explain the nature of the law is not by itself sufficient if the normative function of the law is interwoven with several other principles, such as cultural, religious, social, and ethnic principles. The normative function of the law and other principles are all based on the strong potencies of the love norm, upon which it depends not only for its quality but also for the true essence of all norms that are similar to the law. These include religious modalities, cultural manifestations, social collectivisation, communal interests, proportionate use of the natural environment, and the equal ethical dignity of human beings. These subdivided norms of love are partly the law itself and partly the way in which we understand the law when it comes into contact with our daily activities.

Needless to say, the normative function of law and its subdivided norms are all based on the concept of certain rationales that are readily apparent to the relevant nation. This is the same for the international standard. The combinations of all these rationales together creates a normative norm, which is familiar for all norms, and therefore it is not of any significance from which nation these rules originated.

Yet, as Kant illustrates, any 'knowledge begins with experience'. This means that with experience we realise that norms of law or subdivided norms are not altogether effective without considering the essence of their existence. This joint or united essence is love. I am not basing my argument here on empirical evidence but on the presumption that we are all aware of the fact that, for example, human rights law principles, if they are respected, represent the union of love for all human beings, or—as it is called in Europe—"solidarity." We come now to the question of the recognition of the normative principles of human rights law with the normative essence of reverence for humanity.[11] What we are doing here is questioning the system of criminal law, criminal justice, and law as a whole and answering the question as to whether human rights norms are effective in the system of criminal justice with love.

[11]See Dougan (2008), pp. 617–703 at 669.

3.3 Mixed Theories

Many national and international lawyers' arguments concerning the questions of monism and dualism are proving to be no longer valid. The perspective of both theory and practice is modifying rapidly. Monism asserted that there is no difference between national and international law and that both come from the same source. Dualism expressed the contrary view.[12] Although both theories present powerful arguments, the reality is that most states have adopted a mixed form of both theories. The reason is obvious: national legal systems and public international law cannot survive without their reasoning. States invoke the concept of both theories whenever they consider it crucial for their national or international policies.

This implies the fact that there is a legal, political, juridical, and moral tendency in the external and internal conducts of states that calls upon the realisation or consciousness of the fact that the human, political, or legal community has to obey the power of law and humanity. A state, with reference to its national law, whether Common law, Palestinian law, Israeli law, Iranian law, Chinese law, United States law, or Swedish law, can no longer hide itself behind reasoning that human rights law has been respected when in reality it has not.[13] On many occasions, the Swedish authorities have been recognised as the violators of human rights norms by the European legal system. The Iranian government is continuously violating human rights and public international law, to such an extent that it no longer bears reporting. The Israeli government is guilty of the violation of human rights in its own country.[14] The United States national system is still suffering from unjustifiable decisions against its own African American population.

Moreover, the Australian indigenous population is still struggling for their very primary rights of existence. The Australian Government has decided to hand back the oil documents which it shamefully stole from East Timor's lawyers. It still does not submit itself to a discussion of the recognition of permanent maritime boundaries of the relevant country. South Africa is not free from unlawful discrimination. The Chinese authorities are guilty of serious violations of human rights law against their own people and neighbouring countries. The Syrian leader, although suffering from the unjustified international political conspiracies of the United States government, is himself guilty of violations of the rights of his own people. The Islamic leaders of many states make many empty promises about their own high commitment to human rights practices. The British system, whilst having a tendency towards the implementation of justice with its conscientious judges, operates very inconsistent and capricious policies towards the human rights of foreigners.[15] The

[12]Ross (1946).

[13]Rydenfelt and Larsson (1966), e.g. at 7.

[14]Sunstein (2001), pp. 3–4.

[15]http://rt.com/news/un-britain-human-rights-122/ (Accessed May 28, 2015).

Russian legal system is almost wholly corrupt. Bearing this in mind, what is it that has gone so wrong with our fixed and united theories of justice?

When we call a body of law "human rights law", it has to have the same product and the same effect in all parts of the world. The provisions of the law do not permit us to apply different policies for the same law. However, I am aware that we do. For the same reason, the interpretation of the provisions of the International Covenant on Civil and Political Rights should be the same in our internal and external policies. Any state in the world obviously has a strong duty to maintain international justice and human rights law when it claims it is armed by integrating the rules of international humanitarian law of armed conflict within its jurisdiction, by the provisions of international human rights law, and by legislation developed according to a high democratic standard. This is especially true when the state is an important member of the European Union.[16] It should be the elementary duty of the relevant state not to engage in the manufacture of weapons, export of such weapons, and import of such weapons. If it does, it surely violates its own philosophy of criminal justice. This is how, as I have said repeatedly, the norm of the power of law may take priority over the norm of love.

The conclusion we can draw from all of the facts assembled in the above paragraphs is that a state must be fully aware of the fact that it should not have two different policies regarding the application of monist or dualist theories at home and abroad. If we seek the spreading of human rights law, we should treat all human beings as equals in accordance with the canon of love for justice and the strength of good faith. This includes people who are living in our nations and people who are not in our nations but live in other territories. Love for the substance of justice does not mean love only for those who are a part of our nation, or a part of our union, but love for all people because of the collective and individual meaning of justice for all human beings as a whole.

3.4 Understanding of Norms

Our legal policies, our legal actions, and our human rights practices do not need to be imposed by sanctions but by the understanding of the fact that binding rules of law do not need to be ordered by a court, or by United Nations resolutions, but at our own initiation based on the moral effect of all legal norms. *This is because when a state, a government, or a nation is civilised and understands law and order, justice and injustice, and the bad habits of laws such as degrading references to Islamic law, it has to demonstrate that it has itself a correct national or international policy. It must have good laws and enforce the law for the maintenance of pure justice and its humanitarian intentions. We cannot attack nations just because they are Muslims. We cannot properly criticise the Chinese government's criminal*

[16] Fischer (1998), pp. 663–702 at 702.

actions when we ourselves our doing wrong. The Islamic Republic of Iran cannot state that the United States government is violating human rights law when it itself has hideously violated the entire system of human rights law, including Islamic human rights law, since it seized power. We cannot speak about our high level of democratic morality when we are violating the law in other countries or when we are, by one means or another, following the criminal policy of a superpower. Such examples are the British government, the Swedish government, many of the Arab governments, and so forth. However, I am not referring here to the plea of *tu quoque* and its consequences or relevant judgments.

We should decide whether we are going to apply either unilateral norms, bilateral norms, or multilateral norms. Each one of these norms is valid but under the condition that the norm of love is applied and this norm is not as selective as other norms. This is because international human rights law, international criminal law, international humanitarian law, public international law, Islamic human rights law, European Union law, and European Conventions on Human Rights laws are not only obligatory but also provide an imperative impulsion, if that is not a *dangerous metaphor*.[17] They embrace a variety of fundamental rights, such as the dignity of man, freedom, equality, solidarity, rights of citizens, and justice.[18] According to one philosopher of law:

> it is not easy to quote instances of unilateral norms. They always seem bilateral when they are really binding, and in order to find examples of unilateral norms we must turn either to norms which have never been treated as binding, as is the case of the norm which recommends us to offer the other cheek, or to the norms which have been binding in the past but nowadays are treated as obsolete, as in the norm of 'Honour thy mother and thy father' in those countries where mutual love and comradeship has replaced a hierarchical structure of the family.[19]

A moral norm can be so strong that it can end up being recognised as a binding legal norm. The same legal philosopher clarifies as follows:

> Thus, if the existence of widely experienced claims is decisive for including the given norm in the class of legal norms, among the really binding norms, practically nothing is left to morality. Even the norm recommending love of one's neighbour, always quoted as a typical example of a unilateral norm, can in some cases be bilateral, as e-g., in the case of maternal love. People disapprove of a mother who does not love her child. The child can claim her warm attention, and the mother herself can feel guilty of disapproving these claims, which she considers valid. . . .the distinction of legal and moral rules does not seem operational, since we have always to inquire what is the state of mind of the person who makes use of the norm, and it may easily happen that the same norm, recommended by the same person, is moral at one time and legal at another.[20]

---

[17] Ashworth (2008), p. 20.

[18] For instance, see the European Charter of Fundamental Rights which was proclaimed in 2000 and is legally binding for the EU with the entry into force of the Treaty of Lisbon in December 2009.

[19] Ossowska, p. 256. http://ossowska.isns.uw.edu.pl/pliki/teksty/Moral-and-Legal-Norms.pdf. The article is about the teaching of philosophy by Professor Petrazycki of the University of Warsaw in 1917.

[20] *Id.*

What I have said here is that every person in the world has a valid claim when he or she demands that the norm of love in justice has to be applied. The spirit of the principle of humanity which is regulated in many laws, including public and Islamic international law and European law, requires governmental authorities, executive, legislative, and judicial, in every state to orient the policy of the government in a direction which leads towards the implementation of international human rights law. This should not only be respected in the individual's own country but also in the world. This means that any claim from any government that we are protecting our national interests but at the same time violating the integrity of international human rights law is obviously invalid and does not therefore concur with the norm of love for justice.

3.5 Conjunctis Viribus

As a general norm of law and as a general ethic of criminal law, we are, according to the philosophy of criminal legislation, obliged, regardless of the time and the circumstances, not to violate the main ethic of the law, i.e. *conjunctis viribus*, or its commonly agreed intention. This philosophy applies not only to the order of national criminal law but also to international criminal law. Otherwise, what is the purpose of the principle of *pacta sunt servanda*? If we are not bound by the effect of the ratification of international criminal conventions, we should also not be bound by any resolutions of the General Assembly or the Security Council of the United Nations. If the signatures of our governments are only a gesture, then we are violating the fundamental principles of international law.[21] If love for justice is not a norm of the law, if the norm of legality is the only norm of human rights law, then, in this case, it should be seen as a very serious duty to adhere to the norm of love. One should not ignore this legal fact and the fact that justice is an integral part of this framework of the law.

A very prominent international lawyer correctly refers in his recent book to the fact that Muslims have killed a large number of Muslims themselves.[22] The significance of this statistic is obviously true and relevant for all Muslims and more broadly for the population of the world. However, one problem with this statistic is that it has probably not taken into consideration the fact that the countries or the Muslim groups, which were the target of those attacks to which the writer refers, are not the groups or nations which produced the weapons used against Muslims.

The fact is that none of these Islamic groups has or will have the knowledge to manufacture such weapons. The questions are therefore very simple: why have

[21] For a contrary view, examine Riesman Michael (2008), pp. 132–134.

[22] Bassiouni Cherif (2014), p. 2.

killings amongst these Muslim groups increased?[23] Who distributes these weapons among these groups? In addition to whether or not there is any political interest in the wealth of these countries, the question then arises as to who is behind the conspiracies to pit these groups against each other? Goodwill constitutes the first universal principle of all of these Muslims, and so what are the reasons behind these grave violations of the principle?

In addition, why are all these problems of beheadings, trade in weapons, and continuous armed conflicts carried out solely in the oil-rich regions of the world?[24] How far does the definition of money laundering countermeasures extend to the relevant provisions of the international legal system and to the European Union law?[25] What *criteria* do we use to judge whether we have understood the difference between dirty money laundering, organised criminality, and the trade in blood money from the illegal armaments trade? Why is Australia denying East Timor rights to permanent maritime boundaries relating to its own oil field? An examination of various reports shows that 90 percent of weapons used in the genocide of the population of East Timor came from the government of the United States. Accordingly:

> The United States certainly has not been alone in its criminal complicity. With few exceptions almost all Western countries are guilty of crimes in East Timor. From Australia, France, and Canada to Germany, Japan, and the United Kingdom, narrow economic and political considerations have informed Western practices toward Indonesia and East Timor since 1975. Constâncio's story vividly shows the human costs of such real politick.[26]

Do all these not denote the existence of the principle of *mens rea*? They "DIDN'T mean to do it."[27] They "just didn't think."[28] Without any doubt, here we infringe material and moral elements.[29] The content of an English Court judgement, almost one hundred years ago, indicates that:

> The guilty intent is not necessarily that of intending the very act or thing done and prohibited by common or statute law, but it must at least be the intention to do something wrong. That intention may belong to one or other of two classes. It may be to do a thing wrong in itself and apart from positive law, or it may be do a thing merely prohibited by statute or by common law, or both elements of intention may co-exist with respect to the same deed. There are many things prohibited by no statute...which nevertheless no one would hesitate to call wrong; and the intention to do an act wrong in this sense at least must as a general rule exist before the act done considered a crime.[30]

---

[23]See *infera.*

[24]As Morris shows, most crimes have a strong basis in given economic reasons. Cohen (1949), p. 1005.

[25]Gilmore (2011), pp. 15–21; Mitsilegas (2003), pp. 1–3 and 184–188.

[26]Pinto and Jardine (1997), p. 23.

[27]Hart (2008), p. 136.

[28]*Id.*

[29]Branlard (2014), pp. 17, 219.

[30]*Tolson* (1889) 23 Q.B.D. 168.

The above quotation clearly refers to the intention to do something which is not right. Has our policy a distinctly legal legitimacy in respect to production, manufacturing, and transformation?[31]

We have to understand these questions, and we have to try to find the true answer for the subjects and objects of the violations. That is what I am talking about and emphasising. If we understand the difference between legal and moral norms, which norm is more powerful than the other one, the content of human rights law that contains both norms, and the reason why we have democratic legislation, then we may come to understand many such phenomena. Still, this depends on the condition that we properly understand why we are allies with those who have permanent seats in the Security Council, those in NATO, and those in the European Union and others. Here, we may find out why certain Muslims are, according to the relevant statistics, killing one another, bombing innocent victims in France or Spain, persecuting the Yazidi population, and beheading innocent Christians, too.[32] In other words, we should be *just* before we attempt to condemn other nations.

3.6 Slicing the Love Norms

It is a natural phenomenon that if you put a gun in the hand of a young child, he will play with it and he will eventually be curious to put it in his mouth. If you put the same tool in the hands of a monkey, it will do the same. If you put it into the hands of a thief who is fleeing from a police officer, he will instead use it against the officer. If you put it in the hands of terrorists, they will terrorise you for the purpose of whatever their intentions are. If you transport such guns to insurgency movements, they will immediately use them against the government in power. If you give guns to groups which have very deep-rooted tensions arising from violations against each other, they will point the guns at each other.

In all of the above examples, those who received the killing tool break the law. The result in all cases is the same, but the real imprudence or lack of wisdom does not come from the owners who received the gun or who purchased the gun, but the ones who produced and delivered it to them through malicious political intention for their own economic interests. However, I am not here, by any means, discharging responsibility from those who used the guns.

These types of activities, namely arms trading, are not given attention in our criminal law and are not recognised as violence, based on the fact that we have redefined an illegal norm as a legal norm through our international treaties. We have agreed that the production of guns has a legal nature and is therefore not

[31]*R.V. Tolson* (1889) 23 Q.B.D. 168. Quoted in McAuley and Paul McCutcheon (2000), p. 278.
[32]Hazan (2004), pp. 131–133.

against the norm of love. Our constitutions, legislations, and legislators support the production of armaments. We may be right to say that:

> Collective violence is not a monopoly of underdeveloped societies or despotic governments; it is also practiced by respectable democratic nations such as our own, which has been called ... a Herrenvolk democracy. Witness our bombing in Wold War II of Hiroshima and Dresden, our war in Vietnam, the bombing of Libya, not to mention the legally institutionalized collective violence... inflicted in the last century by whites on Indians and blacks in the form of genocide, expulsion, and slavery. Australia, another liberal democracy, has over the years through its various institutions, as Barta... has shown, effectively committed genocide on the aborigines.[33]

Here, not only has the love norm disappeared but so have the legal and moral norms. The structure of most international conventions and, more obviously, international human rights law govern all of these norms. There may be differences between these three norms of law. One may see the differences in their external form or in their content. Some of us may argue over their origin and under what conditions they are binding. However, we never blame ourselves as the violators of the international legal order.

The reason for this is that the definition and interpretation of law and morality may be different for us than for others. We may therefore articulate that moral norms do not have a binding effect and are therefore not authoritative. For example, it took 60 years for the Swedish government to confess at the Gothenburg International Conference that the Swedish government had been active in *the killing of undefended innocent Jewish populations in Europe. The victims were subjects of all types of violations against themselves, their families, their relatives and, above all, their dear children. Whose eyes did not dare, did not honour, and did not bear tears for those inhuman actions?* It took almost the same amount of time for the United States government to confess that it had had a strong influence in the obliteration of Mohammed Mossadegh's democracy movement in Persia and the overthrow of a democratically elected Iranian government.[34] Both cases refer to gross violations of international criminal law, international human rights law, and international morality, but both confessions were made long after the innocent Jewish population had been almost completely annihilated and the destiny of the Persian population

---

[33]Ladd (1991), p. 20.

[34]Remarks by President Obama in Address to the United Nations General Assembly (24 September 2013), available at https://www.whitehouse.gov/the-press-office/2013/09/24/remarks-president-obama-address-united-nations-general-assembly (Accessed July 25, 2015); Remarks by President Obama at Cairo University, in his 6-04-09, available at https://www.whitehouse.gov/the-press-office/remarks-president-cairo-university-6-04-09 (Accessed July 25, 2015). Dr. Paul Craig Roberts illustrates that "In 1953 the Dulles brothers overthrew Iran's elected leader, Mossadegh and imposed the Shah, thus poisoning American-Iranian relations through the present day. Americans might yet be led into a costly and pointless war with Iran, because of the Dulles brothers poisoning of relations in 1953." Available at http://www.oneworldofnations.com/2014/09/washingtons-secret-agendas-truth-is.html (Accessed January 14, 2016). John Foster Dulles was the U.S. Secretary of State under Republican President Eisenhower from 1953 to 1959. His brother was Allen Dulles.

derailed into Islamic totalitarianism.[35] There are many further cases in which we were partly responsible for the prevention and disruption of democracy, such as in the Congo in 1960.

3.7 Love Embracing the Heart of Criminal Justice

The concept of love in most systems of the world has the function of being the heart of the law or the main gate for the jurisprudence of the law. This is true concerning public international law, Islamic international law, and the European philosophy of law, but we have become used to ignoring its existence in all legal systems. An illustrative example is the division of law into primary and secondary rules by Hart, the combination of which is the "key to the science of jurisprudence." However, he does not refer to the norm of love, but instead he searches to find the heart of the law.

> If we stand back and consider the structure which has resulted from the combination of primary rules of obligation and the secondary rules of recognition, change, and adjudication, it is plain that we have here not only the heart of a legal system, but a most powerful tool for the analysis of much that has puzzled both the jurist and the political theorist.[36]

Any realistic international lawyer is aware of the fact that while the nineteenth-century movements for the regulation of armed conflicts in central Europe at The Hague and Geneva were ostensibly aimed at preventing the unlimited use of force in armed conflicts, they were an expression of the human commitment to and love for justice. Alternatively, let us call it the provision of the security of law for humankind combined with the desire for justice, in order to minimise unnecessary human suffering.

A clarification may be useful here. The reality is that the function of the International Military Tribunal in Nuremberg was to accentuate the intrinsic validity of human dignity.[37] Although Schwarzenberger *correctly* asserts that the tribunal lacked sufficient basic legislative references,[38] it nevertheless referred to the concepts of *human morality*, *human dignity*, *and the natural rights of human beings*

[35]Farhad Malekian, Criminal Responsibility for Core International Crimes Against *Children*, Username: Islamic State Groups, Password: Presidents of the United States of America (2014-10-09). A declaration directed by the Institute of International Criminal Law to the Presidents Barack Obama, Vladimir Vladimirovich Putin; Xi Jinping; David William Donald Cameron; François Gérard Georges Nicolas Hollande; and the General Secretary of the United Nations, Ban Ki-Moon, whose policies of crime prevention are subject to serious questions of morality and legality, p. 6.

[36]Hart (1961), p. 95.

[37]Earl (2009), pp. 296–303.

[38]Schwarzenberger (1968), p. 469.

to live together as a whole.[39] *The question was, how could the international legal or political community of the time pay no attention to the inhuman slaughter of several millions innocent Jewish people and allow it go without retribution?*[40]

This is what I am calling 'the pure theory of *love* of justice', which aims to secure through the law the recognition of the substance of the human soul, the shared nature of humankind, and the union of all individual 'hearts' located within billions of bodies. Righteousness through the power of love may constitute a sense of philosophical justice, which may have no particular definition or place in law, but generally refers to non-violatary conducts or behaviours. Yet, the strength of love may be used positively, negatively, or collectively to prevent human rights violations, such as in the principle of collective defence in Islamic or public international law or the European Union Common Security and Defence Policy.[41]

Thus far, when the power of love comes to the assistance of law or vice versa, it may soon lose its potential validity and we may start again to violate the law whether by resorting to the use of force or aggression. As such:

> Human rights are like love, both necessary and impossible. We cannot live without them, but we cannot have them, either. As soon as we are safely installed in a social order that promises to guarantee our rights, that order starts to appear oppressively totalitarian. We need new rights, or new interpretations of old rights. Routine kills love, as it does to rights-regimes. It is good to struggle for rights, or to reach them finally: in France between 1789 and 1791, in South Africa in 1994, East Germany or Russia for a brief period after 1989. As the tyrant falls, there is dancing in the streets. But the morning after is cold, and certain to come. Why?[42]

Depending on their personal attitudes, a considerable number of international lawyers or politicians may provide different answers to the question "why?" in the above quote. Practically speaking, love or the power of love can never die in a given society, because the objective and operative function of love is respect. The people in a society may become familiar and accustomed to it, and when they have it, they do not need to declare its existence. Love makes possible the law and becomes a part of life, but it exists as part of the inner framework of human society to different degrees. It is like the function of the heart in the human body. Although, we do not talk about our heart in our daily life, we are aware that all its chambers are operating and are an essential part of the human body.

---

[39]*International Military Tribunal, Trial of the Major War Criminals before the International Military Tribunal in Nuremberg* (Publisher not identified, Nuremberg, 1947); Jackson (1946–1947); Ratner and Jason (2001); Sheldon (1946); Ginsburgs and Kudriavtsev (1990); Cassese et al. (1980); Detmold (1984); Fuller (1969).

[40]For example, incitement to commit genocide is one the legacies of the Nuremberg Tribunal. Although, the crime was not dealt with at the Tribunal, its work ended in the preparation of genocide convention with the intention of protecting the first principles of natural rights of man. See Eastwood (2011), pp. 254–255.

[41]See Sects. 2.3 and 2.4.

[42]Koskenniemi (2001), pp. 33–45.

3.8 Boundaries of Criminal Argumentations

The entire system of international criminal justice is based on several concepts of national criminal systems such as the principle of legality, the principle of proportionality, and the principle of *nullum crimen sine lege* or *nulla poena sine praevia lege*.[43] I strongly contend that these principles are not only part of the principle of legality but also the principle of morality. How can we criminalise certain acts without any concept of morality? If a murder or any other crime under a national criminal system was not against the principle of morality in the given society, the act would not be recognised as wrong. In some societies, cannibalism was not a criminal act and was not therefore penalized. In other words, the criminalisation of certain acts is not done solely for the purpose of criminalisation but following the motive that a society considers such acts to be a crime against its moral standards. It is the same under European Union law, Islamic law, Jewish law, United States and Russian criminal law. The criminalisation of conduct under the system of international criminal law also comes from the same theory. That is to say that the system of international criminal human rights law criminalises the commission of a considerable number of acts as a violation of national, regional, or international criminal law. These include apartheid, discrimination, genocide, slavery, torture, and the use of child soldiers.

We may have different interpretations of the principles of human rights law, and we may argue about the boundaries of their imperative position in the system of criminal laws. We may also emphasise that a legal duty constitutes an obligation, but a moral duty does not. For these reasons, we may never accept our responsibilities concerning violations of criminal provisions of human rights law. This means when we deliver guns to certain groups or states or trade in such weapons and, as a result, genocide, crimes against humanity, and war crimes are committed, we may not be accepting our responsibility. We may say that we did so but not with the aim of killing or destroying. We may present various reasons because we want to prove that our conduct was justified, unjustified, reasonable, unreasonable, right, or wrong. All this means that we are aligning ourselves to a code of morality that permits us to perform certain acts, the consequences of which may be killings in other nations. As Martin Luther King said, "There are two types of laws: there are just laws and there are unjust laws... What is the difference between the two? ... An unjust law is a man-made code that is out of harmony with the moral law."[44]

Although we have adopted human rights declarations, they do not have a binding effect and cannot be recognised as valid. This may include not only the American Declaration of Independence 1776 and the French Declaration on the Rights of

---

[43]For the development of the principle of legality consult Rinceanu (2011a), pp. 89–101; Rinceanu (2011b), pp. 73–85.

[44]*Martin Luther King, Jr., 196.* Available at http://mlk-kpp01.stanford.edu/index.php/resources/article/king_quotes_on_war_and_peace/ (Accessed July 20, 2015).

Man, 1789 but also the Declaration of Human Rights announced by the United Nations.[45] We may argue that they express rights but not obligatory law-rights. Finally, one may argue that they are unilateral rules, which do not have a binding effect, and therefore one cannot express a valid claim. Obviously, these statements may be right but not as concerns the content of the declarations, nor the validity of the double nature of norms in human rights law, but instead concerning the fact that they look to human beings as carriers of rights, objects of rights, and reasons for rights, not as the owners of rights.

The distinction between valid and invalid claims constitutes indications of governments' political attitudes. When one talks about humanity, equality before instruments of human rights law, or our constitutions, one does not speak about claims but the facts existing in the law. Rights have not only been a part of morality but are today a part of legality, too. Furthermore, in most situations, it is the concept of morality which defines whether the notion of legality is right or wrong.[46] In addition, "we must live our lives according to our rights."[47] Most of our new laws or regulations have come into existence because we consider certain laws unjust. This means that we have modified the limit and scope of our morality. It also means that many acts which were criminalised earlier may not only now be decriminalised, but we may have also adopted rules of criminal law for their protection. These include marriage between members of the same gender or escaping from slavery. Escaping slavery used to be a crime and created the right for the owner to kill the respective slave, but now criminal law recognises that keeping someone in slavery constitutes a crime punishable by law.

3.9 Variation of Criminalisation

The criminalisation of acts does indeed vary from one region to another and depends upon the standard of morality in each region. A clear example is the regulation of ownership of weapons. In the United States, this ownership not only does not constitute a crime but is also a recognised component of personal integrity, personal protection, defence of the family, and social protection. However, under European Union law, gun ownership constitutes a serious criminal conduct and is punishable by law. It is the same in Russia and many Islamic states. This means that each society, in accordance with its own standard of morality, enacts provisions, rules, or norms that prohibit or do not prohibit certain conduct. Stating that the provisions of criminal law do not follow the standard of morality is akin to saying

[45] However, all these declarations are strongly valid, based on the fact that most of their provisions have been inserted into international law-making treaties, and provisions of the declarations are an integral part of customary international law.

[46] Wendel (2012), p. 17.

[47] Gross (2012), p. 23.

that a law is a law and therefore it is supposed to be a law. It is also similar to stating that there is a law, but without any sense of human nature. Even most of our retroactive laws, which should never have been enforced, were implemented solely on the basis of moral standards, rather than legal ones.

Again, criminal law was not originally intended to be criminal law for punishment; in fact, some of the basic elements of criminal law are rehabilitation, re-education, or the abolition of certain conducts or behaviours that are not acceptable according to the standard of morality in the given society.[48] The purpose of criminal law is supposed to increase the standard of morality, and therefore decrease the degree of criminalisation. However, Kant requires a just retribution for crimes:

> Judicial or juridical punishment (*poena forensis*) is to be distinguished from natural punishment (*poena naturalis*), in which crime as vice punishes itself, and does not as such come within the cognizance of the legislator. Juridical punishment can never be administered merely as a means for promoting another good either with regard to the criminal himself or to civil society, but must in all cases be imposed only because the individual on whom it is inflicted has committed a crime. For one man ought never to be dealt with merely as a means subservient to the purpose of another, nor be mixed up with the subjects of real right. Against such treatment his inborn personality [i.e., his rational capacity] has a right to protect him, even although he may be condemned to lose his civil personality [i.e., his citizenship, liberty, property, or life]. He must first be found guilty and punishable, before there can be any thought of drawing from his punishment any benefit for himself or his fellow-citizens. The penal law is a categorical imperative; and woe to him who creeps through the serpent-windings of utilitarianism to discover some advantage that may discharge him from the justice of punishment, or even from the due measure of it, according to the Pharisaic maxim: "It is better that one man should die than that the whole people should perish." For if justice and righteousness perish, then human life would no longer have any value in the world. What, then, is to be said of such a proposal as to keep a criminal alive who has been condemned to death, on his being given to understand that, if he agreed to certain dangerous experiments being performed upon him, he would be allowed to survive if he came happily through them? It is argued that physicians might thus obtain new information that would be of value to the commonweal. But a court of justice would repudiate with scorn any proposal of this kind if made to it by the medical faculty; for justice would cease to be justice, if it were bartered away for any consideration whatsoever.

Here, we are certainly referring to normal criminal law legislation, provisions, rules, norms, and behaviour. We are not referring to such criminal legislation, the existence of which constitutes itself serious violations of international human rights law, such as the criminal legislation under Stalin, Hitler, and Marcos Duvalier and his son Jean-Claude Duvalier. Nor are we referring to the criminal law provisions of some Islamic nations which violate the principles of morality and human rights legislation, such as those provisions of some Islamic states that do not permit freedom of speech, freedom of assembly, freedom of communications or of the press, or free use of internet services, and prevent gender equality by the harshest methods. A clear example is the Iranian criminal law system, which not only ignores the many shared principles of criminal law between the Islamic legal

[48] Cohen (1949), pp. 989–990.

system and its Western equivalent but also imposes severe torture on political prisoners. Similar views can be held about the Israeli interrogation practices which have been condemned even by the respected Israeli High Court of Justice.[49] This is what Kant says: *for justice would cease to be justice, if it were bartered away for any consideration whatsoever*. The following four interlinked principles constitute the most significant criteria in the system of criminal law:

> *The principle that the criminal law should be used, and only used, to censure persons for substantial wrongdoing*. This principle recognises that the prevention of such misconduct is a reason for criminalising it...
>
> *The principle that criminal laws should be enforced with respect for equal treatment and proportionality*. The implication is that enforcement authorities and their policies out to be reorganised so as to reflect the relative seriousness of the wrongdoing with which they are dealing and should not remain hidebound by traditional divisions of responsibility that fail to reflect proper assessments of the culpable wrongs involved.
>
> *The principle that persons accused of substantial wrongdoing ought to be afforded the protections appropriate to those charged with criminal offences,* i.e. at least the minimum protections declared by Articles 6.2. and 6.3 of the European Convention on Human Rights.
>
> *The principle that maximum sentences and effective sentence levels should be proportionate to the seriousness of the wrongdoing.*[50]

Thus, the principle of *nullum crimen sine lege* or no crime without law is the expression of the moral principle in national and international criminal law. This is because we do not want to punish a person for acts which were not criminalised at the time they were committed. In fact, a statutory text guarantees the application of such principles that are not against the social or moral standards of human society. In other words, we are referring here to the norm of love or a norm which does not accept force, injustice, irregularity, immorality, or replacement of justice by the use of force. Although, the principle of *nullum crimen sine lege* does not address love for justice, its content and its intention is love for the respect of human integrity. This interpretation is also correct in the case of the principle of *nulla poena sine praevia lege* which denotes the application of punishment according to the norms of law.

3.10 The Hidden Mechanism of Love

The intention of the principle of *nulla poena sine praevia lege* is justice, and justice should refer to the existence of the principle of morality and the latter to the existence of certain attitudes in the respective society towards the application of equality. Where domestic governments or international authorities violate the norms of equality, there is another norm which may demand justice by a strong objection to its non-implementation. This is the norm of love, which is a hidden or a silent norm inherent within each human personality. Disappearance of love

---

[49] Gur-Arye and Jessberger (2011), pp. 229–263 at 229–230.

[50] Ashworth (2013), 28–29.

therefore takes place where there is conflict between the norms of law, morality, and love. All three may be misunderstood by the conflicting parties, with the strong reservation that the love norm is the same for both conflicting parties, yet with the difference that they are violating the norm of law and morality in order to achieve their own 'wills'. As Kant says, no political party should for any reason whatsoever cease the application of justice in any circumstances.

This is because the norms of law and morality may vary from culture to culture and may have different degrees of application.[51] However, the norm of love is not a visible regulation of a visible norm of morality within a law alone. Instead, it is a norm existing all the time, within the subjects of the law. In other words, subjects are not born for the law; rather, the law is adopted for the subjects of the law. Consequently, the invisibility of the norm of love is descriptive rather than perceptive in the relevant legal system. For example, no international criminal convention or international criminal justice system mentions the principle of love, the principle of strong will, or the invisible principle of unity of human dignity, but these principles obviously all exist, albeit with the qualification that they do not need to be written with the word 'love.' Nevertheless, they are there in order for justice to be applied, and if justice is not applied, the non-application calls for the enforceability of the principle of *concern of all states or concern of all human beings as a whole*. Judge Weeramantry in his separate opinion concerning the Convention on Genocide argues as follows:

> The Genocide Convention does not come to an end with the dismemberment of the original State, as it transcends the concept of State sovereignty. An important conceptual basis denying continuity to treaties is that the recognition of the continuity of the predecessor State's treaties would be an intrusion upon the sovereignty of the successor State. This would be so if it were a matter confined within the ambit of a State's sovereignty. But with human rights and humanitarian treaties, we are in a sphere which reaches far beyond the narrow confines of State sovereignty, and enters the domain of universal concern. In its ongoing development, the concept of human rights has long passed the stage when it was a narrow parochial concern between sovereign and subject. We have reached the stage, today, at which *the human rights of anyone, anywhere, are the concern of everyone, everywhere*. The world's most powerful States are bound to recognize them, equally with the weakest, and there is not even the semblance of a suggestion in contemporary international law that such obligations amount to a derogation of sovereignty.[52]

This denotes the fact that love is an organised system of law, morality, and will, and it does not necessarily exist in the letter of the law but rather in the substance and the content of the law. We cannot separate the norms of human rights law from the law. Here, again, we are dividing the law into several pieces of legal material. This division is necessary to understand and find the proper function of the law for a better understanding of the norm of love in international criminal law. Some

---

[51] Dan-Cohen (2014), pp. 101–118 at 113.

[52] Emphasis added. Application of the Convention on the Prevention and Punishment of the Crime of Genocide (*Bosnia and Herzegovina v. Serbia and Montenegro*). Separate Opinion of Judge Weeramantry, available at http://www.icj-cij.org/docket/files/91/7361.pdf, 55–56 (Accessed June 20, 2015). See *also* Fournet (2015), pp. 915–921.

philosophers of law may divide the law into primary and secondary law. But, here, I am not dividing law into these two different categories as Hart proposes, and I am not trying to follow what Kelsen says on the pure philosophy of the law or what the problems of philosophy of law are.[53] We simply orient ourselves towards the principle that justice requires love and love comes with justice when it is satisfied for all without any discrimination between races, religions, cultures, nations, or ethnic groups.

3.11 The Machinery of Criminal Justice

My intention is to explain that the norms of international criminal law are not solely the norms of the legal system or a combination of moral and legal norms within an international treaty. They are without doubt also the representation of the system of international criminal law aiming to protect human beings from suffering, and where it does not function and is not effective; its norms may be protected by the norms of love. The key examples are the demand for justice after the Second World War, after the conflicts in the former Yugoslavia, and after the genocide in Rwanda. However, the extreme infanticide in Gaza and the beheading of different groups in Iraq and Syria have not seen justice because of the overwhelming interests of powerful states in the political situation of the regions.[54]

Since the term 'love' is a rather problematic term, international lawyers have only occasionally used the term. For them, the key issue may be how we limit and quantify the tasks of love and law. According to them, love and law are not completely identical because challenges to law cannot be dealt with in the way that Shakespeare suggests. Expressing this in a 'more legal' sense, in the face of misunderstanding the law, the word 'love' may carry no obvious meaning in a hypothetical or practical sense. For them, it may therefore be doubtful that one could explain how the reader or the interpreter should understand this issue of the love norm, or they may express awareness that 'love' cannot easily be compared and contrasted with 'force', 'law', 'justice' and 'rights'.[55] Although these types of arguments may be presented and may also be valid, the question remains to what extent, if any, we are bound by the norms of a law and morality which permit killing.

As I have underlined elsewhere, *a law which defends, for any reason, resorting to the use of force, is itself using force and therefore violates the system of international criminal law and justice. How can we talk about international human rights law, human morality, social legality, high courts of appeal or international courts of justice, if we do not understand that the value of all of*

---

[53] Ross (1952), pp. 701–732.

[54] See, generally, Meloni and Tongnoni (2012).

[55] See *infra*.

these legal systems is based on respect, justice, love, and equality of all men before all legal systems. This equality of men by nature and law is so evident in itself and beyond all doubt that it becomes the foundation of mutual love among men. This love calls upon the duties of men towards one another, and from it "man derives the great maxims of justice and charity."[56] An English solicitor from the sixteenth century judiciously explains this concept of equality, love, and law:

> The like natural inducement hath brought men to know that it is no less their duty, to love others than themselves; for seeing those things which are equal, must needs all have one measure; if I cannot but wish to receive good, even as much at every man's hands, as any man can wish unto his own soul, how should I look to have any part of my desire herein satisfied, unless myself be careful to satisfy the like desire, which is undoubtedly in other men, being of one and the same nature? To have anything offered them repugnant to this desire, must needs in all respects grieve them as much as me; so that if I do harm, I must look to suffer, there being no reason that others should show greater measure of love to me, than they have by me showed unto them: my desire therefore to be loved of my equals in nature, as much as possible may be, imposed upon me a natural duty of bearing to them-ward fully the like affection; from which relation of equality between ourselves and them that are as ourselves, what several rules and canons natural reason hath drawn, for direction of life, no man is ignorant.[57]

If the norm love is very difficult to understand and we criticise it on the basis that it has no legal dimension, legal strength, or legal validity for judges and lawyers, then the question is what is the law? Is it not the expression of our collective wishes, collective responsibility, collective duties, and the communication of our high standards of love? I am not, however, here talking about law which is dictated by different means. Nor am I concerned with law that is enforced by force and which one has to obey under threat of violence, as are the laws in some of the Islamic states. Neither am I referring to law which pretends to be law but which does not respect the rights of civilians, as is the case with many of the rules in Russia, China, the United States, Saudi Arabia. Nor am I speaking of the legislation of parliaments which apply the law with prejudice, such as the serious discrimination practised in Australia.[58]

Lawyers and the international public are accustomed to using the word 'love' mostly in their sexual or social relations, or in connection with the expression of their feelings towards their children or family members. They resort to the word 'love' when the sun is shining—'a lovely day'; when a meal is tasty—'the lovely food'; and so on: 'a lovely girl', 'lovely company', 'a lovely conversation', or 'a lovely friend'. However, if one were to say that a law is a lovely law, this would be a very strange expression. The law cannot be lovely. Of course, all of these lawyers are correct. The reason is very simple: human civilisation has not yet had any law

---

[56]Locke (1689), see Online Library of Liberty, *A collection of scholarly works,* available at http://oll.libertyfund.org/titles/locke-the-two-treatises-of-civil-government-hollis-ed (Accessed March 31, 2015).

[57]*Id.*

[58]For criminal law of this country, see Clough and Mulhern (2004).

which is a comprehensive system of truth, justice, and which can be said to be 'lovely'.

We modify our written laws at all times. The reason is that we are not rational, we will not be rational, and we will forever remain in our law-bound cages. Most of the laws are laws but are surely contaminated, in one way or another, with injustice. That is why the word and philosophy of 'love' has to be integrated into our legal system, although I do not deny the fact that it is already there, but we have to become accustomed to using it for the prevention of serious conflicts before we face more atrocities against humanity.

However, international lawyers may claim that the suggested relationship between love and hurt that is found in a Shakespearean quote does not clarify whether it is a correct or a universal route to clear argumentation. For them the Shakespearean quote may embarrass the human mind and universal validity of love. By the quote, I do not mean the Shakespearean quote alone, but Shakespearean quotes that are integrated into our civilisation. Here, I am not using the Shakespearean quote as a final stage of understanding love, not as an initiation but as a method to connect the mechanism of love to the engine of law.[59] *This means that with the Shakespearean quote I do not presume to further the interpretation of legal rules or provisions but their very great strength for the prevention of violations in order to find universal similarities in the house of love and the heart of human beings.* For example, Mo Tzu (470–391 B.C.) was one of the earliest philosophers who put a high value on the universality of love. He rejected the Confucianist theory concerning personal control, obedience to a social hierarchy, and social and political order. He concluded that the impartiality of justice and the need for "universal love" constitute the most basic values of justice.[60] "When everyone regards the states and cities of others as he regards his own, no one will attack the others' state or seize the others' cities."[61]

Furthermore, the main intention of the *Shakespearean* quote is to highlight the similarities which exist between those who love one another. I fully understand that the interpretation of the word 'love' in normal relations is subjective and thus depends on particular relations, but one should bear in mind that we are not referring to personal love as is commonly understood between two individuals. Rather, we mean the love for justice, for humanity, for prevention of genocide, for elimination of crimes against humanity, and for the fact that peace will never come to our garden of law if the sovereignty of love for justice is not secured by our common understanding and moral or legal interpretations.

---

[59]For a good analysis of Shakespeare's position on law, visit also Mark Andre Alexander, Shakespeare's Knowledge of Law: A journey through the history of the argument available at http://shakespeareoxfordfellowship.org/shakespeares-knowledge-of-law/ (Accessed October 4, 2015).

[60]See Power (2007), p. 97; see also http://oll.libertyfund.org/pages/mo-tzu-c-470-391-bc#_ftn1 (Accessed June 5, 2015).

[61]Mo-Tse (1929), p. 88.

3.12 Love Against Criminal Force

With this discussion of the norm of love, I am not attempting to overcome the question of plurality or provide an overarching interpretative attitude. The existence of the norm of love does not therefore mean that the term 'love' has such a capacity to solve the traditional contradiction between what is right and is not, and when we are permitted to use or not to use force. This means that I do not presume to construct a critique of interpretations of *jus ad bellum*. My intention is to clarify that there exists a norm in law, international human rights law, international criminal law, international humanitarian law, and international criminal justice, which draws our attention to the prevention of all forms of violation or resort to the use of force. I mean that the term 'love' could encourage and direct the awareness and perception of what constitutes a 'good' interpretation for this purpose.

A writer may, by an ideal distinction, claim that the question of the interpretation of the doctrines of use of force is both practical and theoretical. Therefore, when assessing *jus ad bellum*, a distinction may be useful. The expert would examine the threshold as to when law can constitute an option to use force, or *vice versa*. On the one hand, the expert presupposes that this is something that is within his power of choosing. On the other hand, the theoretician would attempt to formulate to what degree law can be taken into account as a critique of force. This means that the theoretician endeavours to exclude specific sanctions through critique. There will be two different opinions concerning resorting or not resorting to the use of force. All this means that there is a longstanding major plurality in opposing perspectives between international lawyers. In particular, this is more tangible concerning the questions of resort to the use of force under international criminal law and guided by the Security Council resolutions under Chapter VII of the organisation.

Again, and this is obvious when we talk about the norm of legality, the norm of morality, and the rule of law, we do not mean a bad interpretation of the law but surely a good interpretation. That is why there are rules and principles for the interpretation of conventional law. These include prevention of the interference of political views as much as possible, the maintenance of the principle of good faith, the principle of language interpretation, the ordinary meaning of the terms, the technical meaning of the phrases, any special intended meaning of a term, and any relevant agreement which may help to reduce contradictions. We therefore call not only upon the principle of legality but also upon the principle of morality and, at the same time, we trust that the interpretations are correct and are not corrupted. Here, we attach to the law all those good principles that we consider at the time to be necessary.

We assume that the Declaration of Human Rights Law contains all the good intentions of negotiators, drafters, and the philosophy of law. In other words, if the Declaration does not include such assumptions, it must be wrong and any revision of this wrong may not be so easy. The same is true of the other laws or constitutions of the world. If European Union law does not have a good intention or if, when it was formulated, there were also bad intentions which were hidden behind its formulation, then we have not achieved a good law but a mishmash of ideologies. That is why when I refer to the norm of love, I do not necessarily mean that we are going to solve the problem of pluralism, positivism, naturalism, communism, Kantianism, Darwinism, imperialism, dualism, monism, Judaism, or Islamism.[62]

However, *I insist that there is a powerful norm in international human rights law, international criminal law, international humanitarian law, and international criminal justice which is called the norm of love. This is a norm which aims to put an end to situations where the divergences between law and morality, conflicting parties, ideologies, religions, and cultures can lead to the destruction of human society, the killing of Jewish, Vietnamese, Palestinian, Syrian, Iraqi, and Afghan children. Even here, the concept of similarity cannot prevent the genocide of our neighbours, including the fleeing of millions of refugees from their homeland. The norm of love is significant here. We cannot sit with the hope that justice will come with the evaluation of the value of the Kantian ideology of separation of law from church, the Hartian view of primary and secondary rules, the Kelsenian view of pure theory of law and basic norms, and the Hegelian system of absolute idealism concerning the relationship of mind and nature. This evaluation also cannot be helped by the dead Scandinavian idea of separating legal justice from morality,*[63] *including also many other philosophies. We have to use the perception or the intuition of our true human nature in order to solve the problem of violations to the greatest degree possible. This is why I say the norm of love is necessary in criminal justice and in international criminal law as a whole.*

3.13 Misapplication of Islamic Criminal Law

Each individual in the world will have a unique understanding of the nature of love and its scope, whether they live in a Muslim or non-Muslim nation, in a European or non-European state, in the United States or outside them, in Australia or Africa and so on. This means that we could provide an endless number of definitions that demonstrate what love is and what its correlation to the law is. That is why, for the sake of practicality, the Universal Declaration of Human Rights constitutes our starting point and the cornerstone for setting the scope of the concepts of law and love.

In Islamic law, the term 'love' has a particular function, which should not be rejected out of hand by its opponents: it is the principle of forgiveness, which constitutes, in all situations, an integral part of the application of the law if it is respected. This means any view expressing that Islamic criminal law is not based on love for humanity is out of step with a modern juridical understanding of the law.[64] Islamic law requires the principle of love to be respected in all aspects of criminal

[62]See Malekian (2009a), pp. 139–215.

[63]Krarup (2006), 19–28 at 19.

[64]See Malekian (1999), pp. 591–628.

justice but not just by legal phenomena and not by the understanding of Islamic law, but also by the *wisdom and vision of the judge*. This means that certain punishments, assured penalties or certain actions are not judicious, and therefore the order of the law should not be a reason for their severe implementation. The legal authorities should respect the proper application of the principle of humanity.[65] As is rightly asserted, "there are good reasons for arguing that the presumption of innocence is inherent in any proper conception of the relationship between the state and its citizens in an open and democratic society."[66]

In several countries, the legal power of a judge may in fact develop case law and bring it into the standard of criminal law. This is evident in the practice of certain member states of the European Union or more particularly in the United Kingdom. An Islamic judge is even responsible for the development of the law, although it has to be within the framework of Islamic provisions. This means that a judge of an Islamic court who applies the provisions of European Union criminal law does not by any means violate the criminal provisions of Islamic law; instead, he has developed the standard of law to the stage of *internationalisation*. This is because Islamic law does not insist on the development of Islamic law, as many lawyers understand it, but on the universalisation of humanity from all aspects of the law.[67] This can be taken into recognition from the provisions of any law, as long as the law does not go against the principles of humanity. For instance, Islamic nations have adopted various international human rights instruments but do not implement their aims regarding certain significant matters of freedom and liberty.[68]

The unfortunate fact is that many lawyers, whether they be British, American, Chinese, European, Latin American, African, Asian, or Arab, are bound by the provisions of their legislations and are not permitted to apply other laws in their decisions. Although Islamic law also has a similar construction and obligations, the essence of the principle of love is much stronger than the law itself if Islamic lawyers properly understand it. However, they do not. Whilst Islamic law is based on a number of sources of *shariah*, the opinion of jurists and the entire intention of Islamic law amalgamate human beings for unity of love, unity of human beings, and the maintenance of justice with ethical and philosophical principles of criminal law.[69] This means that an Islamic lawyer or judge has a particular freedom to interpret the law with a positive approach to the principles of humanity, and as long as the principles of criminal law of neighbouring countries or others do not contradict with the principles of human rights law, they are an integral part of *shariah* law too.[70] The internationalisation of human rights law into Islamic law has

[65]Ashworth (2006), pp. 63–97.

[66]*Id.*, at 73.

[67]See Malekian (2015), p. 833.

[68]Malekian (2009b), pp. 595–621.

[69]*Id.*, at 618–621.

[70]*Id.*, pp. 595–621.

been one of the first concepts in the transformation of positive and natural rights of man into a global perspective.

The fact is that Islamic law consists of three clear norms while most laws of human civilisations apparently consist of two norms. These are the norms of legality, morality, and love. The true norm of love in Islamic law has a number of messages. Some of these are *i)* cultivation of pure equality between genders; *ii)* recognition of the modern development of the theory of law, *iii)* respect for human nature and its existence, *iv)* prevention of impunity, *v)* giving forgiveness from the bottom of heart, *vi)* speaking the whole truth and solely the truth, and *vii)* prevention of all types of use of force. This means that norms of legality and morality in the inner structure of Islamic law have to, in the final stage of their application, be evaluated with the positive structure of the love norm.

As such, the inner structure of human rights in Islamic law integrates the principle of love of humanity into its body too. This is also true regarding the Cairo Declaration of Human Rights Law in Islam. Article 1 (b) of the Declaration vividly refers to the power of the love of the creator. This means that we should love one another according to the provisions of Article 1 (a) in combination with sub-section (b). The article states that:

(a) All human beings form one family whose members are united by submission to God and descent from Adam. All men are equal in terms of basic human dignity and basic obligations and responsibilities, without any discrimination on the grounds of race, colour, language, sex, religious belief, political affiliation, social status or other considerations. True faith is the guarantee for enhancing such dignity along the path to human perfection.
(b) All human beings are God's subjects, and the most loved by him are those who are most useful to the rest of His subjects, and no one has superiority over another except on the basis of piety and good deeds.[71]

Islamic law, if it is understood correctly, does not insist on the application of its laws as the best law for humanity but as the best law which should follow the modern interpretation of humanity's current state of development. On the one hand, at the time of the contemporary development of international relations, a wise Islamic judge or jurist realises the fact that most punishments under Islamic criminal law are not compatible with the principles of humanity and cannot therefore be enforced. In other words, "basic human rights are being ignored when there is serious criminal punishment."[72] On the other hand, Islamic law has adopted a very significant principle regarding the application of the provisions of other jurisdictions within the concept of Islamic territories from the first seed of its inception.[73] A practical interpretation of this principle means that the Islamic jurist

[71]The Nineteenth Islamic Conference of Foreign Ministers (Session of Peace, Interdependence and Development), held in Cairo, Arab Republic of Egypt, from 9–14 Muharram 1411H (31 July to 5 August 1990).

[72]Gross (2012), p. 19.

[73]Malekian (2009b), pp. 595–621.

can also employ the entire system of English Common criminal law as an integral part of Islamic law, as long as it does not violate the principles of equality, justice, humanity, brotherhood, and love.[74] *If it is difficult to understand this simple logic of love for proper justice and respect of the integrity of mankind here and in the lectures of Islamic jurists claiming to teach human rights law; we will, in future, be forced in our class courses to deliver lectures of law without audiences in most universities in the world.*[75] *An Islamic jurist has to come to the vision that human rights are not just integrated into Islamic law, and if that were the case we would be violating all the principles of human rights laws in the world by that law.*[76]

In short, the Islamic system of criminal law must be completely modified and should be almost stagnant in its present theory of application. It should be replaced by the modern rules of criminal law that can be found in the European system of criminal law. The logic is very simple and understandable—none of the provisions of the latter are in contradiction with the former and any rules in the former, which contradict with the latter, are an abolished institution in the entire modern human legal system as a whole.

3.14 Norm of Love: Concern of All States

The norm of love is *a norm of concern of all states* and its boundaries reach even beyond the *erga omnes* principle.[77] The difference is that, for the enforcement of the latter, states are required to react but do not have to do so. A clear example is the International Court of Justice Advisory Opinion concerning the Wall in the Palestinian Occupied Territories which was built by the Israeli government. However, the Israeli government did not respect the decision of the Court. But concerning the former, the strong norm of love not only calls upon all states to react by all means for the prevention of a blatant use of force, but it also manifestly encourages the population of the world to express the norm of love cumulatively embodied in their nature. This is because of the following:

> Too often in the past religious people have equated the law of love with turning the other cheek and passively accepting and submitting to evil. Natural religion today recognizes that to permit people of power to prosecute the weak is to deny love to both the weak and to the people who exploit them. Love is commitment, caring and responsibility. ... To allow some people to abuse others is to allow them to abuse themselves. We cannot deny the law of love to others without destroying a part of our own humanity. Love must be strong enough to protect both the victim and the person who would victimize others.[78]

[74]Malekian (2013), pp. 1220–1225.

[75]*Id.*

[76]Malekian (2009b), pp. 595–621.

[77]See the judgment of the Inter-American Court on the case of *La Cantuta*, Fujimori. IACHR, Case *La Cantuta v. Peru*, judgment of 29 November 2006, Ser. C. No. 160.

[78]Swanson (2010), p. 387.

By this, I mean that there is an invisible body of legislation parallel to the law which is named "love," the legislators and the implementers of which are human beings. There is in fact an invisible international constitution in the legal system of the world which does not obey any other legal system. It is free of the power of any authority. This is the constitution of love based on human commonalities. The norm of love is in fact one of the basic legal philosophies in the jurisprudence of law that has unfortunately not been acknowledged separately and has been integrated or pushed into other philosophies of law. We have to realise this power of the legislation of love which has a legal body, a legal function, and legal requirements for the implementation of justice, peace, reciprocity, and mutual understanding of international problems. This principle of love has to be realised, even though we do not give attention to the significant merit of the principle of *erga omnes* which is the concern of all states.

The concept of *erga omnes* in the system of international law is the modern and most consolidated form of internationally permitted intervention, relying upon the existence of several principles, in particular the principle of *concern of all states*.[79] The principle of *erga omnes* does not really resort to the use of force, the use of terror, or the use of aggressive conduct but puts the truth on the table of negotiation and encourages states to fulfil their international obligations.

This concept constitutes an integral part of the *jus cogens* framework. It denotes the high legal validity of a legal norm that is accepted as a norm from which no derogation is permitted. Here, I am leading a parallel discussion regarding the norms of love, legality, and morality in international justice, including international criminal law and international human rights law. The norm of love is not only included in customary international law but also constitutes also a part of the duty of criminal justice systems of all states from which no divergence is advisable.

All of these demand the existence of a pure theory of love of justice. This is a theory which cannot be reformed by the will of a state, nor can it be changed by the will of a group of states, nor be altered by a nation or nations, nor be dictated by collective human will. The *pure theory of love of criminal justice* is a law, which does not need the consent of states, entities, or groups of individuals. It need not necessarily be relied on by legislation, in juridical or parliamentary decisions, or in the decisions of our various organs. By this I mean, if the rules of law and moral aspects of the rules are strong enough, the love norm will work automatically and consent will appear to be the reason for the existence of the law and at once the primary and simultaneously the most minimum part of love for justice.

[79] IACHR, Case *La Cantuta v. Peru*, judgment of 29 November 2006, Ser. C. No. 160.

3.15 Doubleton Legal Sanction of Love

It is an established legal principle in international law that a state should not bring any allegation against a provision of the international legal system which has a high legal value for the maintenance of international legal order and security of mankind as a whole. The conclusions of the International Court of Justice regarding the Case Concerning Application of the Convention on the Prevention and Punishment of the Crime of Genocide in Bosnia-Herzegovina are very valuable for the treatise of humanitarian love, international human rights law love, international criminal law love as well as international criminal justice love on behalf of the oppressed population. The Court said that:

> That under the current circumstances, the Government of Bosnia and Herzegovina has the right to seek and receive support from other States in order to defend itself and its people, including by means of immediately obtaining military weapons, equipment, and supplies. 5. That under the current circumstances, the Government of Bosnia and Herzegovina has *the right to request the immediate assistance of any State* to come to its defence, including by means of *immediately* providing weapons, military equipment and supplies, and armed forces (soldiers, sailors, air people. etc.) 6. That under the current circumstances, any State has the right to come to the *immediate defence* of Bosnia and Herzegovina – at its request – including by means of immediately providing weapons, military equipment and supplies, and armed forces (soldiers, sailors, and air people, etc.); . . .[80]

The term "concern of all states" actually constitutes one of the maximum and serious questions of the corpus of international legal and political life. The judgements of international courts have dealt with the merit of the term when a matter of high international importance was involved. The term was eventually employed to present the whole theory of international human rights law and its very significant function for the implementation of human rights provisions at a global level. The term 'concerns of all states' constitutes a periphery between violations of norms of legality, morality, and love where the whole substance of law has been ignored and therefore demands its reestablishment with the assistance of public or united power.

This means the theory of enforcement of public international law defends human rights law, and where these rights are systematically the target of attack by the authorities of an offending state, other states may resort, after exhausting all other internationally peaceful methods, to armed use of force in order to protect victims. This is called 'humanitarian concern of all states' in most legal systems. The International Court of Justice (ICJ), in its landmark Advisory Opinion, concluded that the Wall in the Palestinian Occupied Territory infringes the Palestinian people's inalienable right to self-determination. The building of the Wall was, according to the decision of the Court, a violation of the internationally recognized obligation known as *erga omnes*, which is the *concern of all states*:

---

[80]Emphasis added. See Case Concerning Application of the Convention on the Prevention and Punishment of the Crime of Genocide (8 April, 1993, Order), p. 7.

> Given the character and the importance of the rights and obligations involved, the Court is of the view that all States are under an obligation not to recognize the illegal situation resulting from the construction of the wall in the Occupied Palestinian Territory, including in and around East Jerusalem. They are also under an obligation not to render aid or assistance in maintaining the situation created by such construction. It is also for all States, while respecting the United Nations Charter and international law, to see to it that any impediment, resulting from the construction of the wall, to the exercise by the Palestinian people of its right to self-determination is brought to an end. In addition, all the States parties to the Geneva Convention relative to the Protection of Civilian Persons in Time of War of 12 August 1949 are under an obligation, while respecting the United Nations Charter and international law, to ensure compliance by Israel with international humanitarian law as embodied in that Convention.[81]

As a result, the ICJ Advisory Opinion was brought before the United Nations. Due to the urgent situation of the case, Resolution ES-10/15 was passed with an overwhelming majority in the Tenth Special Emergency Session of the UN General Assembly. The legal body of the resolution places emphasis on the significant role of the decision of the ICJ. The decision is certainly a key phenomenon of legal art formulating love for pure justice in the intellectual sphere of the rule of law over the rule of force. It constitutes a balance between the implementation of legal and moral norms on the one side and the call for the enforcement of the principle of love on the other side. It demanded that Israel should comply with the Advisory Opinion.[82] It reads that:

> A. The construction of the wall being built by Israel, the occupying Power, in the Occupied Palestinian Territory, including in and around East Jerusalem, and its associated regime, are contrary to international law;
> B. Israel is under an obligation to terminate its breaches of international law; it is under an obligation to cease forthwith the works of construction of the wall being built in the Occupied Palestinian Territory, including in and around East Jerusalem, to dismantle forthwith the structure therein situated, and to repeal or render ineffective forthwith all legislative and regulatory acts relating thereto, in accordance with paragraph 151 of this Opinion;
> C. Israel is under an obligation to make reparation for all damage caused by the construction of the wall in the Occupied Palestinian Territory, including in and around East Jerusalem;
> D. All States are under an obligation not to recognize the illegal situation resulting from the construction of the wall and not to render aid or assistance in maintaining the situation created by such construction; all States Parties to the Fourth Geneva Convention relative to the Protection of Civilian Persons in Time of War of 12 August 1949 have in addition the obligation, while respecting the United Nations Charter and international law, to ensure compliance by Israel with international humanitarian law as embodied in that Convention;
> E. The United Nations, and especially the General Assembly and the Security Council, should consider what further action is required to bring to an end the illegal situation

[81] Legal Consequences of the Construction of a Wall in the Occupied Palestinian Territory (I.C.J. Reports 2004), Para. 159. See also Tomuschat and Thouvenin (2006).

[82] *Id.* See also the Advisory Opinion of the ICJ concerning the Namibia case in 1971. The Court held that the presence of South Africa in Namibia was illegal and that the State Members of the United Nations should not conduct any act implying recognition of the legality of South Africa's presence.

> resulting from the construction of the wall and the associated regime, taking due account of the present Advisory Opinion.
>
> *Noting* that the Court concluded that "the Israeli settlements in the Occupied Palestinian Territory (including East Jerusalem) have been established in breach of international law".

The violations of the principle of *concern of all states* implicit in the building of the Wall and the Israeli settlement communities in the occupied territories of the West Bank, East Jerusalem, and in the Golan Heights since the end of the 1967 Six-Day War are some of the clearest justifications for evoking the common understating of the principle of love.[83] In 2014, the General Assembly of the United Nations received credible reports concerning the engagement of the settlers in serious violations of the norms of legality and morality.[84]

The Court and the General Assembly verdicts may postulat together a *doubleton legal sanction* for assisting the victims.[85] This means two organs having parallel apposite rudiments for the enforcement of their decisions. However, neither Israel nor any other state complied with the rules sanctioned by the ICJ Advisory Opinion or the General Assembly Resolution. The threat of economic crisis, the risk of losing power, and the military armed forces of two politically strong nations—the United States and Israel—have been the three indispensable factors for the evaporation of the virtue of love for justice. Unhappily, these factors must be enumerated among the things which are requisite for the completion of the Court and the General Assembly decisions.[86]

3.16 Mutatis Mutandis of International Love

The principle of legality is not only applicable to substantive criminal law but also to procedural law. The substantive criminal law concerns the definition of the concept of crimes, responsibility, sanctions, and the relevant punishments in criminal law. The procedural aspect relates to the rules that govern criminal procedure from the time of accusation up until the Court has delivered its judgment in the end and its consequences follow. The system of criminal procedure is in fact one of the most complicated legal systems under national criminal law with the aim of combating offences.[87]

This is also true when one considers the Schengen information system for the fight against crime between the member states.[88] One may also come to similar

---

[83] http://unispal.un.org/UNISPAL.NSF/0/CD39DAA8F9BC342985257DFC005E0F53 (Accessed September 25, 2015).

[84] Ibid.

[85] Malekian (2015), pp. 861–895 at p. 887.

[86] See Ramcharan (2006).

[87] For instance, examine the system of Swedish criminal procedure Lindell et al. (2005), pp. 19 and 20.

[88] See *also* Jareborg et al. (1995), pp. 323–324.

conclusions in the case of civil laws and civil procedures. Both cases mentioned in the preceding section, i.e. Bosnia–Herzegovina and the Wall in the Palestinian Occupied Territory, denote the existence of substantive and procedural aspects of international criminal law. All the relevant provisions may also *mutatis mutandis* be applicable in the case of international human rights law or any part of public international law. The principle of *mutatis mutandis* implies the principle that the relevant given matter has already decided been as a matter of fact, law, or practice.

I shall however emphasise here that the conclusion of the ICJ is just one example of referring to the norm of love and its disappearance in the relevant cases. With their representations here, I do not mean in my remarks that we should give priority to one state and reject the other established state of Israel. I would have put the case forward if the Israelis were Palestinians or *vice versa*. In other words, I would have defended Israel with a full heart and love for justice if it was occupied by the Palestinian state or the barrier was built under the order of their authorities.

The request by the ICJ in both cases, i.e. Bosnia–Herzegovina and the Wall in the Palestinian Occupied Territory, and its statements are therefore a call for humanitarian intervention under public international law which has the character of 'concern of all states' and is also subject to certain conditions. Such immediate assistance would be justified when, for example, people of different ethnic groups or cultures are under pressure, such as in the case of floods, volcanic eruptions, earthquakes, or tsunamis. The conclusion of the ICJ can also be examined under the legal regimes of other states. For instance, the Arab Charter on Human Rights Law, and the International Declaration of Human Rights also point to this significant fact. One may reach similar conclusions concerning the legal character of European Union law and its collective recognition of the circumstances of humanitarian action. Accordingly:

> Humanitarian action is a collective responsibility at an international level, involving many different organisations, governments, local communities and individuals. For the EU, supporting the development of the collective global capacity to respond to humanitarian crises is one of the fundamental tenants of our approach. The EU commits itself not to duplicate existing international mechanisms.

Yet I agree with the fact that the concept of immediate assistance or concern of all states is one of the most controversial questions in public international law.[89] Despite this fact, the United Nations has systematically resorted to armed force for peacekeeping operations, where, according to the UN, there have been systematic violations of the principles of international law.[90] This is with reservation to the fact that the economic and political interests of the Security Council permanent members have often taken priority over other factors. One may assert that, with the odd exception, humanitarian concern constitutes an integral part of *political*

[89]Falk (1981).

[90]The most miserable fact is that the peacekeepers have not been loyal concerning their duties and have been seriously involved in systematic sexual exploitation of women and children.

agendas under the system of public international law today. For example, separatist movements in China, India, Indonesia, Iran, Israel, Japan, Russia, Turkey and other countries have not, for one reason or another, received the assistance of the United States armed forces.

In addition, the recent codification of the system of conventional international law prohibits any form of intervention in the domestic affairs of states which is not the 'concern of all states'. For example, the preamble of the 1986 Vienna Convention on the Law of Treaties between States and International Organizations or between International Organizations expresses vividly that states should respect:

> the principles of international law embodied in the Charter of the United Nations, such as the principles of the equal rights and self-determination of peoples, of the sovereign equality and independence of all States, of non-interference in the domestic affairs of States, of the prohibition of the threat or use of force and of universal respect for, and observance of, human rights and fundamental freedoms for all.

The intention of all these principles is, without doubt, to prohibit resorting to the use of force and balance that aim with love for justice. *At first glance,* one may think that international criminal law permits, in the case of the recent Syria Crisis, for example, resort to the use of force according to the doctrine of intervention for humanitarian reasons, whereby the system of the United Nations may recognise it as unlawful. This doctrine arises from the theory that when there are serious infringements of international human rights law which concern the international community as a whole, states are responsible for taking action. This is particularly imperative when the United Nations Security Council is intentionally incapable of taking a decision for the benefit of the population of the victim state. Clear examples of this are the recent war crimes, crimes against humanity, and grave breaches of the international humanitarian law of armed conflict committed against Gaza by the Israeli Air Force.[91] However, the use of military force has been justified as legitimate use of force in the conduct of the relevant state.[92] Another example is the use of various powerful military forces against the territories of Syria and the devastation of the whole country for economic gain.

At second glance, it is needless to say that the information on the violations of the provisions of human rights law, international humanitarian law, or flagrant violations of the rules relating to the prohibition of the use of certain unlawful weapons during an armed conflict must be reliable and not false. For example, the recent Syrian crisis and the information regarding the creation of the terrorist Islamic State groups revealed that the allegations by the United Kingdom and particularly the United States concerning the use of unlawful chemical weapons

[91]For various significant discussions, see Meloni and Tongnoni (2012).

[92]For resort to the use of force for humanitarian purposes, see https://www.gov.uk/government/uploads/system/uploads/attachment_data/file/235098/Chemical-weapon-use-by-Syrian-regime-UK-government-legal-position.pdf. But see also the last paragraph of subsection 7.3. Use of Unlawful Weapons. See also http://www.independent.co.uk/voices/comment/bashar-alassad-syria-and-the-truth-about-chemical-weapons-8393539.html (Accessed April 1, 2015). See also footnote below.

by the regime against its own population were very dubious.[93] Consequently, an intervention has to be based on correct information and must be of the nature of a *concern of all states* or fulfil, in one way or another, the conditions for a *doubleton legal sanction* as specified in the judgments of the ICJ and resolutions of the General Assembly of the United Nations.[94]

It must be borne in mind that the voting processes for the resolutions of the General Assembly or the European Union are two of the processes most similar to those developed in other legal regimes such as Islamic international law. With these processes, international laws wish to ensure that consensus or a unanimous majority decision for the expression of love for humanity has been achieved through the principle of *concern of all states*. This is a sanction which does not rely on being or not being a permanent member of the Security Council but a "permanent member" of the union of law demanding the implementation of the norm of love for humanity and justice.

References

Allen, W. B. (Ed.). (1988). George Washington, *George Washington: A collection.*

Ashworth, A. (2006). Four threats to presumption of innocence. *South African Journal*, 63–97.

Ashworth, A. (2008). Criminal procedure, human rights and 'Balance': Towards the Dark Night Sea? In *Ikke Kun Straf: Festskrift til Vagen Greve. Jurist- og Økonomforbunds* forlag.

Ashworth, A. (2013). *Positive obligations in criminal law.* Oxford: Hart Publishing.

Bassiouni, M. C. (2014). *The Shari'a and Islamic Criminal Justice in time of war and peace.* Cambridge: Cambridge University Press.

Bentham, J. (2016). An introduction to the principles of morals and legislation. Available at www.earlymoderntexts.com/. Accessed 18 Jan 2016.

Bozbayindir, A. E. (2013). *Turkey and the International Criminal Court: A substantive criminal law analysis in the context of the principle of complementarity.* Germany: Nomos Verlagsgeseells, Baden-Baden.

Cassese, A., Eser, A., Gaja, G., & Conor, R. E. (1980). *Justice at Nuremberg.* New York: Harper & Row.

Clough, J., & Mulhern, C. (2004). *Criminal law* (2nd ed.). Australia: LexisNexis Butterworth.

[93]The British Prime Minister, Tony Blair has after almost fifteen years confessed that he has greatly been wrong about his decisions and information received from the United States about Iraq. His decisions have been one of the most few essential reasons for the devastation of Iraq. Available at www.countercurrents.org/2016/07/09/tony-blair-goes-to-confession/ See 'Tony Blair is World's Worst Terrorist', http://www.telegraph.co.uk/news/2016/07/06/dont-blame-tony-blair-for-the-mess-iraq-is-in-blame-obama/ (Accessed August 4, 2016); and more in Google.

[94]Thus, the legal validity of the accusation of the British memorandum to the United Nations and the White House Statement by Deputy National Security Advisor for Strategic Communications Ben Rhodes on Syrian Chemical Weapons Use is null and void. They violate the principles of the United Nations and Islamic international law, available at http://www.whitehouse.gov/the-press-office/2013/06/13/statement-deputy-national-security-advisor-strategic-communications-ben- (Accessed April 1, 2015). See also *id.* In fact, it is believed that a British defence company, Britam, revealed a plan such that the White House would provide chemical weapons to hired mercenaries to exploit against civilians in Syria in order to have a legitimate reason to justify a direct intervention, as was done in Iraq.

Cohen, M. (1949). Moral aspects of the criminal law. *Yale Law Journal, 49*, 987–1026.
Dan-Cohen, M. (2014). Dignity, crime, and punishment: A Kantian perspective. In M. D. Dubber (Ed.), *Foundational texts in modern criminal law*. Oxford: Oxford University Press.
Detmold, M. J. (1984). *The unity of law and morality: A refutation of legal positivism*. London: Routledge & Kegan Paul.
Dougan, M. (2008). The Treaty of Lisbon 2007: Winning minds, not hearts. *Common Market Law Review, 45*, 617–703.
Earl, J. (2009). *The Nuremberg SS-Einsatzgruppen Trial, 1945–1958*. Cambridge: Cambridge University Press.
Eastwood, M. (2011). *The Nuremberg Trial of Julius Streicher: The crime of "Incitement to Genocide"*. Lewiston: The Edwin Mellan Press.
Falk, R. (1981). *Human rights and state sovereignty*. New York: Holmes & Meier Publishers.
Fischer, M. (1998). The human rights implications of a cultural defense. *Southern California Interdisciplinary Law Journal, 6*, 663–702.
Fournet, C. (2015). The *Actus Reus* of genocide in the Croatia v. Serbia Judgment: Between legality and acceptability. *Leiden Journal of International Law, 28*(4), 915–921.
Fuller, L. L. (1969). *The morality of law* (2nd ed.). New Haven: Yale University Press.
Gilmore, W. C. (2011). *Dirty money: The evolution of international measures to counter money laundering and the financing of terrorism* (4th ed.). Strasburg: Council of Europe Publishing.
Ginsburgs, G., & Kudriavtsev V. N. (Eds.). (1990). *The Nuremberg trial and international law*. Leiden: Martinus Nijhoff Publishers.
Gross, H. (2012). *Crime and punishment: A concise moral critique*. New York: Oxford University Press.
Grotius, H. (1625). *The rights of war and peace* (A.C. Campbell, ed. 1901).
Gur-Arye, M., & Jessberger, F. (2011). The protection of human dignity in interrogations: May interrogative torture ever be tolerated? Reflections in light of recent German and Israeli experiences. *Israel Law Review, 44*, 229–263.
Hart, H. L. A. (1961). *The concept of law*. Oxford: Oxford University Press.
Hart, H. L. A. (2008). *Punishment and responsibility: Assays in the philosophy of law* (2nd ed.). Oxford: Oxford University Press.
Hazan, P. (2004). *Justice in a time of war: The true story behind the International Criminal Tribunal for the former Yugoslavia*. College Station: Texas A & M University Press.
Jackson, R. H. (1946–1947). Forward the Nuremberg trial becomes a historical precedent. *TEMPLE L Q, 20*.
Jareborg, N., Friberg, S., & Asp, P. (1995). *Svensk Internationell Straffprocessrätt*. Uppsala: Iustus Förlag.
Branlard, J.-P. (2014). *Master Droit Pénal: Droit pénal general & Procédure pénale*. Paris: Editions Eska.
Koskenniemi, M. (2001). Human rights, politics and love. *Mennesker & Rettigheder, 4*, 33–45.
Krarup, O. (2006). Justice and legal seismology. In U. V. Bondeson (Ed.), *Law and morality*. Forlaget Thomson.
Ladd, J. (1991). The idea of collective violence. In N. Graver (Ed.), *Justice, law and violence*. Philadelphia: The Temple University Press.
Lindell, B., Eklundo, H., Asp, P., & Andersson, T. (2005). *Straffprocessen*. Justus Förlag.
Locke, J. (1689). *The two treatises of civil government (Thomas Hollis (ed.), Of the State of Nature*, Chap. XVII, section 5, Book II, 1689).
Malekian, F. (1999). International criminal responsibility. In M. C. Bassiouni (Ed.), *International criminal law: Crimes* (2nd ed.). New York: Transnational Publishers, Inc. Ardsley.
Malekian, F. (2009a). The miserable wedding of naturalism into positivism. *ID EST Journal*, 139–215.
Malekian, F. (2009b). The homogeneity of International Criminal Court with Islamic Jurisprudence. *International Criminal Law Review, 9*, 595–621.
Malekian, F. (2013). Islamic criminal justice systems. In J. S. Albanese (Ed.), *The encyclopaedia of criminology & criminal justice* (5 volumes, Vol. III). Wiley-Blackwell.

Malekian, F. (2015). The Canon of love against the use of force in Islamic and Public International Law: Part II: The anatomy of love against violations. *International Criminal Law Review, 15*, 861–895.
McAuley, F., & Paul McCutcheon, J. (2000). *Criminal liability*. Round Hall, Sweet & Maxwell.
Meloni, C., & Tongnoni, G. (Eds.). (2012). *Is there a court for Gaza: A test bench for international justice*. The Hague: Springer.
Mitsilegas, V. (2003). *Money laundering counter-measures in the European Union: A new paradigm of security governance versus fundamental legal principles*. The Hague: Kluwer Law International.
Mo-Tse. (1929). *The ethical and political works of Motse*. London: Arthur Probsthain.
Nussbaum, M. C. (2013). *Political emotions: Why love matters for justice*. Harvard University Press.
Ossowska, M. *Moral and legal norms, the journal of philosophy*. University of Warsaw.
Pinto, C., & Jardine, M. (1997). *East Timor's unfinished struggle: Inside the Timorese Resistance*. USA: South End Press Collective.
Power, J. (2007). *Conundrums of humanity: The quest for global justice*. The Hague: Martinus Nijhoff Publisher.
Ramcharan, B. G. (Ed.). (2006). *Human rights protection in the field*. Leiden: Martinus Nijhoff.
Ratner, S. R., & Jason A. S. (Eds.). (2001). *Accountability for human rights atrocities in international law: Beyond the Nuremberg Legacy*. Oxford: Oxford University Press.
Riesman, W. M. (2008). Learning to deal with rejection: The International Criminal Court and the United States. In M. S. Elis & R. J. Goldstone (Eds.), *The International Criminal Court: Challenges to achieving justice and accountability in the 21st century*. New York: International Debate Education Association.
Rinceanu, J. (2011a). The principle of legality (Nullum crimen sine lege) in Romania. In U. Sieber, S. Forster, & K. Jarvers (Eds.), *National criminal law in a comparative legal context*. Volume 2 (1): *Max-Planck-Institute für ausländisches und internationals Strafrecht* (pp. 89–101). Berlin: Duncker & Humblot.
Rinceanu, J. (2011b). Concept and systematization of the criminal offense in Romania. In U. Sieber, S. Forster, & K. Jarvers (Eds.), *National criminal law in a comparative legal context*. Volume 3(1): *Max-Planck-Institute für ausländisches und internationals Strafrecht* (pp. 73–85). Berlin: Duncker & Humblot.
Ross, A. (1946). *Towards a realistic jurisprudence: A criticism of the dualism in law*. Copenhagen: Einar Munksgaard.
Ross, A. (1952). Retsfilosofiens Problem. 7-9 Svensk Juristtidning 1952, 701–732.
Rousseau, J.-J. (1761). *The social contract and discourses* (1761) (G. D. H. Cole, Trans., London & Toronto: J.M. Dent § Sons LTP § in New York, E.P Dutton & Co, 1923).
Rydenfelt, S., & Larsson, J. (1966). *Säkerhets Polisen Hemliga Register: Om Åsiktfrihet och Åsiktförföljelse*. Uddevalla: Zindermans förlag.
Schmid, A. P. (2014). Austria's reformed law on Islam – A model for Europe? Available at http://icct.nl/publication/austrias-reformed-law-on-islam-a-model-for-europe/?dm_i=1ADT,3FCGN,76AWD2,C9CO7,1. Accessed 1 June 2014.
Schwarzenberger, G. (1968). *International law: As applied by International Courts and Tribunals* (Vol. II: The law of armed conflict). London: Stevens & Sons Limited.
Sheldon, G. (1946). *The Nuremberg trial and aggressive war*. New York: Alfred A Knopf.
Shelton, D. L. (2014). *Advanced introduction to International Human Rights Law*. USA: Edward Elgar Publishing.
Sunstein, C. R. (2001). *Designing democracy: What constitutions do*. Oxford: Oxford University Press.
Swanson, J. (2010). *God, science and the universe: The integration of religion and science*. Eloquent Books.
Tomuschat, C., & Thouvenin, J.-M. (Eds.). (2006). *The fundamental rules of the international legal order: Jus Cogens and Obligations Erga Omnes*. Leiden: Brill.
Wendel, B. (2012). *Lawyers and fidelity to law*. New Jersey: Princeton University Press.

Chapter 4
The Modus Operandi of the Norm of Love in Criminal Justice

4.1 Rule of Love on Criminal Justice

Rule of law constitutes a significant principle for the implementation of the ethics and philosophy of criminal justice. The principle of rule of law or the principle of enforcement of justice in accordance with rules and provisions therefore embraces the entire historical philosophy of law.[1] This historical philosophy of law does not only mean legality but also morality. However, one may strongly violate both these principles of the rule of law in that their prevention may not only be impossible but also unsolvable.[2] Here, the only principle which may be above the principles of morality and legality, is the norm of love. This is the norm of a legal system that can no longer tolerate violations of the principles of morality and legality.

There may not even be any principle of legality that can criminalise criminal conduct like the criminality of the acts of Nazism under the Second World War, the criminality of acts of Stalin during the reformation of the former Soviet Union, or the criminality of acts of the United States in Cambodia. Both international criminal tribunals after the Second World War were not only incapable of finding good principles of legality and morality but were also short of any regulations which could properly cover the criminal acts committed during the wars. The only juridical mechanisms which were functioning here were the norm of love, the power of love, the existence of strong will, the philosophy of similarities, and the strong rejection of the principle of pluralism.

The policies of both tribunals were philosophically against any system which encourages divergences.[3] The ICTY, the ICTR, and even the permanent ICC also

---

[1] Nussbaum (2013), pp. 30–31, 35–39.

[2] *Id.*, at 45.

[3] However, I am fully aware of the fact that both tribunals have had strong political motives. The chief question was not in fact to help the victims but to access the will and interests of the strong

F. Malekian, *Judgments of Love in Criminal Justice*,
DOI 10.1007/978-3-319-46900-3_4

have a similar policy. Their policies require the power of love for justice, respect, and similarities of our good intention with good faith in law. It is however important to highlight here that the policies of these tribunals, in particular the first two tribunals in the world, were indeed arbitrary since the norm of love for justice was only employed against the conquered party and not the victors who were also actually serious violators of the system of legality and morality. Between 20 and 60 million *human beings* alone were murdered in Russia and almost 4 million died from the starvation in India because Churchill stored the Indian food for British soldiers. This was a crime of crimes older than food itself.

All this shows the existence or non-existence of the rule of law at the right time. This is because the whole theory of the rule of law is a hypothetical concept of law. The principle of rule of law can be referred to from two different perspectives. One is the principle of rule of law denotes the existence of a healthy legal and moral system. The other is the rule of law which implies the existence of an ill legal or moral system. However, there is a third body of the rule of law, which does not coincide with either of the first two. This means that the third one has the tendency to be a complete rule of law. A clear example of the first is the international conventions concerning the necessary norms of human rights law. An example of the second is the existence of norms that include rules of force such as the criminal provisions of the Islamic Republic of Iran, China, and Russia. The third refers to the concept of rule of law in some democratic countries.

Although they are based on human rights conventions, their strategic policies are in some instances arbitrary and unjust, such as rules of law in Australia and Sweden. For example, the European Court of Human Rights has not been positive about some provisions of the Swedish legal system. Similarly, the Human Rights Committee of the United Nations and the United Nations Human Rights Council have strongly condemned Sweden for its unlawful immoral political conduct.[4] All these

---

nations. This can be particularly examined in the structure of the Tokyo Tribunal, which demonstrated itself to be a show tribunal in order to gain Japanese gold. In fact, different acts of the military judges corrupted and terminated the entire justice system and prosecution of those who had participated in the killing of millions of people.

[4]For the European Court of Human Rights, see http://www-user.uni-bremen.de/avosetta/hydenconstrights.html (Accessed May 31, 2015); For the Human Rights Committee of the United Nation and serious violations of the International Covenant on Civil and Political Rights, see CCPR/C/88/D/1416/2005 (10 November 2006) or http://docstore.ohchr.org/SelfServices/FilesHandler.ashx?enc=6QkG1d%2fPPRiCAqhKb7yhsh0NOQzIlNsoUFstAtJW4fuo7HcOEe2RBCW3JoVfYCkiyI95uu4vvQbGTkpqAAWg%2f0DZKaNo6qgjQh9hajtajOz9D%2bVZaFfKZZIKLpPm1Ht3CrENInUn9L2LtKvgimI6IA%3d%3d. The above case was brought against Sweden by Egyptian nationals, and Sweden was sentenced and accepted its responsibility for gross violations of the provisions of the Convention. The substantive issues in the Committee were "Torture or cruel, inhuman or degrading treatment or punishment – exposure to a real risk of torture or cruel, inhuman or degrading treatment or punishment and/or manifestly unfair trial in a third State – no respect for due process in process of expulsion of an alien – ineffective domestic remedies against alleged violations – frustration of the right to effective complaint." Sweden finally paid damages. Nevertheless, both victims had undergone severe torture under the supervision of the CIA in Egypt. Available at http://sverigesradio.se/sida/artikel.aspx?programid=83&artikel=1230523; In 2013,

policies imply the existence of the rule of law or the norms of law but to different degrees. To avoid this confrontation between different natures of law, the Secretary-General of the United Nations describes the rule of law as:

> a principle of governance in which all persons, institutions and entities, public and private, including the State itself, are accountable to laws that are publicly promulgated, equally enforced and independently adjudicated, and which are consistent with international human rights norms and standards. It requires, as well, measures to ensure adherence to the principles of supremacy of law, equality before the law, accountability to the law, fairness in the application of the law, separation of powers, participation in decision-making, legal certainty, avoidance of arbitrariness and procedural and legal transparency.[5]

The structure of the Universal Declaration of Human Rights law encourages a healthy form of rule of law, yet one that is almost impossible to implement properly. It expresses that "... it is essential, if man is not to be compelled to have recourse, as a last resort, to rebellion against tyranny and oppression, that human rights should be protected by the *rule of law*..." The norms of the declaration have several natures. These are legality, morality, and love. All these three concepts may overlap and it may not be possible to isolate them from one another because of their very strong correlations. The difference between these three natures is that the former is completely visible whilst the second is integrated into the former and the third is transparency of justice when the first two are grossly violated. Although the third principle is not tangible within the provisions of the Human Rights Declaration, it is always accessible and its absence within the norms of the law does not confirm its non-existence.

We may not properly put into operation human rights law without love. However, we may implement love without law. The term "love" as a norm of law and jurisdiction therefore has a full tendency to help understand the ingredients of justice and jurisdiction. This is not only vital for the entire building of justice, but also for all the theories behind which our judges, prosecutors, solicitors, and advocates present justice. Thus, the term "justice" necessitates the term "love" and the latter the attendance of the former, and justice without love is like a bee without honey and most often synthetic and hazardous. The norm of love may together with justice transparency for the truth and equality of application of law to all criminals coming from all parts of the world.

---

the Swedish Minister of Justice clearly stated that "obviously, it was wrong to execute a deportation to Egypt." The case was the mistake of the whole government. http://www.unt.se/omvarld/bodstrom-angrar-utvisning-2584595.aspx; For Julian Assange case see http://ohchr.org/EN/NewsEvents/Pages/DisplayNews.aspx?NewsID=17012&LangID=E (All accessed February 14, 2016).

[5](Report of the Secretary-General: The rule of law and transitional justice in conflict and post-conflict societies" (2004)).

4.2 Criminal Dimensions of Love

We are aware that one may use the word 'love' with a negative connotation, such as 'love of killing', 'love of destruction', 'love of harm' and 'love of one's country'. The latter implies the fact that one is right within one's own philosophy of international law at any cost.[6] Yet, the positive interpretations of the phrase "for the love of one's country,"[7] have often been practised by various nations. Looking at positive and negative facets of love, the entire nationalism theory was built upon the norm of love and later replaced with the norm of love to an international union of humanity. Examples are the Greek war of independence against the Ottoman Empire in 1821, French Revolution in 1830, and Ukrainian Revolution in 2014. Similarly, one could not establish the European Union as a potential system of collective regional security before the process of nationalism was settled in Europe.

> . . .the growing love for the patria that became the basis of modern nationalism, one finds a potent configuring internationalism as the alliance or the clash of particularisms. There were profound consequences for political good in all of this that cannot ignored as one critiques the ill effects over time including agitation for constitutional and democratic forms of governance. Much of this agitation arose from patriotic loves for one's nation and a commitment to her and to what sort of place she was.[8]

The pessimistic approach to the concept of love is surely contrary to what is generally understood by the word 'love' within civilisation. Such a position may not fall into the field of love in connection to law but rather into the scope of an extreme form of discrimination between inhabitants of the globe. This means a strong form of radical terror. The Spanish and the British enforced such a policy in America against the Native Americans (Indians); several colonial states in Africa against Africans;[9] the United States against the *Indians, Africans*; and

---

[6]A central question is "whether lawyers are consigned to do dirty work "for the love of country" or in the name of political expediency to the detriment of the law, and particularly of international criminal law. The best example of this point is the resurrection of criminal conduct that many of us thought was obliterated by our legal system years ago. Now we are burdened by allegations of torture and cruel and degrading treatment of detainees, and by the legal rationales for such practices, inflicted "for the love of country" during the so-called war on terror." Scheffer (2009), pp. 665–678 at 666–677. Available at http://www.auilr.org/; http://digitalcommons.wcl.american.edu/cgi/viewcontent.cgi?article=1099&context=auilr, (Accessed October 20, 2014).

[7]For example, whilst there were a considerable number of young men in Germany "who, for love of country, threw themselves into death's embrace on the Eastern front in 1942, there were many other men on the Eastern front, or with the *Einsatzgruppen*, or in Poland—for example the 101 Reserve Police Battalion—who, for the same love of country, engaged in the vilest atrocities against civilian men, women, and children." Al-Hussein (2009), pp. 647–664 at 665. Available at http://www.auilr.org/; http://digitalcommons.wcl.american. edu/cgi/viewcontent.cgi?article=1098&context=auilr (Accessed October 18, 2014).

[8]Elshtain (2006), p. 155.

[9]The colonial power by regulating sanitation, health, education, or public conduct started to believe that "they were in Africa for local peoples' own good. The idea rule of law seemed to them to provide evidence of this fact, and it powerfully legitimized colonial rule." Mann and

other ethnic groups; the former Yugoslavia against *the Muslim population;* Europe against the *Jews*; and Israel against foreigners, even including non-native Jews.

Similarly, one can study the policy in the practice of the Union of Soviet Socialist Republics against various different ethnic groups; in the attitude of South Africa against the *black population;* in the invisible regulations of Australia against *the Aboriginal people;* and in the legislation of Iran against *the Baha'i group, Kurds, and against the majority of women in general*. These practices of racial discrimination violate the norms of a considerable number of international conventions. Such are the Convention against Discrimination in Education, 1960; the Convention on the Elimination of All Forms of Racial Discrimination, 1965; the Convention on the Elimination of All Forms of Racial Discrimination against Women, 1979; and the Declaration on the Elimination of All Forms of Intolerance and of Discrimination Based on Religion or Belief, 1981.

Unfortunately, among many peoples, the power of individuals to influence others has not been replaced with the power of love for humanity, equality, brotherhood, and a higher degree of mutual understanding. As it has been justly asserted, "To be modern is to find ourselves in an environment that promises adventure, power, joy, growth, transformation of ourselves and the world—and at the same time threatens to destroy everything we have, everything we know, everything we are."[10] The spirit of love therefore has to surmount the love of control of law. That should be one of the duties of the systems of laws.

4.3 The Monopolization of the Rule of Love

Norms of love are always present within the instruments of human rights law or international humanitarian law of armed conflict based on the fact that the basic philosophy of these instruments is not solely their existence or respect but establishing the borderline of respect, justice, injustice, and grave violations of the norms of love. It is in fact not helpful to say that the rules of law in international humanitarian law of armed conflict regarding grave breaches are the final stage in

---

Roberts (1991), p. 3. One can even conclude that the genocide of almost 800,000 Tutsis and moderate Hutus in Rwanda traces back to the tensions which had been initiated by the Belgian government's colonisation of the two ethnic groups in 1922. The Belgian authorities supported the Tutsi political power and degraded the Hutus by imposing the compulsory use of identity cards for the two groups. These tensions became more and more visible over decades and finally resulted in a Hutu revolution declaration of independence in 1962 and the creation of the international legal personality of the Rwandan Republic. From this time on, the country was engaged in infrequent violence between the Hutu government and Tutsi rebels. The Rwanda Patriotic Front (RPF), formed by Tutsi refugees who had sought asylum with their families in Uganda, invaded Rwanda, starting the Rwandan Civil War in 1990 to 1994. The Tanzanian International Criminal Tribunal for Rwanda prosecuted and punished 93 individuals who had taken part in the 1994 genocide.

[10] Berman (1982), p. 15.

which the norms of love for justice are completely violated by criminal behaviour at the time of armed conflict. It is therefore not without reason that the Charter of the United Nations aims to codify the rules of law in which the rules of morality and love are integrated. The Preamble of the Charter aims to elucidate the norm of love and its significant function for the prevention of injustice. That is why the United Nations Charter has in many articles referred to the maintenance of justice, equality, and peace.

Although we do not object to the fact that the powerful states in the United Nations have different policies regarding the application of justice when their own interests are in question, this should not be a legal factor for the prevention of justice and the implementation of the principle of love. In other words, such policies should not stop the norm of love in the structure of legal discipline. The Charter clearly says that its aim is to save succeeding generations from the scourge of war, which has brought unthinkable sorrow to humanity.

This aim of the Charter can be examined in the provisions of the Declaration of Principles of International Law Concerning Friendly Relations and Co-operation Among States in Accordance with the Charter of the United Nations. The Declaration refers to the core values of the system of international law with regard to the Charter of the United Nations. These include respect for the sovereign equality of states and the principle of non-use of force or threat of use of force between various nations. It also refers to the accomplishment of the obligation of states in good faith, the need to resolve disputes by peaceful means, and the full admiration of the protection of human rights and fundamental freedoms. It also encourages states to avoid acts constituting genocide, crimes against humanity, ethnic cleansing, and war crimes. The Declaration calls upon the core responsibility of states towards their population and their responsibility to the international community as a whole. The Declaration also encourages states to respect the principle of self-determination of peoples.

Despite the fact that there are many international human rights conventions, we are also aware that the five permanent members of the United Nations with their allies have completely monopolized the heart of the Charter. This makes the provisions of the United Nations very difficult and sometimes even impossible to enforce. In other words, the organisation's most significant rules of law are the *personal rules of the five permanent members* which in turn make the application of the principles of legality, morality, and love very intricate. This complicated situation can be seen in the decisions of the Security Council of the United Nations which functions more often for the individual benefit of the five permanent members. For instance, although the provisions of Chapter VII of the Charter were enacted for the prevention of aggression, recognition of the use of force, and elimination of possible commission of international crimes, the permanent members do not respect this policy, and the power of Chapter VII has been used to a contrary effect.

The permanent members have used the relevant provisions of the Charter with the intention to commit war crimes, crimes against humanity, and aggression. One may strongly assert that Chapter VII of the Charter is used to legitimize acts of aggression committed by the permanent members. A quick reading of the history of

Chapter VII implies this unfortunate fact. That is why, when we talk about the norm of love, we do not mean that the Charter of the organisation is presenting these norms but the fact that the permanent members do not defend even the simple merit of legal norms. In fact, the Security Council has frequently infringed the system of international human rights law. This also includes the principles of international morality and the general principles of customary law.

As a result, one can list several parallel types of justice, such as natural, distributive, retributive, retroactive, restorative, reparative, and procedural justice. There are also a considerable number of other concepts of justice like communist justice, imperialist justice, dictatorial justice, spiritual justice, fanatical justice, Stalinist justice, Obama's justice, and Putin's justice. All these relate to justice. Mussolini and Hitler also had their own types of justice. That is why I am speaking about the norm of love as delimitation *between* the negative and the green justice.

4.4 Enshrine the Core Principles

The term "love" constitutes the inner structure of any law that aims for the implementation of justice and equality between nations. Most lawyers believe that the creation of a new law is natural or the way that we promote our social interests and justice together. In that case, the same lawyers should also believe that it is quite natural to speak about love in conjunction with the law in order to achieve the substance of the rule of law. This is because any response to a particular will of the state involves regulating certain matters that we value highly. This new law is not the protection of one individual's right but those of all individuals. According to Aristotle:

> Justice can only exist between those whose mutual relations are regulated by law, and law exist among those between whom there is a possibility of injustice, for the application of the law means the discrimination of what is just and what is unjust. Persons therefore between whom injustice can exist, can act unjustly towards each other... This is why we do not permit a man to rule, but the law, because a man rules in his own interest, and becomes a tyrant...[11]

Even if we suppose that the adopted law is referring to the rights of a single individual, this is still the expression of our social collective love to protect that individual's rights. The law does not obviously refer to a single name but to all of us together. Thus, when one talks about freedom of speech or freedom of movement, this means that one looks for the presence of certain norms of love for justice, which are called freedom or which are rights of privacy. In other words, there exist certain high principles in all laws. These are what we call the norm of love, which must always be inside our decisions.

---

[11] Aristotle, Nicomachean Ethics, Book V, in Morris (1959), p. 21.

For instance, the term 'love' is used in the provisions of the Islamic law of nations in order to avoid any use of force and to make violators cognizant of the reality that the architect of the law does not admire its use to justify violence in order to establish, re-establish, or maintain rights. This principle of love in the law is also significantly important in the criminal law of the same system. The provisions of the law encourage believers to struggle for rights but within the terms of non-aggression, non-use of force, or prohibition of resorting to the use of force. Similarly, the term 'love' in most laws, including European law, international human rights law, or even the Charter of the United Nations, means to give, to have tolerance, to be just when implementing the law, whether for companions, strangers, or enemies, and to believe that conflicts can be resolved by loving the essential substance of one another. In other words, its widest interpretation means that the exercise of any concept of force based on religious rules, the European Union's law, or international human rights law has zero validity.

For this reason, any interpretation of Islamic law, in the shadow of *jihad*, human rights law with the reasoning of Article 51 of the Charter, or violation of the Genocide Convention with reference to a *tu quoque* argument is without valid grounds. Therefore, the theory of permission to use force against one another by defenders of Islam, public international law, or European Union law lacks an understanding of the principle of love. The brutal policies of terrorist groups, such as the Islamic State in Iraq and Syria, are surely the grossest violation of international law. Stating that the criminal conduct of relevant groups is Islamic ideology is really a feeble explanation. It is like saying that the immoral or illegal killing of several millions by Stalin was the idea of Marx and Engels, or that the killing of several millions in Europe during the Second World War was the theory of Immanuel Kant. This has no logical basis. It would also be an unwise idea to express that the destructions of Iraq, Libya, and Syria are the accomplishment of the philosophy of Hart.

Love constitutes not only the threshold of good faith on any given issue but also the necessary threshold to fight against any use of force, crimes against humanity, or war crimes. The numerous rules of jus ad bellum have proven ineffective and have been used arbitrarily to engage in the illegitimate use of force. A clear example is the disproportionate use of force by Israeli military forces in July 2014, leading to the murder of children and innocent civilians in the Gaza Strip. The victims plans to bring the case before the ICC jurisdiction,[12] *however, without any success.*

[12]Palestine has now become as the 123rd State Party to the ICC (1 April 2015). The President of the Assembly of States Parties stated that "The accession of Palestine as the 19th State Party from the Asia-Pacific region and the second from the Middle-East, is a new stage in the quest for universality for the Statute. We hope that it will pave the way for other countries in the Middle-East who, by adopting the Rome Statute, will strengthen the International Criminal Court in its fight against impunity for mass crimes." Available at http://www.icc-cpi.int/iccdocs/PIDS/press/01-04-15-ASP-speech.pdf (Accessed May 20, 2015).

A more or less similar conclusion may be drawn regarding the substance of many regulations in public international law or European Union Law, the original intention of which is to realise the needs of the European people by enshrining the principle of equal justice.[13] An analogous argument can also be concluded regarding the decisions of the European Court of Human Rights and the International Court of Justice. Furthermore, the entire structure of the United Nations should be based on the canon of love, i.e. the firm commitment to upholding justice, security, fairness, and avoiding any decision which generates an inequality of arms between the nations of the world.[14] The Security Council of the United Nations needs to modify and substitute the desire for superior status of the five permanent members with the strength of love for all nations under the direct supervision of the General Assembly. By this, I mean that "love of equality" has to enter the structure of the United Nations as a whole. In other words, the permanent members of the Security Council have to decline their permanent powers so that they can help the posterity of the international community with the legacy of love for justice.

4.5 Cornerstone of Love on Criminal Justice

The principle of love constitutes the cornerstone of the value of the rule of law or the final stage of rule of law which demands fair justice and non-violent behaviour.[15] A concrete example of this situation is the previous position of South Africa and the practice of apartheid against the black population. Almost all resolutions of the Security Council defended, by one means or another, the apartheid regime whilst the General Assembly resolutions were strongly against the practice. The position was clearly the use of radical evil force by the Security Council resolutions against the norm of love in the General Assembly resolutions. As a result, there was evidently a legal and moral fight to achieve justice. Here, it means that the

[13]Creation of an equal justice has been long struggled for against the historical background of Europe. See Cappelletti et al. (1975), pp. 1–14.

[14]According to Article 1 of the United Nations, the purposes of the organisation are "1. To maintain international peace and security, and to that end: to take effective collective measures for the prevention and removal of threats to the peace, and for the suppression of acts of aggression or other breaches of the peace, and to bring about by peaceful means, and in conformity with the principles of justice and international law, adjustment or settlement of international disputes or situations which might lead to a breach of the peace; 2. To develop friendly relations among nations based on respect for the principle of equal rights and self-determination of peoples, and to take other appropriate measures to strengthen universal peace; 3. To achieve international co-operation in solving international problems of an economic, social, cultural, or humanitarian character, and in promoting and encouraging respect for human rights and for fundamental freedoms for all without distinction as to race, sex, language, or religion; and 4. To be a centre for harmonizing the actions of nations in the attainment of these common ends."

[15]Trechsel (1997), pp. 94–119 at 101–105.

resolutions of the General Assembly demonstrated that there is also a norm in international law or in the body of law which is called love. This norm of love was not coming from the words of the GA resolutions alone but was based on the provisions of several international conventions, such as the 1965 International Convention on the Elimination of All Forms of Discrimination and the 1973 International Convention on the Suppression and Punishment of the Crime of Apartheid.[16] The conventions demanded the abolition of the shocking practices of discrimination. Most states of the world ratified the conventions. However, the United States, Israel, and the United Kingdom governments did not ratify the Convention on Apartheid, based on their investment in South Africa.

Here, with the love norms, I have absolutely convinced myself that I mean the final stage of tolerance against brutality of criminal justice; against unlawful rules; against injust decisions; and against barbarous segregations. I also mean love against unequal divisions of social, economic and other services; against civil, criminal, procedural, and juridical humiliation. Love also points to the rules which are against the basic integrity of man, constituting an integral part of human unions. The apartheid system and its abolition are just one example of how the final stage of violence may provoke the power of love for justice, not only in the United Nations General Assembly but also within the civil and cultural systems of most nations in the world. Thus, when the population of the world supported large demonstrations against the apartheid system in their own respective states, they not only proved the existence of the norm of love for justice but also via this power exhibited their own civil rights to express their critical opinion. This means that there is a *green norm* or a line shared between civil codes in one country with those of another, not to mention the civil code under European Union law, which should be almost the same for the whole of Europe.

In other words, when the norm of love was expressed in the General Assembly resolutions in order to achieve justice and eliminate the apartheid system, the civil codes of most states were also indirectly enforced. The power behind the enforcement was set out neither by the application of the United Nations resolutions, nor by the legal authorities of different states in their countries, but by the use of the right to demonstrate, the right to express an opinion, and the right to participate in group activities for freedom, justice, and unity of hearts. These activities were useful and beneficial for the freedom of the black population of the world. *This is the colour which is whiter than white, but which the Europeans' grandfathers incorporated to become darker than dark.* The enforcement of the resolutions also helped to lead the struggles for justice and liberation. This freedom of expression in various countries finally resulted in very serious sanctions against the South African regime and ended the criminal system.

[16]It must be emphasised here that, although the Soviet Socialist Republic was one of the perpetrators of the draft on the apartheid regime, it was itself practicing very serious discrimination against the countries which were occupied by its government.

This was a system where the criminal law was the most dangerous offender with state criminal character, collective criminality, and permitted criminal legal personality secured and guarded by the government. The entire international legal personality of South Africa was used to supporting the criminal system of the white European. Likewise, the assistance, cooperation, and understanding were helpful in the establishment of justice and worked against the monopolisation of the Security Council which was controlled by powerful states such as the United States, the United Kingdom, and Israel. The norm of love in law for justice therefore means preventing any concept of such justice which may create diversity and multiplicity among the members of our national or international society.

I shall repeat myself again: no rule of law is valid if it does not provide justice. No law is law if it brings violations and inequality. Lex injusta non est lex. No civil law is good if its subjects are in prisons. None of the judges and prosecutors of the criminal jurisdictions is perfect if they are still working with criminal cases. No defence is correct if it ends in killings. All these are our fault. All those who are working, by one means or another, in law, have, according to the principle of love for justice, strict liability before all members of our nations if there are violations of law by the same members. We have to be devoted to the system of love for justice as much as the overcoming of violence disappears from our living environment.

A lawyer is not a lawyer if she does not realise that her elegance of knowledge is not based on her income, position occupied, academic institutions, orations, or degrees.[17] *Knowledge of the law is not the knowledge of law if it cannot understand that the law does not need a lawyer with the knowledge of its laws but one with the knowledge of its substance for the morality of justice and for the love of justice.*[18] *As Plato asserts, justice is "one's capacity to think rationally and to be able to follow the proper reasoning based on superior knowledge." These principles are in place in order to find a way to put an end to most reasons that are the basic source for the commission of grave violations of the system of international criminal human rights law.*

War crimes or crimes of devastation are older than civilisation itself. Crime against humanity, the crime of crimes, lives in the structure of human buildings. Genocide, or the massacre of humanity, is a crime that constitutes the visceral nature of civilisation of humankind.[19] This is nonetheless a serious insult to the nature of animals in this treatise. The reason is that most domestic animals live together in groups and are seldom harmful to each other's existence. The system of criminal law is a law which remains more dangerous than its subjects of concern. That is why we search in this exposition for the norm of love in the inner structure of all laws, in particular criminal justice regulations. This also implies the positive obligations of states to fulfil their obligations in a way such that we will not have victims, we will not have problems in re-establishing their violated rights, and so

[17]Shaffer (1997), pp. 963–970.

[18]Examine Shaffer (1997), pp. 963–991.

[19]Boot (2002), pp. 609–631.

forth. For instance, concerning human trafficking, the European Court in *Rantsev* clarifies the following:

> The Court considers that the spectrum of safeguards set out in national legislation must be adequate to ensure the practical and effective protection of the rights of victims or potential victims of trafficking. Accordingly, in addition to criminal law measures to punish traffickers, Article 4 requires member States to put in place adequate measures regulating businesses often used as a cover for human trafficking. Furthermore, a State's immigration rules must address relevant concerns relating to encouragement, facilitation or tolerance of trafficking.[20]

4.6 The Norm of Love Against Criminal Mentality

The technique of war develops very rapidly, and it soon becomes impossible to bring every action under international humanitarian law of armed conflict and even under public international law. There is the possibility that a state may develop a technique which does not fall under the jurisdiction of the international criminal system, international criminal justice, or the United Nations as a whole. The new technique may be of such capability that it does not fall under any rules of international criminal law and therefore its use is not apparently prohibited. When an armed conflict is waged, the relevant state may use the new technique and kill human beings on a massive scale. What is international criminal justice is going to do?

Are we going to say that we do not have any applicable law and law did not prohibit the conduct? Are we bound by the principles of *nullum crimen sine lege* or *nulla poena sine praevia lege*? Have we violated the provisions of the Convention on Genocide? Whatever the answer may be and whatever we are obliged to do in accordance with the attitude of laws, we are surely forced by the principle of human morality and love to assert that such conduct cannot go without accountability. This is regardless of the philosophy of Mohamadism, Kantianism, Kelsenism, Marxism, the theory of our jurisdiction, the ethics of our politicians, the morality of our criminologists, the argumentation of prosecutors, the ignoring of the voice of the victims, and various reasoning presented by the users of the new technique.

We cannot accept at any rate that violators of legalised/illegalised conduct go without prosecution and punishment. *This is what I call the criminal law of morality, the criminal law of our international human conscience, the invisible criminal law expressed by the human mentality of love that the offenders of grave atrocities have to be prosecuted and punished in accordance with the principles of natural law, human rights law, justice without law,* and ethics. *One may ask what the nature of justice without law is. This is a justice which not only relies on the statutory law that is suggested by Hart but also relies on much more. It is a law that*

[20](2010) 51 EHRR 287, para 89.

relies on the substance of all laws, on the statutes of all legislation, on the natural existence of man, on the core principles of the substance of human rights law, and on the strength of justice to achieve its essence.

This is what should be called the encouragement and the strength of all laws of human beings demanding the implementation of criminal justice in accordance with love for human beings. Yet, as Gandhi asserts, the power of punishment is not helpful for the prevention of violations, occupations, or mistreatment of individuals. Punishment may be useful but is not the solution because, since the end of the world wars, the world has seen numerous barbarous armed conflicts. He says, "Power is of two kinds. One is obtained by the fear of punishment and the other by acts of love. Power based on love is a thousand times more effective and permanent than the one derived from the fear of punishment." The philosophy of this international lawyer obviously corresponds to the present position of the repeatedly violated system of international criminal law and justice.

The goal of international human rights law, international humanitarian law, international criminal justice, and the principle of proportionality is love of human beings. By love here we mean the respect of their laws and provisions. These are the highest values of the relevant law. If the value of these laws cannot be respected by superpowers or even by the authorities of any state, Western or Muslim, what is the use of all these provisions? We may realise that the purpose of law is not to be a law, but to gather and protect our human wills and interests. We may also realise the fact that a law is regulated not because it was so demanding but because our need for the *rule of love* with law has increased and became more civilised and lost its savage nature, such as law for the prohibition of all types of sexual intercourse during war times or prohibition of capital punishment.

The reason law exists is not therefore, its existence, but its substance, particularly in the case of international human rights law. This means that the substance of the law has certain aspirations that are not far from our moral justice or cannot be so far from this concept. Under commercial law, when we attempt to buy certain objects, we also attempt to pay. Although we are trying to obtain the highest benefit for our actions, we are also aware that we also have a duty to fulfil the relevant covenant between the two parties. *This means there are certain concepts of moralities that follow our objectives and these moralities tell us what to do and not to do. They tell us the borderline between the interests and integrity of the law. However, a moral norm is not justice and nor is a legal norm. Justice should be the presentation of love for the maintenance of moral and legal norms with the sole intention of creating fairness.*[21] *However, we cannot deny the fact that justice is very easy to sell, but a justice with the passion of the love norm for the real essence of justice is a covenant that cannot sell us down the river, by any man or government.*

[21]Franck (1995).

4.7 Punctuality of Criminal Justice

The norms of law may not always be written within the law but may be extracted from the rules of law, rules of morality, and rules of justice. I am not stating here that norms of law are invisible but saying that most rules of law are subject to interpretation, and the interpretation has to follow the development of the law, the improvement of the rules, and also the enhancement of justice. A clear example of this is the English Common Law legal system or the case law. Similarly, the judgments of the ICTY, the ICTR, and the SCSL, are modifying or creating new interpretations of the rules of international criminal law and justice. It is the same in the procedures of the ICC. If justice is going to be limited by the words or provisions of the resolutions of the Security Council and the decisions of national, regional, or international courts, then we may promote injustice in the system of public international law and we may limit the scope of the application of justice. This is because justice not only has to be punctual but also practical in the circumstances of the time. By this, I mean that we should not ignore justice and permit impunity or permit evidence to be destroyed.[22] One of the main functions of criminal justice is to bring accused persons under the right jurisdiction at the right time.

Punctuality of criminal justice creates trust, ensures that impunity will not increase, and raises awareness that criminal behaviours have to decrease. Above all, punctuality means giving the highest value to the integrity of the victims, which is the most fundamental reason for the existence of criminal law and criminal justice. This means investigation of crimes and gathering of evidence must be started at a reasonable time and not be delayed. The victims must see that justice has been done and that it is done in a reasonable time. The Inter-American Court in its excellent judgment relating to the *Bulacio* case qualifies the rights of victims and underlines that punctuality of criminal justice should always be adhered to in the procedure of justice. It therefore recommends the following:

> This manner of exercising the means that the law makes available to the defense counsel has been tolerated and allowed by the intervening judiciary bodies, forgetting that their function is not exhausted by enabling due process that guarantees defense at a trial, but that they must also ensure, within a reasonable time, the right of the victim or his or her next of kin to learn the truth about what happened and for those responsible to be punished. . .the right to effective judicial protection therefore requires that the judges direct the process in such a way that undue delays and hindrances do not lead to impunity, thus frustrating adequate and due protection of human rights.[23]

In the *Bulacio* case, the Inter-American Court even demonstrated that the state, under which the criminal conduct had been prepared, has the basic responsibility

[22] Roberts (2009), pp. 347–380 at 374.

[23] Bulacio Case, Judgment of September 18, 2003, Inter-Am. Ct. H.R., (Ser. C) No. 100 (2003), paras. 114 and 115. Available at http://www1.umn.edu/humanrts/iachr/C/100-ing.html (Accessed April 29, 2015).

to bring the case into its jurisdiction in order to protect the rights of the victim. This also includes the punctuality of justice and its accuracy.[24] By the principle of accuracy, we mean that law not only has to be just, but its application in the procedure of reaching judgment has to stand with proper evidence in the courtroom.[25] This means that an unjust law is not law at all, i.e. *lex injusta non est lex*.

4.8 Survival of Criminal Justice

We are not talking here about our survival or our existence. Any law which is drafted, adopted, and exercised for the sole reason of our survival has a very poor intention indeed. The main purpose of the law is not at all our survival but the reconstruction of our relations in order to come to more adaptable and acceptable conditions for its subjects. A very good example is some aspects of ancient Roman law, which not only sought the safety of its direct subjects but also that of its indirect subjects. The Roman jurist Gaius expresses that the laws of every person are:

> governed by statutes and customs observes partly its own peculiar law and partly the law common to all mankind. The rules established by a given state for its own members are peculiar to itself, and are called *jus civile*; the rules constituted by natural reason for all are observed by all nations alike, and are called *jus gentium* for this law applies to all peoples. So the laws of the people of Rome are partly peculiar to itself, partly common to all nations.[26]

This means that the epoch of early civilization also had certain recognition of the rights of individuals of other nations. The development can also be seen throughout the civilization of law, its applications, jurisprudence, and the new consolidation of its modernity. This applies to any law in general and in particular to international human rights law, international criminal law, international humanitarian law, and international criminal justice. Their intention is to modify our relations for a better understanding of each other's needs and one another's values of integrity, personality, privacy, and legacy. All these mean a move towards the creation and mobilisation of a norm which has a direct link with our integrity and has the same level of value between all nations of the world. In a Separate Opinion in the Barcelona Traction (Preliminary Objections) case, the court addressed the need for the balance between certainty and justice. It says that:

---

[24] *Id.*

[25] Cryer (2009), pp. 381–400 at 399.

[26] *Gai Institutiones or Institutes of Roman Law by Gaius,* with a translation and commentary by Edward Poste, 4th ed. revised and enlarged by E.A. Whittuck, with an historical introduction by A.H.J. Greenidge (Oxford: Clarendon Press, 1904), 1.

> I am well aware that some consideration should be given to the existence of precedents in regard to a case which the Court is called upon to decide. Respect for precedents and maintenance of the continuity of jurisprudence are without the slightest doubt highly desirable from the viewpoint of the certainty of law which is equally required in international law and in municipal law. The same kind of cases must be decided in the same way and possibly by the same reasoning. This limitation is inherent in the judicial activities as distinct from purely academic activities.
>
> On the other hand, the requirement of the consistency of jurisprudence is never absolute. It cannot be maintained at the sacrifice of the requirements of justice and reason. The Court should not hesitate to overrule the precedents and should not be too preoccupied with the authority of its past decisions. The formal authority of the Court's decision must not be maintained to the detriment of its substantive authority. Therefore, it is quite inevitable that, from the point of view of the conclusion or reasoning, the minority in one case should become the majority in another case of the same kind within a comparatively short space of time.[27]

Here, we are searching for the recognition of a norm which can create a more flexible and acceptable solution for divergences between the family groups of humankind. This is called the central power of all laws which has an abstract character and cannot be real as long as the natural rights of man as not manifesting the power of love for justice and empathy for all human beings. Even though we are following the principle of *stare decisis*, we have to be cautious in our obligation to respect the precedent established by prior decisions. As a matter of principle, all cases must have windows for the evolution and development of law, even though the law does not respect the pure philosophy of love for justice. The body of law inherits the legacy of a special type of understanding of the past, of the present, and of the future. All these are embodied in the structure of law. Even though we cannot easily touch all those in law, the law has obviously inherited the legacy of the preceding rules, the present wills, and the undefined situation in its future. These together, separately, and collectively give us an idea of what justice has to be, how justice has to be respected, and how justice has to be done.

With the norm of love as an integral norm of law, we mean a norm which is mediated solely via justice, and justice cannot be trusted in its absence and therefore it cannot survive long without its presence. A certain law has therefore not been drafted to help our survival and our environment but with the ambition of respect of one another's rights. These rights are followed by duties, the concept of duties brings the concept of responsibility, and the concept of responsibility, if violated, invokes sanctions. However, the sanction of law is not the reason of survival of the law or survival of our existence but the way in which we are drawing a red line between what it is required to be and what should not be. This is what I call the control of our personality in harmony with our given consent, or the culmination of our national and international juridical efforts for the rule of love.

---

[27] Barcelona Traction, Light and Power Company, Limited, Preliminary Objections, Judgement, ICJ Reports 1964, p. 6 at para. 65, Judge Tanaka, Separate Opinion.

4.9 Unjust Employment of the Rule of Law

A norm of law is the transmission of our natural feeling that we would wish certain conduct to be controlled in accordance with the law and that justice has to be given priority in a civilised society.[28] According to one opinion, "Justice is the correct application of a law, as opposed to arbitrariness."[29] Yet I fully understand that sometimes our justice is severely violated by our own decisions or by our own laws. However, to express that "The ideology of justice has. . .no place in a reasonable discussion of the value of laws,"[30] is very problematic and causes the rule of law to lose its validity. This is based on the assumption that the rule of law and justice are not separable, even though they are two different ideas. Again, the idea that one should not assert that "a law is unjust," since that would involve presenting one's own emotional resentment against the law,[31] is obviously an unjust assessment in the system of law and human rights law as a whole. The value of the rule of law can never and should never be evaluated without considering the intention behind it, the substance of its nature, and its possible consequences. In the present position of the international human rights system, a rule of law including a national or regional one, which does not take into consideration the pure philosophy of justice for all human beings, is not law but private machinery. A human rights approach to the body of laws "requires laws to be read, if possible, in a way that is compatible with human rights."[32]

This is essentially relevant at the time of armed conflict. An example is when a war has been waged and young generations who are also the subjects of law are selected and sent out to the battlefields. They are killed for the rules of law. Naturally, this should not be considered just, and obviously, our laws violate the nature of justice for human beings and its high value. The murdering of our nationals has two different characters. The first is when one is sacrificed in self-defence of the natural rights of his nation or one is sacrificed because of our higher interests in wealth, oil, or political strength. However, I am not going to enter into a discussion here of how many individuals from either side of the conflict suffer, or the value of their lives.

Although both types of killing have the same consequences for the victims, the first occurs with love for justice and the other with the hope to replace law with power. Thus, individual values have been used for different purposes of the law. It is here that the power of law, the power of love, the power of justice, and the power of maintaining human integrity have diminished. Society has been given priority over the life of certain members of the same society with the intention of increasing its interests, wealth, and endangering the life of certain members of the same

---

[28] Meyer (1963), pp. 125–134 at 125–126.

[29] Ross (1958), p. 280.

[30] *Id.*

[31] *Id.*

[32] Gans (2012), p. 40.

society. Examples include the killings of American soldiers in many wars and the large killings of other nationals by the same individuals. Both, i.e. violators and victims, are killed because of the standard of the laws. Here, the role of the rule of law is to be against arbitrary decisions of governments or a national society being used with a contrary purpose and against the society itself.[33]

What is significant here is not the proper or improper function of the rule of law but the way in which we use its function. Thus, when we speak about the rules of law, we also aim at different matters and consider whether the rules of law are worth mentioning. It has today become a fashion to speak about the rule of law. By this term, they surely mean that the function of the law has to be given priority over any other matter. The rule of law is particularly relevant in the case of international human rights law. However, whether this rule of law is practical for all subjects of the law is one of the most important questions. The law must not only be rational but also useful for all subjects of its law. Thus, a law which permits killing others or killing of oneself for the purpose of the protection of the law cannot be useful and is therefore hazardous to the principle of morality and the norm of love. One may interpret it not as a good law but as a bad law.[34] I draw this conclusion, especially in the case of international human rights law, international criminal law, and international humanitarian law of armed conflict. By this, I mean that the rule of law not only has the function of protection of its subjects but also has the function of prevention of any crime that can be committed in the name of the law:

> Human rights and humanitarian treaties do not represent an Exchange of interests and benefits between contracting States in the conventional sense, and in this respect may also be distinguished from the generality of multilateral treaties, many of which are concerned with the economic, security or other interests of States. Human rights and humanitarian treaties represent, rather, a commitment of the participating States to certain norms and values recognized by the international community. Stated another way, the personality of the sovereign is not the essence of such an agreement. Multilateral treaties are most often concluded with the object of protecting and benefiting the international community as a whole, and for the maintenance of world order and co-operation, rather than of protecting and advancing one particular State's interests.[35]

The acts which are carried out for the good of the law and for the good of the subjects of the law are still subject to serious question from the perspective of morality when they permit their subjects to use the subjects of the same law for the justification of the rule of law and its protective nature. Although the rule of law does not draw any differences between the law and the law, and the subject and the subject, it shows that, in the final application of the law, each person's intrinsic value is different from the aspect of the law. The law does not say that its subjects have to be killed for the protection of the rules of the law, but it eventually permits

[33]Ashworth (2006), pp. 92–96.

[34]Meyer (1963), pp. 125–134 at 127.

[35]Application of the Convention on the Prevention and Punishment of the Crime of Genocide (*Bosnia and Herzegovina v. Serbia and Montenegro*). Separate Opinion of Judge Weeramantry, http://www.icj-cij.org/docket/files/91/7361.pdf, 55.

such order. This means that we grant a higher value to the rule of the law than human lives, which becomes dangerous to the citizens of the law. This concerns any law, be it a Western or an Islamic law.[36]

4.10 The Criminal Policy of the Rule of Law

We have to realise that killing is not permitted, even in defence of criminal law.[37] *How can we abolish capital punishment,*[38] *but permit the killing of our own individuals by our own laws under the principle of the rule of law in order to fight in other countries? Must everyone always obey the law? If not, when is a citizen morally free to disobey?*[39] *If it is understood by all of us that killing is not permitted for any means, even under the order of a judge or an officially recognised court, then all states are under an obligation to abolish military laws, the killing law, the industrialisation of weapons, and therefore to bring an end to the law of war and atrocities.* This means reflecting and respecting "common values" as is required by the European Court, for example.[40] There are conflicts of legal norms between the systems of our national and international norms, and when two rules or several rules conflict, one or several of them is no longer valid. Has the rule of law that permits killing international validity? Alternatively, has the one that prevents killing an invalid nature?[41] Violations of human rights laws are violations regardless of being committed in war or peacetime, regardless of being the European human rights provisions, or African, Latin American, or Islamic ones.[42] The Trial Chamber of one of the international tribunals asserts the following:

> The violence inflicted on the Muslim detainees of Kaonik prison appears to be a reprehensible infringement of international human rights which would be absolutely unacceptable in times of peace. The Trial Chamber considers that the existence of an armed conflict does

[36] Trechsel (1997), pp. 94–119 at 110–111.

[37] Schabas (2002), pp. 41–43.

[38] Novak (2014), pp. 31–32, 73–74, 125–126.

[39] Dworkin (1996), p. 26.

[40] See http://europa.eu/scadplus/constitution/objectives_en.htm (Accessed May 3, 2015).

[41] Dworkin (1996), p. 26.

[42] "The Union is founded on the values of respect for human dignity, liberty, democracy, equality, the rule of law and respect for human rights, including the rights of persons belonging to minorities. These values, which are set out in Article I-2, are common to the Member States. Moreover, the societies of the Member States are characterised by pluralism, non-discrimination, tolerance, justice, solidarity and equality between women and men. These values play an important role, especially in two specific cases. Firstly, under the procedure for accession set out in Article I-58, any European State wishing to become a member of the Union must respect these values in order to be considered eligible for admission. Secondly, failure by a Member State to respect these values may lead to the suspension of that Member State's rights deriving from membership of the Union (Article I-59)." http://europa.eu/scadplus/constitution/objectives_en.htm (Accessed May 3, 2015).

> not render it tolerable and that it constitutes a grave violation of the principles of international humanitarian law arising from the Geneva Conventions.[43]

Of course, I am aware of economic gains in the essence of the rule of law. I am also aware that our comments are a political letter to persons who cannot see law as a reason for creating justice but justice as a reason to hinder the actual intention of the law. Professor Katouzian, a distinguished Persian lawyer, correctly points this out in his oration on this matter. He points out that, if the purpose of legislation is to find the offender and the reason for the crime, this does not necessarily mean that, if the victim of an adult person's crime is a newborn child, we should ignore the harmful effect of our decision on the victim's life.[44] We have to see if our decision deals with the quintessence of our intended morality relating to justice and the flexibility to reach fairness and not obvious monopolisation of justice inside the legislation's norms.[45] He means that the love for the implementation of the law has to replace itself with the love for quality and the consequences of justice.

Put simply, the question is why in Africa so many indigenous groups are fighting against each other for indigenous priority, land, territory, or sovereignty. Evidently, it is our weapons, laws, and above all our policies that sanction the killing of the population in another part of the globe. How can we speak about freedom, liberty, security and justice, including "Europeanised internal security issues" within European criminal law[46] *but not the Africanised or the Asianised security of their criminal systems without our guns? Can we not see the economic security of Europe with its guns in the other countries versus the pure philosophy of love for justice?*[47] *The law cannot be civilised, territory cannot be saved, nations cannot be in peace, justice cannot be secured, hospitals cannot be free from injured civilians, and gardens cannot be full of useful fruits as long as we are not civilised ourselves and, consequently, if our laws are not civilised. Isn't it a violation of the territorial rights of a nation when we deliver guns to them or when we have sufficient information that there are a considerable number of serious, historical, unsolvable issues between various clans, and still we set fire to the old conflicts? Are they the quality of our human rights law? Or, are they the fable of the wolf and the lamb?*

Frances Wright (1795–1852) correctly enquires "Do we exert our own liberties without injury to others – we exert them justly; do we exert them at the expense of others – unjustly. And, in thus doing, we step from the sure platform of liberty upon the uncertain threshold of tyranny." The Troy pastor—Laocoön—was clearly correct about the quality of the *Trojan horse* gift from the Greeks when he

---

[43]Para. 37. ICTY, available at http://www.icty.org/x/cases/aleksovski/acjug/en/ale-asj000324e.pdf (Accessed April 4, 2015).

[44]Katouzian (2003), p. 361 at 362–3.

[45]*Id.*, at 374–6.

[46]Eckes and Kondtandinides (2011), p. 1.

[47]For the security system of Europe and the externalization of internal security, see Guild (2008).

enthusiastically rushed down from the heights of the castle to prevent the inhabitants of Troy from trusting this human rights gift. He shouted from far off at the crowd, which was hesitant and split by opposing opinions:

O unhappy citizens, what madness?
Do you think the enemy's sailed away?
Or do you think any Greek gift's free of treachery?
Is that Ulysses's reputation?
Either there are Greeks in hiding, concealed by the wood,
or it's been built as a machine to use against our walls,
or spy on our homes, or fall on the city from above,
or it hides some other trick: Trojans, don't trust this horse.
Whatever it is, I'm afraid of Greeks even those bearing gifts.[48]

Obviously, as long as we do not abolish the permission to produce weapons in our country, we cannot be a decent state of justice and peace in accordance with the purity of basic rights. These rights can be seen in the words of the European Union model, the real Islamic Quranic Charter interpretation, the French or the United States Declaration of Human Rights proclaiming fundamental rights of their la paix, la justice et l'amour for *jihad*, the German jihadist human rights law within its constitution and so forth. I am deliberately using the term "*jihad*" here as the *struggle for peace, justice, equality, and even more,* in order to express its wholly independent character in the context of Islam. It is correctly asserted that the term *jihad* "is certainly one of the most misinterpreted terms in a certain Western, anti-Islamic discourse."[49] The term, like many Latin terms, has a universal nature rather than just belonging to Islamic literature.

4.11 Complicity in the Scope of Attack

The definition of an attack is normally direct attack, but the real attacks are mostly indirect. The concept can be seen in most of the draft articles on the definition of aggression presented by the Union of Soviet Socialist Republics in the early establishment of the United Nations and rejected by the United States of America. How can we claim to be just, generous, and helpful in the reducing of attacks and poverty of different nations, but not be just in reality. We should be decent to justice, we should be righteous in our politics, and we should be imperial and royal before we attempt to be *generous*. Our trade in weapons under any name should not

[48]*Virgil, The Aeneid Book II* (Translated by A. S. Kline, 2002). Available at http://www.poetryintranslation.com/PITBR/Latin/VirgilAeneidII.htm#_Toc536009309 (Accessed July 12, 2015).

[49]Statement by Peter Leuprecht in the preface of the book on Zawati (2001) at p. v. See *also* Malekian (1999), pp. 621–622.

kill the nations of the world if there is really a trust in human rights norms and we do not have the intention of indirect attacks. According to natural law:

> We cannot logically declare the children of God to be equal before God and to be unequal before men. We cannot wish our immortal spirit to abjure on earth that gift of liberty which is the source of good and evil in our actions; the exercise of which makes man virtuous or criminal in the eyes of God. We cannot wish the brow that is raised to heaven to fall prostrate in the dust before any created being; the soul that should aspire to heaven, to rot in ignorance of its rights, its powers, and its noble origin. We cannot admit, that instead of loving one another like brethren, men ought to be divided, hostile, selfish; jealous, city of city, and nation of nation.[50]

The new interpretation of the system of international criminal law and its conventions in the international criminal courts clearly confirms that all these acts of trade or others fall under the term "attack." Systematically distributing or selling weapons in a country where the people are suffering from deeply traditional tribal conflicts also constitutes a form of attack. This must be the same in the case of discrimination, apartheid, or torture, which are implemented or executed systematically. In the *Akayesu* case, the ICTR vividly clarifies that:

> The concept of attack' may be defined as an unlawful act of the kind enumerated in Article 3(a) to (I) of the Statute, like murder, extermination, enslavement etc. An attack may also be nonviolent in nature, like imposing a system of apartheid, which is declared a crime against humanity in Article 1 of the Apartheid Convention of 1973, or exerting pressure on the population to act in a particular manner, may come under the purview of an attack, if orchestrated on a massive scale or in a systematic manner.[51]

One of the classical writers of international law has correctly dealt with the concept of crime and its legal reasoning. He says that we agree that robbing is a crime, that killing is a crime, that it is not lawful to take away the property of another under the national legal system, and that nations are equal without any regard to their military power. *He says further that, if those acts are crimes, we should also admit without further proof that the commission of such acts are crimes in another country too. This means that no nation has a right to drive another from the territory which it inhibits, to create terror among its citizens, to sell or distribute without charge weapons among the clans with malicious plans, or to demand respect for the international legal and political order when it itself violates the rights of other nations and laws.* According to John Locke:

> Where-ever law ends, tyranny begins, if the law be transgressed to another's harm; and whosoever in authority exceeds the power given him by the law, and makes use of the force he has under his command, to compass that upon the subject, which the law allows not, ceases in that to be a magistrate; and, acting without authority, may be opposed, as any other man, who by force invades the right of another. This is acknowledged in subordinate magistrates. He that hath authority to seize my person in the street, may be opposed as a

---

[50]Joseph Giuseppe Mazzini (1846). Mastellone (2001), p. 3. See also https://archive.org/stream/newpoliticalecon00roserich/newpoliticalecon00roserich_djvu.txt (Accessed May 27, 2015).

[51]ICTR-96-4-T, para. 581.

> thief and a robber, if he endeavours to break into my house to execute a writ, notwithstanding that I know he has such a warrant, and such a legal authority, as will empower him to arrest me abroad. And why this should not hold in the highest, as well as in the most inferior magistrate, I would gladly be informed. Is it reasonable, that the eldest brother, because he has the greatest part of his father's estate, should thereby have a right to take away any of his younger brothers portions? or that a rich man, who possessed a whole country, should from thence have a right to seize, when he pleased, the cottage and garden of his poor neighbour?[52]

Thus, *we have to come to a better solution for this problem of the law, to this question of the law and that this primitive understanding of the fact that a rule of the law which orders, directly or indirectly, the subjects to kill or to be killed cannot be a good solution for the security of the law. There must be something wrong with the law. One may see this as wrong in the rule of law of many nations. It does not solely concern European Union law, the United States or Australian law, and the Middle East or the Muslim nations' law. This is a general epidemic of all our legal systems. There is a shortage in the formulation of the law, and this problem has to be solved, has to be identified, and has to be treated correctly, not only with the norm of morality but also with the norm of love.*

The preservation of the law should be proportionate, not only in relation to its value but in relation to the protection of the lives of its subjects. We must decide whether it is the law which should have significant value or the justice of the law which gives law value. Those who do not understand that the law is solely a tool for identification, but not a tool of violations, may infringe the law under the jurisdiction of the law, in the courtrooms, and in our prisons all the time. All these violations are serious attacks on the framework of the legal discipline. Here, I focus, *inter alia*, on the torture of our dearest brothers and sisters in any prison, in any part of the world, and for any reason.

I mean those who are condemned to suffer by the rule of the law and their destinies are in danger. We have forgotten the fact that the goal of all laws has to be rational. Here, among others, I particularly refer to the Chinese, Islamic, and certain Latin American criminal practices defended by the political and legal authorities of the relevant countries. They permit torture for political ends, transplantation of organs of condemned prisoners, amputation for terrorising civilians, and degradation of women to create a reason to overcome dissatisfaction. Most perpetrators of white-collar crimes and money laundering enjoy impunity given by the leaders of the aforementioned countries. Such practices of the rules of law have the criminal nature of the attack and violate the norm of love and the soul of criminal justice of the world. Have we achieved justice with love? Can we not see that something is missing in our method of human rights law, including criminal law?

---

[52]Locke (1689), see Online Library of Liberty, A collection of scholarly works, http://oll.libertyfund.org/titles/locke-the-two-treatises-of-civil-government-hollis-ed (Accessed March 31, 2015).

4.12 Criminalisation of Values

My intention here is to prove that, although the rule of law has a very high validity, the value of its subjects is more significant than its own preservation, even if its aim is the protection of its subjects.[53] By the force of nature, the force of the law, and the rule of love, we should understand that those laws, the intention of which is the satisfaction of military tools for the purpose of violations, for producing weapons, and the objective of invading each other's territory, cannot properly be called laws. They are instead an order for the killings of others and us. We have to realize that we cannot by any means and by any law, whether Muslim, European, American, Chinese, Russian or any other, for the reason of our legal order or its survival, kill fellow man.

Unfortunately, most classical writers of international law, including prominent writers, strongly defend the use of armed force and condemn the contrary. For instance, the inspiration for Grotius' book on "*De Jure Belli ac Pacis* was the love of peace, yet he was far from being one of those visionaries who totally condemn the use of armed force and proscribe all wars as wrong and unnecessary."[54] Ian Brownlie has also supported the use of armed force in certain situations in his book *The Use of Force by States* (1963). While their arguments may be crucial and useful in the case of self-defence, there may still be practical problems in their theories for the reason that we have to solve the issues of armament and change it into total disarmament. In other words, all laws that permit killing are illegal and we should not call them law. Furthermore, any law, including Islamic, Scandinavian, European Union, Chinese, Russian, or American law, that permits killing is not a law but an evil interpretation of the law. *Lex injusta non est lex.* Although I am aware that all nations have had laws and have laws which permit killing each other when negotiation procedures do not work, and the fact that the United Nations Charter permits the use of force under certain conditions, these cannot be objective laws but the manifestation of our will to kill. The purpose is solely to convince the opposing party of the conflict.

In contrast, neither the norm of legality nor the norm of morality can alter the norm of love, which goes against killing. Thus, the moral requirements of law should depart from an unqualified imperative that the legal order preserves itself. *The loyalty of law cannot be trusted in the law itself but in the love expressed by its subjects for the proper application of the law. The essential task for the law is the maintenance of the legal norm, even at the price of killing the subjects of the law. Appreciably, the notion of law has to be sincere to the subjects of the law and has to prevent any killings of its subjects; a law which is ratified for the application of justice in the manner of injustice no longer has appropriate legal validity and*

[53] Trechsel (1997), pp. 94–119.

[54] This conclusion is formulated by David J. Hill who has written an introduction to Grotius (1625), p. 8. Available at http://oll.libertyfund.org/titles/grotius-the-rights-of-war-and-peace-1901-ed (Accessed April 27, 2015).

cannot be referred to as the rule of law but rather the imposed order. The standard and abstract frameworks of rules—the intention of which is to perpetuate themselves with individualistic views of the law—can no longer be considered practical and expedient in a world in which the rule of law is spreading into international spheres and forging national character models similar to international ones.

A clear example is the establishment of the European Court of Human Rights based on articles of the European Convention on Human Rights. The Convention orders the Court to ensure that the state parties to the Convention and its protocols have adopted the necessary measures for the implementation of its provisions. The Lisbon Treaty has even developed a new system of individuals' rights.[55] Has the question of morality and legality of the Convention truly been represented in its whole policy? On the one hand, states are required to apply the provisions of the Convention and respect, as far as possible, the rights of their individuals in their national or regional relations. This pattern of the law is highly appreciated and fully logical.

On the other hand, the European states permit their guns, their soldiers, and their politics to be used against their own or other states. An illustrative example is their participation in the criminal acts of NATO and the killing of thousands of innocent individuals in other states.[56] Does this need further proof? For example, their soldiers, military machineries, politics, law and morality were used against innocent Afghan people in assistance and cooperation given to the United States. Yet, the US has given continuous financial aid to the Pakistani government in secret, solely for killing. Their policies here and in other places bring into question the standard of their laws, morality, and justice. The rule of law orders them to participate in the killing and destruction of other societies with the logic that they are preventing criminal behaviour, terrorists, and helping humanity. Jean Racine, the French writer, pertinently says that "*there are no secrets that time does not reveal*." The Christian lawyer, philosopher, and theologian—St. Augustine—continues further, "the truth is like a lion. You do not have to defend it. Let it loose. It will defend itself."

In addition, many cultures in the world speak of humanity and its very high value within their systems. These include European Union Law, Islamic law, Jewish law, and the Chinese communistic regulations. Article 2 of the Treaty on European Union consolidated by the Treaty of Lisbon affirms that 'The Union is founded on the *values of respect for human dignity, freedom, democracy, equality, the rule of law and respect for human rights*, including the rights of persons belonging to minorities.' The pioneer position of this value for human beings is encouraged by the provisions of other articles.[57] Ironically, the respect for these values can also be found in the provisions of other laws in the world, including Islamic law. Many Muslims are not only violating the system of international human rights law, but

[55]Hinarejos (2009), p. 19.

[56]Hazan (2004), pp. 131–133.

[57]Hinarejos (2009).

also the Islamic legal system, based on very old interpretations of religious rules that have long been abolished in the civilisation of man as a whole. One may therefore draft several questions. For instance, do those nations, those theories, and those governments respect these values on all sides?

Grotius correctly asserts that:

> Sometimes indeed men are so circumstanced, that to relinquish a right becomes not only a laudable act, but a debt of respect to that law, which commands us to love our enemies: a law to be respected and obeyed not only for its intrinsic value, but as being a precept of the gospel. By the same law, and for the same reasons, we are commanded to pray for and to promote the welfare. . .These, and these motives alone, when they can safely be complied with are sufficient to keep the sword within its scabbard. For the debt of love and forbearance to our enemies is an obligation which it is honourable to discharge.[58]

I am not however encouraging gospel or similar theories here, but aiming at the inherent theory of law for the maintenance of appropriate justice. Evidently, here we must have different definitions of values and respect. One is the value of individuals in Europe that must not be violated by any means by the member states. This recognition of the value of individuals is certainly good and is parallel to the provisions of international human rights law about which the European Union law is proud, arrogant, and self-righteous. The other is disrespect of the value of other states that is dramatically demonstrated by our military, economic, and political standards. I have similar critical conclusions regarding Islamic states, communist states, Arab states, and the states of Latin America—most of which are corrupted by the rules of law, rules of legislation, and the rules of government. My conclusion is the same for the criminal conduct of the Israeli government. Beside all these, one should not orient my words against the honourable populations of these nations. What is significant here is not the political standard but the legal standard, which expresses full love for its own individuals and full inhumanity and immorality towards the individuals of other states or its own whenever it considers it necessary.

4.13 *Mens Rea* Affecting Values

The concept of *mens rea* constitutes one of the significant elements of the system of criminal law and criminal justice.[59] The element is also discussed in conjunction with the principle of *actus reus* or the physical element of the crime.[60] Similarly, *actus reus* may be an act or an omission.[61] It may also include the results of the act

[58]Grotius (1625), p. 281; available at http://oll.libertyfund.org/titles/grotius-the-rights-of-war-and-peace-1901-ed (Accessed April 27, 2015).

[59]See the excellent views on Badar (2015); McAuley and Paul McCutcheon (2000), pp. 273–312 and also 721–729.

[60]*Id.*, at 309.

[61]Walsh (2006), p. 53.

and the surrounding circumstances.[62] Thus, mere proof of the accused's action may suffice for the commission of an offence.[63] The *mens rea* element has also to some extent entered into the structure of international criminal law and criminal justice. The element refers to the mental intent to commit crime. However, the element is not necessary for the identification of all crimes in national and international criminal law. In other words, a guilty mind for the commission of crimes may vary. Offences such as those which are categorised under omissions do not necessarily qualify as this element.[64] Similarly, international criminal law does not identify certain international crimes such as genocide, rape, or torture due to the provisions of the mental element.

The element of *mens rea* in fact denotes the principle of criminal responsibility in criminal procedural law.[65] This should not be interpreted such that, if the concept of *mens rea* does not exist, the concept of criminal responsibility does not arise either. The element means that the person who carried out the act was aware that his or her conduct was criminalised under the law. The act needs a guilty state of mind in order to identify the crime and attribute the concept of criminal responsibility. Still, some crimes such as murder require a malicious state of mind but other states of mind may also fall under the *mens rea* concept. These states are: knowingly, purposely, carelessly, hastily, tacitly, and recklessly.[66] All these also constitute the *mens rea,* but with a strong/decisive or a weak form of non-clear guilty mind, which may be proven by evidence under the procedures of justice.

The concept of *mens rea* may also be examined in the conduct, policies, and divisions of the big political parties and states in international law. In particular, this is significant when the question relates to the trade of weapons, distribution of weapons, and causing of serious conflicts in the internal situation of a state, nation, or region in order to monopolise economic income, territories, oil, gas, or gold resources. All these indicate not only the existence of *mens rea* but also the process by which we come close to our main criminal intention. This is what may be called white crime, black crime, governmental political crime, permitted crime, and state crime, but not the red crime in the philosophy of criminal law. The reason is very simple and clear—the power of criminalisation of criminal conduct is given to those who have the authority to codify the law and apply it as they see fit, and therefore the concept of the theory of *mens rea* obviously depends on their criminal policy and the mental element of the crime seems absent. A similar theory can be seen in the case of national criminal law.[67] For instance, political crimes are of these categories.[68] Evidently, if a revolution or a coup "is successful, or if the distribution

---

[62]Hanly (2006), p. 48.

[63]*Id.*

[64]For a discussion on the concept of guilt, see Ross (1975), pp. 1–12.

[65]Coffey (2010), p. 181. See also Hanly (2006), pp. 73–95.

[66]Hanly (2006), pp. 73–77.

[67]McIntyre et al. (2012), pp. 52–53.

[68]Ingraham (1979), pp. 1–8.

of power is changed in other ways, yesterday's political offender may be today's head of state. The uneasy political situation in Europe during recent generations clearly exemplifies this."[69] Here the principle of *culpability* is also ignored because of the restructuring of the political authorities and re-modification of criminal legislation.

Has any state of Africa against the historical background occupied any state of Europe and sold Europeans as slaves or the contrary? Has any state of Asia attempt to occupy the European states' territories or the contrary? Has any state of Asia and the Middle East occupied the United States of America or the contrary? Has any state of Africa, Asia, or the Middle East prosecuted and punished the European or American leaders for their grave violations of international humanitarian law of armed conflict or the contrary? Hypothetically, the Afghan people and the Syrian population could not and cannot come to destroy Europe, but certain powerful states of Europe can destroy and have destroyed the above states. What is again of significance here is not the politics but the standard of love or our interests towards ourselves and individuals of other nations and committing a type of conduct which varies between crime and omission. This means we apply the norms of legality, morality, and love to different degrees. One is the criteria of mens rea at home and the other is the criteria of non-mens rea outside our borders.

By this, I mean that there is a particular norm integrated into certain laws, the high value of which can only be measured in times of crisis. In other words, when we refer to human rights law, it is not really of any value if we do not show that, in practice, we are respecting the provisions of certain laws of other countries for the protection of their fundamental rights. Human rights cannot just be practised at home; in that case, we would not call it human rights law but the rights of our population. Human rights law norms should surely have international standard of application. Those norms are not necessarily for the purpose of application but provide crucial moral, legal, and love knowledge that has to be learned by all governments.

Legal and moral norms are therefore integral parts of our laws.[70] Nevertheless, the standard of morality and legality can only be measured against the expression of our love in their practical enforcement. Put simply, norms of legality and morality are, in their final stage, bound by the norms of love. We express these norms at the time of their very serious breach or in the course of the application of justice. Thus, when we say that the norms of international human rights law are excellent and they have high values, we do not really mean at all times but rather at certain times and periods when they are connected to our political standard. Otherwise, a country that claims to respect humanity, human morality, and human law courts cannot or should not have different applications or understandings of human rights law. This by itself is thoughtless and tacitly an attack against the system of international human rights law. *An example is a human rights law, which is for the home and does not permit the possession of weapons on the national level, whilst the law of*

[69] Andenaes (1965), p. 52.

[70] According to one view, legal norms are either rules or principles. See Alexis (2002), p. 44.

the same nation permits the transport of the same cargo to other nations or states of the world such as Germany, Sweden, the United Kingdom, France, Canada and China. What comes out of this double morality of human rights law?

If a state exercises a certain double standard of humanity, it is applying the law, not because it is law but because of the choice and love of the country. Thus, there is a norm here, called love. However, this is the love of a country for its population but not love for the substance of the law. The same country may differently understand the principles of international human rights law concerning other countries which are the targets of its attacks. This understanding is not based upon the norms of love in order to secure justice but solely on the norm of legality and probably the code of morality that the relevant state decides and uses to form its own definitions of international human rights law. *One may say a radical propensity to evil justice. If this is not* mens rea, *if this is not a crime, if this is not violation of the principles of the Charter of the United Nations and Human Rights law, then it is a clear contradiction between the principles of legality and morality of the law. Obviously, the norm of love which is elucidated in this book, will also be contrary to the policy of such laws.*

Clear examples here are the frequent references made to the principles of human rights law by the high legal authorities of the United States. They talk about humanity and its great value for the understanding of the dignity of man. The most notable of these are the speeches delivered by the current president of the United States. Most of these speeches have strong references to the principles of international human rights law and their great value for the maintenance of justice and peace. But a close examination of these principles of human rights law which are based on the principles of legality and morality demonstrates that these principles have, in practice, different values, and these values are interpreted within the inner structure of national and international political consideration. Thus, a reference to values by the highest supreme authority in the United States may have several aspects.

Human rights principles may not have any value in relation to the states in which the United States has great interests such as Syria. In addition, the double standard of value can be seen in the practice of the United States in Iraq.[71] This country has been the target of brutal armed attacks by other states solely based on oil interests. In fact, the long strategy of human rights violations in the region constitutes one of the most serious issues of human rights law in the world. The United States succeeded, by the monopolised resolutions of the Security Council, to get away the dictator of the time—Saddam Hussein—who had been working for the CIA for a long period for the CIA. I am not lecturing here about the Gulf Crisis and inhuman attacks by the United States armed forces with close complicity of the United Kingdom.[72] The United States government promised to bring peace to the Iraqi population but the result is indeed more than simply a catastrophe. It cultivated

[71]Malekian (1993), pp. 1–10.

[72]Particularly see the recent confessions of the British Prime Minister, Tony Blair, and his great regret for the destruction of Iraq.

terrorists in the relevant country for the sake of its *oil* interests, i.e. ISIS. This means that we may politically interpret the principles of legality, morality, love, and *mens rea* at a different level.

4.14 Arbitrary Deprivation of Life

The problem of *mens rea* in the case of the application of human rights principles with two different policies is not a new situation in the political history of the world and in the practice of the permanent members of the United Nation. However, the situation may be analysed from different angles. One may also see such double policies in the body of international conventions or human rights law. Firstly, we are aware of the fact that there are many instruments applicable to human rights law. These are, e.g., the Universal Declaration of Human Rights of 1948; the International Covenant on Civil and Political Rights of 1966; the International Covenant on Economic, Social and Cultural Rights of 1966; the Convention against Torture and Other Cruel, Inhuman, or Degrading Treatment or Punishment of 1984; and the Convention on the Rights of the Child of 1989. To these instruments, one may also add the regional treaties. These are, e.g., the European Convention on Human Rights of 1950, the American Convention on Human Rights of 1978, the African Charter on Human and Peoples' Rights of 1986, the Cairo Declaration on Human Rights in Islam of 1990, and the Arab Charter on Human Rights of 2004, which contain more or less the main principles of international instruments. Secondly, a significant basic principle of all these instruments is the right to life.[73]

The right to life or the supreme right in human rights law means an effective guarantee for human beings that their lives will not be endangered by any means, *especially by laws*. This right is not limited to a particular time or period; it is of a perpetual nature and is a legal right which has to be respected by all states or organisations, even though they may take a strong political decision against their enemies.[74] That is why the international humanitarian law of armed conflict is added to the general body of international human rights law.[75] For example, Article 6.1 of the ICSPR states: "Every human being has the inherent right to life. The relevant law shall protect this right. No one shall be arbitrarily deprived of his life." The words of this article are very clear. Protection of human life is a necessary mandate. By this, the legislator surely means all human beings and not part of one country and not another part. This rule should also be valid internationally.

It is a generally accepted rule of law that one should make no distinction between the life of a person who is born in the United States and a person who is born in Palestine or Pakistan. Nor should there be a distinction between those who are

---

[73]For most of these instruments, see Malekian (2007).

[74]Examine Eser (2009), pp. 163–190. www.freidok.uni-freiburg.de/volltexte/9800. Consult *also* Eser and Rettenmaier (2009), pp. 222–237.

[75]Examine also Goodale and Merry (2007).

Jewish or those who are Christian, Buddhist, or Muslim. With the phrase protection of life, we also mean that the protection of the life of a black person who is born in the middle of Africa and a white person who is born in the same region should be the same. The guarantee is international and does not have any limitation. This philosophy also constitutes the basic philosophy of the relevant law. As has been stated elsewhere, the purpose of international human rights law is to create equal respect and with this policy is not meant to limit the boundaries of its application in one area and diminish it in another area. This is what we call international love for the life of all human beings. The right to life is the expression of legal, moral, and love norms that no one should be killed.

However, the expression 'arbitrarily deprived of his life' in Article 6.1 of the ICCPR has been subject to strong criticism. The same criticism can also be applied to Article 4 (1) of the American Convention on Human Rights. This is because, when we articulate that no one shall be arbitrarily deprived of his life, we may mean we permit it if it is not done arbitrarily. This is *argumentum a contrario*.[76] The philosophy behind this expression is against the principle of life and the principle of love for human dignity. Because the principle of life is a protected principle, with a perpetual nature, with a permanent character, and with a high level of international human rights law recognition.

One can particularly examine this serious problem of protection of the dignity of the life of a person in the provisions of Article 6.2 of the same instrument. This article permits killing. "Countries which have not abolished the death penalty, sentence of death may be imposed only for the most serious crimes in accordance with the law in force at the time of the commission of the crime and not contrary to the provisions of the present Covenant and to the Convention on the Prevention and Punishment of the Crime of Genocide." The provisions of the Covenant have permitted the right to kill and obviously go against the established principle of the abolition of capital punishment. Killing is therefore legitimised which is a theory against the principle of love that is integrated into the principle of the abolition of capital punishment. It also goes against the established principle of *mens rea*, which involves mental intention. To put it another way, the content of the article deactivates the concept of criminality and the concept of *mens rea* or culpability, all of which constitute an integral part of *jus cogens*.

4.15 Criminality of Judges Applying Capital Punishment

As a rule, punishments of all types have to be replaced with the force of love if the intention is to decrease violations and increase the effect of rehabilitation.[77] Love is the only legal medicine for healing.[78] This has to be understood by all legal systems

[76] Römer (2010), p. 94.

[77] Shay (1994).

[78] Consult Gilligan (1996–1997).

and lawyers.[79] Even the concepts of Christianity, Islam, Buddhism, and Hinduism, along with the philosophy of scholars from different disciplines like Erich Fromm, Karl Marx, Simone Weil,[80] and Paolo Freire, emphasise the significant value of love for justice and a reason for decreasing violations.[81] Fromm asserts that love is a very difficult norm unless one tries more actively to develop one's "total personality, so as to achieve a productive orientation; that satisfaction in individual love cannot be attained without the capacity to love one's neighbour, without true humility, courage, faith and discipline."[82]

As I have emphasized elsewhere, capital punishment is an abolished institution, as are torture and slavery. One may even conclude that since *jus cogens* law prohibits the application of capital punishment, any judgment which permits such inhuman conduct violates the following legal orders too. These are law-making treaties, customary international law, general principles of law, the law of the permanent International Criminal Court, the ICTY, the ICTR, the SCSL, European Union law, African laws, Antarctica laws, most Asian laws, Australian law, most North American and South American law. Evidently, the authorised judges in charge who sanction such cruel punishment are guilty of violating international criminal law. This means without any hesitation, the respective judges should bear criminal responsibility, not only before their wrongful national criminal courts but also before the jurisdiction of other national courts.

For example, this principle also applies to those judges who contributed to the Saddam Tribunal and ordered his and other persons' executions. This is not to say that we are protecting, by one means or another, the notorious Iraqi criminal, but we are emphasising that justice has to be carried out on an equal footing and with love for justice. The plea of superior order or order of the law should no longer be tolerated as a reason to permit the impunity of those judges. This means that the judges of courts in Iran, Iraq, Yemen, Saudi Arabia, China, Libya, the United States, North Korea, Syria, Somalia, Afghanistan, Pakistan, Vietnam, or Bangladesh who order the application of capital punishment are considered, under the principle of universality of the abolition of capital punishment, *hostis humani generis. They are prosecutable as well as punishable under any jurisdiction which does not permit the application of capital punishment. Our theory is very simple. A judge should not work in a criminal court which legitimates capital punishment. How can a judge decide on capital punishment against a person who*

[79] DeValve (2014).

[80] "At the bottom of the heart of every human being, from earliest infancy until the tomb, there is something that goes on indomitably expecting, in the teeth of all experience of crimes committed, suffered, and witnessed, that good and not evil will be done to him. It is this above all that is sacred in every human being."

[81] For the development of love in religion see Turner (2014), pp. 135–153; Gorsky (2014), pp. 43–55; Barnes (2014), pp. 11–42; Elior (2014), pp. 103–134; Andreopoulos (2014), pp. 57–71; Chittick (2014), pp. 155–180; Shah-Kazemi (2014), pp. 73–101; see also Lumbard (2016); Pour-Golafshan (2012); Kamal (2014); Awadallah (2005).

[82] Fromm (1956, 2006), p. xvii.

has seriously violated a national order, but he himself gets away with violations of international criminal obligations? Is the situation morally correct? The ethical question is whether the national legal order is beyond the international criminal order of jus cogens law or the vice versa.

A judge may give a considerable number of reasons for her/his engagement in criminal cases which lead to the death penalty. Nevertheless, the *jus cogens* law accepts no excuse. This legal philosophy of *jus cogens* is quite exceptional in that it does not treat the relevant judges by means of *argumentum ad hominem*, but as an *ex concessis* of what has been consolidated in the system of international human rights law. *Furthermore, the decision of a judge, which gives permission for the application of capital punishment, goes strongly against the principles of jus naturale. Human beings should not avert the principles of jus naturale and neither can jus naturale follow human being's natural rights.*

A reason given by a judge in self-defence is simply not to be found guilty of international crimes. Obviously, the written judgment of a judge is an *intentional erratum* carried out with full consent with due regard for the principle of *mens rea*. A reason is often an explanation that is expressed by most of us in order to justify our wrongful conduct or fault. Its basic intention is to minimise the borderline of responsibility by freeing ourselves from moral accountability. Most judges of those states that have implemented capital punishment give amnesty and forgiveness to themselves by reasoning that they were carrying out their duties. This is particularly notable in the case of replacing the old regime with a new one.

A duty which goes against the pure philosophy of love for justice, love for the implementation of jus cogens law, love for the application of the basic principles of human rights law, and love for the appropriate application of European criminal law can no longer be called a duty. It is instead a serious violation of the principle of universality of abolition of capital punishment. The term love here means a norm that is clearly the intention of a particular norm of law presented in the substance of the relevant law for the proper implementation of the purpose of its object. These are the non-derogable purpose of prohibition of capital punishment, non-excusable implementation of torture, or non-acceptable impunity in the case of sexual offences in war and peacetime. All these mean a borderline between what is permitted and what is not permitted by international law. Here, I am not only focusing on the law of all states—Western or non-Western—but also those cruel Islamic provisions that have become reasons for the application of capital punishment, stoning, cutting off hands and entire arms.

I really wonder what the nature of law is. Is law the manifestation of the concept of morality? Or, is morality the law? Can a violation of law be qualified as a violation of a legal system? Or, may non-violation of law be qualified as a violation of moral norms? Obviously, the law may not represent morality, but morality definitely symbolizes the real virtue of the law. *By all these, I mean that the norms of law which present injustice, and even those norms which apparently present justice, may not be considered the obvious norms of legality if they do not fulfil the standard of international legalisation of law. This means, inter alia, good faith in the natural substance of the law; the intention of achieving good results regardless of the purpose of the law; demanding the full standard of human justice for the subjects of the law; and creating the atmosphere of objectivity for the law. The standard of international legalisation of law also means not containing any political deceptions; giving birth to the creation of justice with tolerance for other ideologies; quality of pure human rights law over quantity of the same law; and preventing criminal justice from any possible criminal behaviour against the machinery of judgment, i.e. the pillar of acquisition with love.*

4.16 *Jus Cogens Enshrining* the Love Principle

The question that arises is how we can violate the established principle of *jus cogens*—the respect of which is obligatory for all states and is considered *erga omnes*.[83] The norm of love is the 'concern of all states' and cannot be derogated to the contrary effect. This means that the provisions of sub-paragraphs 4 to 6 of Article 6 of the International Covenant on Civil and Political Rights of 1966 (discussed above) mislay all their intentions.[84] In a case before the Human Rights Committee of the Latin American region, the legitimate or illegitimate understanding of the position is considered with the following words:

> The right enshrined in . . . article (6) is the supreme right of the human being. It follows that the deprivation of life by the authorities of the State is a matter of the utmost gravity. This follows from the article as a whole and in particular is the reason why paragraph 2 of the article lays down that the death penalty may be imposed only for the most serious crimes. The requirements that the right shall be protected law and that no one shall be arbitrarily deprived of his life mean that the law must strictly control and limit the circumstances in which a person may be deprived of his life by the authorities of a State.[85]

Apparently, the Human Rights Committee of the Latin American region, like other committees in human rights law, promises the abolition of capital punishment. Similarly, other entities for the protection of the supreme right of human beings, side by side, of different organisations of the United Nations promise the full protection of the same right. However, this policy may change because of ambiguous language in the relevant provisions for the abolition of capital punishment. Eventually, the protection loses the power of love and replaces it with the power of application of the death penalty in limited situations.[86] Therefore, although we assert that no one shall be arbitrarily deprived of his life, we permit the legal authority or judicial machinery of a state to deprive an individual of his life

[83]See the judgment of the Inter-American Court over the case of *La Cantuta*, Fujimori. 11 IACHR, Case *La Cantuta v. Peru*, judgment of 29 November 2006, Ser. C. No. 160, para. 160.

[84]Ramcharan (1985).

[85]Human Rights Committee, Communication No. 45/1979: Colombia, 31/03/82, CCPR/C/15/D/45/1979 Colombia, 31/03/82, CCPR/C/15/D/45/1979 (Jurisprudence), 31 March 1982, available at http://www.ohchr.org.

[86]Römer (2010).

when it seems necessary. Furthermore, we permit our national, regional, or international committees to apply the illegitimate use of the death penalty or capital punishment. This policy decreases the legal and moral validity of the principle of the right to life and banishes the love norm. The expression surely legitimises the killing of a man by judicial process.

The problem here is obvious. The law encourages violations of the law. In other words, *if the use of force is prohibited by all means, it cannot be permitted by any means. If the application of capital punishment is abolished, it cannot be justified in any situation, as is the case in Article 6 of the Covenant. If the norms of legality are correctly divided into primary and secondary rules, then we cannot deprive them of their high human values. Likewise, if Islamic law is a permanent brotherhood, then it cannot be removed from this significant principle. If the communist idea is to share common interests for humankind, then it cannot be isolated from other theories. The norm of love is built on the strength of justice and our ability to understand that if every human being has the inherent right to life, freedom of speech, and marriage, this is a collective inheritance, and therefore no human being should be isolated from this right by any means.* Particularly, the above rights are an integral part of peremptory norms of international law.

There are several criteria for the recognition of the principle of *jus cogens*. These are *i)* the common characteristics of the norm, *ii)* the interests of all human beings as a whole, *iii)* the concern of all states, *iv)* the protection of individuals, groups, or nations in absolute terms, *v)* the lack of a right of derogation, *vi)* the prohibition of renunciation of fundamental rights recognised by the basic instruments of human rights law, *vii)* the high validity of certain norms, *viii)* the superior character of a norm for human personality, *ix)* the massive gravity of criminal acts against human beings, and *x)* consensus among the majority of states to prevent such conduct. All these show the common human interest in preventing injustice and in transmitting the principle of love for justice with full protection. This is because *jus cogens* norms are not a matter of utility or private interests but about the high value of morality that has to be protected in the international legal and political community of states. This is regardless of whether a state agrees or disagrees with the principles of *jus cogens* such as the abolition of capital punishment or genocide.

References

Alexis, R. (2002). *A theory of constitutional rights* (Trans.). OUP.

Al-Hussein, Z. (2009). For love of country and international criminal law. *American University International Law Review, 24*(4), 647–664.

Andenaes, J. (1965). *The general part of criminal law of Norway*. London: Sweet & Maxwell Limited.

Andreopoulos, A. (2014). Exchange of life: The Love of God in the Orthodox Christian tradition. In S.T. Hidden (Ed.), *Jewish, Christian, and Islamic mystical perspectives on the Love of God* (pp. 57–71). Springer.

Ashworth, A. (2006). Four threats to presumption of innocence. *South African Journal*, 63–97.

Awadallah, I.Z. (2005). Islam, civil and political rights and the universal declaration of human rights. Florida International University. http://digitalcommons.fiu.edu/etd/1347. Accessed 11 Sept 2016.

Barnes, M. (2014). Between task and gift: Jews, Christians, Muslims, and a spirituality of dialogue. In S.T. Hidden (Ed.), *Jewish, Christian, and Islamic mystical perspectives on the Love of God* (pp. 11–42). Springer.

Badar, M. E. (2015). *The concept of Mens Rea in International Criminal Law*. Oxford: Hart Publishing.

Berman, M. (1982). *All that is solid melts into air: The experience of modernity*. New York: Simon and Schuster.

Boot, M. (2002). *Genocide, crimes against humanity, war crimes: Nullum Crimen Sine Lege and the subject matter jurisdiction of the International Criminal Court*. Cambridge: Intersentia nv.

Cappelletti, M., Gordley, J., & Johnson, E. (1975). *Toward equal justice: A comparative study of legal aid in modern societies*. New York: Oceana Publications.

Chittick, W.C. (2014). Themes of Love in Islamic Mystical theology. In S.T. Hidden (Ed.), *Jewish, Christian, and Islamic mystical perspectives on the Love of God* (pp. 155–180). Springer.

Coffey, G. (2010). *Criminal law*. Round Hall: Thomson Reuters.

Cryer, R. (2009). A message from elsewhere: Witnesses before International Criminal Tribunals. In P. Roberts & M. Redmayne (Eds.), *Innovations in evidence and proof*. Oxford: Hart Publishing.

DeValve, M. J. (2014). *A different justice: Love and the future of criminal justice practice in America*. Carolina Academic Press.

Dworkin, R. (1996). *Taking rights seriously* (8th ed.). Duckworth.

Eckes, C., & Kondtandinides, T. (2011). *Crime within the area of freedom, security and justice*. Cambridge: Cambridge University Press.

Elior, R. (2014). The Love of God in the Jewish mystical tradition: Mysticism of freedom and commemoration versus mysticism of hope and redemption. In S.T. Hidden (Ed.), *Jewish, Christian, and Islamic mystical perspectives on the Love of God* (pp. 103–134). Springer.

Elshtain, J. B. (2006). Concrete levels of being and their political implications. In D. Browning (Ed.), *Universalism vs. Relativism: Making moral judgments in a changing, pluralistic, and threatening world*. England: Rowman and Littlefield Publishers.

Eser, A. (2009). Human rights guarantees for criminal law and procedure in the EU-Charter of Fundamental Rights. *Ritsumeikan Law Review, 26*, 163–190.

Eser, A., & Rettenmaier, F. (2009). Criminality of organizations: Lessons from domestic law – A comparative perspective. In A. Noellkaemper & H. van der Wilt (Eds.), *System criminality in international law*. Cambridge: Cambridge University Press.

Franck, T. M. (1995). *Fairness in international law and institutions*. Oxford: Oxford University Press.

Fromm, E. (1956, 2006). *The art of lovıng: En enquiry into the nature of love*. New York: Harper.

Gans, J. (2012). *Modern criminal law of Australia*. Cambridge: Cambridge University Press.

Gilligan, J. (1996–1997). *Violence: Reflections on a national epidemic*. New York: Putnam.

Goodale, M., & Merry, S. E. (2007). *The practice of human rights tracking law between the global and the local*. Cambridge: Cambridge University Press.

Gorsky, J. (2014). Maimonides spirituality: Intellectual mysticism and the Love of God. In S.T. Hidden (Ed.), *Jewish, Christian, and Islamic mystical perspectives on the Love of God* (pp. 43–55). Springer.

Grotius, H. (1625). *The rights of war and peace* (A.C. Campbell, ed. 1901).

Guild, E. (Ed.). (2008). *Security versus justice? Police and judicial cooperation in the European Union*. Hampshire: Ashgate.

Hanly, C. (2006). *An introduction to Irish criminal law* (2nd ed.). Dublin: Gill & Macmillan Ltd.

Hazan, P. (2004). *Justice in a time of war: The true story behind the International Criminal Tribunal for the former Yugoslavia*. College Station: Texas A & M University Press.

Hinarejos, A. (2009). *Judicial control in the European Union: Reforming jurisdiction in the intergovernmental pillars*. Oxford: Oxford University Press.
Ingraham, B. L. (1979). *Political crime in Europe: A comparative study of France, Germany and England*. London: University of California Press.
Kamal, M.H.M. (2014). International legal personality of Prophet Muhammad International Islamic University Malaysia. http://www.ocis.org.au/files/pdf/full-papers/ocis14final00103.pdf. Accessed 6 Aug 2016.
Katouzian, N. (2003). The quality of justice in judgment. *The Journal of Faculty of Law and Political Science (Persian language), 62*, 361.
Locke, J. (1689). *The Two Treatises of Civil Government (Thomas Hollis (ed.),* Of Tyranny, Chap. XVIII, section 202, Book II, 1689).
Lumbard, J.E.B. (2016). *Ahmad Al-Ghazali, remembrance, and the metaphysics of Love* (Sunny Series in Islam). State University of New York Press.
Malekian, F. (1993). *Condemning the use of force in the Gulf crisis*. Almqvist & Wiksell International.
Malekian, F. (1999). International criminal responsibility. In M. Cherif Bassiouni (Ed.), *International criminal law: Crimes* (2nd ed.). New York: Transnational Publishers, Inc. Ardsley.
Malekian, F. (2007). *Documents on the principles of international human rights*. Stockholm: Norstedts Juridik.
Mann, K., & Roberts, R. (1991). *Law in Colonial Africa*. Heinemann Educational Books.
Mastellone, S. (2001). *Thought upon democracy in Europe*. Florence: Cntro Editoriale Toscano.
McAuley, F., & Paul McCutcheon, J. (2000). *Criminal liability*. Round Hall, Sweet & Maxwell.
McIntyre, T. J. McMullan, S., & Togohda, S. O. (2012). *Criminal law*. Round Hall, Thomson Reuters.
Meyer, P. (1963). Justice in politics. In *Legal essays to attribute to Frede Castberg on the Occasion of his* 70th *Birthday*. Universitetsforlaget.
Morris, C. (Ed.). (1959). *The great legal philosophers: Selected readings in jurisprudence*. Philadelphia: University of Pennsylvania Press.
Novak, A. (2014). *The global decline of the mandatory death penalty: Constitutional jurisprudence and legislative reform in Africa, Asia and the Caribbean*. Surrey: Ashgate.
Nussbaum, M. C. (2013). *Political emotions: Why love matters for justice*. Harvard University Press.
Pour-Golafshan, F. (2012). *Love of Jesus and Mary in Islam: An enlightening course for all, including Islamists and Islamophobists*. Independent Publishing Platform.
Ramcharan, G. B. (1985). *The right to life in international law*. Dordrecht: Martinus Nijhoff Publishers.
Roberts, P. (2009). Why international criminal evidence. In P. Roberts & M. Redmayne (Eds.), *Innovations in evidence and proof*. Oxford: Hart Publishing.
Römer, J. (Ed.). (2010). *Killing in a gray area between humanitarian law and human rights: How can the National Police of Colombia Overcome the Uncertainty of Which Branch of International Law to Apply?* Heidelberg: Springer.
Ross, A. (1958). *On law and justice*. London: Stevens & Sons Limited.
Ross, A. (1975). *On guilt, responsibility and punishment*. London: Stevens & Sons Limited.
Schabas, W. A. (2002). *The abolition of the death penalty in international law* (3rd ed.). Cambridge: Cambridge University Press.
Scheffer, D. (2009). Tenth annual Grotius lecture response – For love of country and international criminal law, further reflections. *American University International Law Review, 24*(4), 665–78.
Shaffer, T. L. (1997). The legal ethics of radical individualism. *Texas Law Review, 65*.
Shah-Kazemi, R. (2014). The metaphysics of oneness and sanctifying Love in Islamic mysticism. In S.T. Hidden (Ed.), *Jewish, Christian, and Islamic mystical perspectives on the Love of God* (pp. 73–101). Springer.

Shay, J. (1994). *Achilles in Vietnam: Combat trauma and the undoing of character*. New York: Scribner.

Trechsel, S. (1997). Why must trials be fair. *Israel Law Review, 31*, 94–119.

Turner, D. (2014). The uniting wisdom of Love: The story of a late Medieval controversy. In S.T. Hidden (Ed.), *Jewish, Christian, and Islamic mystical perspectives on the Love of God* (pp. 135–153). Springer.

Walsh, M. (2006). *Criminal law*. Dublin: Thomson, Round Hall.

Zawati, H. M. (2001). *Is Jihad a just war? War, peace, and human rights under Islamic and Public International Law*. Lewinston: The Edwin Mellen Press.

Chapter 5
The Right to Demand Love in Criminal Justice

5.1 Requisite Faculty of Love

The legend of the mill of Sanssouci, the palace of Frederick the Great, and the miller who was threatened by the king that his mill would be destroyed since it was disturbing his privacy, is a clear example of how a court should be trusted by citizens and refrain from any personal prejudice or bias. The miller replied to the king that if Frederick destroyed the mill, he would bring the case against his majesty before the Supreme Court of Berlin. The mill was never destroyed. This is a narrative example of the right to demand fairness, trust in justice, and live without being afraid of the authorities. The concept of human rights may sound different. Many books and articles adorn themselves with the concept. Many philosophers and theologies query its nature. However, in law, the concept has been given more consideration when there has been a violation of rights. It is based upon this theory that the term or the word 'humanity' has taken shape in the body of law. Thus, from the commencement of civilisation (where the law began its role), human nature has been the focus, but to different degrees. Therefore, what was considered to be the concept of humanity in the Babylonian and Hammurabi Codes has emerged into a different feature in the present structure of law and particularly in international human rights law. All these evaluations of the term humanity have helped to protect its nature than to destroy it. This protection can be seen today within the provisions of most international conventions. Thus, the character or the personality of human beings has come into law, not as a subject of obliteration, annihilation, or humiliation, but as a secure subject of law based on the high value of its integrity. Kant described humanity as:

> The idea of humanity in its complete perfection supposes not only the advancement of all the powers and faculties, which constitute our conception of human nature, to a complete attainment of their final aims, but also everything which is requisite for the complete

F. Malekian, *Judgments of Love in Criminal Justice*,
DOI 10.1007/978-3-319-46900-3_5

determination of the idea; for of all contradictory predicates, only one can conform with the idea of the perfect man.[1]

In particular, the concept of humanity has been one of the most significant issues in the system of public international law in relation to its branches, such as international criminal law and international criminal justice. The term 'humanity' in these bodies of laws has not meant the protection of the physical bodies of human beings alone, but also their mental, cultural, ethical, religious, linguistic, and other similar factors. Although these protections are of different quantities, they have one quality alone and this quality has to be based on a strong notion of human nature, human ability, human will, and human intention. I call this the principle of love and justice. This is because we cannot talk about humanity, human dignity, or human values by any means if there is no love for it. In fact, the norm of love is the first reason that human beings have organised most of the realistic laws, have codified rules, have formulated conventions, have created international humanitarian law and so forth. Here, I am not engaging in discussions about dictatorial laws or laws governing slavery, permission of torture, application of severe penalties, or capital punishment. I have addressed them in other parts of this volume.

5.2 Revocation of Penalties

It is commonly believed that the substance of natural law is love of mankind and justice for all. The natural law also has a norm of love, which is necessary for its existence. If the norm of love and the centralisation of all powers of the universe are not based on magnetic fields, then there should possibly be another power which has such a strong capacity to keep the natural environment of the universe. This should be a positive and not a negative norm. This norm must be more powerful than other norms of the universe that are visible, tangible, solid, and join the somatic universe.

The great classical writer of the European law of nations, Grotius, treats the question of love as a priority within his writing. He looked on the question of love as a principle from the natural law point of view. According to him, the norm of love is the first norm of law which was created by God. He says, "from this fact the old poets and philosophers have rightly deduced that love, whose primary force and action are directed to self-interest, is the first principle of the whole natural order."[2] However, his thought and his arguments have sometimes been misunderstood. Some writers believe that he was solely looking for self-love.[3] One of the reasons for this misinterpretation may be the heavy emphasis on elucidation of the scope of natural law knowledge. This is a law which is associated with spiritual and also non-spiritual principles. Yet, according to the same debaters, Grotius produced "a

[1]Kant (2014), p. 333. Available at http://www2.hn.psu.edu/faculty/jmanis/kant/critique-pure-reason6x9.pdf (Accessed December 27, 2014).

[2]Grotius (eBook, 1603, http://oll.libertyfund.org/titles/1718) (Accessed March 28, 2015).

[3]von Lockey (2006), p. 198. See *also* p. 201.

radical redefinition of natural law and natural rights."[4] "Natural law was the dictate of right reason involving moral necessity, independent of any institution – human or divine."[5] Grotius also clarifies his position by stating that:

> Love, then, is twofold: love for oneself, and love for others. In the former aspect, it is known as "desire"; in the latter, as "friendliness." While a certain form of friendliness is discernible even within inanimate objects, and more clearly so in the lower animals, this manifestation of love burns most brightly in man, as in one who is peculiarly endowed not only with the affections shared in common with other creatures but also with the sovereign attribute of reason: that is to say, as in a being derived from God Himself, who imprinted upon man the image of His own mind.[6]

What I am talking about here is obviously not the questions of natural law and natural love or God's love or "God himself when he acts as Judge,"[7] but the love that is permanently integrated into our legislation with the intention of keeping our wills and our legal order. By this, I mean all laws. I am not speaking here about courts of love either. I have discussed these courts in Europe in another section. What we are aiming at here, in our discussion, is to understand that the norm of love has been one of the most significant norms of the metaphysical science of law. In other words, human beings have within their laws, the right to demand *the right of love*. This right of love in reality constitutes an integral part of the natural rights of man and should not be ignored by the legislation of our governments.[8]

To quote the title of a work by an excellent American philosopher of law, Lysander Spooner, namely Natural Law; or the Science of Justice: A Treatise on Natural Law, Natural Justice, Natural Rights, Natural Liberty, and Natural Society; showing that all Legislation whatsoever is an Absurdity, a Usurpation, and a Crime, may be sufficient to demand justice with love. The implementation of this justice is necessary for every person in the world.[9] This right is also integrated into our criminal law, in particular our modern criminal law which not only envisages the legal point of view but also criminological points of view of the law, including psychological and sociological aspects. Some clear examples are harsh punishments, long imprisonment, and capital punishment, which are disappearing, and treatments including reintegration of the offenders into our social system, which are becoming stronger than ever before in the system of criminal justice. However, there is yet another serious difficulty with our system of criminal justice and the weakness of love for justice.

For instance, the severity of imprisonment is one of the serious problems of our criminal legal system by which we seek the establishment of the security of the national legal system. The application of severe punishments such as

---

[4]von Rovira, p. 61.

[5]Hannikainen (1988), p. 30.

[6]Grotius (eBook, 1603, http://oll.libertyfund.org/titles/1718) (Accessed 28 March 2015).

[7]Grotius (eBook, 1603, http://oll.libertyfund.org/titles/1718) (Accessed March 28, 2015).

[8]Marcin (1984), pp. 363–391. See *also* http://scholarship.law.edu/cgi/viewcontent.cgi?article=2126&context=lawreview (Accessed June 12, 2016).

[9]Spooner (1882), available at http://oll.libertyfund.org/titles/spooner-natural-law-or-the-science-of-justice-1882 (Accessed on May 17, 2015).

imprisonment for most crimes causes the infringement of personal liberty and goes against the principle of love for justice. "Criminal punishment is by far the worst thing the law allows."[10] We are to learn that imprisonment should only be used for the most serious crimes, such as sexual assault which is associated with the personal integrity of a person. Consequently, by giving effective and proportionate balance to the crime, its nature, and the evidence against the offender, we may prevent the total loss of liberty of a person and the violation of human rights principles.

5.3 The Right to Petition in Criminal Justice

In our preceding discussion in the above section, we underlined the existence of an element called *the right to demand the right of love*. The question then arises as to what *the right of love in law* is. By the phrase 'the right of love in law,' we mean the right of every human being to demand justice, to demand equality, and to demand the abolition of cruel treatment of humanity under the law due to the principles of justice such as *jus cogens principles*. The right of love creates for all human beings a right to petition for an appropriate application of the law, a human implementation of the law, a just jury, an impartial court, a rightful presentation of evidence by judges or the prosecutor, the appropriate right to appeal unlawful decisions and so forth. For instance, according to the Basic Law of the Federal Republic of Germany, a "petition committee" of the German Bundestag is responsible for preparing decisions on complaints pursuant to Article 17 of the Basic Law which deals with the right to petition. It is a right to protest individually or collectively a case if the decisions are in contradiction with humanity.

> **Article 17**
> Every person shall have the right individually or jointly with others to address written requests or complaints to competent authorities and to the legislature.
>
> **Article 45 c**
> (1) The Bundestag shall appoint a Petitions Committee to deal with requests and complaints addressed to the Bundestag pursuant to Article 17.
> (2) The powers of the Committee to consider complaints shall be regulated by a federal law.[11]

The right of love therefore implies the existence of a norm of justice that cannot and should not be violated by the proceedings of jurisdiction. A clear example is the application of unequal norms of law under the criminal legislation of some Islamic states.[12] The *principle of the right to love* means, *inter alia*, that a person who has been brought before a criminal court, a political court, a civil court, a tribunal, or

[10] Gross (2012), p. 7.

[11] The Basic Law of the Federal Republic of Germany.

[12] Malekian (2015).

any other hearings can entirely reject the system of criminal justice which is based on cruelty, inhumanity, and rules that are not following the principles of human rights law. A recent synonym for the development of the principle of the right to love is the arrival of the "right to hope." In the case of *Vinter and Others v. the United Kingdom*, the concurring judgment of the Grand Chamber of the European Court of Human Rights articulated clearly that *Article 3 of the European Convention on Human Rights* concerning the application of the prohibition of inhuman or degrading treatment evidently maintains the right to hope for every human being. The Court in its strong yardstick of equality between all men, regardless of their offences, clarifies that:

> The judgment recognises, implicitly, that hope is an important and constitutive aspect of the human person. Those who commit the most abhorrent and egregious of acts and who inflict untold suffering upon others, nevertheless retain their fundamental humanity and carry within themselves the capacity to change. Long and deserved though their prison sentences may be, they retain the right to hope that, someday, they may have atoned for the wrongs which they have committed. They ought not to be deprived entirely of such hope. To deny them the experience of hope would be to deny a fundamental aspect of their humanity and, to do that, would be degrading.[13]

Similarly, a concurring opinion of the Chamber of the European Court of Human Rights in the *Trabelsi v. Belgium* case motivated its judgment to be comparable to the *Vinter case*. It emphasised that the *Trabelsi* extradition to the United States, with due regard to the situation in which the applicant faced the possibility of life imprisonment without parole on his arrival, was also against the provisions of Article 3.[14] With reference to the earlier judgment, the Court argues that:

> in the light of the Vinter requirements, the risk of ill-treatment derives not from concrete facts such as torture during the applicant's interrogation or denial of access to a lawyer, but from the mere idea that his life sentence might appear irreducible to him at the time of sentencing, thus depriving him of a "*right to hope*" inherent in human dignity.[15]

This means that a law that attributes penalties such as cutting off parts of the body, torturing, abusing, negating, humiliating, degrading, depriving, mortifying, corrupting, shaming, defaming, dishonouring, embarrassing, insulting, and distressing a person who has come before the criminal justice system, is invalid. However, justice has to be very careful not to violate the natural or legal rights of man by its legislative power. Human beings should not be forced to accept the old legal systems by the force of guns. This includes religious or non-religious systems.

---

[13]Concurring Opinion of Judge Power-Forde, the Grand Chamber of the European Court of Human Rights (9 July 2013) (Applications nos. 66069/09, 130/10 and 3896/10) http://hudoc.echr.coe.int/fre?i=001-122664#{%22itemid%22:[%22001-122664%22]} (Accessed October, 2015).

[14]Concurring Opinion of Judge Yudkivska, the Grand Chamber of the European Court of Human Rights (9 July 2013), Application no (140/10), JUDGMENT. This version was rectified on 7 October 2014 under Rule 81 of the Rules of Court (Strasbourg, 4 September 2014) Final (16/02/2015). This judgment has become final under Article 44 § 2 of the Convention. http://hudoc.echr.coe.int/eng?i=001-146372#{%22itemid%22:[%22001-146372%22]} (accessed October 2, 2015).

[15]Italics added.

Even systems which depend on jury decision or the decision of the majority of judges should be aware of the fact that:

> A man cannot see by another's eye, nor hear by another's ear; nor more can a man conclude or infer the thing to be resolved by another's understanding or reasoning; and though the verdict be right the jury give, yet they being not assured it is so from their own understanding, are forsworn, at least in foro conscientiae.[16]

In the United States, the right to petition exists within the constitution. According to this right, Congress is prohibited from modifying the right of people to petition the government for a redress of grievances. The right to petition therefore constitutes a fundamental right which cannot be ignored. This means that the right to petition is the final stage at which the machinery of justice cannot go against complainants, according to which love of justice and transparency has not been respected.

Similarly, all the discussions in the above paragraphs together and separately create the right to petition. All these conducts against the fundamental rights of man violate the term 'love of justice'. Likewise, all these behaviours, such as torturing the offender, abusing the accused, shaming, and distressing a person, can, for example, more or less be found, varying from case to case, in the legislation and practices of the Islamic Republic of Iran, Saudi Arabia, Afghanistan, the United States, China, and many Western and non-Western states. This means that judgments, proceedings, and jurisdictions have lost their goal of the implementation of the aims of justice. The implementation of the law has become more powerful than the soul of justice, the strength of fairness, the value of the legacy of jurisdiction, the respect for human dignity, and the merits of the case.

5.4 The Right of Love in Law

With the term "right of love in law," we mean that law has in its organised method a system of norms that is beyond the norms of legality and morality. It creates for us the right to protest against immoral interpretations of law and justice by legal authorities or politicians. This system of norms is called the norm of love. The right of love exists within all legal systems, particularly in the system of international humanitarian law of armed conflict. It also exists within the law of the United Nations Organisation against the use of force and the implementation of aggressive conduct carried out by permanent members under the provisions of Article 51 of the Charter. This means that the Security Council of the United Nations is not permitted to use force against any state by resorting to unlawful sanctions adopted within

[16]Bushell's Case, 124 Eng. Rep. 1006, 1013 (C.P. 1670). See *also* A complete collection of state-trials, and proceedings for high-treason, and other crimes and misdemeanours: from the reign of collection King Richard II. to the end of the reign of King George I. With two alphabetical tables to the whole (20 Volumes, Vol. xvii, London, 1816), p. 716.

its resolutions. When a sanction of the Security Council does not respect the real spirit of the Charter or the rights of civilians in their own home states, and violates the right of love for justice, it is not any longer a sanction but rather an obstacle to justice. The Gulf Crisis in 1991 proved to be one of those examples of violation of the norm of the right to love in criminal justice systems of the world. The unlawful occupations and attacks have created the ISIS in Iraq, Syria, and Libya, which is part of strange chain of events shaped by the United States' hidden policy for the oil region of Arab-speaking nations.[17]

The right of love in law also displays the inadequacies of our national and international legal systems on the rightful application of law or the monopolisation of criminal law by politico-legal control. I trust that one should raise the question of why we are permitted to produce weapons if our laws are connected to a system of healthy law, i.e. law that does not license production of any type of weapons. This is law that strains the application of proper democratisation of law. If a system of law voices the democratisation of law, it means it is adorned by the world of love for justice for all and it rejects any personal monopolisation of law.

A system of law that claims to present democratic rules and habits has to be democratic in its practice, in its views, and in its hidden political policies. *A democratic law, which opens windows to the sun of justice for its own land by the lawful/unlawful killing of others and opens the gate of injustice by the export of weapons of all kinds, cannot be called a democratic system but a devaluation of humanity, democracy, equality, and love for justice for all human beings. What we*

[17]See articles by Professor Michel Chossudovsky, available at http://www.globalresearch.ca/when-terrorism-becomes-counter-terrorism-the-state-sponsors-of-terrorism-are-going-after-the-terrorists/5496051. See *also* article by Dr. Paul Craig Roberts, '*Washington's Secret Agendas - Truth is Being Disguised to Suit'*. Roberts puts clearly that "The public fell for the lie that the Taliban in Afghanistan are terrorists allied with al Qaeda. Americans fought a war for 13 years that enriched Dick Cheney's firm, Halliburton, and other private interests only to end in another Washington failure. The public fell for the lie that Saddam Hussein in Iraq had "weapons of mass destruction" that were a threat to America and that if the US did not invade Iraq Americans risked a 'mushroom cloud going up over an American city.' With the rise of ISIS, this long war apparently is far from over. Billions of dollars more in profits will pour into the coffers of the US military security complex as Washington fights those who are redrawing the false Middle East boundaries created by the British and French after WW I when the British and French seized territories of the former Ottoman Empire. The American public fell for the lies told about Gaddafi in Libya. The formerly stable and prosperous country is now in chaos. The American public fell for the lie that Iran has, or is building, nuclear weapons. Sanctioned and reviled by the West, Iran has shifted toward an Eastern orientation, thereby removing a principal oil producer from Western influence. The public fell for the lie that Assad of Syria used "chemical weapons against his own people." The jihadists that Washington sent to overthrow Assad have turned out to be, according to Washington's propaganda, a threat to America. The greatest threat to the world is Washington's insistence on its hegemony. The ideology of a handful of neoconservatives is the basis for this insistence." Available at http://www.oneworldofnations.com/2014/09/washingtons-secret-agendas-truth-is.html. See *as well* https://docs.google.com/viewer?a=v&pid=sites&srcid=ZGVmYXVsdGRvbWFpbnxoYWlkZXJub3Rlc3xneDo3NDEwMDI3NjViZTNjODZm (Accessed December 25, 2015). For a useful analysis see http://www.politico.eu/article/why-the-arabs-dont-want-us-in-syria-mideast-conflict-oil-intervention/ (Accessed March 4, 2016).

advocate here is that democratic reciprocity needs love. One may ask why the formulations of basic principles of human rights law are not sufficient. The reason is that, although the basic principles address the respect for human beings, the theory still does not have an appropriate balance unless love can be reinvented in such a way that it does not make the people obsess about how to nourish the hierarchy of justice and personal balance.

In the contemporary position of international human rights law, any act which results in the killing of others is illegal and not allowed by law. One cannot, without having any problem, advocate a theory that legitimises killing. In fact, the distinction between the terms "lawful and unlawful" has lost its validity in the system of national, regional, and international law. Again, one cannot divide the conduct of man, especially acts carried out under the legal personality of entities or military operations, into lawful and unlawful conduct. All acts of killing are prohibited and therefore unlawful. Any other interpretation goes against the norm of love for justice. I am not talking here about individual or collective self-defence, which may be absolutely necessary due to the circumstances of a particular case. However, I have a strong objection even to the question of self-defence when it is carried out with weapons of war.

My objection is simply based on the fact that if we do not manufacture weapons, we do not need to be involved in such lawful/unlawful killings. Resorting to self-defence may seem necessary, but it is not always crucial in order to solve problems which can instead be solved by peaceful methods. The history of civilisation has demonstrated the fact that war has never been the key to the treatment of justice like the Swiss Saridon medical tablets used to relieve mild pain, such as menstrual pain, toothaches, headaches, and also mild fever from colds and flu. One was never released from aches and pains; the medical treatment was a temporary prevention of pain in the organic body. In order to be released from menstrual pain, a woman normally has to suffer until she is at least 50 years old. I am not here promoting or demoting the use of a medical tablet, but aiming at the fact that the world of law has to realise that *the distinction between lawful and unlawful is no longer valid.* This is if, and only if, capital punishment, the killing of individuals, terrorism, and the use of force are all prohibited in the system of international human rights law, the European human rights standard, the declaration of human rights announced by Islamic and Arab states, the Latin American declaration of human rights law, and so forth. If a system of law propagates rights and duties but does not imply the transparency of the law or its application in practice, such law is against its own function. This in turn reduces the right of love in law and therefore constitutes a restriction of individual rights.

5.5 The Court of Love for Justice

The expression 'court of love' is the appellation for a court that is not ruled by the law of a sovereign but by the law of conscience. This is where the law is silent and cannot, for one reason or another, investigate moral and oral contracts between parties. The purpose of a court is not to gain money from a conflict by the judges or barristers of the court. It looks upon humans as one of the integral parts of humanity and not as subjects of law and legal order. This does not mean that it ignores law; on the contrary, it puts heavy emphasis on the law of morality, which is the first source of legal discipline. Most modern regulations of criminal law are also based on this source. By this, we do not mean that morality should be the first stage of the creation of new rules; if this were the case, many laws would not be developed, such as the alterations which have come into the law of marriage, resulting in marriage between members of the same sex. This is partly the expansion of law and partly the modification of morality.

The court of love was established where the law did not acknowledge its norm of love for justice or interruption between norm and judgment. The court of love is a feminist court which has long been exercised in Europe and was officially established on *St. Valentine's Day*, 1400 by Charles VI of France.[18] He promulgated a statute which established the *Cour Amoureuse* or a *High Court of Love* in Paris.[19] The practice of the court also traces back to the Common Law system. This court intended to solve disputes between lovers by peaceful methods. It puts heavy emphasis on the existence of the power of love between two or several people and not on the norms of legislation which are practised today.

The judges of the court consisted of ladies, who were married or widowed, and belonged to high nobility. There were around ten to sixty of them. In particular cases, there could also be a man, too. The objective of the court of love was to rule cases like a "lady's behaviour to a nobleman."[20] Or, they could "legislate on all questions regarding love, to settle disputes between lovers, to pass sentence on any lover who was in the wrong, and generally to establish a system of jurisprudence, which would be useful in solving problems which might arise between lovers, thus leaving the tribunals only as a last resort."[21] This meant to avoid civil courts, which could not realise the love norm within the inner structure of the legal norm that connected the parties. The whole idea was also a female jurisdiction. The following observation was made:

---

[18] Goodrich (2006), p. 1.

[19] *Id.*

[20] http://www.globalresearch.ca/when-terrorism-becomes-counter-terrorism-the-state-sponsors-of-terrorism-are-going-after-the-terrorists/5496051 and https://docs.google.com/viewer?a=v&pid=sites&srcid=ZGVmYXVsdGRvbWFpbnxoYWlkZXJub3Rlc3xneDo3NDEwMDI3NjViZTNjODZm (Accessed February 14, 2015).

[21] *Id.*

> A minor jurisprudence is one which neither aspires nor pretends to be the only law or universal jurisprudence. Its referent is a law whose jurisdiction is neither jealous of other jurisdictions nor fearful of alternatives disciplines. It represents strangeness of language and so the possibilities of interpreting as also of plural forms of knowledge. A minor jurisprudence, and in the example given in a feminine justice, is a challenge to the science of law and to its monopoly of legal knowledge. It challenges the law of masters, the genre and categories of established institution of doctrine and its artificial proceeds upon a different view, it is predicated upon a politics of the literary practice of law and upon the existential commitments of writing: where one believed there was the law, there is in fact deserted and desire alone. Justice is desire and not law.[22]

The supreme effect of a court system, which based its jurisdiction on the rule of love, was welcomed positively in the history of courtship in the whole of Europe.[23] The legal problem of the court of love was that it went beyond the boundaries of state law and did not search for legislation but the essence of the lovers' trust. In other words, the courts of love constituted the courts of conscience, which were connected to the prerequisite of conscience alone and therefore developed their rule through the sphere of the spirit. However, the position depended on the fact that the ethic of scruples neither barred grounds of causes nor did it dissociate the *raison d'être* of spirituality from the practice of law. While the courts of conscience, also so-called spiritual courts, slowly and with the passing of time were substituted by common law, their positive effect and improvement of justice should not be misjudged. "The spiritual courts not only preceded the common law and ethical and hierarchical terms but also had the power to take cognisance of a wide range of speculative and institutional causes."[24]

It is worth mentioning here, as a starting point to understanding the substance of a case that two expressions were used in order to advocate the significant value of the justification for the jurisdiction of love. These were the concept of *regulae amoris* and the concept of *Le Jugement du roy du Behaigne*.[25] Both of them implied an important justification for the jurisdiction of love. They gave an opportunity to the parties to the conflict not to ignore the substance of the principle of love perused and suggested by the court. "Courtly love defied the social order by making love more important than politics or religion. It became, in its own right, a political power and a new religion."[26] This became one of the serious reasons that the court of love was systematically erased from the legal history of European nations.[27] The relations between the conflicting parties were not seen as a matter of the letters of the law but as a matter of the substance of the case, their relations, children, and also culture, art, and the beauty of love. This meant, "Love is preferred over

---

[22]Goodrich (2006), p. 2.

[23]*Id.*, p. 1.

[24]*Id.*, p. 25.

[25]Goodrich (2006), p. 52.

[26]Graybill, available at http://www.illinoismedieval.org/ems/VOL5/graybill.html (Accessed March 29, 2015), p. 95.

[27]von Lockey (2006), p. 198.

marriage."[28] We call this another side of the norm of love for justice. The court of love was directed by women and was a series of minor decisions that escaped the phantom of a sovereign and strict unitary law.

This means the norm of love searches for the soul of judgment and not the role or rule of judgment. It also searches for the application of friendship, respect, and service for justice with the dedication of love. This also includes proceeds from love in the devotion to moral relations. The principle of love in justice and legal systems empowers victims, witnesses, and the accused; uses their courage, strength, and love as the greatest advantage for the system of the machinery of justice; and allows the case to be presented and heard with full purity.

5.6 Positive Obligations of Justice for Humanity

Justice today is not just part of listening to the heart, but a part of our collective consent to the common position of humanity in our heart. It is addressed to the nature of humanity and its significant value before the jurisdiction of love. Many lawyers misplace the position of the term 'humanity' because of the reasons that we all consider a law as a law, a law as an order, a law as an institution of restrictions, a law as a statute of discovering different crimes, and a law as the way to obtain the satisfaction of justice. These have been our theories, our understanding of the reality of the law, and our central issue to use the law against one another when it seems necessary regardless of whether we violate the law by our own motives. Therefore, our governments enhance various perceptions by claiming that the protection of law is the first necessary condition for the protection of human beings and not us as individuals. For this reason, there have been strong reactions to abhorrent practices committed by fellow man, by local neighbours, by our territorial neighbours, and by regional and international neighbours. As Grotius asserts, "we are bidden to love our neighbours that the term 'neighbours' obviously includes every human being."[29]

We have taken every reaction as a protection of the law without realising that the whole system of law is based on love for justice, and this canon of law, which is called love, should not be violated by any of us in any part of our family world.[30] Western, Eastern, and Muslim perceptions have not taken into account the fact that the differences between our base theories are not the reasons for the differences in love for the nature of man or humanity in terms of human, social, and economic development. My full intention here is to say that the power of love and justice exists within our laws, but we should understand by the force of the same love that, because of the very dangerous technical development of military forces, it is time to

[28]von Lockey (2006), p. 198. See *also* p. 201.

[29]Grotius, p. 434. Available at http://oll.libertyfund.org/titles/1718 (Accessed May 3, 2015).

[30]*See generally* Roback (2001).

give appropriate attention to these positive obligations of love as the power of humanity. They should function as the centre of positive obligations of justice and a positive powerful sanction against violations or the victimisation of man. What is at stake is that with the power of positive obligations of love for humanity, with the strength of positive obligations of love for justice, and with the command of our positive human inspiration, we should understand that the norms of our human rights law may not be pure. This is true if we violate the positive obligations of the norms of love for other countries. To quote, the cultural achievement of Tibet may be relevant here:

> First, look at the dying person in front of you and think of that person as just like you, with the same needs, the same fundamental desire to be happy and avoid suffering, the same loneliness, the same fear of the unknown, the same secret areas of sadness, the same half-acknowledged feelings of helplessness. You will find that if you really do this, your heart will open toward the person and love will be present between you. . . . The second way . . . is to put yourself directly and unflinchingly in the dying person's place. . . . What would you most need?[31]

Most lawyers who read the above quote argue that this is a religious inspiration and not law. They ignore the fact that most regulations of the civilisation of man have been inspired from the code of various political theories of theology. Even the great philosopher of Europe, Emanuel Kant, was and was not affected by the concepts of theories expressed by the Churches. On the one hand, religious codes are not law, nor are they orders, nor do they have the value of defence due to the present modernisation of international human society. On the other hand, they are the inner structure of most philosophies of development of law, the development of the idea of natural law, natural existence and the basic background for the development of criminal law, including international criminal law.

The term 'humanity' has come into the law and the law has been organised for that purpose. Almost all laws deal solely, in one way or another, with the questions of human beings. This means organising the matter of love and humanity. I am obviously aware of the fact that there are also laws that are not only disturbing the norm of love, but also our complete existence. I am not referring here to the concept of love that is expressed in romantic terms but love as a central energy for the entire human existence and its shared values. In order for laws to be healthy, we must encourage the potential values which do exist in the intention of our laws, our aims, our motivations, and our integrities, such as a justice with love, harmony with love, understanding with love, generosity with love, and brotherhood with love.[32] All these types of love mean the strong will and potential pure energy for the realising of the truth. If I use the word brotherhood, one should not associate it with Muslims, as the term exists within all civilisations; its meaning is equal, its effect also has to be equal, and its practice must be the same. I shall therefore say that goodwill, brotherhood, sisterhood, friendship, neighbourhood, and globality are all equal internationally.

[31]Rinpoche (2002).

[32]Hora (1986), p. 19.

5.7 Avoiding Criminal Contradictions

Contrary to what many may believe, the power of law is not solely centralised in legislation, positive obligations, statutes, or within the hands of our civil or criminal courts, but rather the first power of law is the power of integrity of man. That is why law contemplates humankind and its behaviour and conduct. Similarly, the interconnectedness of all human spirits seeks to find the best alternative for their relations. The intention of the law is not therefore to have rules but to avoid contradiction between human nature, which is the same nature within all human beings.

This notion of interconnectedness elucidates why the remedy for prevention of violations is not more violations, or why the remedy for pluralism is not to find more pluralist opinions, theories, ethical reasoning, philosophical argumentation, killings, or attacks on our individual civilization. However, the accurate remedy is certainly love as a central measure of justice and as a basic element of jurisdiction of humanity, or as a norm that should be located in the hearts of all men, in the centre of all laws, in the heart of justice, and in the wishes of all human beings with the same intentions. By the norm of love here, I neither mean nor support the philosophy of kindness or theory of compassion, sympathy, or gentleness.

Although I fully understand that the norm of love may be translated into all these synonymous and other words, I do not in any case mean that we are to be kind to our fellow men; kindness may, in some cultures, be defined as foolishness and stupidity. Consequently, with the use of the term 'norm of love' I mean a powerful basic element which should exist and is in the inner structure of all men in order to see fair justice for all of us, without any discrimination between one man and another.[33] Therefore, by law, we mean human relations and these laws aim to remove fears and violations. Both these terms 'fears and violations' are analogous to darkness, which explains to us how love has disappeared from their nature and therefore illness, injury, genocide, atrocities, crimes, and infringement of human nature are their fruits.

Here, we need a similar norm or similar powerful convergence. This norm works its magical power against the glimmer and darkness. This norm presents the pure theory of love. It aims at human unity against illogical acts of violation, ill treatment of human nature, crimes against humanity, and against all types of aggression against human generations. As the international lawyer Martin Luther King proclaimed, "Darkness cannot drive out darkness; only light can do that. Hate cannot drive out hate; only love can do that." In other words, if there is only one natural form of creation of which we are all a part, which is called the human race, we want it to be as protected as possible. This means the need to qualify its existence with the same quality and increase its value with the same degree of recognition which is significant for us. In order to help the infringed position of man, we need a powerful connection and not more infringements. Put it this way, if

[33]Trechsel (1997), pp. 94–119.

we connect ourselves to the canon of love, fear will not be present or decrease. If the norm of love is the objective subject of the law and legal regulations, we must add similar norms, not fear.[34]

5.8 A Process of Loving Justice

All these argumentations mean that the principle of love embraces the entire human community. The whole nature of law, including civil, criminal, family, and procedural law, are in the service of man and the intention is to mobilise this potential power of love to prevent authorities from violations of our similarities. When a law does not permit violations and cultivates fairness and equality for all human beings within its jurisdiction, the law not only encourages legal and moral norms but also the norm of love. If humanity in law is linked juridically with the basic requirements of non-violation and justice for all with love, it means we embrace the fundamental human rights law that concerns all races solely because they exist for this reason. This means the law is enforceable to all men from all cultures and backgrounds.[35] A well-recognised international lawyer asserts this more clearly:

> Whether humanity will consciously follow the law of love, I do not know. But that need not disturb me. The law will work just as the law of gravitation works, whether we accept it or not. The person who discovered the law of love was a far greater scientist than any of our modern scientists. Only our explorations have not gone far enough and so it is not possible for everyone to see all its workings.[36]

I do not mean by this a criticism of opinions that struggle for the maintenance of their cultures, for the keeping of their own legacy or ethnic originality, but *I suppose that a critical inquiry into the real function of our legal system is indeed vital if not welcomed. One can observe that our legal norms, including national, regional, and international ones, are giving more priority to the validity of the law than the validity of their real intention for the maintenance of justice with love. This is one of the serious sicknesses of our legislation. I refer here to the real cognition of the law, or our awareness of the reality of the existence of the law, including our way of argumentation, reasoning, and delivering judgment on the nature of the law. I mean that, if the nature of law is peace and if the nature of legislation is to keep the value of human dignity, then the principle is that law is created for the needs of humanity and humanity is our need combined and organised with love, whether we sometimes call it morality or sometimes legality. Whilst they may be different from one another, their perspective is to realise what is possible and what is not possible*

[34] See Atwell (2008), pp. 501 and 505.

[35] *Id.*

[36] Mahatma Gandhi.

or what is against the nature of man, humanity, or the power of all laws that may be called love.

We do not aim here to solve all the problems of law, nor do we need to prove which law is more important than another law or which is more reliable than the other. Many philosophers including Plato have evaluated this theory of discovering the nature of law.[37] They all aimed to come to a point that can help us to understand how we can trust the nature of law. Although these speculations among various philosophers and writers are of the highest significance to the development of the philosophy of justice, legality, and morality, they are still not settled because of the variety of our differences and explanations of their theories. The force of time and the force of the inspiration of the logic of philosophers and ourselves should come to a solution that can reduce our differences and understand that the nature of all laws has incorporated some parts of the nature of man, and its aims bind us. Those aims which are integrated into the law by force or are interpreted by antagonist mentality or political systems cannot continue when the law is presenting one central power of the law and that is love for justice. As is rightly stated *"humanity is not saved by ideological manifestos, but by the 'acts…of love."*[38]

Again, I am not looking here to suggest that we should go against our traditional sovereign interests, but at the same time I am concerned by the fact that all laws have their own sovereignties, and the intention of all these laws should not and cannot be against each other. This is when we reflect on the sphere of humanity in the world or the value of human nature in the statutes of international organisations. By drawing attention to these values and listing them as provisions of our international conventions and interpreting them by different methods of dualism or monism, we are saying that there is a central value in the system of law which is the nature of law or relevance of law that I call the final stage of the law. This pinpoints the fact that, by all these international conventions regarding different matters such as international criminal justice, we are creating a process to express that the nature of law should be enforced by the nature of love for human beings in order to keep its integrity and protect its international values by the power of sovereignty of the law.

5.9 Treating International Criminal Justice with Love

We should accept the fact that the intention of international conventions governing the area of human rights principles, justice, and criminal law is to serve human beings. This means that we should try as much as possible to avoid seeing the system of law as a system of engineering, which is served by the lawyers and court authorities for their clients. We should not wait to face violations and then apply the

[37] Andersen (2011), pp. 76–78.

[38] Ward (2001), p. 946.

nature of the law or face the power of the law and the authority of the ICC. In other words, we should realise the fact that law is not only a social science and human knowledge but also the apparatus in which we have certain shared power that is formulated into law. Thus, when the principles of international criminal justice are violated, we are facing not only the violations of the law but also the fact that our powerful norms or shared values are violated.

A clear example is the strong protest against the real value of the International Criminal Court. This is because, when one sees that the system calls for the prosecution and punishment of certain criminals and releases, by one means or another, other criminals or those who are accused of committing international crimes, one may consider this problem to be an infringement of the court's own rights. This is because we suppose that the system of international criminal justice exercises its judicial power with the same eye of the law. It means in turn that we seek to find the shared values of the criminal justice system. This is what may be called again the norm of love for justice.

As a whole, the ICC has a duty for all international violations which fall under its statute. This means that the ICC is, according to its provisions, responsible for trying those who have committed international crimes under its jurisdiction for the purpose of prosecution and punishment. Various bodies, including states, groups, organisations, and even the Prosecutor of the ICC, may call upon this responsibility. As I will demonstrate in Part II, it is the duty of the relevant bodies not to present incorrect information or bring an inappropriate accusation before the Court. The purpose is to keep the principle of justice non-violated and not cause injust decisions. This means that we are trying to keep the idea of justice authentic and the central power of law, which is called love for human beings, functional. We are also ensuring that our own prosecutors do not violate the central power of the law or love of justice and humanity.

One of the tasks of the Prosecutor is to examine the scope of evidence and to keep her/his objectivity about the merits of any case submitted for investigation by a member or non-member state. By this, I mean calling upon the responsibility of the Prosecutor or the entire Court constitutes one of our duties, and these duties are a part of our international obligations that require the power of the law or the power of human beings to prevent violations against the norms of love. Neither the Prosecutor nor any bodies of the Court are permitted to act against the principle of objectivity, and this strategy of objectivity has to be the main policy of the ICC into which the canon of love is integrated. This principle would also seem to be a basic requirement for all other national, regional, and international judgments. This means that in each case we are looking to implement the power of the law that is correlated to our personal integrity as a whole.[39]

The body of law, in particular the body of most international conventions relating to the relationships between human beings, is organised to secure love for justice to be done in order that the value of human dignity is respected. This

[39]Consult chapters ten and eleven.

reference and argumentation may not seem enough for the proof of the norm of love. Whether I am right or not, I am trying to estimate the causes and consequences of the non-existence of the norm of love in the system of law, or human rights law. This means we have to find a reasonable theory to prove that the norm of love does not exist in law or *vice versa*. Without attempting to answer this question, which is already done in other parts of this volume, I have examined the norm of love in the light of the principle of the pure theory of love or how to achieve pure justice which is not tied up with various forms of restrictions.

This means again, without entering into contradiction with other matters, we must see which reason is much stronger than the other reason and which one fails in the end. Without any doubt, and without going into the merits of each instance case by case and the problems which may exist in the truthfulness of each case, we should assume that all cases which have been brought before the jurisdiction of international criminal courts have the intention of settling and finding the truth and application of appropriate punishment. These courts include the ICC, the ICTY, the ICTR, the SCSL and others. This positive intention should be found in the procedures of the courts, the mentality of the judges, the horrible legacy of the victims, and the bad memories of the witnesses too.

This means that there is a strong interconnectedness between the entire machinery of justice and the whole intention of the injured society to express their love for the victims. We did not establish international criminal courts simply because we wanted to establish such courts; the reason for the establishment of the courts was the implementation of our sincere love for justice to be done.[40] *This implies the fact that there is an interconnectedness among human spirits to discover the cause of the actions. What is the nature of this interconnectedness, which exists in our mind, in our heart, in our actions, or in our essence? Should we call it law? However, the law does not exist as long as we have not drafted its shape. It is still an abstract form of existence. There must be another matter which is surrounded by our law, by our regulations, by our courts, and by our judgments. This is what I call the norm of love. In other words, a judgment is not the heart of justice, but if love for justice is done with the sole intention of fairness, it constitutes the heart of pure judgment.*

However, I do not reject the fact that we have not established the courts to show our love but to show the power of justice. Therefore, an attempt to find a single document, which discusses that tribunals are being established in order to manifest love, would be in vain. This argument may be true but may not take into account the fact that, in our ordinary lives and relations, we do not speak about the concept of love all the time or about our great feelings for every member of society but the fact is that love exists. We only experience love more effectively when a violation has been occurred. The reality is that a misconception exists concerning the understanding of the true nature of love, not only between individuals but also between entities and, more strongly, between states of the world. It is not our duty to prove how this misconception of the legal interpretation of the law has come into

[40]See Malekian (2014a).

existence, but it is our very central duty to understand that most laws are without doubt bound by the concepts of fairness, egalitarianism, consensus, equality, impartiality, equal opportunity, and classlessness. The amalgamation of all of these may be called the norm of love for justice. This means that the word love not only represents the norm of love but also the norm of *unity*.

5.10 Rightfulness of Love for Criminal Justice

It is not easy to describe what the rightfulness of love for criminal justice is. However, it certainly refers to positive and trustable obligations for the maintenance of criminal justice. We are bound to find a pure reason that is common or has a magnificent operation in human nature that challenges the application of love and the maintenance of justice based on the power of our national or international legislation. If the reason of our argumentation is not sufficient, the problem rests on the fact that we have always dealt with the law as an instrument of order and not as a tool of recognition of our inner strength for ascertaining and discovering truth with love for human beings. "I have never yet been able to perceive how anything can be known for truth by consecutive reasoning - and yet it must be. Can it be that even the greatest philosopher ever arrived at his goal without putting aside numerous objections?"[41]

Whilst I am saying this, I must also admit that we are also obliged by the philosophy of reason to see what the nature of law or the sole metaphysics of law is. As we have noted earlier, it is not self-evident that all legal positivism ignores the moral content of law—to the extent that the debate concerning what is essential or necessary for the metaphysics of law is not and will never be settled. The essential features of the law, therefore, might be seen from the growing nature of international conventions to sometimes bind themselves in social, political, and teleological terms. Legal positivists, however, do not have a tendency to search for deep teleological concepts of law, but this does not necessarily mean that they deny such metaphysical intention of the law.

We are therefore obliged to find the reason for the law. Is the reason for the system of international conventional law protection of humanity by humanity or is it to keep humanity in order? Clearly, in the word 'reason,' we also include the main intention of the law and, with intention, we mean the goal or rightfulness of the law. The *raison d'être* has therefore been to express that we dislike violations against human beings. We dislike violations not only against our nearest fellow man but also against those that are far from us. The logic is very simple: we love fellow man because we would like to be loved in return, as happens in reality. This means that we have a strong reason in our law, in particular our international criminal law,

[41]Letter from John Keats to Benjamin Bailey (Nov. 22, 1817), in Rollins (Ed.) (1985), p. 185. See also http://www.john-keats.com/briefe/221117.htm (Accessed June 4, 2015).

international criminal justice, and international human rights law to implement the strength of our love for human beings, which is the soul and the intention of the law at the same time.

Although I humbly confess that proof of humanity has been very poor in the world of justice and in the practice of most states of the world because of the double moral standard between ratified papers and policy, this does not hinder us from recognising the fact that humanity rests on love. In addition, *the basic institution of most law is love or has to be love, if it is going to be effective*. Therefore, it is not so essential to know if the relevant authorities are correctly practising the law but if the reason or the essence of the law is correct. We are hence bound to work for the strangeness of the operation of this reason of the law. Consequently, if human beings who are the subjects of the law are not the subject of the love, the position of the law or the nature of the law will be modified such as not to be a law but authoritarian regulations.

Our aim must not be arbitrary when we analyse the quality of the law, because the nature of cognition for the security of man requires that we should have some more effective reasons for the regulations of the law. This must be the rightfulness of love for justice. *As I have stated elsewhere, pure love is the indispensable condition for clear and fair judgment. A judgment cannot be authentic if it does not follow the reason of its existence whether by law or by custom. Knowledge of the law or its cognition cannot be solely established on the basis that there has to be a law because we desire a law. There must be a priori justification for its adoption, which is necessary for its drafting, building, adoption, and implementation. If that is not love for justice, what could it be?* For example, the body of international humanitarian law is based on prior or posterior grounds that were necessary for its formulation within the system of international criminal law. The same argument can be made in relation to the system of international criminal justice or the crime of genocide. Both have been adopted or regulated within our international legal system not because we wanted them to be created, but because a number of people were killed by atrocities against the seeds of civilisation.

5.11 Deterrence of Crimes with the Norm of Love

Many international crimes, such as crimes against humanity, war crimes, and aggression, provided strong grounds for the formulation and establishment of the permanent International Criminal Court.[42] The function of the Court is to uncover international crimes after their commission. This is one of the most miserable features of the Court. The Court, as we will discuss later, should operate for the full deterrence of crimes with the norm of love for justice *before* their commission. I am not here specifically drafting any philosophical question, but I am convinced

[42] Consult Bozbayindir (2013), pp. 20–21.

that none of our laws could come into force without a prior ground that was seen as necessary and a reason for its establishment. This is also true for any laws, particularly those laws, the intention of which is our full physical security.

My purpose here is, therefore, not to convince international lawyers or the judges of the national and international courts that there is a strong norm in law which is called love, but I certainly fear and I am concerned about the fact that law which does not base its elementary raison d'être on love for human beings cannot survive appropriately. Therefore, the structure of the law is always in very serious danger. When we speak about the genocide law and its relevant regulations in the system of international law of *jus cogens*, we are trying to say that its elements are certainly based on love for human nature and humanity as a whole. The intention of the relevant law is clearly to prevent certain acts that are against human beings as a whole and is vital for justice.

A similar investigation into other laws implies the same fact. Examples are conventions regarding torture, discrimination, apartheid, children's rights, and the prevention of rape. My purpose here is to say that we have to realise and understand the fact that our laws cannot be proper law if there is no soul in their creation. If we discover this soul and teach it to our own family or our neighbours all over the world, we may prevent differences and aggressiveness with an understanding of our similarities, *before* our legal and intellectual relations can be violated. In other words, it is rather imperative to come to a solution towards understanding the faculty of peace and justice with love, since neither of these two—justice and peace—can be seen if we do not see the strength of love for their establishment, theories, and jurisdiction. When war rages between several indigenous or native groups in a society as it did in Rwanda, it means that the law has been misunderstood and love for neighbours has been replaced by hostility. What is really missing here is the pure understanding of the reason for its creation.

Not all members of the groups were surely aware of the fact that there is a law about crimes against humanity or a law about a crime called genocide, a crime of crimes more massive than crimes against its victims. This ignorance might have existed in Rwanda, and ignorance of the crime of genocide may exist in other societies in the world. Nonetheless, the fact is that the members of the relevant groups who committed genocide in Rwanda cannot reject the general fact that exists within the law of all civilisation of the world that killing is not an expression of love, and such conduct is in fact against the principle of respect and creates more killings. *By this, I mean that the objective validity of love and the objective invalidity of killings are prior conceptions within our civilisation that cannot be ignored by us through posterior argumentation that love does not constitute a norm in law. When we kill, at the same time we are lulling the soul of the norm of love.*

My proposition is to specify that knowledge of the main reason for the law constitutes the most significant tool for the recognition of the nature of the law and one of the essential reasons for its proper development and use. That is why I speak about the philosophy of love, the norm of love, and the pure theory of love as the main gateway to mobilising law - not only be used as the rule of law but also love for its intention. Therefore, a pure understanding of the theory of love opens the window to its legal possibility and its power of cognition, from a subjective point of view, to control violations in their infancy.

This means that if most laws are thought of as love statutes and not legal order, and if most laws are seen as purity and not curity, we may prevent many serious international crimes by the norm of love. It means we, by the logic of awareness, ought to look at the basic reasons for the law and not the procedural successfulness of the relevant law whether it is accepted as a part of our legislation or not.

5.12 Institutionalising Justice with Love

We view at the principle of non-violation from two perspectives. One is that a violation is not permitted in its entirety by any system of law and the other is that a violation is against the universal harmony of the human spirit. This implies the fact that we are searching to find the pure philosophy of the existence of relevant law, and this attitude cannot be separated from its goodwill for the well-being of human beings. By this method, we are able to differentiate between the prevention of a single murder and the prevention of a million murders. Although both principles involve the same injury to the victim(s), the difference lies in the fact that the former has a more personalised character while the latter is related to the international standard of humanity arising exclusively from the principle of the spirit of man. If my assumption is wrong and if there is a parallel assumption that the harm, which we experience from different crimes, is the same, then we are bound to change our legal theory and point to the principle that a single crime of murder is equal to the killing of a million people. Although I am fully aware of the fact that any murder constitutes a crime against humanity, the degree of harm must be quite different for the murder of a million people, taking into consideration that crimes against humanity, war crimes, and genocide are considered a great breach of international criminal law and justice.

My attempt here is not to introduce a revolution into the system of law but just the realisation that the reason behind the recognition of such crimes is based on love for justice. Those crimes are practically out of our control and are committed because of the disappearance of understanding or fear of differences that exist. At the same time, we have to understand that there has not been any appropriate encouragement for different groups to recognise the pure theory of love, which exists in their culture, language, ethnic origin, and law. These shortcomings have been one of the basic reasons that the groups run away from the concept of unity. They have forgotten the fact that the confrontation with opponents can only be conquered 'with love.'[43]

In my opinion, there is also a strong connection between the metaphysics of the law of one civilisation with the law of another civilisation, which brings them into

[43]Mahatma Gandhi.

one unity of law or harmony; they should thus respect one another, solely on the ground of similarities. For example, the European Union system does so.[44] However, a good number of international lawyers may ask what the real value of this unity is and what type of help this principle of love in the system of law and international criminal justice can produce. A cursory view of the principle of love may prove to be merely emotional and not semantic. It may prove to be unrealistic since it is arguing the feelings of individuals or spiritual nature. A lot of such reasoning may be disputed because of non-identification of the norm within the legal system, and therefore it may be asserted that its legal notion is negative and may even jeopardise our legal system of legislation. In contrary to these argumentations, the principle is not only not emotional but also realistic. It is realistic since it bases its conception on the first principle that is given to man and is required by man and that is the final stage of man's will. It is positive since it evokes a strong gravitation towards or a powerful sanction against grave violations of the system of international criminal law and humanitarian law of armed conflict. Its virtue is not just a moral code but a definite code of collectiveness to achieve justice or to stop violations.

By all this, I am not criticising by any means any international lawyer or anyone who has to deal with the law; my intention is also not to criticise legal works or the inner structure of our international conventions at all. With the principle of love in law, I am examining the whole system of law, be it national, regional, or international. I am not only thinking about the inspiration of our legal system but also the existence of our moral system. As a rule, any legal system is valid and enforceable as long as it relies on rational grounds in accordance with certain principles. However, there has never been an assessment of its substance with the power of love. We seldom examine law with the essence of our own nature but with the essence of social relations between people and authorities. Thus, the private scope of the love norm remains undistorted because of its absence in the provisions of law. I mean within its provisions. No lawyer, judges, or judgment speaks about the norm of love.

The truth is that the legal, moral, and love norms cannot be proven as material. They are all hypothetical or alien, so long as we are not involved with them. Their existences are only proven when there is an act or conduct which brings them into being. All three demonstrate a response to certain matters of interest. Nevertheless, the difference between these three norms rests on the fact that the legal norm is a copy of the moral code and these two together constitute an integral part of the love norm, which is the basic reason for the existence of both norms. Even a very dictatorial legal norm represents the moral code of relevant authorities who are in power and both of them represent the negative aspect of love for power. Here, the conscience of man is killed and replaced with ill thoughts that are hazardous for others and for man himself.

[44] Klaus Stern, 'From the European Convention on Human Rights to the European Charter of Fundamental Rights: The Prospects for the Protection of human Rights in Europe' in Blanke and Mangiameli (2006), pp. 169–184.

Consequently, one may miscalculate the concepts of the terms "law," "criminal justice," "criminal proceedings," "criminal responsibility," and "criminal penalty." The fact is that they are conceptual figures, which do not exist at all. For example, the term "criminal justice" is the imagination of certain conduct or habits that we are accustomed to recognising as law. Thus, the law comes into existence with the reasons for certain conduct. This means the principles of legality and morality are imputed into the law at particular times. It also means that the philosophy of law varies from time to time, as does the philosophy of legality and morality. Therefore, we have to strengthen the power of law, the security of law, and trust in justice. The existence of the norm of love in criminal justice creates and teaches its subjects to trust the potential validity of jurisdiction and decreases tensions between its objects.

Whenever tensions increase in a society, faith in justice has decreased. For instance, one of the strongest reasons for the decrease in trust in the Security Council of the United Nations is the decrease in confidence and assurance of justice with love under its governance. Again, the norm of love means how we understand the relationship between justice, legality, morality, and love. For example, the laws governing the crime of genocide, crimes against humanity, war crimey, and the prohibition of capital punishment are all abstract regulations which are impossible to see as long as they are not committed. The norm of love contains substances that cause these abstract regulations to be present at all times because the norm is a combination of reality and intellect. This means that even a single individual in our societies clearly knows that violence is not permitted due to the first principle of social relations between members, and this need not necessarily be based on the provisions of law, but the norm of respect for all individuals' rights.[45]

5.13 Relatability of Love with Criminal Justice

I do not want to and I cannot affect by any means the rule of law, which already prevails, in our society. I also do not intend to defend myself in front of so many good and excellent theories of laws. When I am discussing these issues of the relatability of love to criminal justice, it should not be understood that I am trying to convince the law or the people, but I have consented myself to the law of love, given that nothing in the law can be more powerful and effective than the norm of love itself. It is for this reason that the norm constitutes the substantive part of the power of justice. That is to say that the relatability of love to justice is something impossible to be denied if the philosophy of justice is not solely based on the implementation of strict legal concepts of the law. This relatability is also powerful

[45] *Id.* pp. 169–171.

if the theory of fundamental rights of man is valid and if the inherent right of man has to see the face of justice.[46] Justice has to be accompanied by love and love has to be truthful and reliable for everyone.

This theory is not based on any means of intuition that love is stronger than the law itself, but the theory is itself an integral part of the norm of law. That means that our substantive theories of the law are, in one way or another, based on the philosophy, power, or strength of love. If the philosophy of criminal justice or criminal fairness has the primary function of the understanding of our interconnectedness, it should also have the function of the understanding of our heart, mind, and virtue, all of which are based on the canon of love for one another. Therefore,

> There is an earthly sun, which is the cause of all heat, and all who are able to see may see the sun. And those who are blind and cannot see him may feel his heat. There is an Eternal Sun, which is the source of all wisdom, and those whose spiritual senses have awakened to life will see that sun and be conscious of His existence; but those who have not attained spiritual consciousness may yet feel His power by an inner faculty which is called intuition.[47]

By all these argumentations in this volume, I am exposing myself to many critical climates that are not welcomed by most international lawyers and also layman. However, I am convinced that I have to do this job, even though I will be the subject of more attacks than the law itself. I do it because I trust the notion of love in law and the fact that appropriate justice is interwoven with love. In fact, it is a right of every citizen of the world to demand love in criminal justice and justice as a whole. Here, the necessary required tools are very simple, although their policies are complicated because of the non-existence of the theory in writing. International lawyers extend or limit the concept of international law in a way they consider logical for requirements of thought. As is asserted, "international law is nothing more than the way that those who call themselves international lawyers look at international relations."[48]

Arguments about the sovereignty and the meaning of justice evidently have a direct bearing on how we fathom the rule of love with the law's content and the indulgence of criminal justice. *If a criminal justice theory does not have such dispensation for the implementation of justice with just norms, a just approach, and a just theory of recognition of the principle of mens rea, varying on a case-by-case basis or based on the nature of the crime, then it is based on the lovelessness of its legislators and applicators. We mean those who did not realise that justice does not consist of different mathematical figures but of understanding of the reason of justice to identify its intention in each relevant case by the theory of love.*

For instance, *if criminal law is about the punishment of criminals, if criminal law permits punishment of children under 18, 15, or 12 years of age, the responsible judge has to realise that such criminal provisions are against the provisions of the*

---

[46] Malekian (2005), p. 721.

[47] Paracelsus (1493–1541).

[48] Carty (1986), p. 21. See *also* Charlesworth and Chinkin (2000); Bederman (2002); Koskenniemi (2005); Marks (2000); Meron (2006). Goldsmith and Posner (2007); Chayes and Chayes (1995).

Convention on the Rights of the Child and cannot be implemented. This is regardless of whether the legislation of the relevant state permits it.[49] *This means the judge must have the skill of differentiating between legislation and punishment and between the requirements of the judgment and the requirements of love for justice. The norm of law here cannot go against the norm of love, which is integrated into the provisions of the relevant convention. Underpinning the subjectivity of the theory of justice to the concept of the love norm means, therefore, empowering judgment with a norm that demands justice, equality of arms, and adherence to the rule of law.*[50] *Consequently, the norm of love encourages positive obligations of relatability between the means and the end to justice. The norm love is about the natural rights of man.*

This is also the case in relation to fundamental rights in European constitutions, in the United States constitution, the Islamic constitution of *Shariah*, and most constitutions of the world. What we really mean with fundamental rights is nothing more than the full freedom of a person to require love over all violations. This means any person in our international social community has the right to demand love in criminal justice and justice as a whole. Clearly, this arises from the fact that national and international justices have to be fair and correct and not ignore the fundamental rights of man for the substance of justice by the rule of law and irrational judgment.

5.14 Replacement of Genocide with Love

The concept of pure justice has been heavily criticised. This is because, although we have an increasing number of regulations for the prevention of crimes at national, regional, and international levels, the commission of crimes around the world has also increased. Many millions have been killed since the ratification of the United Nations Convention on Genocide such as in Iraq, Rwanda, and Bosnia Herzegovina. One of the most serious incidences of genocide occurred against the Aboriginal children in Australia by the government's plans between 1910 and 1970. Almost 100,000 Aboriginal children were kidnapped and forced to live with white families. In 2008, the Australian government confessed all this immoral conduct but did not describe it as genocide. However, Article 2 (e) of the Genocide Convention clearly provides that genocide means 'forcibly transferring children of the group to another group.'

---

[49]Mission for Establishment of Human Rights in Iran, available at http://www.google.de/url?sa=t&rct=j&q=&esrc=s&source=web&cd=1&ved=0CCIQFjAA&url=http%3A%2F%2Fmehr.org%2FIslamic_Penal_Code_of_Iran.pdf&ei=uSpvVYbDA4bfUayBgdgN&usg=AFQjCNHhVkRBVR1-Gx-4IMUToSeIhg_uTA&bvm=bv.94911696,d.d24 (Accessed June 3, 2015); Malekian (2014b), pp. 31–69; Malekian and Nordlöf (2012a), pp. 1–3; Malekian and Nordlöf (2012b), pp. 1–5.

[50]For instance, see Fedorova (2012), p. 11.

In the first and second civil wars, between 1955 and 1972, and 1983 and 2005, almost two and a half million people were killed in Sudan. In addition, 4 million people were displaced. The international community has not yet identified the genocide of indigenous people in Brazil between 1957 and 1968. The Chinese genocide against the Tibetan population and the eradication of their culture between 1959 and 1966 is another example of the fact that provisions of international criminal justice are not effective. Half a million people were killed in the Indonesian genocide between 1965 and 1967. This was the plan of an anti-communist attempt to establish a new order. The victims were members of the Indonesian Communist Party. They were killed simply because of their ideological views.

The Nigerian-Biafra War in Nigeria and the genocide of 30,000 as well as one million that died of famine between 1967 and 1970 was the result of the British colonial period which led to Nigerian independence in 1960. This war was waged between different groups and was due to economic and political tensions, including the long shadow cast by the exit of the colonial powers in the region who were there for Nigerian oil. The genocide against Aché Indians between 1968 and 1978 is another example of the disappearance of justice. The Paraguay government pacified the four ethnically nomadic Indian tribes which were linguistically diverse from other citizens. They lived in the forest and their territories were very important for economic reasons, as they could be sold to western global investors. The Guatemalan civil war and genocide against the Mayan indigenous people by the armed forces is another example of justice based on the principle of legality. Another picture of violations of law and morality is the Bangladesh genocide in 1971 by the central government of Pakistan.

The genocide by Idi Amin, the president of Uganda, against the Acholi and Lango tribes between 1971 and 1979 is another instance of violation of international criminal law. In Burundi, the conflicts between different ethnic groups brought on the mass killing of Hutus in 1972. The Cambodian people witnessed the killing of 2.2 million under the Khmer Rouge regime between 1975 and 1979. Likewise, the Sri Lankan civil war between 1983 and 2009 caused the killing of many civilians, ending with the defeat of the insurgency. Another example of violations is the Khojaly Massacre against ethnic Azerbaijani civilians from the town of Khojaly in Azerbaijan in 1992. This was carried out by Armenian and Russian armed forces during the Nagorno-Karabakh War. The war in Bosnia and Herzegovina between 1992 and 1995, in Darfur by Sudanese armed forces, and in Rwanda in 1994 are should also be mentioned. In North Korea, several million people have died of starvation since the mid-1990s. Atrocities in Libya and Yemen in 2011 and in Iraq are other clear examples. The Russian and Ukraine crisis is yet another example of violation of international personality since 2013. The Syrian unjust war amid superpower politics in order to gain oil pipelines is going on with the complete destruction of Syrian civilisation and killing in large numbers.

5.15 The Magnetic Awareness of Love

Looking comprehensively, it was solely due to the misuse and misinterpretation of the first two norms of law, i.e. legality and morality, that the United States and the Union of Soviet Socialist Republics seriously violated many international criminal conventions immediately after the establishment of the United Nations. A survey of their actions raises awareness that justice should not solely be served to the international public by legal or moral codes. On the one hand, both codes were and are violable due to the very feeble structure of their interpretative mechanisms. On the other hand, since both predictably force themselves on the philosophy of law and have a strong settled position among lawyers and judges of our legal machinery, they are not being debated as to their dominance but as to the means of their development. Although the method of their development is historical, they are no longer practical for the machinery of the jurisdictions of the world, where many sanctions imposed by the United Nations have the semblance of superpower interests and not pure theory of love for justice and humanity. This means the legal system, which was established in the interests of human beings, is in practice being employed for other purposes where the actions and decisions of the authorities do not coincide with the concept of love for human beings. As has been rightly stated by Mother Teresa, "We don't need bombs and guns to destroy, to bring peace - just get together, love one another, bring that peace, that joy, that strength of presence of each other in the home. And we will be able to overcome all the evil that is in the world." As de Vattel further asserts "we ought to hate the crime, but love the man, since all mankind ought to love each other."[51]

If human beings did not have love for human beings, they would never have drafted international human rights codes. However, they did, and they express love through the relevant conventions, which means that love is present in the soul of the law. Again, for the same reason, legal, moral, and love codes have been established on a firm basis to follow and support the theory of law. The advantages of the third norm, as we have explained elsewhere, are that it gives the power of understanding, the power of prevention, the power of justice, and the power to force the big violator into the hands of a trustable justice.

A pure power of law is magnetic and does not rest on statutory power, constitutional strength, sanctions to be adopted, judgments of courts, enforcement by individuals or collective self-defence, or on European Union law, Jewish traditions, Latin American decisions, or Arab Union commitment. Although all these are all fully respectable and understandable, they involve the enforcement of law in very limited measure rather than a putative one. By magnetic we mean that love is a form of awareness which always has a demanding power of enforceability, if not a dogmatic flexibility. Lord Hewat's statement in *R.v. Sussex Justices, ex parte McCarthy,* which is often quoted in Anglo-Saxon discussion and is also integrated

---

[51]Vattel (1844), para. 231, p. 108. Available at http://www.loc.gov/rr/frd/Military_Law/Lieber_Collection/pdf/DeVattel_LawOfNations.pdf (Accessed December 16, 2016).

into the European Court and the Commission of Human Rights, maybe useful here. "It is not merely of some importance, but it is of fundamental importance that justice should not only be done, but should manifestly and undoubtedly be seen to be done."[52] This phrase perceptibly refers to a third norm of law that is the norm of love, or security for the implementation of justice.

The love norm does not let the legal authority take a decision which is against the power of law or the power of human integrity, which has been the basic reason for the adoption of the law. This means that we can achieve progress in the law by pure recognition of the fact that the norm of love constitutes the main possible presumption, which is derived from human reason for its inspiration, integrity, and commonality.

Thus, with the spontaneous power of love, we are aiming to find the best solution for the enforcement of those human rights principles that are not possible to enforce by our legal institutions, by the resolutions of the United Nations, and by the efforts of different bodies of the organisations. The human rights principles also have not been powerful in the works of different national groups concerning the prevention of genocide, crimes against humanity, war crimes, aggression, or torture. My purpose is here to prepare, if and only if possible, a semantic groundwork for the development of a legal philosophy of love and a legal understanding of the subject within the framework of our international legal system. *If love for human beings, for justice, and against grave violations cannot perform its task, how can those legal norms to be effective? And, why are violations of international crimes increasing?*

5.16 Transformative Power of Love

Here, I am not speaking about the fixed principle of legality or morality but a fixed principle of powerful love in our legal system, which is indeed necessary if the concept of justice in international criminal law is going to be efficient and prevent grave breaches of the law. For example, it has been proven that the international humanitarian norms cannot truly be powerful through the norms of legality and morality. This was proven over the course of many wars that have led to the creation of several *ad hoc* or hybrid international criminal tribunals.[53] Some examples of hybrid tribunals are the Special Court for Sierra Leone, the Extraordinary Chambers in the Courts of Cambodia, the Special *Panels* of the *Dili* District Court or East Timorese tribunal, the Bosnia War Crimes Chamber, the UNMIK Court in Kosovo, and the Special Tribunal for Lebanon. The jurisdiction of the courts shows that legal and moral norms have been evaluated to different degrees by the conflicting parties

---

[52] *R.v. Sussex Justices, ex parte McCarthy* (1924) I.K.B.256, p. 259.

[53] Fichtelberg (2015).

and have therefore had very catastrophic results.[54] It means that both norms had more of an aspiration character rather than the cancellation of unjust decisions.[55]

I am not suggesting that, when the norm of love is understood by our legal system, it will prevent violations entirely or that it is going to cure all the problems of unjust decisions or even that it will secure peace and justice. But the fact is that it is the only norm which does not need to be evaluated by the conflicting parties due to the reason that each member of the conflicting parties and non-combatants are cognisant of the reality that they like that their first principles to be respected. These are the rights not to be raped, not to be forced into sexual slavery, not to be attacked against their civilian installations, not to be gang-raped, not to see their children killed, and that all those who they love do not undergo malicious crimes. The classical writer of international law, Pufendorf, puts this significant question of the transformative power of love in our nature, in our natural law, and in our law of nations in this way:

> Man has this in common with all living things to whom it has been given to realize their own existence, that he loves himself most, is zealous to protect himself in every way, and strives to acquire the things which seem good to him, and to repel the evil. And commonly, indeed, this love of each man whatsoever towards himself is so great that any and every inclination towards any and every other man yields to it. At times some seem, indeed, to embrace others with a more tender affection than themselves, and to rejoice more in the blessings of others than in those which are especially theirs, and to grieve more over the ills of others than over their own. Thus, frequently parents would prefer to have transferred to themselves the pain which they see their children suffering. Thus, it is well established that many have met death with equanimity, in order to save others united to them by a special bond.[56]

He goes further and clarifies:

> But, in truth, this was done either because, as the result of an intimate relationship, they regarded the good or evil of others as their own, or else because, by that display of affection or fidelity, they were on the way to acquire some special good for themselves. Thus some parents rejoice more effusively in the blessings of their children than in their own blessings, because the blessing which affects equally both themselves and their offspring is in their judgment doubled. Thus we would often be willing to redeem the suffering of one of our loved ones by our own suffering, because the weapons, as it were, which seeks us would be inflicting a more severe wound by passing through so dear a body. And he who does not refuse to die for another, either hopes for so much glory from that act that he judges he can well afford to pay for it with his life, or else he fears that on the other's death such evil would come upon himself that life would no longer be worth living for him.[57]

The intention here is to realise that the pure reason of love is necessary for the nature and character of human beings. This is in order to stop violations. I am therefore aiming in the complicated system of criminal law, international criminal law, and justice to find the *raison d'être* for the non-effectiveness of the law from the viewpoint of motive or the simplest norm which is understandable by every human being and by every lawyer and judge. It is my ambition to be sure that there

[54]Fichtelberg (2015), pp. 182–185.

[55]*Id.*, pp. 177-8 & 179, 185.

[56]von Pufendorf (1931), p. 315.

[57]*Id.*

is enough confidence in the understanding of the norm of the primary logic of human beings and by the fact that the scope of the legal realist or moral realist is not violated by this principle, based on the fact that the principle is not volatile but instead original and decent.

Therefore, the discussion is not based on opinion or experience but the evidence which exists in the understanding of the nature of law and the reason for its policy prevention. My intention is also that we all become aware of the fact that the presence of legal or moral norms is more evident than the norm of love. *The first two are part of the law when one reads the law, but the third norm relies on the transformative power of the law when the first two norms are lacking proper function. This is because the norm of love is solely a human reason and therefore constitutes the invisible power of human law. Beyond this argumentation, one may think that the love norm is powerful because human beings may fight for it and demand its implementation. Such arguments cannot be strong because the naked norm of love does not rest on fighting, conflicts, guns, resorting to the use of force, use of various military techniques, or political organisational motives. It does not rely on our personal desire either. With the term 'naked norm of love,' I mean the norm, which is not covered by radical evil propensity interests in the innateness of man.*

A norm of love is a non-violative norm, which goes against any type of violation, including the use of force. Its purpose is therefore not to empower a law of armed conflict or a law of armed attack, but rather its intention is to put a stop to any kind of violation or any act whose law permits its violation. Its motive is therefore to empower the legal and moral codes through prevention of inhuman acts. Thus, the norm of love stands for a solely peaceful method such as arbitration, negotiation, and, if needed, forgiveness in order to come to a better, comprehensive result. The norm may even go well beyond the norms of justice and create efficiency, trustworthiness, reliability, and composure for the institutions of reconciliation, mediation, and restoration. This is what I call the necessity for the recognition of justice with love.

5.17 The Paradox of Choice Against Love

I am bound here to explain that I am aware of the fact that we are, most of the time, looking to find an absolute norm, provision, principle, rule, or regulation that can be associated with human beings. A lawyer in a conflict wants to know what the law is and not what the philosophy behind the law might be.[58] Therefore, she/he seldom puts the question of reason but rather the question of how to win the case and succeed in the relevant proceedings. This normally means we have *lost sight of the* ultimate objective because of *a one-eyed justice*.[59] *If an attorney does the work, the*

[58]Martin Luther King. See also Vischer (2014), pp. 39–41.
[59]*Id.*

client pays the attorney's hourly charges. Therefore, the attorney has to obey the conditions. Normally, for the lawyer, it is not the norm of love which is important but the norm of cash, which brings her/him more clients and reputation.

To win a case is thus a principle for which most lawyers fight, and the morality of the case is hardly questioned by them. Her/his question is normally how you would like to recover but not to discover the basic hidden reasons in the case between the conflicting parties. She/he solely pays attention to the client's argumentation but not to the opposite party. The attorney does not properly see the practical effects, the practical loss, or the real nature of the relations.[60] One cannot deny the fact that there may be other situations in which the lawyer truly works for the love of justice or a combination of both. However, the general practice is the first instance. This means it will be a very difficult job for us to realise the most significant power behind a law. Here, I will present an example, in order to clarify the situation.

In 2004, the United States government, with the assistance of its intelligence agencies, drafted a plan to bring Saddam Hussein under national prosecution and punishment. The aim was that the president of Iraq not be prosecuted by an international court, based on the fact that Saddam would release secret information about his prolonged complicity with the United States concerning certain international matters that would not have a good outcome for the United States' foreign policy.[61]

Consequently, the United States drafted a national criminal court idea in order to prosecute Hussein and other relevant accused authorities. This became a show tribunal having power over the accused people. Therefore, the Government of President Bush decided to train the prosecutor and judges of the Tribunal in London. This was because the judges and the prosecutor of the Special Tribunal for Hussein did not have the requisite knowledge of national or international crimes. It was hence necessary for the United States to demonstrate to the world that the Tribunal was a real Tribunal similar to the International Criminal Tribunal for the former Yugoslavia. This meant they decided to invite and hire those who could come to give lectures to the judges of the relevant tribunal.

In practice, it meant that the Tribunal machinery was using certain internationally known lawyers to broadcast and give the impression that the Tribunal's function was real and supported by those who were delivering the lectures. The search started among international lawyers to find those suitable for the job. I personally was in Peking, China, attending the meetings of the International Penal Association, where a number of international criminal lawyers were discussing questions relating to juvenile justice, trafficking, and the principle of *ne bis in idem*. It was at this time that the General Secretary of the United Nations Mr. Kofi Annan asked international lawyers not to give a positive response to the request of the United States government to teach in the tribunal. This was because

[60]Some psychologists may also have a similar policy without measuring and solving the internal position with love.

[61]Malekian (2005), p. 691.

the General Secretary considered the tribunal to be monopolised by the superpower political diplomacy.

Sometime latter, I followed a TV program in which a well-known Swedish international lawyer who had participated in the drafting of the permanent International Criminal Court had given a positive response to the task of teaching in London. The reporter, who disliked the position taken by the lawyer, raised the question: 'are you aware of the fact that the Secretary General of the United Nations has required international lawyers not to give a positive response to the request of the United States government?' The lawyer answered the question by stating, *"I couldn't turn my back on the request."* Here, obviously the lawyer was not only ignoring the very respectful official statement of the Secretary General of the United Nations concerning the illegality of the Special Criminal Tribunal for Saddam Hussein but was also strongly engaged against the principle of love for justice, love for human beings, and love for international criminal courts. He did not show at any level or to any degree a true love for international human rights law, although he was working on the drafting of a convention governing crimes against humanity in Nuremberg.[62]

Equally, before agreeing to the lecture, the lawyer should have known about the opinion of Hans Blix, who is a Swedish international lawyer and known for his strong statements against the propaganda mechanism by the United States government against Saddam Hussein. Accordingly, the United States articulated that Saddam had in his possession chemical weapons of mass destruction. In addition, the very significant position of the Secretary General and his statement should have been obvious to the lawyer. Since he was also an official diplomat of the Swedish government, he should have known about the Saddam regime's complicity with the CIA over several decades. He should also be aware of the fact that the United States' government sanctions against Saddam were based on political conspiracies in order to access oil resources. To this, one should also add the suffering of over 550,000 children because of the sanctions enforced by the United States policies during the Gulf crisis. Obviously, the lawyer knew about all these facts. If he did not know, he could not be a diplomat. One may raise the question regarding what the real reason was for ignoring all these aspects and yielding oneself to enticement of lecturing the members of a court whose basic education was mostly car parking penalties. The phoniness of the tribunal is completely clear to any realistic international lawyer today.

Apparently, if the United States loved justice, it would not establish a show tribunal and the situation would be quite different. Nor would a Swedish well-known Swedish diplomat-lawyer be engaged in the teaching of immoral ethics.[63] "What is wrong with lawyers' ethics?"[64] Alternatively, what is the real strength: to love justice or to be a hardhearted person who lacks the capacity for genuine

[62] *Id.*, p. 690.

[63] For the morality of lawyer, consult Pepper (1986), p. 613.

[64] Wendel (2012), p. 1.

compassion with true justice?[65] However, lawyers may yearn to access justice by identifying its legal merits.[66] But in the present case, the lawyer ignored the real face of justice by viewing "clients as walking boundless of legal rights and interests rather than as whole persons whose legal issues come deeply intertwined with other concerns relationships, loyalties, hopes, uncertainties, fears, doubts, and values – which shape the objectives they bring to legal representation."[67] In addition, a lawyer is morally accountable for the advice she/he gives or fails to give.[68] This is particularly significant in the case of *international crimes with complicity* of the United States that were committed by the Iraqi president.

References

Andersen, P. (2011). Klassisk og Kristen Naturret. In O. Hammerslev & H. P. Olsen (Eds.), *Restsfilosofi – ecntrale tekster og temaer* (pp. 71–96). København: Hans Reitzels Forlag.

Atwell, B. L. (2008). The jurisprudence of love. *University of Detroit Mercy Law Review, 85*, 495.

Bederman, D. J. (2002). *The spirit of international law*. The University of Georgia Press.

Blanke, H.-J., & Mangiameli, S. (2006). *Governing Europe under a constitution: a hard road from the European treatise to a European constitutional treaty* (pp. 169–184). Erfurt: Springer.

Bozbayindir, A. E. (2013). *Turkey and the international criminal court: A substantive criminal law analysis in the context of the principle of complementarity*. Germany: Nomos Verlagsgeseells, Baden-Baden.

Carty, A. (1986). *The decay of international law?* Manchester University Press.

Charlesworth, H., & Chinkin, C. (2000). *The boundaries of international law: A feminist analysis*. Manchester: Manchester University Press, Melland Schill Studies in International Law.

Chayes, A., & Chayes, A. H. (1995). *The new sovereignty: Compliance with international regulatory*. Cambridge: Harvard University Press.

Fedorova, M. (2012). *The principles of equality of arms in international criminal proceedings*. Cambridge: Intersentia.

Fichtelberg, A. (2015). *Hybrid tribunals, a comparative examination*. Heidelberg: Springer.

Goldsmith, J. L., & Posner, E. A. (2007). *The limits of international law*. Oxford: Oxford University Press.

Goodrich, P. (2006). *Law in the courts of love: Literature and other minor jurisprudences*. The Politics of Language.

Graybill, R. V. Courts of love: Challenge to feudalism. In *Essays in Medieval Studies* (Vol. 5).

Gross, H. (2012). *Crime and punishment: A concise moral critique*. New York: Oxford University Press.

Grotius, H. *Commentary on the Law of Prize and Booty*.

Hannikainen, L. (1988). *Peremptory Norms (Jus Cogens) in International Law*. Helsinki.

Hora, T. (1986). *Beyond the dream: A wakening to reality*. The Crossroad Publishing Co. 1996.

Kant, I. (2014). *The critique of pure reason* (J. M. D. Meiklejohn, Trans.). An Electronic Classical Series Publication.

Koskenniemi, M. (2005). *From apology to Utopia*. Cambridge: Cambridge University Press.

[65] Luther King (1963), p. 6.

[66] Simon (1998), p. 138.

[67] Kruse (2010), p. 393.

[68] Pearce (2002), p. 1807.

Kruse, K. R. (2010). Lawyers in character and lawyers in role. *Nevada Law Review, 10*, 393.
Luther King, M., Jr. (1963). *Strength to love*. United States: Fortress Press.
Malekian, F. (2005). Emasculating the philosophy of international criminal justice in the Iraqi special tribunal. *Cornell International Law Journal, 38*(3), 673–723.
Malekian, F. (2014a). *Jurisprudence of international criminal court*. Cambridge: Cambridge Scholars Publishing.
Malekian, F. (2014b). The international criminal law of children on war crimes. *Prawa Dziecka i Ich Ochrona, Horyzonty Wychowania, 13*(25), 31–69.
Malekian, F., & Nordlöf, K. (2012a). *The sovereignty of children in law* (pp. 1–3).
Malekian, F., & Nordlöf, K. (2012b). *Confessing the international rights of children* (pp. 1–5).
Malekian, F. (2015). The canon of love against the use of force in Islamic and public international law: Part II: The anatomy of love against violations. *International Criminal Law Review*, 861–889.
Marcin, R. B. (1984). Justice and love. *Catholic University Law Review, 33*(2), 363–391.
Marks, S. (2000). *The riddle of all constitutions: International law, democracy, and the critique of ideology*. Oxford: Oxford University Press.
Meron, T. (2006). *The humanization of international law*. Netherland: Martinus Nijhoff Publishers.
Pearce, R. (2002). Model Rule 1.0: lawyers are morally –accountable. *Fordham Law Review, 70*, 1805.
Pepper, S. L. (1986). The lawyer's amoral ethical role: A defence, a problem, and some possibilities. *American Bar Foundation Research Journal*, 613.
Rinpoche, S. (2002). *The Tibetan Book of Living and Dying: A spiritual classic from one of the foremost interpreters of Tibetan Buddhism to the West*. CPI Cox and Wyman, Reading, RG1 8EX.
Roback, M. J. (2001). *Love & economics: Why the Laissez Faire family doesn't work*.
Rollins, H. E. (Ed.). (1985). *The Letters of John Keasts, 1814–1821* (Vol. 1).
Simon, W. H. (1998). *The practice of justice: A theory of lawyers' ethics*. United States: Harvard University Press.
Spooner, L. (1882). *Natural law; or the science of justice: A treatise on natural law, natural justice, natural rights, natural liberty, and natural society; showing that all legislation whatsoever is an absurdity, a usurpation, and a crime. Part First*.
Trechsel, S. (1997). Why must trials be fair. *Israel Law Review, 31*, 94–119.
Vattel, M. (1844). *The law of nations or the principles of the law of nations applied to the conduct and affair of nations and sovereign* (6th American Addition, A new edition by Joseph Chitty).
Vischer, R. K. (2014). *Martin Luther King Jr. and the morality of legal practice: Lessons in love and justice*. Cambridge: Cambridge University Press.
von Lockey, B. C. (2006). *Law and Empire in English Renaissance Literature*. Cambridge: Cambridge Publications.
von Pufendorf, S. (1931). *Two books of the elements of universal jurisprudence* (1660) (W. Abbott, Oldfather, Trans.).
von Rovira, M. G.-S. *The project of positivism in international law*. Oxford: Oxford University Press.
Ward, I. (2001). Universal jurisprudence and the case for legal humanism. *ALTA Law Review, 38*, 941.
Wendel, B. (2012). *Lawyers and fidelity to law*. New Jersey: Princeton University Press.

Part II
The Rule of Love in the Aquarium of International Criminal Procedures

This part lectures the theory that the entire system of criminal law, including the system of criminal justice in Europe, Islamic nations, and international criminal law, is like a frangible aquarium which can easily be broken into pieces if the system is not governed by the norm of love. This is a norm which is much more crucial than any legal and moral norm. Its duty is to simultaneously keep and change the entire criminal system. A number of fishes float in the aquarium, whose names are provisions, obligations, rules, norms, principles, legislation, and statutes. Some are armed, some are waiting to be armed, and some are disarmed. Montesquieu describes this international aquarium like the pretext of a useless battle between Spain, Portugal, and Turkey or a fishing competition between the Dutch, English, and French on the one side against the Italians and Spanish on the other side.[1] He concludes that in "a well-ordered monarchy, the subjects are like fish in a big net: they think they are free, and yet they are caught. . ."[2] He continues:

> The men who enjoy the government I have spoken of are like fish who swim in the sea without constraint. Those who live in a prudent and moderate monarchy or aristocracy seem to be in large nets, in which they are caught, though they think themselves free. But those who live in purely despotic States are in such tight nets that they feel themselves to be caught right at the outset. A free government can be compared to a big net in which fish move around without thinking they are caught.[3]

This fishing has altered its features under the contemporary system of international law. Fishing is today like finding and hunting conflicts and distributing weapons among the relevant populations of the conflicting parties for state interests. A clear example is the emergence of pirates on the coast of Somalia. The prolonged war in the country caused the illegal fishing off the Somalian coast by the foreign

---

[1] de Secondat and de Montesquieu (2012), paras. 262 and 345.

[2] *Id.*, para 597.

[3] *Id.*, paras. 828 and 874.

boats.[4] This illegal fishing resulted in lost fishing income to Somalia.[5] In order to gain back the income, the anglers formed armed groups to prevent the foreign ships from pirating their natural resources. This means that the Somali pirates were organised because of international piratical conduct. Their acts may fall under the defence of inherent rights for economic self-defence under Article 51 of the United Nations Charter and the provisions of international customary law.[6]

I am not here encouraging the criminal acts of pirates at all but pointing towards the fact that there were obviously certain basic reasons for the criminal conduct. In other words, the elementary human rights law of the Somali people was already violated before the piratical conduct being carried out by the Somali anglers, including juveniles. As the German Institute for Economic Research aptly puts it, there was also a "hidden agenda" for control of Indian Ocean that created all these events.

Regrettably, most international provisions are disregarded by the states manufacturing weapons for their economic reasons. The most fantastic part is that they are waiting with their fishing tackle box in which they have extra hooks, bobbers, sinkers, lures, and sharp hunting knives, without considering that it is solely them and solely the production of their weapons which create conflicts of armed force, pirates, and terrorists. Still, all these fish in the frangible aquarium of criminal justice are controlled by the big fish or the real whales whose flapping is out of control. From time to time, the legislators of the aquarium move inside and outside of the aquarium whenever they think it is necessary. *In order to save the heritage of humankind and the life of those who are outside the aquarium, we have to entirely abolish the production of weapons as well as create equality of arms before the criminal justice system. We will do this if we do not wish to have more violations, victims, offenders, and anti-terrorist propaganda concerning 11 September, counterterrorism, and ISIS movements.*

---

[4]German Foreign Policy: *The Advantage of Piracy 2010/09/03*. http://www.german-foreign-policy.com/en/fulltext/57866 (Accessed January 18, 2016).

[5]Waldo (2009). The German Institute for Economic Research clearly indicates that piracy in Somalia was about the economic conditions in Somalia. According to it "International pirate fishing and organized toxic waste disposal off the Somali coast has deprived the population of the coastal regions of their livelihood" "Piraterie ist nicht nur für die Somalier ein gutes Geschäft"; DIW Wochenbericht 29/2010, 21.07.2010, http://www.diw.de/sixcms/detail.php?id=diw_01.c.358585.de (Accessed January 18, 2016). The toxic waste articles were dumped onto Somalia's shores by different national groups, for instance, by the Italian mafia.

[6]In 2011, the Report of an African Development Bank describes, "Fishermen, dismayed at the inability of the central government to protect their country's EEZ, and at the number of foreign fishing vessels illegally exploiting their traditional fisheries, took matters into their own hands. Initially arming themselves to chase off the illegal foreign fishing vessels, they quickly realized that robbing the vessels was a lucrative way to make up for lost income. Seeing their success, land based warlords co-opted some of the new pirates, organizing them into increasingly sophisticated gangs." In Joshua Keating, What You Won't Learn About Somali Pirates From *Captain Phillips*, *available at* http://www.slate.com/blogs/browbeat/2013/10/11/captain_phillips_true_story_of_somali_pirates_is_complicated.html (Accessed January 18, 2016); For some other discussions see Gaswaga (2013), p. 277.

Reference to any law in this book does not mean that the relevant law is more important than other laws. I look at serious violations of the international legal system, not only from a legal conception of different branches of public international law, but also from the concept of different philosophies of law expressed by different writers such as Grotius, Vattel, Pufendorf, Kant, Beccaria, Hart, and Rawls. Their observations concern the persistent questions surrounding the relationship between the principle of morality and the principle of legality or primary and secondary rules. The idea has also been developed by the works of the international criminal tribunals. This hierarchy of norms in European law can also be seen in cases presented before the European Court. These are primary law, secondary law, and provisions derived from rules of procedure.[7] Yet "the Court of Justice has fallen critically short of the ideal of an independent judiciary, whilst the failure to respect the barest notions of democracy and citizenship has emerged as a crippling weakness."[8]

The intention of the analysis in this part is not to intensify or reduce the power of any law but to open a window to the jurisdiction of love norms. The function of this norm is to call upon all laws to end divergences and lend a hand to the understanding of the similarities of the law and the heart of the law. This means attaining the real strength of law. "The drift of this lecture is that a cherished value, with fundamental international recognition and strong justifications, it being undermined through the alleged imperatives of governance in the risk society."[9] As we will see, the norm of love constitutes the ultimate stage of respect of human integrity and value when the law is seriously violated and injustice has occupied the security of justice. This part concentrates on the development of criminal justice with the principles of legality, morality, and love. It also looks at the structure of criminal justice in the international courts, the concept of philosophy of law, and the principle of impartiality, including the concept of *a one-eyed justice* in the permanent International Criminal Court (ICC). Part II also contains a concluding chapter about the whole volume.

References

Ashworth, A. (2006). Four threats to presumption of innocence. *South African Journal*.

de Secondat, C. L., & de Montesquieu, B. (2012). *My thoughts (Mes Pensées)* (trans. H. C. Clark in http://oll.libertyfund.org/titles/2534#P828 (Accessed July 25, 2015)).

Gaswaga, D. (2013). Does the International Criminal Court have jurisdiction over the recruitment and use of child pirates and the interference with the delivery of humanitarian aid by Somali Pirates? *International Law Students Association Journal of International and Comparative Law, 19*, 277.

---

[7]Wägenbaur (2013), p. 2.

[8]Ward (2003), pp. 19–20.

[9]Ashworth (2006), p. 97.

Wägenbaur, B. (2013). *Court of the European Union* (p. 2). C.H. Beck/Hart/Nomos.

Waldo, M. (8 January 2009). *The two piracies in Somalia: Why the world ignores the other. WardheerNews.com*. Retrieved 22 January 2011.

Ward, I. (2003). *A critical introduction to European law* (3rd ed., pp. 19–20). Cambridge: Cambridge University Press.

Chapter 6
Underpinning the Criminal Philosophy of Justice with the Norm of Love

6.1 Pure Theory of Reason

We should remember that law is one of the oldest subjects that has survived since the existence of civilisation of humankind. It has always been modified or abolished, not because we wanted to modify the law but because our understanding and our moral values have been modified by the change of times and by various national, continental, and regional revolutions. These modifications were not made for the reason of not being loved by our fellow man but for the reason that the boundaries of our morality and love of human beings have been improved by the advancement of knowledge based on the pure theory of reason.

It is the better understanding of reason that brings the enhanced understanding of human relations to law and to fellow man. This reason shapes our common values and our widespread integrity. The reason into which love is integrated is practically foremost for the understanding of our problems. If we do not put confidence in common reason, how can we offer self-assurance to our law which is based on us as its subject? Is man the servant of the law? Or, is law the servant of man? Should love be the servant of the law or should the law be the servant of love for justice? Some may search for the answer to these questions, some may not, and some may discard the total structure of the questions. The reason is that we wish to know the truth by referring to the legal code of the law and sometimes to the moral code of the relevant law. We do not take other discussions so seriously. The fact is that the law is generally conservative and does not overlap with love. Although positivism and naturalism operate in a manner similar, much evidence proves that there is always a serious conflict between them.

It appears to me that the problem of naturalism and positivism has been more obsessive than radical. They have both fought for the same reason but with the difference that one looks at the law as a document written by man as special rules while the other looks at the law, not because it is to be made into rules in a document, but because of its nature. They seldom look at the fact that there are

F. Malekian, *Judgments of Love in Criminal Justice*,
DOI 10.1007/978-3-319-46900-3_6

so many similarities between both theories that there is no effect if we call positivism naturalism and naturalism positivism. This theory proved to be reality when it came to the drafting and adoption of a considerable number of international conventions on human rights law. The entire body of this law is without any doubt a combination of natural law and positivist law. It is difficult to differentiate between them because human rights law has not been successful in preventing grave violations of the system of international criminal law. This sudden revolution between the two legal systems, which started officially in 1948, focuses our attention on the indispensable conditions of the change in the theory of law.

6.2 Sanity of Justice

In all societies, justice is always a matter of necessity. No human society can strongly assert that it does not need the application of *real* justice or humanity for all. Justice can be a combination of capacity, empathy, and compassion in order to achieve direct objectivity called blindness of justice.[1] One may even suppose that justice is always applied in all aspects of family, clan, group, domestic, and international relations. This is what we may call the *automatic* application of justice or humanity. Why do we speak of humanity? The reason is that justice is the foremost principle of humanity, and its concept and spirit cannot survive without kindness, charity, compassion, thoughtfulness, gentleness, empathy, and many other sensations, including the proper understanding of the rights of human beings and their putative dignity.[2] As Rawls expresses it:

> Justice is the first virtue of social institutions, as truth is of systems of thought. A theory however elegant and economical must be rejected or revised if it is untrue; likewise laws and institutions no matter how efficient and well-arranged must be reformed or abolished if they are unjust. Each person possesses an inviolability founded on justice that even the welfare of society as a whole cannot override. For this reason justice denies that the loss of freedom for some is made right by a greater good shared by others. It does not allow that the sacrifices imposed on a few are outweighed by the larger sum of advantages enjoyed by many. Therefore in a just society the liberties of equal citizenship are taken as settled; the rights secured by justice are not subject to political bargaining or to the calculus of social interests.[3]

Thus, when one discusses justice, one does not necessarily allude to the establishment or creation of rights but the feeling that a common thread should exist throughout the lives of all human beings. If this is not true or is something impossible to attain, it should in any event be the normal expectation of human beings. This is because justice is, in its final stage, the application of ultimate good dreams in our mind for others, us, and for nature and animals. Even if we are mad in

[1]Roberts (2014), pp. 129–56, 132–134. Jackson (2009), p. 7.

[2]*Id.*, Jackson, pp. 9, 13 and 23.

[3]Rawls (1999), p. 3.

the scope of our justice, this can also be justice as long as the reflection of the substance of justice is not mad.[4]

Yet, what is the concept of *real* justice and its automatic application? Naturally, the concept of justice differs from case to case and from culture to culture.[5] The fact is that there is no particular framework for setting up the context of justice. Every culture and domestic society has its own pattern of justice.[6] Cultural attitudes may be different for particular social questions. For instance, we permit sexual relations before marriage in Europe. A couple may not even need to get married during their united relations. They may have children and may be the proper parents of the child. A clear example is the legislation of Scandinavian countries and their full acceptance of non-married couples. Couples of the same gender have recently received similar legal rights. According to the old traditions of Europe, the relations of the latter group were not accepted as correct and were not only condemned by most citizens of Europe but also by social authorities. The idea that their relationship could be accepted as normal and be officially recognised for the adoption of a child was impossible to imagine.

The situation for the victim was unjust and immoral whilst for most of the European population, it was just, was the application of appropriate justice and defended the basic principles of morality in Europe. This meant that to understand the situation and improve the condition of the victim, basic morality in Europe had to change in order to adapt to the given circumstances. It required shifting from several hundred years' cultures and traditions to a new modified culture, not only among the citizens of Europe but also within the files and papers of the social authorities. This was probably to reach out to the heart of justice and to develop a better understanding of the truth and application of real justice for all, rather than specifically for same sex relations.

The issue is, however, relatively different in many other countries in Africa, Asie, and particularly in the Middle East. The latter countries may consider the adoption of children by couples of the same gender not fair and therefore unjust against children whilst the Europeans may be of the view that the position of such children is just and follows the provisions of domestic legislations in *democratic* states. Yet, many countries in Asia may not only reject marriage between people of the same sex but may also condemn any sexual relations between them. The legislation in a considerable number of states may even demand serious punishment for such conduct.[7] A clear example of this type of regulation can be seen within the legislation of many Africans states, Iran, Iraq, Afghanistan, and Pakistan. Both Eastern and Western may claim that their laws and interpretations, including their

[4]The problem of the scope of justice and its definition becomes more serious and complicated when we use medical/technical developments for the purpose of identification of criminals. See Karimsky and Simoncelli (2012).

[5]Dan-Cohen (2014), pp. 101–118, at 113–116.

[6]Dan-Cohen (2014), pp. 101–118, at 113–116.

[7]Fischer (1998), pp. 663–702, at 675.

cultural norms, are right and therefore apply the concept of real justice to have achieved the heart of justice.[8]

Consequently, the concept of real justice may vary from one nation or culture to another.[9] Interestingly, in the *United States v. Bauer case,* "the defendants' moral blame, viewed from behind a veil of ignorance, changes when it is revealed that marijuana is part of their religion. Since the defendants are not violating any human rights, there is no barrier to preclude them from presenting this evidence."[10] Different cultures may have different interpretations and definitions of the concept of justice. Thus, real justice may not be real within the norms of another culture. This is because the concept of genuine justice is not based on the cultural norms of one nation or another, although both sides may strongly assert that their understanding of the concept of true justice concerning certain matters is fair. Therefore, the question is what are the concepts of real justice, criminal justice, and as international criminal justice? All these require definitions. Although all three pertain to justice, they can be different from each other.

The reason is that, in the first instance, we need to describe the concept of justice in general. In the second instance, we need to give a definition of criminal justice. This may be in relation to national relations. The third relates to the concept of criminal justice in international relations. All three have to be fair, although they may indicate different cases or different perspectives of the term justice. Nevertheless, it should initially be clear that cultural differences should not be against the cornerstones of the international legal system integrated into human rights law.[11] Let us say, "'evidence' or a 'cultural defense' as a justification, excuse, mitigation, or other means to avoid (full) liability."[12]

Still, from the perspective of judgement, they may be different from one another but are still required to fulfil certain conditions for the definition of justice.[13] Even if we find a definition of justice, it would still be doubtful, as "few, if any, lawyers would accept the view that justice is confined merely to what the law lays down, that is, justice according to law, but what is this justice beyond the law?"[14] One may even ask what the substance behind the law is. There is even the possibility that national criminal justice varies from country to county. A case which has been brought before an Islamic nation's criminal justice system may never be brought to criminal justice in the United Kingdom or *vice versa.* For instance, a man may be condemned for having a few bottles of wine at home by an Islamic criminal court, while the drafting of such an idea in a European criminal court, may create the right

[8] *Id.,* pp. 678–679.

[9] *Id.*, p. 678.

[10] *Id.*, pp. 681–682.

[11] *Id.*, p. 702.

[12] Kymlicka et al. (2014), pp. 1–14, at 2.

[13] *Id.,* pp. 8–9.

[14] Lloyd (1963), pp. 111–124, at 112.

to defamation. Therefore, national criminal justice may have different identities, and different interpretations.

Justice is a little word indeed but also the greatest of all fine words which man cannot hear without feeling better. The word is actually stronger than armed forces, by virtue of hope for justice. The term 'justice', as we will examine later, is very difficult to define. The difficulty is not because it has a limited scope of applicability or a limited function; on the contrary, it is a very broad and demanding term. This makes the definition of justice very tricky and controversial, particularly when it comes to criminal justice. Ross, who belongs to the positivism class goes even further and believes that sometimes any approach to justice makes its definition much sceptical. He says:

> To invoke justice is the same thing as banging on the table: an emotional expression which turns one's demand into an absolute postulate. . . . It is impossible to have a rational discussion with a man who mobilizes 'justice,' because he says nothing that can be argued for or against. His words are persuasion, not argument. The ideology of justice leads to implacability and conflict, since on the one hand it incites to the belief that one's demand is not merely the expression of a certain interest in conflict with opposing interests, but that it possesses a higher, absolute validity; and on the other hand it precludes all rational argument and discussion of a settlement.[15]

The controversy is not based on the subject of justice but the result, its consequences, or its application. It is the application of justice which creates conflicts and ultimately wars. In any event, justice should struggle for fairness; even its practical implementation should be fair. The vision of justice demands that it be rational, lawful, and universal. It should never be subordinate to other political manoeuvres.[16] When a man has been denied access to justice because he is a Jew, Muslim, Christian, Chinese, Russian, or American, then the concept of love for the universality of justice is lost, and every citizen of the world must be seen to have been denied justice. When the overwhelming weight of evidence is for the implementation of appropriate justice and that is rejected by any organisation, then justice's rationality is perceptibly denied.[17]

6.3 Trust in Criminal Justice

In the United States system, justice is proclaimed and is supposed to be 'the truth, the whole truth, and nothing but the truth'. The criminal justice system in the US postulates the theory that the criminal justice system should enforce a punishment that is proportionate to the criminal conduct. The classical aspects of the words surely refer to the significantly higher value of justice and the respect for its

---

[15]Ross (1959), pp. 274–275.

[16]Hoffman (1980), pp. 94–95.

[17]*Id.*

integrity. A court of appeal in the United States has examined the full validity of the interpretation of the above phrase concerning the important function of morality in the definition of justice. This occurred when *U.S. v. Ward*, a tax-evasion case involving a Las Vegas publisher named Wallace Ward, refused to use the word 'truth' and wanted to replace it with the phrase '*fully integrated honesty*'. In 1992, the court concluded that the accused had aptly demanded in the court of first instance "a moral or ethical sense of right and wrong" with his proposed term. This means that, according to the Court, justice presents the philosophy of appropriate moral or ethical considerations, which is the requisite corollary of distinguishing between right and wrong, and *it may have a higher value than the truth*. It is a fully integrated honesty.

Justice is definitely not self-satisfaction. If this were the case, simply everyone fighting everyone else could achieve justice. Nor is justice the giving or receiving of sadness, otherwise the philosophy of justice would always be in danger, not only for suspected persons but also for the victims. It is not easy to define the term "justice." In general, "justice" is a term of art. It is designed neither to create happiness nor to generate sadness. Its function is to find the truth. Everyone is in reality subject to justice, but the reverse may not be true. Justice cannot and should not be subject to anything—this includes a material object, a physical person, an entity, or a state. If these substances or concepts bind it, the notion of justice loses its moral and judicial validity. Justice should thus have its own sovereignty, its own legal territory, and its own autonomy. In fact, the moral and legal values of justice are based on its self-governing status. This means that the sovereignty of justice should be so strong that no monopolization of its strength can occur. Still, we should be very cautious in our demand concerning the definition of justice. To keep insisting against other individuals, by trusting solely in our own definition of justice, may lead to implacable hostility between the relevant parties.[18] Alf Ross, the Scandinavian scholar, masterly writes that:

> To invoke justice is the same thing as banging on the table: an emotional expression which turns one's demand into an absolute postulate. . . . It is impossible to have a rational discussion with a man who mobilizes "justice," because he says nothing that can be argued for or against. His words are persuasion, not argument. The ideology of justice leads to implacability and conflict, since on the one hand it incites to the belief that one's demand is not merely the expression of a certain interest in conflict with opposing interests, but that it possesses a higher, absolute validity; and on the other hand, it precludes all rational argument and discussion of a settlement.[19]

In addition, justice is not the concrete knowledge of empirical laws, legislative frameworks, or a collection of particular norms. In each social case, it has its own

[18]Marcin (1984), pp. 363–391. Available also at http://scholarship.law.edu/cgi/viewcontent.cgi?article=2126&context=lawreview (Accessed June 12, 2016), 366–7.

[19]Ross (1959), pp. 274–275. (Quoted in ibid, 366). However, Ross ignores the fact that a settlement, which ignores the real understanding of justice with love, may create, in the final stage, many more conflicts between the conflicting parties. Here, Ross apparently refers to the question of a settlement between Palestine and Israel, but with a one-eyed justice.

way of reasoning, approach, understanding, theory, philosophy, and conclusion. Through all these issues of presumptions, justice should have one aim. This is what we call protection of its subjects and the truth. Justice must have full substance of authenticity in order to be trusted by the national, regional, or international community as a whole. For instance:

> Show trials, like that of Saddam Hussein, do not deliver justice simply by being held in the country where the crimes were committed. Similarly, prolonged and distant trials such as Milosevic's in The Hague, despite satisfying notions of procedural fairness, do not satisfy the desire for accountability. Not only must justice be done; it must also be seen to be done. There is no geographic formula for justice. If justice is not delivered in a way that builds the trust of the society that demands it, it's not genuine justice and may prove detrimental. Politics in disguise as justice, as some claim is the case at the Bangladesh war crimes tribunal, is not justice. Lingering doubt follows proceedings that are marred by corruption, as those at the Khmer Rouge tribunal. It will be tempting for Libya to give Saif (Gadaffi) a show trial, orchestrated to deliver a predetermined outcome. But in a country that remains divided, a show trial would prolong discord.[20]

Therefore, protection or trust appears to be the first philosophy of justice. Based on this philosophy, justice may achieve a convincing result. In civil, criminal, or procedural matters, the first primary function of justice is also to ensure protection. This may include protection for victims, suspected persons, and witnesses. The second function of justice is the acquisition of a protective judgment. This means justice has to be very cautious in delivering a decision. The reason is that the decision has to be formulated within a specially articulated policy that should not harm any of the subjects of justice, i.e. the accused, the victim, and witnesses. However, the function of justice as a means of protection does not end with the delivery of the decision; justice has to be vigilant to prevent any misunderstanding of its own function, philosophy, and misinterpretation. When new evidence becomes available, the previous judgment may be overturned and the previous evidence becomes invalid. This is because the principles of accurate justice require the appropriate application of the *status quo*.

6.4 Understanding Victims

It is correctly stated "justice system shall reduce suffering in society. The best justice system is that which results in crime being as low as possible, so that there are fewer victims."[21] Even in the case of retribution for victims of injustice, we have to deal with the accused, convicted persons, victims, and witnesses equally. The implementation of international legal and moral norms should not discriminate between victims by any means. The power of the victims should not play a

[20] http://www.theguardian.com/law/2012/jan/24/show-trial-saif-gaddafi-libya (Accessed December 12, 2014).

[21] Greve (2005), p. 516.

significant role in the compensation of wrongs and criminal behaviour. Justice has to be done for every victim, and the world of justice should not wait and weigh the strength of the victims to see if the victims are strong enough to bring the criminal case to a court. For instance, justice did not treat the victims of the Second World War equally. The victims of Europe, because of their influential political position in Great Britain and the United States, received a much higher degree of reparation compared with Japanese victims.[22] This meant that the norms of legality, morality, and love were divided into different portions. Why did the Burmese, Cambodians, Filipinos, Indonesians, Malays, and Vietnamese, most of whom had a Chinese ethnic background, receive less compensation? This may be partly based on the fact that they were from third world developing countries and therefore their lives were not as highly valued as those of the other victims and, as a result, justice could be varied. This means that the strength of justice, legality, and morality was very low and not sufficient to establish proper compensation with love.

However, the system of international criminal justice has tried not to repeat its previous mistakes and has adopted many rules relating to the victims and witnesses of armed conflicts.[23] This means, we are trying to come to a better understanding of international morality, and the problems of the victims are no longer just a question of legality. They exact a high understanding of the question of morality so that what we are doing with victims is morally permitted. I am not by any means building here the concept of morality and rejecting the concept of legality or the necessary questions of *de lege lata*, but I am trying to establish the fact that when we are dealing with the questions of victims, human morality has an intense influence on the concept of legality.[24] A clear example of this is the very serious moral questions which were raised in the reparation for Gaza victims in 2014.

Obviously, none of the victims of the intense killing of civilians, injuries, and destruction were compensated by the Israeli government. Several donor governments increased their contributions because of the principle of morality and love to human beings, or possibly also on the political diplomacy of give and take. The governments, which assisted the victims, could not sit and wait for the victims or the international legal community to bring the perpetrators of grave international crimes under the jurisdiction of the International Criminal Court for prosecution and punishment. Such an idea was and is at present very idealistic when the world powers have monopolised criminal justice, not only in the United Nations Security Council but also in the practice of international criminal courts.

Although the Palestinian state has become a member of the ICC, there is still a long way to go. The sole alternative was the strong presence of the feeling of morality and love as legal norms in order to compensate the victims of the crimes against humanity, war crimes, and genocide. Again, none of those countries, which gave the highest financial help, was apparently under obligation to do so. Here, the

[22] See Seagrave and Seagrave (2003).

[23] Fournet (2014), pp. 56–80, at 56.

[24] *Id.*, pp. 56–80.

only matter, which was significant, was the principle of unity of man, unity of love, unity of pain, and unity of assistance to the neighbour, as jurists express it. However, there was a serious facet of justice which was ignored by all donors. The reference here is to the time under which the criminal conduct of superpower states was carried out against the victims, but they did not receive any practical assistance for their prevention, with reservation to the Persian government's humanitarian assistance.

6.5 Inquiry into Gain

It is not at all imperative to specify here that one should have the same cultural, religious, linguistic, and ethnic background in order to assist or to receive support. The significant question in the Gaza financial aid case was not the norm of love for human beings in accordance with the principles of international human rights law or others but the question of highly realising the fact that those human beings unjustly suffered from the criminal behaviour of the neighbour's government. Human rights law does not and cannot force any nation or state to help another state because it is the victim of unlawful violations. That is why, when we speak about the norm of love, we approach the high stage of humanity where criminal suffering or other catastrophes need urgent help. However, I clearly understand the issues of politics.

Another clear example concerns our help to the victims of natural catastrophes. Here, it is the principle of love, which is working very intensively, and not the question of legality. Almost no state, nation, or entity is under any particularly enforced responsibility to participate in the process of recovery for natural catastrophes, although I fully understand that there are certain relevant rules of the United Nations organisation. What we are doing and what we are contributing materially and financially is solely based on the questions of love for humanity, moral justice for victims, and understanding the question that we do not here need any legal or juridical order as is, unfortunately, required by Hart and others under the principle of primary or secondary obligations.

The point is that those respectful international philosophers did not care about the questions of love for justice when Martin Luther King and others spoke about their merits. Even the movements by the two other international lawyers, Mahatma Ghandi and Nelson Mandela, were not only based on questions of legality but also morality and love. This was because both these international lawyers considered the legality of the actions of the Security Council of the United Nations in each case to be doubtful. In addition, the decisions of governments such as the United States, South Africa, Israel, and the United Kingdom were against the fundamental principles of morality and love for human beings. They were protecting the large investments that they had in the relevant country and the large gains from slave labour of the black population of the world.

These gains were obviously not a question of right and wrong since they directly violated the provisions of all international conventions relating to labour law. *This means that by the principle of love, I mean the inner substance of our shared interests and the inward structure of human rights intentions to bring justice to peace and legality to justice for all individuals. In other words, if the function of law is to arrange regulations for certain behaviours of individuals and the implementation of those regulations, the function of the norm of love is to humanise and regulate the law for better understanding of the terms law, morality, and justice. These brief remarks, taken in connection with what we have already seen above, show that love is an enquiry into our gains. The soiled character of such gain can be seen in the structure of the Socrates talk with the Friend, which may be interesting to read here:*

> *Socrates*: Well now, ask me on my side whether I do not likewise: for I shall agree with you, for my part, that I love good things. But besides you and me, do you not think that all the rest of mankind love good things, and hate evil things?
>
> *Friend*: It appears so to me.
>
> Socrates: And we admitted that gain is good?
>
> *Friend*: Yes.
>
> *Socrates*: On this new showing, everyone appears to be a lover of gain; whereas, by our former way of arguing, no one was a lover of gain. So on which of the two arguments are we to rely, in order to avoid error?
>
> *Friend*: What has to be done, I think, Socrates, is to conceive the lover of gain rightly. The right view of the lover of gain is that he is one who concerns himself with, and thinks fit to make gain from, things from which honest men do not dare to make gain.[25]

6.6 Unity of Love

I have discussed the question of certain matters as a concern of all human beings in another section. However, it is relevant that I complete here the fact that the power of our understanding of the term love is connected to the principle of concern for all human beings, which gives the principle of love much more motivation and presents the fact that the principle of love cannot be treated in isolation as the principle of legality or morality. The interpretation of the last two principles can vary from one nation to another but the former, however, may vary in isolated interpretative tactics; *it is an obvious veracity that the basic principles of humanity which are similar to one another cannot be different from one another's theory*. This is what is called the unity of love. The significant strength of the principle of unity between men is described as being the reason for our development. It is suggested that man should be educated from the beginning as one unity.

> In an improving state of the human mind, the influences are constantly on the increase, which tend to generate in each individual a feeling of unity with all the rest; which, if

[25] http://www.cakravartin.com/wordpress/wp-content/uploads/2008/08/plato-complete-works.pdf (Accessed December 27, 2014).

perfect, would make him never think of, or desire, any beneficial condition for himself, in the benefits of which they are not included. If we now suppose this feeling of unity to be taught as a religion, and the whole force of education, of institutions, and of opinion, directed, as it once was in the case of religion, to make every person grow up from infancy surrounded on all sides both by the profession and the practice of it, I think that no one, who can realise this conception, will feel any misgiving about the sufficiency of the ultimate sanction for the Happiness morality.[26]

The unity of love concerns the substantive parts of a legal system. This not only embraces moral and legal sagacity but also the equanimity of the jurisprudential discipline of the system. *It calls upon our legal, moral, and global responsibility for our wrongful actions. That is to say, superiors and subordinates are both responsible for their actions in the case of a grave violation of the system of human rights law or international criminal law if they act aggressively against the unity of love of human beings.* In the *Barrios Altos v. Peru case* relating to killings committed by death squadrons of the Peruvian armed forces in their alleged fight against the Sendero Luminoso guerrillas, the Inter-American Court clarified that:

... all amnesty provisions, provisions on prescription and the establishment of measures designed to eliminate responsibility are inadmissible, because they are intended to prevent the investigation and punishment of those responsible for serious human rights violations such as torture, extrajudicial, summary or arbitrary execution and forced disappearance, all of them prohibited because they violate non-derogable rights recognized by international human rights law.

... Self-amnesty laws lead to the defencelessness of victims and perpetuate impunity; therefore, they are manifestly incompatible with the aims and spirit of the Convention. This type of law precludes the identification of the individuals who are responsible for human rights violations, because it obstructs the investigation and access to justice and prevents the victims and their next of kin from knowing the truth and receiving the corresponding reparation.[27]

A clear example here concerns criminal violations carried out by the Israeli authorities in the Gaza Strip in the summer of 2014. The crimes were committed under the legal authority of Israel's, laws, which were legitimate due to the national legal order but were unlawful because of their contradiction with the system of international criminal law. This meant that the crimes were violating the unity of love for human beings and the unity of law for protection. A united international movement against the Israeli government finally prevented the crimes. One should not interpret the movement to be against any political party in Israel but against the criminal conduct of the state. Consequently, the opposition was a clear movement organised by the power of love against grave violations which were carried out mostly against civilians. *This unity of love can also be seen in the decisions of the international legal and political community when several million Jewish people*

[26]Utilitarianism by John Stuart Mill (1863), Chapter 3: *Of the Ultimate Sanction of the Principle of Utility, available at* https://www.marxists.org/reference/archive/mill-john-stuart/1863/utility/ch03.htm (Accessed June 10, 2015).

[27]Inter-American Court of Human Rights (IACHR), Case *Chumbipuma Aguirre and others (Barrios Altos) v. Peru*, judgment of 14 March 2001, Ser. C No. 41 and 43.

were barbarously murdered under the orders of the Nazis. Here again, we needed an international movement to prosecute and punish those who had committed these murders against the union of love. With reference to 1915, we find that the international community could not accept the genocide of Armenians by the Turkish government and finally declared those actions to be crimes against humanity or crimes against the unity of love. Kant draws the correct conclusion by addressing *humanity as the union of dignity*:

> Every human being has a legitimate claim to respect from his fellow human beings and is *in turn* bound to respect every other. Humanity itself is a dignity; for a human being cannot be used merely as a means by any human being (either by others or even by himself) but must always be used at the same time as an end. It is just in this that his dignity consists.[28]

By all this, we mean that the unity of love is a union in which we see law and justice united with the principles of love for human beings, humanity, and the ultimate stage of human nature which no longer tolerates violations against human dignity, human morality, and the natural existence of man.

6.7 The Mirror of Criminal Justice

True justice is a combination of true love for victims, the accused, and witnesses. Victims are very significant subjects of human rights law and are entitled to compensation, including material, financial, and if possible, physical compensation. This means that we cannot isolate love from justice and justice from love. It also means that the question of compensation of victims is not a private one, but one of a highly international character. Although we understand that many victims in the history of humans did not receive justice and their rights for compensation were ignored by legal authorities who were responsible for reimbursement, this does not necessarily mean that they were not fulfilling the requirement for compensation but that their cases were not presented by strong voice. That is why, when we are speaking about the norms of love and morality in law, we are not aiming at moralisation or localisation of love in law but to remember that legal norms may not be sufficient for compensation when a nation is politically weak. We are obliged to demand justice with love for all without giving any weight to rights or wrongs. This means that, although love, justice, legality, and morality are four separate questions of the philosophy of science, they are still relevant to one another and cannot be completely isolated from one another's substance.[29]

---

[28] Kant (1996), p. 209.

[29] A clear example is the fact that many academics in law still isolate themselves from questions of criminology and do not bring the science of criminology under the scrutiny of law. It is, however, a fact today that neither the science of criminology nor the concept of pure legality can be treated in isolation.

Justice cannot be right when it has been proven to harm its subjects. In a well-organized society, the principles of justice are publicly known and are understandable to the layman. Those principles have evolved out of the social attitudes of that society. Even so, the principles may not be modified by the will of the legislature; there must be a certain code of conduct within the social structure of the given society that demonstrates the need for modification or a complete change of the principles of justice. This may result in a different understanding of the core principles of justice, and a comparative examination of the issue may demonstrate that the principles of justice differ from one society to another.

Nonetheless, *an inquiry into the laws of various civilizations proves that the differences between the principles of justice do not prevent the application of the theory of fair and objective justice. The basic principles of justice are the same in all societies. The reason for this is that they all want to achieve a reasonable decision in accordance with the evidence. This may be called the powerful intention of love that justice be done. However, the intention of the norm of love is twofold. Justice has to be accompanied by confidence and independent legal personality, and no justice should be deprived of love for the immutability of equality. This aspect of equality should be regarded as an integral part of peremptory norms and an integral part of all science.*

Any attempt by any lawyer or philosopher to say that a theory of law is independent of other theories or science is refutable. Most sciences of law and philosophy are interrelated. This is based on the fact that although we are presenting a new method of thinking, we may, at the same time, use other methods or philosophies, whether as a positive tool of our argumentation and development of the idea or as a negative tool to prove the contrary.[30] *We do not separate the norm of love from other sciences. This means that all sciences are interrelated, including hypothetical, metaphysical, and physical sciences. I am elaborating here the fact that we are bound in law as in other sciences to use the necessary knowledge which may be required for the proof of our intention and the mirror of equality. By this, I also mean that the love norm exists even within other sciences such as natural, medical, and physical sciences.*

The entire natural environment is based on the philosophy of goodness and light. Our natural forest does not like fire in its wood, but water in its roots. That is why pollution constitutes one of the most serious diseases for our natural environment. Medical science, as I have demonstrated in another chapter, benefits from love and love constitutes one of its important principles of equality in the human body. Physical science also cannot be separated from the basic philosophy of love as the centre of its emotion. By this, I mean that the norm of love is not just present in the human spirit, but it is a principal strength in other branches of knowledge. If a theory of love does not have consistency in the science of law, then it must be weaker in the theory of natural law or medicine because the former is our own creation, which is not only drawn from our own nature but also from our instincts. If

[30] Aubert (1963), pp. 41–63, at 41.

we start to understand the very significant nature of this powerful gift in our nature and in our collective decisions, *we may conclude that love is the only norm of the mirror of justice, which not only relies on any prior agreement but on the objectivity of goodwill and not on good faith. This is because the territory of good faith is much more theoretical than practical.*

In respect of this theory, I am aiming to specify the fact that, most of the time, the norm of love does not need, for the implementation of its power, to be given orders by authorities, by sanctions, by legislators, by the Security Council, and by General Assembly resolutions. It also does not need to be supported by Islamic jihad, by European Union jihad,[31] *by Latin American jihadic organisations, by Arab states orders, by African Union approbation, by Jewish traditions of communality, by communist parties' unilateral decisions, or by Indian, Bangladeshi, or Pakistani verdicts.*[32] *The norm of love is self-assurance. This means that when the law is empowered by the force of love, this force is itself self-productive and has self-understanding of the fact that there is a limit to violations and when that limit is violated, it concerns all human beings as a whole.*

The principle concern of all states calls for all nations, all human beings, all cultures, and all rules of law to demand the visibility of love for justice, love for peace, and love for humanity. This principle was announced by the International Court of Justice (ICJ) in the case of the Wall in Gaza and was affirmed by General Assembly (GA) resolution. Although the words of the ICJ and the GA were not respected by the occupying state, it proved that when the law is very seriously violated by any state, justice and injustice no longer have two separate definitions because of the cruelty of the particular conduct. That is why the international lawyer Martin Luther King also referred to the significant message of non-violent behaviour. According to him, 'at the centre of non-violence stands the principle of love ... Love is the only force capable of transforming an enemy into friend.' Obviously, both entities, i.e. the ICJ and GA, could no longer tolerate heavy use of force against the victims. Here, the mirror of justice is worn out.

6.8 Monitoring Criminal Justice

Justice has to guarantee protection for all its subjects, and this protection should not be affected by variations within its principles. Thus, while individual state laws may be wrong or unjust, it does not necessarily mean that the administration of justice as

[31]Jihad here means to work together collectively. See *also* Zawati (2001), pp. 7, 8 and 111–112. "For many centuries most Europeans believed that Islam was a religion of violence which spread by the sword. This was part of the distorted image of Islam, which, as I have argued elsewhere, was the negative identity of Western Europe or Western Christendom—a picture of what it considered itself not to be." Montgomery Watt (1976), p. 390. See *also* Arnold (1961), pp. 115–119; Montgomery Watt (1972), pp. 72–84.

[32]Malekian (2015), pp. 841–842.

a whole is wrong or unjust. Dealing with the principles of justice requires access to the spirit of justice or the strength of a rational mind. Thus, the principles of justice may be slightly different from one another, but the spirit of justice remains the same, yet only if the authority to judge is not misused or misunderstood by judges. The subjects of justice should not be harmed by different principles of justice, and the integrity of justice, as well as judgments, must always be respected by human morality and not just legality. Thus, appropriate justice has to be the cornerstone of the protection of social institutions and their evolution.

Even in a dictatorship, a judge yielding to pressure from politicians or religious groups, etc. should not devalue justice. Justice should always be impartial, and the provisions of legal orders should be interpreted in such a way that a judgment reflects the content or the intention of justice. This means that protecting the subjects of justice should be given priority and any dictatorial rules interpreted in such a way that justice is not devalued by rules which are unreasonable, irrational, illogical, and unfounded within the general theory and policy of justice.[33] That is why the institution of justice should not violate the mirror of justice or purity.

The theory of justice in fact has a very complex structure, consisting of principles, norms, rules, and provisions. They may have an independent characterization, or maybe dependent, although this legal personality of justice does not necessarily have anything to do with its intention and inspiration. The common understanding of the theory of justice demonstrates that there must be reasonable or logical harmonies between its individual parts for protecting its subjects; this means that such harmonies should not devalue the subjects of justice. They have to be used or interpreted in the ethical or legal personality of a person. Justice should remember that each person has her/his own social equality compared with others and is not subject to the imposition of power. This is because, as a general rule accepted by most civilizations, the possession of the power of justice is not encouraged within the theory of pure inspiration of justice.

In other words, the institution of justice may be in danger and may infringe the theory of the protection of different subjects of justice if the power of justice is used in contrast to the motivation of justice. The security of the theory of justice and its principles concerning understanding the rights of its subjects should be guarded within all institutional services of law. This may be more necessary in the case of those who are weak, minor, or dependent. This is because the whole theory of justice is to deliver unwariness, immunity, and love for its subjects. If justice is not based on trust, it will be very difficult to impose and to find the truth. Therefore, one of the basic functions of justice is to create confidence through love for its subjects, including society.

Most significantly, justice must be based on goodwill, good interests, and good results. By "good" we do not necessarily mean the requirements of a good test or good as opposed to bad. 'Good' is meant to represent certain highly qualified values that bring trust and enlightenment to the machinery of justice, to the administration

---

[33]Fischer (1998), pp. 663–702, at 700–702.

of equality, and to the consolidation of the rights of individuals. In fact, looking at the concept of justice and its theory of existence, the ideal result would be the achievement of a just and fair society in which all individuals are respected as full subjects of law with no racial discrimination.

The role of justice is thus to create a balance between what we want and what justice sees as essential for our nature. The concept of justice should not depart from its subjects, black or white, healthy or sick, alive or dead. It should not ignore their personalities, characters, or natures. This is because the theory of justice recognizes that its subjects are not always equal in terms of reasoning, age, or ability. These differences should not be essential for justice and should not make one subject better than another. Love of justice has to be divided for all without any particular privileges. This means that impunity has to be avoided and everyone must be considered the owners and the pillars of justice. The role of the norm of love is to empower the forum of judgment and humanise justice from all malicious treatment.

Thus, the function of the norm in criminal justice is to put a heavy emphasis on the prevention of impunity and bring criminals under the jurisdiction of national, regional, and international courts. The norm of love in law may therefore be defined as a norm that is more than justice, which not only belongs to the knowledge of justice but also to the legal personality of the jurisdiction of a court in order not to be corrupted, deleted, or yield its judgment to the decisions of superpowers. Such is the case concerning the intimated tribunal established for the prosecution and punishment of Saddam Hussein. All these intend the protection of the philosophy of judgment. Thus, justice may be corrupted, the moral norm can be removed, the legal norm can be discharged, conscience can be extinguished, but the love norm of law cannot get rid of the eyewitnesses of human beings as a whole. This means a service from humans to humans in order to observe whether a judgment has been carried out for the sake of justice or for the sake of politics.

6.9 The Rule to Love Justice

With the term ‘justice’, we may have different aims for the protection of the code of ethics, morality and order.[34] The term also has civil and criminal connotations.[35] For instance, the intention at the core of the English and Welsh criminal justice system is to reduce crime by bringing more offenders to justice. The aim is to raise public confidence that the system is accurate and fair and protects all citizens. Whatever the definition of justice may be in the English legal system, the system traditionally relies on legal and moral support. In my opinion, the English system might have a tendency to consider the norm of love a principle. However, by

[34]Roberts (2014), pp. 129–156, at 149.

[35]*Id.*

reducing its subjects, such as witnesses, it has been a "deeply unsatisfactory" system.[36] Although it is true that "a general feature of all branches of English law is its materialistic approach," much of the high reputation of the law rests on the quality of its criminal justice.[37] In addition, the English system of human rights does not necessarily represent the Scottish system. They have two rather different histories. Civil liberties have been defended by "remedies" in English law whilst in Scotland law by "bills of rights."[38] Human rights are an integral part of Scottish law today.[39] Unfortunately, English law is a legal system redressing mostly material loss. "It does not directly deal with abstractions like honour, prestige, general comfort."[40] In any case, the system includes law and justice as part of a package to its citizens, and citizens are those who have drafted the will of justice. There is, therefore, a connection between the integrity of citizens and the practice of the courts to maintain this integrity. However, I will not mention here a considerable number of violations against foreigners through deportation under the English legal system that have been brought before the European Court of Human Rights.[41]

Although we understand that English Common Law is directed and made by judges who apply the legal precedent, *stare decisis*, to the evidence presented to them, this does not reduce the normative aspect of the principle of justice. This is because decisions of the Supreme Court of the United Kingdom or the Court of Appeal are binding for other courts, and judges are then obliged to uphold the necessary requirement for the application and satisfaction of the principle of fairness and not violate the criteria of the truth, trust, accuracy, and impartiality.[42] Hence, the judge has to demonstrate her/his high objective morality with full interest when implementing justice and recognising what constitutes a crime. According to one opinion, even supposing that a court could articulate that the conduct of the defendant would constitute a crime solely in the future but not in the given case, this method of proceeding is still not consistent with the notion of a democratic system.[43]Therefore, a sharp view of the English legal system is that it violates the principle of *de lege lata* and gives a wide authority to the judicial power to create new offences.[44] The English legal system has hence assimilated to "the whims of man"[45] and more specifically "as a man treats his dog, hitting him every

[36]Roberts (2014), pp. 129–130.

[37]Duncan and Derrett (1968), pp. 177–179.

[38]Boyle (2002), p. 1.

[39]Murdoch (2011), pp. 1–7.

[40]*Id.*, p. 178.

[41]Ashton and Finch (2002), pp. 51–54.

[42]It should be bear in mind that, for instance, murder constitutes a Common law crime rather than one established by an Act of Parliament. However a Common law principle may be modified or abolished by the British Parliament. The crime of murder, for example, can no longer be punished by the death penalty but by a life sentence.

[43]Fitzgerald (1962), p. 10.

[44]*Id.*, p. 9.

[45]*Id.*

time he does something to which the master takes exception."[46] More recently, it has been pointed out that pragmatism "appears to be open to doubt whether it should still serve as the basis of an entire legal system in the twenty-first century, especially when it involves sending people to prison."[47]

This means judges must love justice and not hurt the body of justice by their words which will be law. This can be seen in the moral approach taken by the English lawyer Lord Atkin concerning the concept of liability in tort law, which relates to the duty of care and our responsibility for what we have selected or have committed to perform. He stated the following:

> At present I content myself with pointing out that in English law there must be, and is, some general conception of relations giving rise to a duty of care, of which the particular cases found in the books are but instances. The liability for negligence, whether you style it such or treat it as in other systems as a species of "culpa," is no doubt based upon a general public sentiment of moral wrongdoing for which the offender must pay. But acts or omissions which any moral code would censure cannot, in a practical world, be treated so as to give a right to every person injured by them to demand relief. In this way rules of law arise which limit the range of complainants and the extent of their remedy. The rule that you are to *love* your neighbour becomes in law, you must not injure your neighbour; and the lawyer's question, 'Who is my neighbour?' receives a restricted reply. You must take reasonable care to avoid acts or omissions which you can reasonably foresee would be likely to injure your neighbour. Who, then, in law, is my neighbour? The answer seems to be – persons who are so closely and directly affected by my act that I ought reasonably to have them in contemplation as being so affected when I am directing my mind to the acts or omissions which are called in question.[48]

The above text recalls the concept of our responsibility on a religious, theoretical basis. However, in the contemporary modern relations of states, lawyers, judges, prosecutors, and writers, it is an unworkable question when the philosophy of law and justice is analysed in combination with the philosophy of religion. A lawyer is allowed in his legal writing, which is indeed a *political letter,* to refer to any legal philosophy but not the basic principles of religion, even though similar principles may be found in the work of modern writers. However, it is obvious that no principle, even one coming from religious conceptualisation, can be restricted, since it is not the home of its originality which makes sense but the message or the content of the relevant principle.

6.10 Love as a Legal Attitude

The parable of the Good Samaritan has an excellent philosophical definition of neighbour, law, custom, responsibility, and love as an imperative norm of justice, not only to prevent violations but also to cure the injuries caused to the victims.

---

[46] *Id.*, pp. 9–10.

[47] Bohlander and Birkett (2014), p. xxiii.

[48] Donoghue v Stevenson (1932) AC 532, 580.

However, this does not mean that one has to follow it by force of law but by the logic of understanding. The excellent work of Florence Nightingale, the Red Cross, Amnesty International,[49] Human Rights Watch, and United Nations peacekeeping groups originates from the story. It says that a lawyer asked Jesus the following:

> What I shall do to inherit eternal life.
>
> He said to him, what is written in the law? How do you read it?
>
> He answered, you shall love the Lord your God with all your heart, with all your soul, with all your strength, with all your mind, and your neighbour as yourself. He said to him, you have answered correctly. Do this and you will live. But he, desiring to justify himself, asked Jesus, Who is my neighbour?
>
> And Jesus answering said, A certain man went down from Jerusalem to Jericho, and fell among thieves, which stripped him of his raiment, and wounded him, and departed, leaving him half dead. And by chance there came down a certain priest that way: and when he saw him, he passed by on the other side. And likewise a Levite, when he was at the place, came and looked on him, and passed by on the other side. But a certain Samaritan, as he journeyed, came where he was: and when he saw him, he had compassion on him, and went to him, and bound up his wounds, pouring in oil and wine, and set him on his own beast, and brought him to an inn, and took care of him. And on the morrow when he departed, he took out two pence, and gave them to the host, and said unto him, Take care of him; and whatsoever thou spendest more, when I come again, I will repay thee.
>
> Which now of these three, thinkest thou, was neighbour unto him that fell among the thieves? The lawyer said, He that shewed mercy on him.
>
> Then said Jesus unto him, Go, and do thou likewise.

The discussion taken up by Lord Atkin and the above narrative reinforce the fact that justice and love of justice constitute the first necessary clause when establishing an international humane society in which every person is treated equally with dignity and integrity. They denote the fact that justice cannot be achieved with blind eyes but rather by looking at the situation with the concept of love for human beings and by the enforcement of the rules of morality and legality with equity, fairness, and the protection of individual rights. This means that there is a rule to love true justice. Kant's interpretation of the above paragraph is, however, somewhat different. According to him, a superior cannot order the implementation of the norm of love, even though it has the purpose of better treatment. The good nature of the norm has to be understood by man himself and not by the extraneous force of a superior order:

> It is doubtless in this sense that we should understand too the passages from Scripture in which we are commanded to love our neighbour and even our enemy. For love out of inclination cannot be commanded; but kindness done from duty although no inclination impels us, and even although natural and unconquerable disinclination stands in our way is practical, and not pathological, love, residing in the will and not in the propensions of feeling, in principles of action and not of melting compassion; and it is this practical love alone which can be an object of command.[50]

---

[49]For an examination of the term "amnesty," its nature, character, discipline, and some other legal effects, such as releasing a person from criminal or civil consequences, consult O'Shea (2002).

[50]Kant (1948), p. 71.

This philosophy of Kant and his position regarding the norms of love and legality (that we cannot command love) elicited both positive and negative reactions. A number of writers believe that one cannot achieve the concept of love for justice by the force of law or by moral force. Love is just a personal feeling that one has voluntarily taken into consideration.[51] Charles M. Taylor illustrates this more precisely by saying that love and compassion are passions, not actions, and are, therefore, subject to no terms of duties or moral obligations. According to him, "Love, as a feeling, cannot be commanded, even by God, simply because it is not up to anyone at any given moment how he feels about his neighbour or anything else."[52] However, according to other opinions "Kant, and at least some of those who agree with him, have been wrong about love. I want to submit that there is a significant sense in which love may fairly be commanded, and . . .feeling love as an emotion may be a moral obligation under certain circumstances."[53] Joseph Raz also takes the term love into close consideration. He judges that the concept of love is a question of attitude, and it therefore creates moral obligations. Consequently, he argues that some people "believe that there cannot be a duty to love someone. The common reason for this supposed impossibility is that love is an emotion and the emotions cannot be commanded. This is a misguided view of both love and the emotions. Love is an attitude, not an emotion."[54]

Hans Kelsen examines the situation by evaluating and dividing a norm into a minor norm and a higher norm. He therefore goes into the analysis of the sermon. According to him, the validity of the love norm cannot be separated from its authoritative character. For him, all commands cannot be valid and fulfilled; this is because only a competent authority is empowered to create valid norms, and this authority is itself subject to a higher authority. The Jesus commandment in the biblical sense is subject to divine law, and in written law, this power of legislation comes from the political authority in force, which receives its authority from the international legal personality of the state. From his interpretation, it seems that Kelsen does not separate the norm of love from true justice. He indicates that:

> A norm which represents the reason for the validity of another norm is figuratively spoken of as a higher norm in relation to a lower norm. It looks as if one could give as a reason for the validity of a norm the circumstance that it was established by an authority, human or divine; for example. . .'Men ought to *love* their enemies, because Jesus, Son of God, issued this command in his Sermon on the Mount.' But in both cases the reason for the validity is not that God or his son issued a certain norm at a certain time in a certain place, but the tacitly presupposed norm that one ought to obey the commands of God or his son. . . The norm whose validity is stated in the major premise ("One ought to obey God's commands") is included in the supposition that the norms, whose reason for validity is in question, originate from an authority, that is, from somebody competent to create valid norms: this norm bestows upon the norm-creating personality the "authority" to create norms. The mere fact that somebody commands something is no reason to regard the command as a valid norm, a norm binding the individual at whom it is directed. Only a competent

[51]Taylor (1970), p. xii.

[52]*Id.*, pp. xii, 252–3.

[53]Sankowski (1978), pp. 100–110.

[54]Raz (1994), p. 11.

> authority can create valid norms; and such competence can only be based on a norm that authorizes the issuing of norms. The authority authorized to issue norms is subject to that norm in the same manner as the individuals are subject to the norms issued by the authority.[55]

Martin Luther King, the *true international lawyer* with the theory of the power of love for justice, refers to the same narrative for a better understanding of life's paths and prevention of constant violations against human beings. "True compassion is more than flinging a coin to a beggar; it is not haphazard and superficial. It comes to see that an edifice which produces beggars needs restructuring."[56] This edifice refers, *inter alia*, to the building of our morality, legality, justice, and the disappearance of love in the basic structure of justice. He goes further and clarifies that:

> Power properly understood is nothing but the ability to achieve purpose. It is the strength required to bring about social, political and economic change. ... What is needed is a realization that power without love is reckless and abusive, and love without power is sentimental and anaemic. Power at its best is love implementing the demands of justice, and justice at its best is power correcting everything that stands against love.

Summing up all these opinions, none of the above philosophers or lawyers may object to the fact that the rule to love justice is certainly not emotion. Kant and Taylor want love not to constitute command but a perpetual virtue of justice. Raz sees it as a moral obligation. This is because love is attitude and this can be attitude for justice, too. Similarly, King draws the conclusion that the strength of love demands good power of justice. *One may also draft and debate many other views here. If we suppose that the term love unavoidably involves having certain emotions, one cannot easily disprove its commandability by purporting that love is solely an attitude. Many of these conclusions may overlap one another, and the term love may have both emotional and ultra-functional layers at the same time. Whatever the physical or geophysical nature of love is, the fact is that with the term "love" we mean the way to achieve true justice. Love of justice therefore constitutes an imperative necessity if our purpose is to achieve the substance of justice with transparency and transparency alone.*[57] *The metaphysics of love and justice have to be the same.*

6.11 Homogeneity Between Criminal Justices

Whilst it is true that the word justice has different definitions, it should still be fair and the non-existence of fairness cannot be called the existence of fairness. This is what we call the fine line between the identities of the word justice in all legal

[55]Kelsen (2016).

[56]Luther King (2008), p. 31.

[57]Mendus (1999), pp. 57–75.

systems. Criminal justice, which permits the application of capital punishment, is not and cannot be said to be fair and just. The relevant authorities of a given society, who base their arguments on different philosophies, may object to this idea. Whatever the argumentation of these philosophies may be, it is a fact that a dispute, which is based on the killing of a person because he or she has committed murder, is naturally against the basic fundamental values of human rights law. *A human rights law principle cannot permit the killing or murdering of a person who has committed murder. Such interpretation must be seen as a violation of the rights of the accused person and is consequently subject to retribution. As we have said elsewhere, in the present development of international human rights law conventions, no killing of a person is legal, especially when the machinery of criminal justice carries it out.*

This means that there are similarities between justice in the United Kingdom and justice in Iran; justice in Sweden and justice in Nigeria; justice in the Netherlands and justice in Iraq; justice in the United States and justice in Kuwait; justice in Canada and justice in Rwanda. This is called the first principle of humanity and is recognised by most states and cannot be diminished by those states, which are not yet parties to certain international conventions. Here, we are addressing our arguments to the authorities and lawyers who demand the application of capital punishment in the realm of a particular jurisdiction. Justice also relies on several facts, *inter alia,* the principles of *jus cogens,* the principle of *concern of all states*, the principle of human requirement for the unity of the same object, and the principle of *humanisation*, all of which denote the proper application of justice and prohibition of the application of cruel punishment.

A criminal justice system which permits torture and sanctions its application is obviously not fulfilling the first principles of fair justice.[58] *Such a criminal system, whether it's called Scandinavian democracy, Commonwealth law, Chinese communistic monopolisation, the Latin American system, Islamic law transmission, or Israeli law enforcement, surely violates the principles of similarities in a fair criminal justice system. There should not be any difference between the first fair principles of justice in one nation with those in another. This is regardless of whether justice is applied by a Jewish criminal court or by an Islamic criminal system.* They have to preserve or respect the fundamental principles of justice. This is what I call the basic similarity principles, which are crucial for the definition of a fair criminal justice system and the expression of love for human dignity. In 1988, the Inter-American Court of Human Rights delivered its first judgment in the controversial case of *Velasquez v. Honduras State*. The case related to the commission of grave human rights violations, such as systematic forced disappearances by the State of Honduras. With respect to the rights and freedoms recognised by the Convention and the duties of the state to ensure the free and full exercise of those rights by every person subject to its jurisdiction, the Court came to the conclusion that:

[58]Trechsel (1997), pp. 94–119, at 100.

> This obligation implies the duty of the States Parties to organise the governmental apparatus and, in general, all the structures through which public power is exercised, so that they are capable of juridically ensuring the free and full enjoyment of human rights. As a consequence of this obligation, the State must prevent, investigate and punish any violation of the rights recognised by the Convention.[59]

Evidently, the Court did not solely address its decision to the Latin American States; it concerns all states. The Court refers to the obligations of any state to prevent violations of the fundamental rights of individuals which have been globally recognised under various international conventions on human rights. It even clearly stated that a state not only has obligations for the omission of international human rights law carried out by its entities but has also recognised obligations in the case of crimes committed by private individuals. The Court went on to say that "An illegal act which violates human rights and which is initially not directly imputable to a State, can lead to international responsibility of the State, not because of the act itself, but because of the lack of due diligence to prevent the violation or to respond to it as required by the Convention."[60] This text passage from the Court obviously connotates the homogeneity which has to exist between the criminal justice systems of different nations with the core intention of the protection of human rights principles.

Unfortunately, the Court did not force the state of Honduras to implement the criminal proceedings in order to arrive at its decision. It only asked the state to pay a fair compensation to the relatives of the victims. This meant that criminal proceedings for the prosecution of the accused persons were not truly established. Regardless of this shortcoming of the Court in the application and implementation of its judgment, the decision of the Court refers to clear obligations of states to hinder any violations of fundamental rights of their inhabitants. Here, I intentionally choose the word inhabitants and not population with the intention to emphasise that the latter may not cover all persons who may be under the territorial, civil, or criminal jurisdiction of the state in question. The term "inhabitants" may also include all foreigners or visitors who are in the territory of the state in question. In any event, the Court aimed at homogenisation of criminal justice and its high moral and legal validity.

I am aware that the principles of justice are grossly violated in many states, for example, in Iran, U.K., Canada, Russia, China, Saudi Arabia, and North Korea.[61] The principle of love or the norm of love for justice, humanity, and respect in the above-mentioned countries is not only infringed but is even prevented. In other words, justice is regarded as a matter of satisfaction of the sovereign's constitution, and the latter as the way to control the relevant system, and the system as the way to improve personal requirements of the leaders, and the leaders as the way in which

---

[59] I/A Court H.R., *Velásquez Rodríguez Case*, Judgment of July 29, 1988. Series C No. 4, para. 166.

[60] I/A Court H.R., *Velásquez Rodríguez Case*, Judgment of July 29, 1988. Series C No. 4, para. 172.

[61] Examine also Goodale and Merry (2007).

justice, love, humanity, respect, and morality are interpreted in criminal and civil courts. In fact, the interpretations of constitutions have become a personal matter for the leaders. We may also list several Latin American countries whose soldiers have carried out similar violations against their own population.[62] This means that the rule of love has been replaced with the rule of personal power and the substance of justice has not only been corrupted in the court of jurisdiction but also by the legislative power.

6.12 Judgment

As a phenomenon of our natural being, judgment is one of the integral parts of our capacities. We are thus able to express our opinions concerning certain matters of interest. This ability is employed during the whole of our lifespan. Recognition of justice is not solely restricted to the persons who are dealing with questions of prosecution and punishment within the decisions of the civil or criminal courts. All of us judge, all the time. Actually, an individual's judgment starts from one's earliest days of life and continues throughout the rest of her/his life for the simple reason of preservation. An individual receives love and gives love, not for the reason of legal or moral requirements but because she/he wants her/his rights not to be violated under the given social circumstances. We demand our natural rights via positive law. These natural rights of individuals, which are today an integral part of human rights law, are expressed in the following excellent philosophy of Lysander Spooner:

> Children learn the fundamental principles of natural law at a very early age. Thus they very early understand that one child must not, without just cause, strike, or otherwise hurt, another; that one child must not assume any arbitrary control or domination over another; that one child must not, either by force, deceit, or stealth, obtain possession of anything that belongs to another; that if one child commits any of these wrongs against another, it is not only the right of the injured child to resist, and, if need be, punish the wrongdoer, and compel him to make reparation, but that it is also the right, and the moral duty, of all other children, and all other persons, to assist the injured party in defending his rights, and redressing his wrongs. These are fundamental principles of natural law, which govern the most important transactions of man with man. Yet children learn them earlier than they learn that three and three are six, or five and five ten. Their childish plays, even, could not be carried on without a constant regard to them; and it is equally impossible for persons of any age to live together in peace on any other conditions.[63]

Yet we not only judge everything that happens during our daily life, but we also reassess some of our daily judgments, even when we are taking a break or resting for the night. This is because we take, all the time, certain necessary decisions for certain actions which seem to be important for us. These decisions contain our

---

[62]*Id.*

[63]Spooner (2015), p. 9.

personal judgment. Obviously, our judgement not only considers directly or indirectly the questions of legality but also the moral consequences of our decisions. Our decisions are, in other words, a combination of all these matters. Of course, some of our judgements affect only our own interests, but some may seriously involve others, too. That is why, by the force of law and morality, we consider the consequences of our decisions and judgements. The following section may illustrate the situation.

6.12.1 Personal Judgement

In 2014, a Swede in Stockholm assisted a very seriously handicapped 92 year-old woman to reach her flat because of very heavy snow in the street which made passage impossible, not only for cars but also for pedestrians. He was unable, because of the circumstances, to park his car in an appropriate spot. As a result, he was penalized for the position of his car. The Swede complained to the courts of first and second instance, but they rejected his applications. Finally, he submitted a complaint to the Supreme Court, which overturned the decisions of both courts and declared that, because of the circumstances, the penalty-holder had to assist the handicapped 92 year-old woman and therefore the penalty should not have been awarded. Here, there are several matters at issue.

The court considered the principle of morality and the principle of love to help our neighbours as two of the most significant reasons to assist the elderly woman. The offender has to give priority to one of the principles of morality, legality, and love. Evidently, since he was driving a car, he was aware that there would be a penalty for the wrong position of the car. He had to decide several matters in a very short time. This meant that when he made his decision, he had to ignore the law in force because of the circumstances and serious danger for the elderly handicapped woman. His decision could not create any *danger* for anyone. Apparently, personal morality took priority over legal norms, and this morality was not against the law since many international conventions encourage giving cooperation and assistance to disabled persons. Furthermore, regardless of her physical condition, she was a 92 year-old woman who needed immediate help because of the snow and frozen condition of the environment.

The court decision relied on observation of a particular situation involving the concept of morality rather than by a rigorous set of legal or ethical reasoning. Still, the judgment of the court did not harm the legal norm, since the intention of the law (that one has to park his car in particular location) is not to harm its subjects but rather to create good order. In certain situations, a judge has to decide whether the substance of the law has to be fulfilled for the jurisdiction of justice or whether the order of the law should be fulfilled as such. The intention was to bring the situation to a greater good. Sure, the moral judgement here was a decision taken by the offender, but not a conclusion, since the latter had to be taken back by the authority who wrote the penalty or by the court. As one philosophy puts it, we should seek the well-being of people rather than loving legal principles or our superior order and further that only "one thing is intrinsically good, namely, love: nothing else. Love, in this context, means desiring and acting to promote the well-being of people."[64] Here, every piece of the case comes under the provisions of the Convention on the Rights of Persons with Disabilities and its Optional Protocol of 2008.

6.12.2 Nobility of Judgment

We must admit that sentiment implies judgement manipulated or caused by emotion. One of our most normal judgements starts from our personal sentiments towards one another. The actions of certain individuals may be very familiar to us, even though some of their actions may not be correct for us. A clear example of this is our feelings towards our parents, our children and so forth, or our repugnance concerning certain matters. However, we still do not protest against those who we like, even though we do not like their actions. Although we may sometimes, in certain situations, protest against them, this is mostly to advise them, and it is personal.

One of the strongest reasons for our soft judgements concerning the people nearest to us rests on the fact that we are accustomed to their actions and therefore their actions do not bother us. That is why in certain criminal procedures, although one may know about the ill of the actions of the accused and its effects on society, a person who knows about the criminal behaviour may not come to the court as a witness to testify against the offender. Therefore, the judgment may not be appropriate. The non-appearance of the person does not mean a refusal of her/his duty to give testimony but simply the administration of a justice one may not know about her/his valuable position concerning the case. This is a kind of cooperation, complicity, assistance, or at least a protection of the criminal actions of the accused. However, it is also true that if the witness is the victim, the situation may be completely different. That is why I draw attention to the fact that there are three norms of the law which are visible or invisible depending on the circumstances of the case.

Although these three norms may be an integral part of the same packet, they may function differently. The legal norm calls on us to speak and rely on proper information. The moral choice may assist us in helping the person who is accused and has a close relationship with us. The love principle weighs all matters, as the legal and moral principles do, but with the difference that the love norm may evaluate the configuration of the consequences of the causes of the situation

[64]Joseph Fletcher. For civil rights, see also Ricardo Juan Sanchez, Access to Spanish Civil justice by means of Prosecution Services for the protection of the social and economic rights: legal possibility and structural determinants (2015), available at https://www.researchgate.net/publication/277570894_Access_to_Spanish_Civil_justice_by_means_of_Prosecution_Services_for_the_protection_of_the_social_and_economic_rights_legal_possibility_and_structural_determinants_Acceso_a_la_justicia_civil_espanola_ (Accessed August 10, 2016).

which is raised and whether such acts were really strong violations of human rights or humanitarian laws. These are all our personal judgement but may not yet be our final decision. For instance, sexual violence is an inexcusable infringement of moral codes and public international law. Such criminal conduct affects the entire life of the victim of an international armed conflict.[65] It is here that, if the violation is grave and systematic, like genocide, it strongly calls upon our sentiment that the violation has to be prevented, prosecuted, and punished.[66]

Here, human beings are thinking in the same way, as they feel that the shared dignity of human beings has been violated and has to be given attention.[67] *This strong will falls under the love norm. Thus, justice becomes a requirement for love of human beings and love becomes a response to help justice. This means that there is a visible and an invisible power in the norm of love connecting with our core values in legal regulations and our judgements. These guide us to recognise good and bad acts such as rape, torture, or murder.*[68] *That means that there is an energetic vibration in our will in order to find the truth and to prevent the darkness of injustice.* According to Plato, who is an enthusiast of the unity of man and the universe, justice has to keep its *nobility* and love for the truth; otherwise, it loses its validity and strength:

> There are many noble things in human life, but to most of them attach evils which are fated to corrupt and spoil them. Is not justice noble, which has been the civilizer of humanity? How then can the advocate of justice be other than *noble*? And yet upon this profession which is presented to us under the fair name of art has come an evil reputation. . . . we are told that by ingenious pleas and the help of an advocate the law enables a man to win a particular cause, whether just or unjust; and the power of speech which is thereby imparted, are at the service of him who is willing to pay for them. Now in our state this so–called art, whether really an art or only an experience and practice destitute of any art, ought if

---

[65]The Preamble of G.A. Res 61/143, (19 December 2006) reads that "Recognising that violence against women is rooted in historically unequal power relations between men and women and that all forms of violence against women seriously violate and impair or nullify the enjoyment by women of all human rights and fundamental freedoms and constitute a major impediment to the ability of women to make use of their capabilities." The definition of sexual violence was first formulated in the *Prosecutor v. Akayesu,* Judgment, Case No. ICTR-96-4-T, 2 September 1998. Similarly, in the *Prosecutor v. Kvocka et al.,* Case No. IT/98-30/1-T, 2 November 2005, the court stated that "The Tribunal considers sexual violence, which includes rape, as any act of a sexual nature which is committed on a person under circumstances which are coercive. Sexual violence is not limited to physical invasion of the body and may include acts that do not involve penetration or physical contact." para. 598.

[66]See the ICC Elements of Crimes, UN Doc. PCNICC/2000/1/Ass 2(2000), sexual violence, as an enumerated crime against humanity in Article 7(1)(g)-6 and as war crimes Article 8(2)(b)(xxii)-6 and (2)(e)(vi)-6.

[67]For example, in the consideration of the establishment of the Yugoslav Tribunal, Security Council Resolution 820 of 17 April 1993 condemned: "All violations of international humanitarian law, including in particular, the practise of "ethnic cleansing" and the massive, organized and systematic detention and rape of women, and reaffirms that those who committed or who have committed or order or ordered the commission of such acts will be held individually responsible in respect of such acts."

[68]See *Prosecutor v. Tadic,* Judgment, Case No. IT-94-1-A, 15 July 1999, para. 222.

possible never to come into existence, or if existing among us should listen to the request of the legislator and go away into another land, and not speak contrary to justice.[69]

Discussions contrary to justice are contrary to our personal dignity and violations of the norms of love for justice. At the same time, we must not forget that our judgement is not free of our personal capacities. Some of our most important capacities are our social, economic, political, academic and/or cultural knowledge. Surely, all of us have all these kinds of capacities, depending on our personal understanding of acquired knowledge and experience. One may obtain one's knowledge from different colleges or from other independent sources. Still, most people may not have academic knowledge but may have a high degree of understanding of social, economic, political, moral, and international values and are capable of distinguishing criminal behaviour. *We should not forget the fact that most of the population of the international village is not educated in law but has a natural education in love. If the world were in the hand of judges, prosecutors, and judges, it would only subsist in aggressive war.*

It is also a basis for criminal justice that almost any person who has, reached the legal age in a given society has the capacity to distinguish between right and wrong and must be recognized as being accountable for any wrongful conduct. This is regardless of the fact that our personal judgements may differ from one another. Yet, even if one is a very highly educated person or expert in law, this does not necessarily mean that the relevant person is more reliable than other ordinary people are. It is here that we speak about the three norms attaining different levels of understanding in our judgements.

6.12.3 Disobedience to Criminal Judgment

The president of a country may have a highly recognised juridical education, but this does not mean that the person is capable of good judgement or has a good moral understanding of the rights of others. It is also true that one may often find the most powerful code of morality, hospitality, or expression of practical love among the citizens of villages or small cities. Different factors are decisive here. A person may kill, or give the order for killing or the destruction of the civilisation of neighbouring countries without feeling that he is violating the system of the international criminal law or fundamental principles of human rights law.[70] You may still respect her/him.

---

[69]http://www.cakravartin.com/wordpress/wp-content/uploads/2008/08/plato-complete-works.pdf. (Accessed May 20, 2015).

[70]See, for instance, *Prosecutor v. Furundzija*, Judgment Case No. IT-95-17/-A 21 July 2000; *Prosecutor v. Krstic*, Judgment, Case No. IT-98-33-T, 2 August 2001; *Prosecutor v. Kvocka et al*, Judgment, Case No. IT-98-30/&-T, 2 November 2001. A clear example here is the British Prime Minister Tony Blair and his grave breaches of the system of international criminal law and the general principles of law in Iraq.

> It really pays to murder, and when a thing pays, it becomes respectable. Your old-fashioned murderer killed from fear, from hate -- or even from love, very seldom for substantial profit. None of these reasons is quite -- respectable. But to murder for position -- that's different, because when you've gained the position, nobody has a right to criticize the means. Nobody will refuse to meet you if the position's high enough. Think of how many of your statesmen have shaken hands with Hitler.[71]

According to some criminal lawyers, a law is a law and we should respect its content. An example is the criminal law of Iran. This means, for instance, if the criminal law of a state makes alcohol consumption or possession a criminal offence, the courts of the relevant state have to follow the law, even though such regulations are against the fundamental principles of international human rights law and freedom of individuals. These are freedom of speech, freedom of assembly, and freedom of practising one's beliefs.[72] It means they see the application of punishment as the proper implementation of the law because it is law, order, and legislation of the country. This is the case even if the punishment is severe, such as imprisonment, capital punishment, or corporal punishment, e.g. whipping and cutting off members of the body. For these criminal lawyers, the law is a superior order or discipline which should not only be fulfilled by laymen but also by judges and prosecutors. This means that the judge should use love for the maintenance of law and not love for the reason of implementation of appropriate justice, morality, and the real value of law for the upholding of dignity of man.[73]

Again, the relevant criminal lawyers believe that we should respect a superior order at all times and to the highest degree. Although one may understand the views of these lawyers, it may not be possible to implement the basic structure of their argumentation at all times and it may endanger the security of humans. Providing three examples may be necessary here. *One example* may come from the *ad hoc* jurisdiction of a considerable number of international criminal tribunals which have come to the conclusion that, even if fulfilment of superior orders is a necessary corollary of national legislations, subordinates should still give proper consideration to the structure of an order.[74] At first glance, carrying out an order to murder, rape, or commit genocide against the population of a village may seem necessary by the subordinate officers.[75] At second glance, the subordinate is personally

---

[71]Graham Greene, The Ministry Of Fear (1943), 47.

[72]*Torture and Modernity: Self, Society and Iran* (1993).

[73]For instance, Judge *Salevati* is one of the notoriously known Iranian judges who entirely obeys the Islamic regime's criminal system. Cases in which other judges would not dare to be involved are addressed to his office. He sentences almost every accused to the death penalty without *hearing* the case page by page as normal justice usually requires.

[74]*Prosecutor v. Furundzija,* Judgment Case No. IT-95-17/-A 21 July 2000; *Prosecutor v. Krstic,* Judgment, Case No. IT-98-33-T, 2 August 2001; *Prosecutor v. Kvocka et al,* Judgment, Case No. IT-98-30/&-T, 2 November 2001.

[75]Article 7(3) of the ICTY Statute captures indirect criminal responsibility in these terms: 'The fact that any of the acts referred to in articles 2 to 5 of the present Statute was committed by a subordinate does not relieve his superior of criminal responsibility if he knew or had reason to

responsible for evaluating the content of the order.[76] This is because such reasoning does not release the subordinate from criminal responsibility for her/his criminal behaviour under international criminal law.[77]

The subordinate must consider the order and must see whether the implementation of the order is necessary for the strategy of war or justice.[78] An order for massive killing of civilians and any disobedience against such criminal order may not endanger the position of a conflicting party. Besides this, an order which in itself violates the provisions of the international humanitarian law of armed conflict or is against the basic principles of international criminal conventions or international human rights law cannot be regarded as a lawful order.[79] Although we are aware that a subordinate may not have the right to question the substance of the order, it is still the duty of all persons to evaluate the essence and purpose of the orders.[80] The principle of disobedience was encouraged "as a weapon against British rule in India" by Gandhi. The principle was called *satyagraha* or insistence on truth. It consists of four elements. These are:

(a) One's duty to struggle against unjust laws by civil disobedience. (b) Our disobedience should solely be based on the codes of non-violence and love. (c) The participants should see their struggle as offering their bodies for the soul of justice and the reestablishment of their natural rights by natural law. Finally, (d) the total amount of these reactions should change hearts, minds, and laws. It is only in this case that one can say that the principle has been effective.[81]

The *second position* is when a superior gives a person an order to push a button for the use of an atomic bomb against another nation. Such orders are naturally against love for justice and against the legality and morality principles. Such orders are evidently invalid even if we present them under the auspices of self-defence. Dropping an atomic bomb against any nation or group is clearly against all moral and legal principles of human civilisation and cannot be defended by any legal, moral, or love principle.

The *third example* relates to a Swedish police order. The police, in order to arrest a driver suspected of not having paid for his petrol in a petrol station, ordered the security officer at a bridge to open the bridge. This was in order to prevent the driver

---

know that the subordinate was about to commit such acts or had done so and the superior failed to take the necessary and reasonable measures to prevent such acts or to punish the perpetrators thereof.'

[76]Knoops (2008), p. 251.

[77]Article 7(3) of the ICTY Statute.

[78]See Rasim Delid, Case No. IT-04-83-T, Trial Judgement, ICTY, (15 Sept. 2008), paras. 364–368.

[79]Gaeta (1999), p. 172, at 188–191.

[80]*Id.*, pp. 188–189.

[81]Gandhi (2001, 2015). Martin Luther King. See also Vischer (2014), p. 211.

from escaping. Unfortunately, the driver continued his speed and both passengers died in the car because of the order. The question is whether the police could give such an order or whether the security guard for the bridge had to follow the order to carry out such a request.

Government authorities may know about the unlawful activities of their own government inside or outside the country but may choose to be silent, even if they know that speaking up might prevent the death of even a single human being. However, they may still choose to be silent in order to protect their own position. A highly distinguished judge for the prosecution of those who paid for sex in Stockholm was himself actually paying for sex on weekends and has still kept his position.[82] A chief prosecutor who was prosecuting people for paying for sex was himself engaged in the same business by using the computer in his office in the court to view child pornography and purchase.[83] Likewise, a chief police officer involved in reporting sex crimes and assisting women was himself engaged in forcing and threatening young women to sell him sex in the same country.[84] In 2015, another prosecutor who was involved in over 50 instances of sex crimes, including against children, came under criminal prosecution. Here, I am presenting one of the most highly developed democratic countries in the world. This means that when we refer to personal judgements, we do not mean that all judgements are correct and are bound by moral or love codes. Obviously, neither the judge, nor the chief prosecutor, nor the police officer had any respect or love for justice, nor did they have any respect for the law or nature of the Swedish regulations.

6.12.4 Capacity of Judgement

I must assume that having knowledge of the law does not necessarily mean that we can judge much better than others do or render accurate decisions. This is because judgement is not just a question of knowing the law but also a question of the moral and social capacities of a person and her/his attitudes towards an equal understanding of the values of social norms, natural phenomena, and the standards of moral and love codes for justice.

The anatomy of our judgement is the composition of our personal understanding of evidence and our understanding of the law and the integration of both these understandings into one single conclusion, but this does not mean that we should violate the principles of legality, morality, or love. The reason is that, although these principles may not be the conditions for our judgement, international human

[82](18-05-2007), http://www.aftonbladet.se/nyheter/article11071478.ab, (Accessed May 19, 2015).

[83](26-02-2013), http://www.dn.se/sthlm/aklagare-kopte-sex-pa-stockholmshotell/. (Accessed May 19, 2015).

[84](28-06-20110), http://www.expressen.se/nyheter/polischefen-kampade-for-kvinnors-ratt--och-kopte-sex/ (Accessed May 19, 2015).

dignity requires of us that the judgement has to be fair, impartial, true, and rational. This is what I call love for justice, love for truth, and love to keep human beings from unlawful suffering, which is an integral part of the provisions of international criminal law, international human rights law, international criminal justice, European Union law, and the Islamic and the Jewish norms.[85] If these laws are not incorporating these very basic building blocks of justice, they are obviously violating their own system of jurisdiction and "such situations are invalid."[86]

The fact is that the question of civil, criminal, and personal judgements is so sensitive and so imperative that one can never reach an absolute conclusion. This is especially true in the case of statements of a witness before a criminal court. A personal judgement not only varies on mental abilities but also on physical capacities. By physical capacities, I mean, *inter alia*, the physical conditions of a person.[87] Thus, a person who is suffering from a constant pain and various diseases may express his judgement in accordance with his pain.[88] This is why we have a number of rules concerning medical judgments and consent given by sick or very ill people.

A clear example is the Helsinki Declaration on Medical Ethics of 1975.[89] A person who is raped during armed conflict or has been subjected to sexual abuse has a high degree of experience of what is meant by rape. Yet, a person who only has one leg and lost his leg during an armed conflict may have quite different opinions concerning the rules of warfare. This is because his judgement concerning the rules of humanitarian law of armed conflicts is affected due to the amputation of his leg. Moreover, I may say that a person who is looking at the works of Pablo Picasso, Leonardo da Vinci, Vincent van Gogh, and Salvador Dali has quite different opinions from a person who has just one eye. Similar conclusions may be drawn concerning people who are suffering from colour blindness. They may have a different opinion concerning the art of the above artists.

My conclusions are also similar to the above concerning the sound of musical instruments and musical symphonies, which depend on different people's physical capacities and understanding of classical music. Our judgement may vary all the time and to varying degrees, depending on the circumstances of the time.[90]

[85]There is actually an established legal duty for the members of the European Union to deliver fair judgment. Lagerwall (2014), p. 11, at 11–12.

[86]*Id.*, p. 11.

[87]Engelhardt and Spicker (1976), pp. VII and XIII. xv.

[88]For instance, see Conley et al. (1992).

[89]www.wma.net/e/policy/b3.htm. (Accessed March 8, 2015).

[90]Similarly, our judgment is the same concerning our interpretation of love. Due to certain situations, our judgment is so strong and ambitious that we may express it through loving a person. Examples are our pure love towards a girl or a boy, towards our children, towards our parents and friends. All of them express our love and our deep concern and shape our tendency concerning certain important judgments. I say that I love this girl or boy because I judge her or him to be an admirable person. Yet one must not forget that our judgment can also be affected by the judgments of the person that we love. But by these loves, we cannot and we should not hinder the value of human integrity.

This is also true in the case of our opinion as a witness in a criminal case. In some circumstances, like the war in the former Yugoslavia, there may be many indigenous peoples with different backgrounds and different cultural and religious attitudes towards the methods and the concept of war crimes.

This means that, although the testimony of a witness for the implementation of justice is substantially useful and productive for the discovery of the crime and proof of guilt, other mentioned factors may also affect the value of the testimony. In other words, the witnesses must neither control justice, nor be controlled by justice, nor should they be controlled by the accused person's social, economic, and political positions or power. The purpose is to keep the objectivity of witnesses during the criminal proceedings. This is a difficult task of justice and proceedings in a criminal trial: to access authentic evidence and appropriate testimony of witnesses.

6.12.5 Keeping the Quality of Judgment

To understand the nature of judgement, one may introduce a chain of people with different legal and moral abilities. Here, the most important matter is that all those people have the capacity of judgement, capacity of understanding to think, and the capacity of taking decisions but with different codes of ethics. One important thing is that we have different types and degrees of capacities for our judgements. Also important to these capacities is our capacity to judge criminal cases and criminal matters, although we may not have the required knowledge of criminal law, such as when we protest against genocide, crimes against humanity, and crimes committed in Syria and Iraq. Regardless of this shortcoming in our juridical and criminal knowledge, our opinion or testimony may still be of practical value for the machinery of jurisdiction, for the International Criminal Court, for the prevention of international crimes by our governments, and for the reduction of discrimination.

It is our purpose to discuss the fact that, although legal and moral codes are based on certain reasons and certain ethical, philosophical, or theoretical principles, they still have to keep their objectivity regarding certain very grave violations of the system of international human rights law. We understand that norms of law are norms of law and obligatory, but the fact is that the putative norms of morality are highly recognised criteria for stating the content of the norms of law. This is because we may revalidate norms of law with our interpretation and disregard them in different ways.

The Court's judgments are based on official evidence, personal judgements are based on ethical reasoning of human nature, and international judgements of populations of the world are generally based on principles that are the same within most cultures and have, more or less, the same values within the civilisations of humans. "It is pleasing to remark the similarity, or, rather, the identity, of those conclusions which pure, unbiased reason, in all ages and nations, seldom fails to draw, in such juridical inquiries as are not fettered and manacled by positive institutions."[91] Here we are not just referring to law and morality but the very high value of the principle of love in our juridical system which has to be recognised if we are going to save humanity from grave violations by our own governments. We have to realise that our judgements, laws, and conducts cannot be proper without love.

A secured justice is love and when we have justice, we have shared love with human society, human integrity, and the value of unity of man. This means that love is fundamentally the value of appropriate justice. Whether I have succeeded in what I professed to tell here is for the reader to decide. However, with the norm of love we are facing only one unity and that unity is human value, and human value is our dignity and our dignity the existence of a national justice, the prediction of a regional justice, the notion of an international justice and, finally, the existence of the universality principle of love for justice. This is in order to live in peace with our similarities.

The idea that our understanding of the basic needs of human beings is the same is a fact and a reality that cannot and should not be rejected by us as an integral part of human society. Again, I am aware of the fact that judgements have different meanings, depending on the extent of our ability to realise justice in accordance with our experience, knowledge, and cultural norms. One may base, one's judgement on deduction and reasoning, while the reality can be based on the existence of obvious visible facts or, as I have called them, norms of similarities.

The validity of a judicial judgment is not therefore based on quantity but rather on quality of the judgment. This means that a judicial judgment, which puts an end to the violations, brings peace and justice, establishes rights and compensation for the victims, secures the principles of fair justice, prevents genocide, atrocities, murder, beheadings, and devastation of our civilisation, has an excellent quality.

I mean that if the norms of law are applied with the intention of prevention of discrimination, love for justice, and not love for power, many problems of unnecessary suffering of human beings would end. For example, such a problem as the drowning of 800 innocent refugees who tried to cross the Mediterranean from Africa in Italian waters would never have occurred in 2015. Or the killing of innocent French people by ISIS in Paris and Nice would never be taken place if their government would put all information about the involvement of the CIA in terrorist attacks on the table. An American author correctly describes world politics and crimes in his recent article and points to the fact that we have been fighting in the Middle East for 65 years in order to establish an oil pipeline. Accordingly, this is

> the only paradigm that explains why the GOP on Capitol Hill and the Obama administration are still fixated on regime change rather than regional stability, why the Obama administration can find no Syrian moderates to fight the war, why ISIL blew up a Russian passenger plane, why the Saudis just executed a powerful Shiite cleric only to have their embassy

[91]Statement by Sir William Jones, an English judge in India, and one of the most learned judges that ever lived, learned in Asiatic as well as European law. Jones on Bailments, 133. Available at http://oll.libertyfund.org/titles/spooner-natural-law-or-the-science-of-justice-1882 (Accessed June 23, 2015).

burned in Tehran, why Russia is bombing non-ISIL fighters and why Turkey went out of its way to shoot down a Russian jet. The million refugees now flooding into Europe are refugees of a pipeline war and CIA blundering.[92]

Human beings are not created to hate or to fulfil a singular judgement of one nation over another; in other words, the law is not formulated to create rights to destroy, kill, or discriminate between groups, nations, or justice. Laws, in particular laws which are against the principle of our similarities, theorists who are against human characteristics, decisions which permit occupation, and opinions which create violations are not laws but an individualistic understanding of our social existence which changes the level of our judgement, the result of which ignores love for justice, love for peace, and love for equality. Law always has the right to prevail but not with the violation of human integrity or human love for justice. Such law is considered lex iniusta non est lex. Any law, which imposes its rules by force, is invalid and null.[93] *Or, an unjust law is not law.*

References

Arnold, T. W. (1961). *The preaching of Islam: A history of the propagation of the Muslim faith* (pp. 115–119). Lahore, Pakistan: Muhammad Ashraf Publications.

Ashton, C., & Finch, V. (2002). *Human rights & Scots law* (pp. 51–54). Edinburgh: W. Green/ Sweet & Maxwell.

Aubert, V. (1963). The structure of legal thinking. In *Legal essays to attribute to Frede Castberg on the occasion of his 70th birthday* (pp. 41–63). Universitetsforlaget.

Bohlander, M., & Birkett, D. (2014). *The codification of criminal law* (p. xxiii). Ashgate.

Boyle, A. (2002). In A. Boyle, C. H. Worth, A. Loux, & H. M. Queen (Eds.), *Human rights and Scots law: Introduction* (p. 1). Oxford: Hart Publishing.

---

[92]Robert F. Kennedy, *Why the Arabs don't want us in Syria: They don't hate 'our freedoms.' They hate that we've betrayed our ideals in their own countries—for oil*, available at http://www.politico.eu/article/why-the-arabs-dont-want-us-in-syria-mideast-conflict-oil-intervention/ (Accessed March 4, 2016).

[93]Dr. Paul Craig Roberts correctly asserts that "Many still believe Washington's lies, but increasingly the world sees Washington as the greatest threat to peace and life on earth. The claim that America is 'exceptional and indispensable' is used to justify Washington's right to dictate to other countries. The casualties of Washington's bombings are invariably civilians, and the deaths will produce more recruits for ISIS. Already there are calls for Washington to reintroduce 'boots on the ground' in Iraq. Otherwise, Western civilization is doomed, and our heads will be cut off... Secret agendas have prevailed for so long that the American people themselves are now corrupted. As the saying goes, 'a fish rots from the head.' The rot in Washington now permeates the country." Available at http://www.oneworldofnations.com/2014/09/washingtons-secret-agendas-truth-is.html. (Accessed January 14, 2016). See *also* the very interesting case concerning unlawful deprivation of personal freedom of Julian Assange and the very demanding statement of the Working Group on Arbitrary Detentions, United Nations Human Rights Council report. Available at http://ohchr.org/EN/NewsEvents/Pages/DisplayNews.aspx?NewsID=17012&LangID=E (Accessed 13 February 2016).

Conley, R. W., Luckasson, R., & Bouthilet, G. N. (1992). *The criminal justice system and mental retardation*. Baltimore: Paul H. Books Publishing Co.

Dan-Cohen, M. (2014). Dignity, crime, and punishment: A Kantian perspective. In M. D. Dubber (Ed.), *Foundational texts in modern criminal law* (pp. 101–118). Oxford: Oxford University Press.

Duncan, J., & Derrett, M. (1968). *An introduction to legal system* (pp. 177–179). London: Sweet & Maxwell.

Engelhardt, H. T., & Spicker, S. F. (Eds.), (1976). *Mental health: Philosophical perspectives* (pp. VII and XIII. xv). Dordrecht: D. Reidel Publishing Company.

Fischer, M. (1998). The human rights implications of a cultural defense. *Southern California Interdisciplinary Law Journal, 6*, 663–702.

Fitzgerald, P. J. (1962). *Criminal law and punishment* (p. 10). Oxford: At the Clarendon Press.

Fournet, C. (2014). The human body: Victim, witness and evidence of mass violence. In E. Anstett & J.-M. Dreyfus (Eds.), *Human remains and mass violence: Methodological approaches* (pp. 56–80). Manchester: Manchester University Press.

Gaeta, P. (1999). Defence of superior orders: The statute of the international criminal court versus customary international law. *European Journal of International Law, 72*, 188–191.

Gandhi, M. K. (2001). *Non-violent resistance (Satyagraha)*. Ahmedabad: Jitendra T. Desai.

Gandhi, M. K. (2015). *The story of my experiments with truth*. Ahmedabad: Jitendra T. Desai.

Goodale, M., & Merry, S. E. (Eds.). (2007). *The practice of human rights tracking law between the global and the local*. Cambridge: Cambridge University Press.

Greve, V. (2005). Sheep or wolves. *European Journal of Crime, Criminal Law and Criminal Justice, 4*, 515–532.

Hoffman, R. L. (1980). *More than a trial: A struggle over Captain Dreyfus* (pp. 94–95). New York: Free Press.

Jackson, T. P. (2009). *The priority of love: Christian charity and social justice* (p. 7). Princeton: Princeton University Press.

Kant, I. (1948). *Moral law: Groundwork of the metaphysics of morals* (H. J. Paton, Trans., p. 71). New York, NY: Routledge.

Kant, I. (1996). In M. Gregor (Ed.), *The metaphysics of morals (1797)* (p. 209). Cambridge: CUP.

Karimsky, S., & Simoncelli, T. (2012). *Genetic justice: DNA data banks, criminal investigations and civil liberties*. New York, NY: Columbia University Press.

Kelsen, H. (2016). *The reason for the validity of a normative order: The basic norm*. http://www.philosophy.hku.hk/courses/law/KelsenNormValidity.htm. Accessed 18 March 2016.

King, Jr., M. L. (2008). A time to break the silence. In D. A. Hicks & M. R. Valeri (Eds.), *Global neighbours: Christian faith and moral obligation in today's economy* (p. 31). Eerdmans Publishing.

Knoops, G.-J. (2008). *Defenses in contemporary international criminal law* (2nd ed., p. 251). Leiden: Martinus Nijhoff Publisher.

Kymlicka, W., Lernestedt, C., & Matravers, M. (2014). Introduction: Criminal law and cultural diversity. In W. Kymlicka, C. Lernestedt, & M. Matravers (Eds.), *Criminal law and cultural diversity* (pp. 1–14). Oxford: Oxford University Press.

Lagerwall, A. (2014). The duty not to recognize unlawful situations and the European court of human rights. In C. Binder & K. Lachmayer (Eds.), *The European court of human rights and public international law: Fragmentation or unity* (p. 11). Nomos.

Lloyd, D. (1963). Legal and ideal justice. In *Legal essays to attribute to Frede Castberg on the occasion of his 70th birthday* (pp. 111–124). Universitetsforlaget.

Malekian, F. (2015). The canon of love against the use of force in Islamic and Public International Law: Part II: The anatomy of love against violations. *International Criminal Law Review*, 861–889, 889–892.

Marcin, R. B. (1984). Justice and love. *Catholic University Law Review, 33*(2), 363–391.

Mendus, S. (1999). The importance of love in Rawls's theory of justice. *British Journal of Political Science, 29*(1), 57–75.

Montgomery Watt, W. (1976). The significance of the theory of Jihād. In *Akten des VII. Kongresses für Arabistik und Islamwissenschaft, eds. Herausgegeben Von and Albert Dietrich* (p. 390). Göttingen: Vandenhoeck and Ruprecht.

Montgomery Watt, W. (1972). *The influence of Islam on Medieval Europe* (pp. 72–84). Edinburgh: The University Press.

Murdoch, R. R. J. (2011). *Human rights in Scotland* (pp. 1–7). West Sussex: Bloomsbury Professional Ltd.

O'Shea, A. (2002). *Amnesty for crime in international law and practice*. Hague/London/New York: Kluwer Law International.

Rawls, J. (1999). *A theory of justice* (revised ed., p. 3). Oxford: Oxford University Press.

Raz, J. (1994). *Ethics in the public domain: Essays in the morality of law and politics* (p. 11). Oxford: Oxford University Press.

Roberts, P. (2014). Theorising procedural tradition: Subjects and values in criminal adjudication. In P. Roberts (Ed.), *Theoretical foundations of criminal trial procedure* (pp. 129–156). Farnham: Ashgate.

Ross, A. (1959). *On law and justice* (pp. 274–275). Berkeley and Los Angeles: University of California Press.

Sankowski, E. (1978). Love and moral obligation. *The Journal of Value Inquiry, 12*(2), 100–110.

Seagrave, S., & Seagrave, P. (2003). *Gold warriors: America's secret recovery of Yamashita's gold*. Verso.

Spooner, L. (2015). *Natural Law; or the Science of Justice: A Treatise on Natural Law, Natural Justice, Natural Rights, Natural Liberty, and Natural Society; showing that all Legislation whatsoever is an Absurdity, a Usurpation, and a Crime. Part First* [1882] (p. 9). Available at http://oll.libertyfund.org/titles/spooner-natural-law-or-the-science-of-justice-1882. Accessed 18 May 2015.

Taylor, R. (1970). *Good and evil* (p. xii). New York, NY: Macmillan.

Trechsel, S. (1997). Why must trials be fair. *Israel Law Review, 31*, 94–119, at 100.

Vischer, R. K. (2014). *Martin Luther King Jr. and the morality of legal practice: Lessons in love and justice* (p. 211). Cambridge: Cambridge University Press.

Zawati, H. M. (2001). *Is Jihad a Just War? War, peace, and human rights under Islamic and Public International Law*. Lewiston: The Edwin Mellen Press.

Chapter 7
Dimensioning the Quality of Criminal Justice with Love

7.1 The Middle Value of Love

One cannot deny the fact that the metaphysics of real love, which is integrated in all human beings, are always collective and not isolated. As the people of the world can never come to an agreement to commit genocide against all human beings in one part of the world, they can also never be separated from this powerful law of love which exists in all of us and is integrated into our law. It is almost impossible to say that the majority of people in the world have a love of power—the contrary is true. Therefore, the power of love is the process of self-renewing the power of law in a positive and simpler way to achieve its goals. For example, punishment has been one of the chief tools of the machinery of justice, but it has shown itself to be very ineffective and irrational since it has never been useful. That is why we have modified the mechanism of punishment and modified it all the time, to the point that punishment of torture, which constituted one of the most significant tools of retribution and revenge for several thousand years, is one of the most brutal forms of jurisdictional outcome today. A number of international conventions have also declared its abolition.

The reason is very simple. We have realised that torture of offenders not only is not useful but also is hazardous to the social structure of human beings and against moral and legal codes. Therefore, the doctrines may not safely claim that the concept of torture is the best alternative for the prevention of criminal violations. The strength of moral and legal codes forces them to confine themselves to the elaboration of the fact that severe punishment is not recommended by the force of love for human nature. This is regardless of the crimes that offenders have committed. Here, I am seeking to find the way to the threshold of human nature and the law, where both are based solely on the power of love. One can also examine this philosophy in the practice of three prominent international lawyers whose policy of integration of love and law proved to be the only threshold for the maintenance or establishment of justice for the majority of the population of the world. They are Mahatma Gandhi, Martin Luther King, and Nelson Mandela. The idea behind their

F. Malekian, *Judgments of Love in Criminal Justice*,
DOI 10.1007/978-3-319-46900-3_7

theory was so simple and logical that international lawyers could not digest it. They imparted the main key of law—the norm of love—to the international public. We cannot evaluate the rightfulness of their theory by the logic of law but by the logic of great movements of love in the history of civilisation.

The struggle by the lawyers mentioned above was against discrimination and freedom from the statute of slavery. Here, as I have stated elsewhere, the colonial power consider all legal norms to be a favour for the relevant colonial society. It did not see this as humiliating for the cultural norms or legal merits of society and its relevance to people. The colonial power clarified discriminatory treatment as the way in which that society should be treated or understood by the occupying power. A clear example is the occupation of many states by the European states, whether in Africa or in Asia, such as the occupation of India by the United Kingdom.[1] The occupying power believed that it was their right, based on their military strength, to undermine how those countries and their population should behave. This meant it decided upon the level of positive morality which led to the positive legality of legislation.

The weak states suffer from the theory of strong power even today. This may be observed in a new case brought by East Timor against Australia before the International Court of Justice concerning disputes over its maritime boundaries. The case vividly clarifies "that the seizure of another state's property is as much a violation of international law as would be the seizure of any part of another state's territory – it is a matter of scale, not of quality."[2]

Another example is the occupation of Palestinian territories by a Zionist government, with the assistance of the British government, and various plans for the occupation of the remaining Palestinian territories.[3] All these occupying powers had and have the opinion that they are maintaining and holding the required standards of justice and the core concept of morality. The recent inhuman killing of children in Gaza was not seen by the occupying power as a humiliation of the dignity of humanity nor as serious violations of international human rights law, as grave violations of the international humanitarian law of armed conflict, and not as war crimes, crimes against humanity, genocide, infanticide, or aggression.[4] One also did not consider that it was a crime against the philosophy of natural or positive law.[5]

Yet, in the opinion of the Israeli government, all views expressed love for Zionism or love for Israel or love of one's own country. One can perceive all these possibilities in the actions of the country. The Nazi government expressed

[1]See Mukerjee (2011).

[2]Statement by Sir Elihu Lauterpacht, acting as one of the lawyers appearing at the court for Timor-Leste. http://www.theguardian.com/world/2014/jan/21/australia-has-violated-timor-lestes-sovereignty-un-court-told (Accessed September 12, 2014).

[3]Malekian (2012), pp. 827–69, 829.

[4]For serious violations of international humanitarian law of armed conflict in Gaza, *see* Devers and Mendes-France (2012), pp. 61–75, 71–2.

[5]*Id.*, pp. 841–842.

similar opinions when it started its infanticide against the *innocent Jewish population, which had deep root of civilisation in Europe*.[6] Here, as we can see, such actions integrate three concepts of norms. These were the norms of legality, morality, and love. Nazism had its own concept of legality, morality, and expression of power to control human minds. It is true that Nazism and relevant integrated bodies changed the concept of morality in most of Germany. Their speeches show that the law was morality and morality the whole law, and the latter the presentation of the entire philosophy of how man should and should not behave and what the pure meaning of the term "need" was.

We are cognisant of the fact that violations, decisions, or conducts, which are not based on the obvious reason of human beings' need, cannot be good choices for the structure of law and are therefore legally or philosophically invalid. One should not force human beings to accept conditions which are not fair and not based on the power of love for justice. Thus, we need a scrupulous examination of the growing improvement of international criminal law in order to understand why we have not succeeded by legal and moral codes in implementing the system among different civilisations and why the quality of criminal law and international criminal law has to be measured by the canon of love. Unfortunately, the norms of international criminal law and human rights law and the entire structure of United Nations law are becoming a question of quantity rather than quality today.

7.2 Depowering Interrogation with Love

The basic similarity principles between the laws of different nations involve the fact that no human society in the world is free to disobey such principles. If the existence of such principles is challenged by an Islamic state defending itself with regard to Mohammedan law, such law is abolished and is against humanity and therefore not valid. Similarly, if such laws are present in the Latin American states or the Chinese criminal system, they are also invalid and not fair. Consequently, when we discuss a Chinese provision of criminal law which sanctions harsh treatment against prisoners by the enforcement of torture, the relevant provision is not only violating Chinese obligations of criminal law with regard to its international duties but is also violating shared similar principles in the criminal justice system in any civilisation of the world.

In addition, the application of torture and capital punishment have been identified as a crime against justice.[7] When an Islamic state authorises stoning a person for adultery or imposes similar abolished penalties, such as cutting off parts of the body or capital punishment, it is not only violating its own criminal sanctions

[6]Malekian (2014), pp. 31–69, 48.

[7]di Beccaria (1872), pp. 58–59; Available at http://oll.libertyfund.org/titles/beccaria-an-essay-on-crimes-and-punishments (Accessed 27 April 2015).

relating to human rights law but also the principles of criminal law in the European Union criminal law system. This includes the Common law system and the criminal law of other states, too. Here, I am obviously aware of the fact that the European criminal law system is not applicable in an Islamic state or *vice versa*. However, we should remember that the metaphysics of law reveal the elemental essence of law and that should be similar in all legal systems if the purposes of international human rights laws are correct.

I am also aware of the fact that the European system of criminal law does not sanction capital punishment, does not permit torture, and does not cut off parts of the body or stone criminals. Here, I am not speaking about the darkness of the criminal justice system in Europe, such as underground policies of torture or maltreatment of accused people because of their nationality or ethnic background. We are focusing here solely on the criminal justice system that is present in public and not the hidden criminal policies in Islamic states, in European states, in the Latin American states, in the Jewish state, in communist states or in other countries.

The practice of criminal justice and criminal provisions may be quite different from the political criminal policy of a state. For example, the British criminal system may to some degree be healthy compared with other legal systems but its policy of torturing Irish prisoners is one of the most recognised criminal political policies in Europe. In 1971, the Irish Government on behalf of its population brought a case against the UK before the European Commission of Human Rights, alleging serious human rights violations by the British army in Northern Ireland during the Troubles.

The case arose from the internment of Irish nationals, and a particular emphasis in the proceedings was on the use of the notorious 'Five Techniques' of interrogation under which 14 detainees suffered from torture.[8] Although the European Court did not recognise the five different criminal actions by the English authorities as constituting torture, it clearly stated that deprivation of sleep and subjecting prisoners to various hazardous noises constituted degrading treatment of the Irish prisoners. In 2015, the Irish government was again asked to bring the case before the European Court of Human Rights to ask it to revise its manipulated judgment. This means that what the Irish government is seeking to address is the misuse of judgment and its misapplication. In other words, the judgment of the European Court of Human Rights missed out on the requirements of the third norm of law, i.e. love for justice.

I have reached a similar conclusion about the legal system of the United States, although some writers may have other views regarding "the quantity and quality of legal services" of the relevant state. They may claim it creates "equal justice."[9] However, I strongly doubt whether cases relating to Irish Case, Abu Ghraib Prison scandal or the Guantanamo Bay Detention Camp, which intended the humiliation of humankind, created any sense of justice.[10] These three cases together also denote

[8]Malekian (1991).

[9]Cummings (2011), p. 4.

[10]Examine Rejali (2007).

the non-existence of love for justice and humanity in the policies of powerful states. I would also like to draw your attention to the illegal nature of the Evin Prison in Tehran, where the prisoners are not only tortured, but even the building of the prison is clear evidence of criminality of the criminal law, criminal justice, criminal lawyers, criminal judges, and criminal prosecutors. It is here that Shakespeare properly asserted that "the first thing we do, let's kill all the lawyers." A long time ago, the following passage rightly concluded the barbaric nature of torture:

> The torture of a criminal, during the course of his trial, is a cruelty, consecrated by custom in most nations. It is used with an intent either to make him confess his crime, or explain some contradictions, into which he had been led during his examination; or discover his accomplices; or for some kind of metaphysical and incomprehensible purgation of infamy; or, finally, in order to discover other crimes, of which he is not accused, but of which he may be guilty. . .No man can be judged a criminal until he be found guilty; nor can society take from him the public protection, until it have been proved that he has violated the conditions on which it was granted. What right, then, but that of power, can authorise the punishment of a citizen, so long as there remains any doubt of his guilt? The dilemma is frequent. Either he is guilty, or not guilty. If guilty, he should only suffer the punishment ordained by the laws, and torture becomes useless, as his confession is unnecessary. If he be not guilty, you torture the innocent; for, in the eye of the law, every man is innocent, whose crime has not been proved. Besides, it is confounding all relations, to expect that a man should be both the accuser and accused; and that pain should be the test of truth, as if truth resided in the muscles and fibres of a wretch in torture. By this method, the robust will escape, and the feeble be condemned. These are the inconveniences of this pretended test of truth, worthy only of a cannibal; and which the Romans, in many respects barbarous, and whose savage virtue has been too much admired, reserved for the slaves alone.[11]

The intention here is to emphasise that justice has to be fair regardless of its territories of application, its cultural motivations, its ethnic origins, any shortcomings in the relevant statute, and any condition of the relevant criminal justice system's philosophy. It also has to be beyond any discrimination between legal systems. The line of similarity means that there is a norm which accumulates one another's natural requirement in every legal system of the world, in every culture of our civilisation, in the spirit of the ethnic novelty of different groups, in the strength of civil or criminal jurisdictions, and in the general recognised principle of objectivity of judges or courts. This is the norm of love for justice.

7.3 Searching for Similarities with the Mentality of Love

This very similarity between our legal systems and us is integrated into the substance of man, whether as a social animal, as a legal person, or as an integral part of the spiritual nature of humanity. This similarity, which here I call love imposes not only legal and moral force for the enforcement of fair justice but also keeps the souls of justice immaculate with the norms of humanity. The purpose of

[11] di Beccaria (1872), pp. 58–59.

Lady Justice and the Roman goddess of Justice is also to demonstrate the importance of moral force in the judicial system: that is why they are depicted wearing a blindfold.[12] Lawyers, prosecutors, and judges of a court should therefore be aware of the fact that the mentality of justice is different from the attitude in a legal statute, presented evidence, proceedings of the court, the philosophy of punishment, and finally the framework of a judgment.

Although evidence in a case may be touchable, it is mostly intangible because the souls of justice are not within the evidence or in the relevant decree. Thus, all this encourages us to apply the principle of similarities for the most appropriate definition of a fair criminal justice system. The theory or the principle of love is the same in the case of procedures in all criminal justice systems, the proceedings of criminal jurisdiction, and the application of irrational punishment without love.

This implies the fact that there are and there should be certain principles that are to be protected in any legal system, be it based on the Islamic jihad, European law or United States law. *An administrative justice system or a legislative power which provides the right of choice and legitimises the violation or application of certain cruel provisions not only violates its own rules of criminal legislation but is against the principle of the norm of love which is oriented and supported by any law. This means that a policy of an Islamic state or a European state, which permits violation of the basic rights of women or basic rights of refugees recognised by international human rights conventions, is in contrary to the system of fair criminal justice. Two clear examples are the gross violations of the rights of women in the Islamic Republic of Iran and the major embarrassing violations of the basic legislation of refugee law in Australia.*

When considering all these matters, one has to define the norm of love in justice. The norm may be defined as a system of fairness in which no rule violates the principles of similarities shared by all legal systems. This means that justice is a fair legal, moral, or love system in which we seek to protect our human integrity that is not to be traded, questioned, or offended by any legal system in the globe. By this, we mean that all legal systems ought to secure the basic principles of similarities which are accepted by the sources of the law, such as conventional law, general principles of law, custom, judgments, and opinions of jurists. This implies that violations of justice cannot be permitted and should not be accepted in any legal system of any nation. It is clear that the rules of law and principles of morality cannot be replaced by the rules of injustice, principles of fanatical morality, or principles of the dictatorship. That is why, when a state system violates those primary rules of justice, it has resorted to the use of force against justice and the legal and natural integrity of man. This is by itself an aggressive attack on the international public order.

I mean here that the use of force is not solely resorted to by one state against another or *vice versa*; instead, it can be used by a state against the basic principles of criminal justice systems accepted by most nations of the world. I call this use of

[12] Wägenbaur (2013), p. 12.

force a *hostile* attack against the similarity principles. In its traditional meaning, writers employed the term "use of force" in the case of use of armed force by one state against another. Ultimately, states permitted and did not permit resort to the use of force. Use of force actually had two features. These were the legitimate and illegitimate use of force. There was a limit to injustice. It is for this reason that, in comparison to the problems of the use of force, I have drawn this conclusion pointing to the fact that a conduct, which violates the principles of similarities, constitutes an illegitimate use of force.

7.4 Invisible Sovereignty of Love in Justice

The philosophy of law may not be the application of a fair legal system at all. This philosophy may even be dictatorial and counterproductive. For that reason, we should, by the force of moral norms and by the power of the norm of love, realise that we ought to find the green/fine lines that are acceptable to all nations, all cultures, and all moralities, and are respected by all men. That is why, in order to find those similarities, which are the central norms for the development of fair justice, we are requested to access those similarities via individuals', groups' and states' tolerance. *In other words, similarities bring recognition, recognition creates vision, vision opens closed windows, and the windows become, if we wish, the gate for unity of fair recognition of the power of justice. As long as we have not secured the positions of similarities, we have not come to the right recognition of law, morality, and love norms.* The light of love has to be the reason to depart from polarisation launched by a nuclear warhead. In addition, "if any country is worthy of the love of its people, surely it is the country distinguishing itself among all of the 193 countries in the world today by offering humanity a more mature and hopeful future."[13]

This means also that, as long as we are fighting for divergences and we are trying to convince others that one legal system is better than another, or that the Islamic legal system is fanatical or that the European legal system is overemotional, we are certainly far from the legalist, the moralist, and the love-related points of view. This means prevention of the consolidation of a fair definition of justice. *If the norms of law are norms, if legal norms are divided into various branches of legal disciplines, if each discipline has its own legal validity, and if all these jurisdictional or procedural norms are following our philosophy of legal perception, then there should be no essential reason to prevent us from discovering our similar norms. This means accepting the theory that all these disciplines have certain norms that are present in our common understanding of the reality of human nature.*

These norms are the same for human mentality, human dignity, and human substance all over the world. Historical records demonstrate the fact that we not only try to

---

[13]Al-Hussein (2009), p. 664. Available at http://www.auilr.org/; http://digitalcommons.wcl.american.edu/cgi/viewcontent.cgi?article=1098&context=auilr, (Accessed October 20, 2014).

find similar norms in the substance of man but also defend those norms in different situations. For example, when grave crimes are committed against human beings as a whole, our reaction is to stop such criminal behaviour, although the crimes may not concern our region or could be far from our territories, such as crimes committed in Rwanda and Sierra Leone. *However, what our purpose is in conjunction with the word "far" is itself a serious philosophical question. There is no distance in human hearts and love. In reality, the distance does not exist at all. Here, the reason that we react is not our legal system or their legal system, or the moral or legal shortages of the relevant system; it is rather the sovereignty of love for each other's human integrity which has to be respected, and, when the violation is gross, it draws our reaction towards the invisible norm of love. We react to the violation of our integrated love under the relevant legal system by the relevant authorities.*

7.5 What Is International Criminal Justice?

International criminal justice may define the fruit of transcultural morality, cooperation, assistance, reciprocity, mutual and multilateral tolerances, and a combination of different political necessities. It is, moreover, inspired by ideals of fairness, reparation, and rehabilitation. When we refer to the principles of international criminal justice, we do not necessarily mean only the judgments that may be delivered by international criminal courts but also the living structure of international criminal law as it exists in the international relations of states. International criminal justice is, therefore, not just a matter of criminal jurisdiction.

The term "international criminal justice" has its own framework of recognition of what is right and what is wrong between different nations. That is why we discuss the general principles of law and their effects on the system of international criminal law. The rights secured by the principles of criminal law obviously should not be subject to political interference by any state or authority. As a recognised principle of justice, criminal rules should be applied equally to all individuals, whether they are weak or powerful. The rationale behind these principles is to provide effective measures against violators of international law and to consolidate the principle of non-impunity. National or international criminal jurisdictions should follow this philosophy.

Obviously, the purpose here is not devaluing criminal justice systems of any states, regions, or the writings of many international lawyers about how they perceive the situation of international criminal justice. Instead it is to say that not only in international law are there *comitas gentium*, constituting a species of accommodation within a system of international relations such as the exemption of diplomatic envoys from customs duties, but also that there are certain comities in national, regional, and international criminal jurisdiction that should not be forgotten by the good reputation of our judges. In international law, according to the principle of comity, the courts of one jurisdiction may accede to the laws or decisions of another in certain necessary circumstances. This is not to satisfy the opposing parties but to emphasise that certain provisions of such jurisdiction are more or less equivalent to our own presentations, interpretations, or conclusions.

Apparently, when we are defining the concept of a fair legal system or a fair definition of justice, which is acceptable in accordance with the principles of similarities, we are also accessing the definition of the principle of justice in criminal law. Thus, criminal justice is an integral part of the general definition of justice. This is based on the fact that the concept of any form of justice is not independent of the original concept of justice and the norm of love. We are aiming at the supremacy of fair justice which ought to be the same in any given society. Here, I am not necessarily speaking about qualitative or quantitative justice but about the concept of the rule of law that is a part of fair principles of similarities and is expected to be applied to any legal system. This is what I call the integration of law, morality, and love to reach a better understanding of the rule of law and reduce international conflicts between various nations or groups in the world.

We are not using the doctrine of judicial precedence which is located at the heart of the common law system concerning rights and duties. We are also not binding national courts to the prior decisions of superior courts or other cases. But, I do not deny that my aim is to adhere to the objects of fair justice, e.g. a regime of stable, similar principles for the security of individuals', groups', and nations' rights that are being practised in the criminal justice of most states of the world. At the same time, I also aim to ensure that the implementation of the law is in accordance with the changing perceptions of the community needs and therefore fulfils the moral expectations of the community of human beings as a whole. This need may be identified by the code of love. "Love, it seems, is the key not only to the personal happiness of the central characters, but to the happiness of all, of the whole community."[14] A system of jurisdiction, based on precedents of a fair criminal justice adopted and applied by the nations of the world will be an opportunity to use the human experience of fair justice. It will be more human in order to detect legal issues and resolve intricate legal problems that it is not possible to solve by old legal systems.

7.6 Comity of Cultivating Justice with Love

In legal language, comity specifically refers to legal reciprocity, friendship, consensus, unanimity, unity, connection, sympathy, empathy, solidarity, understanding, peacefulness, and fraternization. All these mean that we respect one another in good faith and with good intentions and love or trust for justice. The purpose is to build a welcoming social harmony between our laws and the laws of other nations, and to find a way to build our legal relations. That is why we have recognised general principles of law as one of the basic sources of international criminal law or

[14]Nussbaum (2013), p. 28.

international human rights law. Article 38 of the Statute of the International Court of Justice (ICJ), which is generally accepted as a formative common assessment of sources of international criminal law among publicists, has clearly stated this fact. By 'general principles of law,' the Statute not only focuses on sources but also gives us a guideline on how to deal with those basic rules of legal philosophy that can be found within different cultures.

These civilizations may be Islamic, Indian, Chinese, European, Australian, American, or African. Furthermore, the Statute of the ICJ emphasises that we should not give priority to the rules of one region of law and breach the rules of another. We have to follow the norms of the law. This includes legal, moral, and love norms. In other words, morality in justice should not be violated at any level or to any degree. The dissenting view in *The Prosecutor v. Germain Katanga* correctly states that:

> This raises the question by which standard fairness and justice should be evaluated. My view is that the trial must be first and foremost fair towards the accused. Considerations about procedural fairness for the Prosecutor and the victims and their Legal Representatives, while certainly relevant, cannot trump the rights of the accused. After all, when all is said and done, it is the accused - and only the accused who stands trial and risks losing his freedom and property. In order for a court of law *to have the legal and moral authority to pass legal and moral judgment on someone*, especially when it relates to such serious allegations as international crimes, it is essential, in my view, to scrupulously observe the fairness of the proceedings and to apply the standard of proof consistently and rigorously. It is not good enough that most of the trial has been fair. All of it must be fair.[15]

The ICJ's intention is clearly to find similar rules of justice with the sole purpose of cultivating peace, fairness, and reciprocity between the laws of all nations. Clearly, if by 'general principles of law,' the ICJ has been given permission to discriminate between various regions of law and their rules, the Court would exercise justice unequally. Undoubtedly, the Statute of the ICJ and the Court itself are not presenting such an illogical idea. As a result, the question may arise whether we should follow or develop the standard of the Court and the merits of its general principles of law regarding the evolution of international justice or whether we should solely deal with the concept of 'general principles of law' in a very restricted way.[16] One may therefore argue that, in particular contexts, rules of interpretation of law have to express the criteria of good faith and truth in the recognition of criminals.[17] This is what we call the duty of the Prosecutor of the ICC or any other prosecutor, national or regional, in the world.

For example, how can we argue that the decisions of all prosecutors of criminal courts in certain Islamic countries are correct and fair when the prosecutors constantly see the violation of national and international rights by the leaders of

---

[15]*The Prosecutor v. Germain Katanga*, Minority Opinion of Judge Christine Van den Wyngaert, ICC-01/04-01/07-3436-AnxI 07-03-2014 1/170 NM T, available at http://www.icc-cpi.int/iccdocs/doc/doc1744372.pdf (Accessed April 4, 2015), para. 311, 166/170. Italics added.

[16]See *also* Kelsen (1957, 1967).

[17]*Id.*

the national authorities? The first duty of a prosecutor is to examine whether the weak and the strong fulfil the principles of justice. With the same logic, how can we say that the prosecutors of most courts of European states are acting in good faith and with love for justice when organisations, groups, and individuals submit many complaints against the criminal conduct of certain powers in certain territories to them, but they simply ignore the cases by different policies? Morris rightly answers this issue: "Judges and jurists are tempted to take the position that they have to deal only with the existing law and need not be concerned with what the law should be."[18]

Thomas Aquinas (1225–1274), the Italian philosopher, undoubtedly refers in his theory to the comity of cultivating justice with love. He rightly asserts that no human conduct is morally good or right, in the sense of not wrong, unless it has the natural characteristic with love of one's neighbour. *Equal division of love has to be the main intention of the conduct. This means that the conduct should contain the basic aspects of the well-being of each and every human being at the same level and to the same degree. The conduct should not only comprise* the *intentions which it is assigned but should also cultivate justice, love, and friendship.* Aquinas based his argument on the well-known principle of *bonum ex integra causa, malum ex quocumque defectu.* The principle means a conduct has a good quality when it has a good quality in every respect of its implementation, and the conduct has a wrong quality when it has a wrong quality in every respect of its implementation, too. *There is a fundamental asymmetry between good justice and feigned justice. In other words, the circumstances under which the conduct is performed should be in conformity with reason; otherwise it does not fulfil the requirements of the principles of accurate, impartial justice. The worst form of injustice is feigned justice.*

7.7 Justice with the Passion of Trust

If a system of justice is fair, it has to be fair not just for its subjects but also for the objects of its subjects. If a subject's voice has not been paid enough attention to in the criminal justice system of the subject's own country for the love of justice, for the truth to be realised and released, or for the protection of victims and witnesses, how can we proclaim that our criminal system of jurisdiction is reasonable? How can we assert that it is organised by the system of positivism and naturalism morality? If the concept of love for justice is not contemplated in the system of justice, in particular in the system of international human rights law and criminal law, the relevant law is not accurate law but the serious allegations of the principles of morality and legality. Sidney correctly interprets the reality of reasons for justice, true law, and the norm of love:

[18] Cohen (1949), p. 998.

> That familiar distinction of the Schoolmen, says he, whereby they subject kings to the directive, but not to the coactive power of the law, is a confession, that kings are not bound by the positive laws of any nation, since the compulsory power of laws is that which properly makes laws to be laws ... If this were so, the governments of the world might be justly called magna latrocinia; and men laying aside all considerations of reason or justice, ought only to follow those who can inflict the greatest punishments, or give the greatest rewards. But since the reception of such opinions would be the extirpation of all that can be called good, we must look for another rule of our obedience, and shall find that to be the law, which being, as I said before, sanctio recta, must be founded upon that eternal principle of reason and truth, from whence the rule of justice which is sacred and pure ought to be deduced, and not from the depraved will of man, which fluctuating according to the different interests, humours and passions that at several times reign in several nations, one day abrogates what had been enacted the other. The sanction therefore that deserves the name of a law, which derives not its excellency from antiquity, or from the dignity of the legislators, but from an intrinsic equity and justice, ought to be made in pursuance of that universal reason to which all nations at all times owe *an equal veneration and obedience*.[19]

A qualified justice is a justice which does not, at first glance, violate the freedom of speech of its members. We recognise justice, not only by Lady Justice but also "by her voice;" this is 'the voice that I love', you love, and we love.[20] *However, I am sure that we have mostly quantitative justice rather than qualitative justice. This is a fact that does not need to be proven by evidence. This is also a reality, such that we are accustomed to it and cannot perceive its defects.*

If the proper interest of criminal justice in the United Kingdom, Sweden, Denmark, Norway, Finland, Brazil, Germany, Austria, France, Russia, Italy, Spain, or many others was right and lawful and for the maintenance of the goals of the norms of love for justice, it would be demonstrated, at least in application by their relevant prosecutors. Our very respectful prosecutors would confirm that many of acts of different powerful states are criminal conducts and fall into their jurisdictions.

This is what I call the true function of a prosecutor who has a love for the interest of justice and not love for his position. A Scandinavian or United States prosecutor easily discusses crimes committed by Islamic regimes but never at all brings a case before her/his respective court against her/his own government or neighbours concerning their involvement in the unlawful production of weapons. Which law and which authority or morality can fully guarantee that the treaties or agreements regarding the manufacture of weapons are correct and do not violate the original text of European or American declarations of human rights law. My conclusions are the same about a German or a British prosecutor.

In this chapter, I should mention the fact that there is unfortunately already an excessive competition between lawyers in the world to get jobs in the ICC. Many lawyers take into account the big income from the Court without considering the precarious justice that comes from the Court. *The purity of a sanction that deserves*

---

[19]Sidney (1698), Available at http://oll.libertyfund.org/titles/sidney-discourses-concerning-government, (Accessed April 3, 2015), section 11.

[20]Nussbaum (2013), p. 35.

the appellation of justice should not derive its motivation from income from the court or from the prestigious position in the Court but from an inherent theory to lay down love for the power of secure justice for all humanity, even at the price of one losing one's job and entire income forever.[21] This is what I have been into for at least the last 10 years. We have to follow the substance of true blind Lady Justice, but solely the naked one. Historically, it was properly stated that "Advocatus sed non latro, res miranda populo - A lawyer and yet not a thief, to the wonder of the people."[22]

7.8 The Master Piece of Justice

We have to realise that we have not studied law to learn law, to learn rules, to punish others, to be judges, lawyers, or prosecutors and earn money by being a successful barrister. If these are our first ambitions and our final intentions, let it be known that we learn the law, not because of justice but because of justice for us, due to the crimes or violations of others. We should learn law for the reason of justice, for the reason of humanity, for the reason of understanding, and for the reason of knowing that all of us together create justice and love. We should realise the fact that the most well-known philosophers of law did not even have a legal education.

A considerable number of professors of human rights and justice are representatives of love for the fundamental human rights law. However, they have been involved in the actions of criminal organisations such as SAVAK, the CIA, and Herasat, and dictatorial regimes. They have acted as diplomats but in reality, when the regime was discarded, they came to European or other states to lecture international or human rights law. When one asks them the substance of their justice, they ignore the question by saying that it is not true. They actually have two types of love: love for the power of that which was in power and love of the position that they maintain today. This is what one of the honest lawyers in international criminal law, namely Albin Eser, calls "double morality." He clarifies how one of his best tutors taught them natural law justice with love but later on, it was revealed to the

[21]"It may also be the case that the same lawyers simultaneously pursue different – and perhaps – competing projects. For instance, their actions may both enhance civil and political rights while undercutting economic and social ones; they may both promote access to justice through pro bono service while undermining it through practice restrictions. This duality also leaves open the possibility that individual lawyers may believe that they are advancing the cause of justice, when other observers would argue that they in fact are thwarting it. This disagreement could be a result of contested normative views – a liberal lawyer's project clashes with her conservative counterpart's. It could also be a product of false consciousness on the part of lawyers, whose subjective beliefs about the social value of their professional contributions could be falsified by objective measurement." Cummings (2011), pp. 2–3.

[22]The expression concerning SaintYves, Patron Saint of Lawyers quoted by Cappelletti et al. (1975), pp. 11–12.

students, that he was a member of the Nazi party in his earlier career. Bentham, a well-known English philosopher, clarifies his own views concerning the academic position of Beccaria in the history of legal jurisprudence by proclaiming that:

> Oh my master, first evangelist of Reason, you have raised your Italy so far above England, and I would add above France, were it not that Helvetius, without having written on the subject of laws, had already provided you with your fundamental ideas;... you who have made so many useful excursions into the path of utility, what is there left for us to do? – Never to turn aside from that path.[23]

What Bentham is really propagating here is not admiration of Beccaria but his theory of love for justice against the sanctioning of criminal actions in the apparatus of criminal law. One should also remember that Bentham was against the natural law theory and labelled human rights "nonsense upon stilts."[24] This was his description of unwritten law.[25] There are international reasons in the international community of human beings which all nations at all times are obliged to pay sufficient attention to and comply with. Mannheim has correctly explained the situation:

> During the seventeenth and eighteenth centuries the earlier attempts to define the conception of *bellum justum* and *jus ad bellum* had to give way to discussions on the *jus in bello* – i.e. on the rules applicable to warfare without any regard to the justness of a particular war. In other words, ever hope had to be abandoned of solving the real problem of war. Working out in immense detail the technical rules of the *jus in bello*, international lawyers had found a field of activities where they could engaged themselves with less personal risk and more profit...Apparently international lawyers of certain previous generations found themselves too much handicapped by the fact of their being appointed by the princes whose actions they were expected to justify. If the teachers of criminal law had had to depend for their livelihood upon the generosity of the most successful criminals in their districts, the results of their labours might well have been equally unsatisfactory. Today we are inclined to be angry at the manifest failure of all those experiments, made before the present conflagration, to outlaw unjust wars.[26]

One should especially not lose sight of the fact that most states show interest in integrating those significant norms of international criminal law into their systems. This is what I call fairness with unfairness: when a judge sees that the Afghan population is not only suffering from its own cultural problems but also from the USSR and the United States and their allies' criminal conduct, but such a judge is

---

[23]Quoted in Young (1983), pp. 317, 318; also in E Halévy, *The Growth of Philosophical Radicalism* (M Morris trans, 1955), 21. I have quoted originally from Harcourt (2014), pp. 59–78, at 43.

[24]Germy Bentham, Anarchical Fallacies (written 1791–1795, published 1816). See *also* Schofield (2003), pp. 1–26. Available at http://www.google.de/url?sa=t&rct=j&q=&esrc=s&source=web&cd=1&ved=0CCIQFjAA&url=http%3A%2F%2Fjournals.cambridge.org%2Farticle_S0953820800003745&ei=dlGEVdauL4PXUZa7gKAK&usg=AFQjCNExs2PvnCBVdYYp-hr-WWvMGhp-yzA&bvm=bv.96042044,d.d24 (Accessed June 19, 2015); Bentham (2002), pp. 317–401.

[25]See Hart (1982), p. 79.

[26]Mannheim (1940), pp. 19–20.

doing nothing more than trying to seem elegant or intelligent. This is also what I call the primary rules and the secondary rules of the law, in contrast to what was presented by the respectful English philosopher, Hart. *A lawyer should realise the fact that it is not the compulsory power of law which makes it law. On the contrary, it is reason, truth, purity, and harmony which make justice reliable, desirable, and digestible.*

If the nature and the character of a legal norm is true, if the legal norm is not a collection of savage norms, if the spirit of moral norms in the culture of the law is not monopolised by bad norms, if the law understands the difference between the vocabulary of justice and injustice, then such norms are love norms. If a norm realises the reasons for hearing and non-hearing or admission and non-admission of a case in a court, the dominance of the rich, weak, and the position of the accused persons, then such law ought to also understand that prosecuting the big criminals is not solely a duty but a mission of justice for love.

How can, for example, Swedish or German law, including criminal law, present the wills of democratic or federal society but at the same time violate justice with love by the production of weapons. *How can the same societies and their neighbours claim jurisdiction over all acts of dull Muslims but not over the barbarous criminal actions of the big political powerful nations. Do they not know the reality behind the events of September 11 and the fake? As the prominent international German lawyer Georg Schwarzenberger rightly states it, international relations are the monopoly of the big, powerful nations. If the interest of justice is love, if attentiveness of justice is legality, if justice is morality, if justice is Scandinavian realism rejecting any concept of morality, if justice is not to enforce our own opinion over another's without the existence of appropriate judgments and decisions, then the issue is how can we forget our own duties and tasks?*[27] *Naturally, beating around the bush in relation to our neighbours will not help justice or our relationship in the end.*

7.9 Inherent Veracity of Elements of Love

However the philosophy of law expresses it, whatever Plato inscribed concerning republic, justice, and a just man almost 400 years B.C.; whatever Aristotle,[28] Cicero,[29] Augustine,[30] Thomas Aquinas,[31] Suarez, Grotius, and Fredrick the Great argued about the vicissitudes and outcomes of the effort towards the prohibition of unjust wars; a law has to present the principle of *equality of arms*. Again, anything the theory of Kant calls for, whatsoever the Hegel argumentation exhorts

[27]Inger (2011), pp. 308–309.

[28]Andersen (2011), pp. 79–82.

[29]*Id.*, pp. 85–87.

[30]*Id.*, pp. 87–90.

[31]*Id.*, pp. 90–94.

about the separation of the power of state and church, and whatever the Mohammedan idea requires for admission into the spiritual law, it is a fact that access to justice should be required not only by victims or witnesses but also by our respectful judges and prosecutors. In addition, access to real justice should also be asked from those who claim to be educated in highly recognised European institutions, are qualified through Harvard Law School, or are the negotiators in the formation of the international criminal courts, the ICC, or resolutions against cybercrime and crimes against humanity. They can also be those who are highly recognised international criminal judges in Yugoslavia, Rwanda, the ICC, the ICJ, the ICSR, the Cambodia Court, or advisers to the United Nations to stop future genocide, or advisers to the same organisation to discover chemical weapons. They may also be experts in criminal and procedural rights of children in Europe and so forth.

As the prominent prosecutor of the International Criminal Court, Robert Jackson, remarked almost seven decades ago, we should be aware that we would be judged tomorrow by the law which we prosecuted and punished today. For the information of this international lawyer, the correct judgment with love for justice has not yet come into existence. This is regardless of the fact that we have developed international criminal conventions to the extent that they are impossible to be controlled by an international prosecutor or judge. The reason is again very simple. We codify the law for the law's purpose but not with the full intention of the prevention of injustice.

If injustice is going to be eliminated, if prejudice is going to be prevented, and if the accusation is going to be the last mission of justice, we have to realise that justice does not draw closer with the formulation, codification, drafting, modification, and adjustment of new international conventions. But by the fact that the interests of justice are not a gift, then love has to be the first elementary principle of justice if peace is going to be obtained and the unintelligent Muslim is going to be wise and if the impure diplomacy of the Western nations is going to be clean. This is solely a wish in the theoretical nature of the law and not reality. The fact is that the most important laws have almost never been applied realistically and justly. This not only includes the perception of Western law but also Islamic law, and the excellent Marxist idea of equality between leaders and workers for the sake of love for justice. Martin Luther King's dream of acquisition of social rights and John F. Kennedy's marvellous emotional speech clearly point to the fate that "the rights of every man are diminished when the rights of one man are threatened." A Chinese lecture's statements may be relevant here:

> I was having a hard week trying to put myself together after I arrived the university, it disappointed me. You see my degree is criminal law and now they want me to teach constitutional law and some crazy Marxism morality, I am not sure if I can zip my mouth not to make any anti-communist speech, which might not be safe cause, beside the Chinese crazy Marxism ideology. *The constitutional law is quite controversial in China; the party just fired any judge who dares to cite any right from the constitutional law. So we only have the constitutional rights in books instead of in reality.*[32]

[32]Email weoljin.1949cupl@qq.com (2015-09-12-14:33 (WEST)). I have manipulated the email address.

Several facts are decisive here. On the one hand, the authorities of most nations want to conquer the situation by power of law or more precisely by the power of their own interpretation. This means that they present the purpose of the law with different interpretations that meet their own desires. Thus, one of the most serious problems of the systems of law in the world is not the matter of having or not having a sense of humanity or love for justice, and not the philosophy of dealing or not dealing with the questions of unity of man or universality of human rights law, but that of intentional personal interpretation. By personal interpretation, we not only mean the personal will of a particular authority in any legal system like Latin America but also intergovernmental wills. On the other hand, states want to prove that the interpretations of law by other states are incorrect and problematic. They ignore all other interpretations. This is particularly evident in the case of the permanent members of the United Nations and their allies. This means that we kill the norm of love and replace it with the power of force and eventually guns.

7.10 The Disguise of Criminal Justice

I even wonder in this book if committing genocide is really prohibited. Any lawyer may argue that it is not prohibited to commit genocide based on the fact that the provisions of the 1948 Genocide Convention contradict with the provisions of many international conventions, which permit the manufacture of most types of weapons. In reality, we cannot have an international convention that strongly prohibits the criminality of the commission of acts of genocide and simultaneously have international conventions, which permit the production of weapons for mass destruction and are not a positive cultivation of justice.[33]

The capacity of a weapon to kill more than one man is no longer for self-defence but a tool of power politics. We should not put weapons of mass destruction into the hands of authorities who are the representatives of members of our population and then say to them that their intensive use constitutes genocide. If the intention of genocide is killing, then the weapons are the tools of such killing. If possession of any type of weapon is internationally permitted, then killings at any level and degree are also homogeneously permitted. Ironically again, if speed limits are 110 or 180 km, then cars capable of driving much faster should not be produced. On the one hand, one should remember that contradiction of any law with the prohibition of the crime of genocide is itself a serious indirect encouragement and conspiracy to commit genocide. This may be called the standard of *human animality violating the lesson of human equality.*[34] Of course, "No nonhuman animal denies that it is an animal, hates being an animal, shrinks from others of its kind

[33] Nussbaum (2013), pp. 133 and 177.

[34] *Id.*, p. 154.

because they are animals."[35] This is what Kant calls "radical evil." Or "perversity of heart, which, on account of the result, is also-called a bad heart." Further:

> The depravity of human nature, then, is not so much to be called badness, if this word is taken in its strict sense, namely, as a disposition (subjective principle of maxims) to adopt the bad, as bad, into one's maxims as a spring (for that is devilish); but rather perversity of heart, which, on account of the result, is also called a bad heart. (42) This may co-exist with a Will ["Wille"] good in general, and arises from the frailty of human nature, which is not strong enough to follow its adopted principles, combined with its impurity in not distinguishing the springs (even of well-intentioned actions) from one another by moral rule. So that ultimately it looks at best only to the conformity of its actions with the law, not to their derivation from it, that is, to the law itself as the only spring. Now although this does not always give rise to wrong actions and a propensity thereto, that is, to vice, yet the habit of regarding the absence of vice as a conformity of the mind to the law of duty (as virtue) must itself be designated a radical perversity of the human heart (since in this case the spring in the maxims is not regarded at all, but only the obedience to the letter of the law).[36]

On the other hand, the problem is that we have almost never heard in political situations of the world of a government or authority accepting that it has misinterpreted the law. In reality, it is ineffective to admit unresponsiveness to such enquiries, the intention of which is to hide humanity with fallacy. Besides, these authorities may try to disguise their policies with the assumption that they are right and the majority is wrong. When they do not realise that they are violating the merit of the law, or they are committing international crimes against their own law as well as the dignity of human beings, the law becomes loveless and undesirable. This includes Western and Muslim states' laws. At the same time, this indifference, which can be scrutinised in the sphere of interpretation of law by state authorities, which directly or indirectly concerns criminal atrocities such as genocide or crimes against humanity, makes the application of love for the interests of justice impossible. A state or a government does not really need to have a systematic plan for what it is doing and is committing under its international legal personality. In the Blaskic case, the ICTY Trial Chamber defined the word systematic as:

- the existence of a political objective, a plan pursuant to which the attack is perpetrated or an ideology, in the broad sense of the word, that is, to destroy, persecute or weaken a community;
- the perpetration of a criminal act on a very large scale against a group of civilians or the repeated and continuous commission of inhumane acts linked to one another;
- the preparation and use of significant public or private resources, whether military or other;
- the implication of high-level political and/or military authorities in the definition and establishment of the methodical plan. This plan, however, need not necessarily be declared expressly or even stated clearly and precisely.[37]

[35]*Id.*, p. 159.

[36]Immanuel Kant, *Religion within the Bounds of Reason Alone*.

[37]*Prosecutor v Tihomir Bla[ki]*, case no IT-95-14-T (3 March 2000), paras 203–204.

It is here that we examine the reason why we have a law that cannot be enforced by ordinary sources, by our police officers, by investigators of the courts or judges or any other national or international body. This also includes the Security Council of the United Nations. In other words, any self-examination of the law, and any official examination of our laws, supports the fact that the relevant law is not implemented in accordance with the substance of love for justice. Consequently, the power of justice is under the control of our own authorities. The concept of love for justice cannot be worked out in a system of jurisdiction in which personal interests have been given privilege over any other matters relating to humanity. This is the same in international legal relations and under the restricted power of the ICC.

7.11 Violations of Women's Rights Against Love

Generations of women have always been discriminated by most international societies. A piece of legislation which emphasises in its provisions that a woman is worth half a man, the value of man in engaging in social activities is above that of a woman, or that a woman does not have the full capacity to judge is without any doubt against the fundamental principles of human rights law. Such a system violates the general aspects of human ethics and is not valid in today's enlightened age.[38] A clear example is the systematic force against Persian women by the internal authorities of Iran which constitutes crimes against humanity.[39] This is also the case for stoning them or preventing them from occupying juridical positions such as prosecutors, lawyers, judges, ministers of justice, or being the leader of the Islamic nation.

This is regardless of the fact that such provisions exist in European Union law or in the interpretations of the Quranic codes. Such legislation is not only invalid but violates the basic ethics of human dignity. The ambition of the Quranic code has not been to keep females from judgment or to establish an inferior position for women. The Quranic code has to be read with the historical events of time and not with the present position of the development of the law. Likewise, the judges and legislators of Islamic states must consider three significant positions and see which one of them takes priority. These are the rule of the law, the rule of judgment, and the rule of love for justice. If the answer is the first two, then I am giving a fully wrong opinion and I am barking up completely the wrong tree. However, we know the favourite adage of Queen Christina of Sweden—aquila non captat muscas.

The logical interpretation of the Quranic code is, therefore, the metaphysics of time and not the metaphysics of historical events, i.e. the time in which Arabs buried their daughters alive and it was wrong to have a female child. Such cultural assumptions only had to face such rules that could be accepted by the majority of

---

[38]Consult Malekian (2011), pp. 3–22.

[39]http://www.al-monitor.com/pulse/originals/2015/05/iran-womens-magazine-zanan-emrooz-suspended.html (Accessed May 24, 2015).

the population. The Quranic codes left the concept of equality between genders to the slow evolution of cultural morality and love for all without any discrimination between men and women. It was also in this context that the value of testimony could vary depending on the sex of a witness. The practice was not a matter of principle but rather a seed that would develop progressively into equal opportunities for both women and men. Otherwise, how can the Quranic codes equally enter both sexes into a theoretical heaven but keep inequality on earth. The basic source of Islamic law, in version 40:40, clearly provides that '...whoever does good, whether male or female,... shall enter the garden.'

The spirit of justice has surely banished such an obvious misunderstanding of the meaning of inequality under Islamic law. Accordingly, "whatever wrongs took place in the days of ignorance are abolished by Islam [...] and whatever wrongs take place in Islam may be abolished by repentance."[40] This means that, in certain cases, sources of Islamic jurisprudence have recommended gradual modification of the law. *The relevant law of the Islamic Republic of Iran is indisputably violating the concept of love for justice, even in the inner structure of Islamic interpretation and is, therefore, responsible before the substance of general cultural morality of the world and the system of international human rights law as a whole. This is particularly the case when one considers that these acts are permanent, systematic, and against a group of inhabitants in the relevant country.*

One of the reasons may be that historically, direct "interference in legislative processes, in the determination of legal doctrine, and in the overall internal dynamics of the law was nearly, if not totally absent." However, the gap between the period of direct interference and the period of tacit interference changed by the gaining of political power by Islamists in 1979. Therefore, "The modern state, ...arrogated to itself the status of a legislator, an act that assigned it a place above the law. Legislative interference, often arbitrary, has become a central feature of modern reform and in itself is evidence of the dramatic shift in the balance of legal power."[41]

Beyond all this, Islamic nations are bound to accomplish their international obligations under certain international conventions such as the Convention on the Elimination of All Forms of Discrimination Against Women, widely known by the acronym CEDAW. However, we are also aware of the fact that Islamic nations have *systematically* violated the provisions of the CEDAW in their practice. A cursory investigation into the practice of Arab states demonstrates the commission of *crimes against women or humanity*.[42] In most instances, the systematic practice of Arab states has proved "their retention of nonconforming domestic standards."[43] They have pretended to exercise "reforms in the direction of affording women's

[40]*Taha Jaber Al-Alwani*, "The Testimony of Women in Islamic Law", available at www.alhewar.com/ Taha Testimony.htm 28 k, (Accessed May 29, 2015).

[41]Hallag (2004), pp. 21–53, 22.

[42]Mayer (2004), pp. 133–160, 133.

[43]Mayer (2004), p. 156.

equality."[44] However, in reality, they are "corroding the legitimacy of their discriminatory laws."[45]

The question how an act of state or its entities can become relevant in a systematic violation of international criminal justice or *crimes against humanity* has recently been taken into consideration in a report by the Australian Human Rights Commission. According to it, there is a strong case that the mandatory detention of illegal immigrant children, which is the current policy of the Australian Government, meets the relevant criteria to be deemed a crime against humanity in violation of Article 7(1)(e) of the Rome Statute and section 268.12 of the Commonwealth Criminal Code.[46] Consequently, crimes against humanity constitute crimes against the international community of states as a whole and are violations of legal and moral standards of human civilisation.[47]

Evidently, I do not aim here to criticise our legal systems, our legislations, our prosecutors, judges or lawyers, but I am making an enquiry into the abilities of the law and the reason of the law, with reference to the knowledge of the fact that love constitutes a part of our legal system. This is regardless of the name of the law, and therefore reference to the existence of the norm of love should be in the substance of any law. However, it is not. This is particularly evident in the case of Muslim women and violations of their rights by the majority of Islamic states.

7.12 Accusation by and without Criminal Procedures

In the hidden vocabularies, cultures, as well as behind closed doors and windows of buildings of the world, many nations accuse each other because of their theoretical, religious, or social backgrounds. If the theory of justice, the development of human rights norms, the extension of non-discrimination slogans, the happiness of our own legacy and morality in Europe, the United States, Australia, Canada, the Middle East and other parts of the world is based upon an accusations of others, then let us be accused. If the courts of criminal justice in Europe are happy with the criminalisation of acts of individuals of other nations, then let us again be accused, let us be condemned, let us be prosecuted, let us be punished and let ourselves be prisoners in the prisons of most united civilised states. What comes of it? Obviously, there will not be peace, justice, humanity, and the norm of love but rather the norms of conflict and war.

---

[44] *Id.*

[45] *Id.*

[46] Submission to the Australian Human Rights Commission Concerning the Inquiry into Children in Immigration Detention 2014, available at https://www.humanrights.gov.au/. . ./Submission%20 (Accessed April 25, 2015).

[47] See Article 53 of the 1963 Vienna Convention on the Law of Treaties. The article addresses the peremptory norms.

If terrorist activities, attacks, and explosions are condemned according to the principles of justice in the world; if human rights law of European states continuously struggles for the discovery of wrongs; if the human rights courts of European governments are finding groups guilty and banning their members from engaging in certain conduct; then, what is going wrong with positivism? If the leading function of international legal instruments, including international legal bodies, is to secure justice, humanity, peace, brotherhood, and trust in international relations; if the European central government/European Union is begging for regional justice among its member states, including for foreigners; then why have they not them been successful in reaching their goals?

If the established international institutes in the Netherlands—particularly The Hague—or the British Institute of Comparative law in London, which are conducting research and are delighted to invite us to Grotius lectures or seminars on fighting terrorism whilst respecting fundamental rights are serious,[48] *then why have they not themselves been constructive in enforcing their demands? If the contemporary respectable heads of many international criminal law institutes in Europe contribute to international justice and prevention of cybercrime, but at the same time receive honourable doctoral degrees from the monopolised universities of criminal regimes, then how can they think offences should not be committed by the accused?*

The core question is, how can the arming of other states by our own machinery of guns and by the manufacture of weapons of mass destruction in order to improve our economy in Europe, Canada, the US, China, Japan, Russia, and so forth not come under different accusations and criminal law labels?

Which philosophies, moralities, ethic, logic, and reasoning should be recognised as legal and which as illegal? If the September 11, 2001 terrorist attacks mean to accuse Muslims, if morality means arming others, if honesty means selling weapons to those who cannot produce such advanced technical tools, if philosophy of law has in practice another mirror of reflections of the truth, let us be accused. If Kantianism or utilitarianism means happiness has to be at the price of the destruction of other values and lives, including those of innocent Jewish people or Muslims, then let us accuse together all Muslims or Jews of being terrorists and say that these terrorists are acting under the principle of international legal personality of their own groups or states. Fromm gives an excellent explanation:

> A person who has not been completely alienated, who has remained sensitive and able to feel, who has not lost the sense of dignity, who is not yet "for sale", who can still suffer over the suffering of others, who has not acquired fully the having mode of existence - briefly, a person who has remained a person and not become a thing - cannot help feeling lonely, powerless, isolated in present-day society. He cannot help doubting himself and his own convictions, if not his sanity. He cannot help suffering, even though he can experience

[48]Lehto (2010), pp. 107–108. See *also* the recent Security Council resolution demanding fights against terrorists. They have forgotten that they were the reason for the creation of terrorism since the outbreak of the first Gulf War in Iraq. Available at http://www.un.org/en/ga/search/view_doc.asp?symbol=S/RES/2249(2015), (Accessed March 12, 2016).

> moments of joy and clarity that are absent in the life of his "normal" contemporaries. Not rarely will he suffer from neurosis that results from the situation of a sane man living in an insane society, rather than that of the more conventional neurosis of a sick man trying to adapt himself to a sick society. In the process of going further in his analysis, i.e. of growing to greater independence and productivity, his neurotic symptoms will cure themselves.

If one does not want to see, if one does not like to follow the fact, or one does not want to open one's eyes to witness that it is European weapons that are sold to these groups and not vice versa, so let them be accursed. If moralities of the European philosophers such as Emanuel Kant, Friedrich Wilhelm Nietzsche Jeremy, Bentham, Hugo Grotius, Charles Robert Darwin, Erich Fromm, Karl Marx and Fredrick Engels, Hurt, and even Rawls (US) have such a definition and effect that allows the production of weapons of mass destruction of any form, any type, or any effect, so let them be accursed.

There must be a total misunderstanding of the philosophy of the law, of the theory of ethics, of the attitude of justice, of the values of humanity and its dignity, of the logic of teaching, of the integration of equal interests of man, and of the maintenance of the rights of men and women in the world. There must also be a serious misapprehension of the values of the lives of children in Europe compared with those in other parts of the world such as the Middle East, Africa, and Asia. Why are our children are killed with their weapons and their children are not killed? Why are the children of the presidents of the United States protected and not discriminated against because of their skin colour but our children are killed in millions. Do Iraqi, Afghan, Palestinian, and Syrian children have less worth? Was not September 11 a show to kill more and receive more oil? A proper law has to be realistic, has to be just, and has to be full of love for humanity and for the truth.

Above all, if the teaching methods, literature, and other doctrine in European law schools or European political science institutions have produced lawyers, judges, prosecutors, military officers, police officers, and other social authorities of such quality that they are blind to the fact of violations, then let them be accursed. If the European population does not realise that it is the fault of their own laws, regulations, economic interests, and other matters that terrorist behaviour is increasing and Islamic State groups are being created, then let them to be accused. The well-known European philosopher *Tomas Hobbes* in his social contract correctly asserts that:

> From this fundamental law of nature, by which men are commanded to endeavour peace, is derived this second law: that a man be willing, when others are so too, as far forth as for peace and defence of himself he shall think it necessary, to lay down this right to all things; and be contented with so much liberty against other men as he would allow other men against himself. For as long as every man holdeth this right, of doing anything he liketh; so long are all men in the condition of war. But if other men will not lay down their right, as well as he, then there is no reason for anyone to divest himself of his: for that were to expose himself to prey, which no man is bound to, rather than to dispose himself to peace. This is that law of the gospel: Whatsoever you require that others should do to you, that do ye to them. And that law of all men, quod tibi fieri non vis, alteri ne feceris. To lay down a man's right to anything is to divest himself of the liberty of hindering another of the benefit of his

> own right to the same. For he that renounceth or passeth away his right giveth not to any other man a right which he had not before, because there is nothing to which every man had not right by nature, but only standeth out of his way that he may enjoy his own original right without hindrance from him, not without hindrance from another. So that the effect which redoundeth to one man by another man's defect of right is but so much diminution of impediments to the use of his own right original.[49]

What is really the logic of law, the logic of morality, the philosophy of human rights law, and the meaning of unreasonable monopolization in the United Nations Charter within its Chapter VII? If peace means monopolization, if the interests of justice means having five permanent seats in the heart of the largest international peaceful union in the world, so let us have an inferior seat, let us be Muslim, and let us be a Jew. Even let us be animals, and let it be realised by others that they can give us any inhuman title that they hope, wish, and implement according to their human rights law. Schwarzenberger rightly asserts, "the existing framework of organised international society is merely a precarious international quasi-order." Alternatively, let us see the cruelty of the Charter of the United Nations more clearly—a hegemony of "a world order under law."[50]

7.13 Burning the European and Islamic Constitutions

It is more sensitive to say that, when political situations get harder and are aggravated through double morality, without the realisation of the truth behind government policies, the first attacks or threats are made against the *Quran*, the spiritual constitution of Islamic law. Historically, the President of the United States, Eisenhower advised the CIA agency, "We should do everything possible to stress the 'holy war' aspect," between Muslim nations.[51] This can be acts covering insult, abuse, maltreatment, and creating conflicts between different groups such as in Iraq, Syria, Africa, and Afghanistan. The conflicts have even been enlarged by threatening to burn the book in public. This is not a new method but an old one, which is also resorted to in Muslim countries, even by Muslims and more remarkably by a *mullah* (Islamic priest). *A group of Muslims in Persia unjustly murdered Ahmed Kasravi, a man of knowledge, a philosopher, and an excellent historian in 1946.* He was actually an Islamic priest in his youth but rose against the interpretation of Islam.[52] He was also a lawyer who taught national integration law at the University of Tehran.

One of his suggestions was to burn the *Quran*. Although one can fully understand his broad knowledge in various areas, in particular the development of the political history of Persia and the creation of the new philosophy of constitutional legislation, some of his opinions were actually against the core principles of the

[49]https://ebooks.adelaide.edu.au/h/hobbes/thomas/h68l/chapter14.html (Accessed June 23, 2015).

[50]Schwarzenberger (1968), p. 783.

[51]Kennedy (2016).

[52]Jazayery (1973), pp. 190–20, 191–192. See *also* http://www.jstor.org/stable/162242 (Accessed June 9, 2015).

Declaration of Human Rights law. The Declaration formulated the respect of all religious theories in 1948. He should have understood that the way to justice, peace, equality, humanity, re-education, reproduction, re-modification, complete abolition, and also evolution in thought, mind, and philosophy does not come through burning but by understanding that the book is respected by a large population of the world.

If any laws, rules, or principles are going to be changed, one cannot amend them by burning or increasing offensive behaviour against them but by decreasing the offensive acts, respect, understanding, the development of social structure, increasing human ability, and access to the heart of the people, by admiration and love. Education is the only way to prevent bloodshed. Similar offensive reactions to burning the *Quran* have recently been experienced in the United States and other parts of the globe. Kasravi was, together with his secretary, unjustly shot to death in a court. In addition, an Islamic group immediately and inhumanly attacked them with knives in the court. They were buried some hours later. The history of knowledge of man will never forgive this tragedy, even by the power of love.

What should be burnt is not a book but ignorance. Burning regulations do not bring new regulations but hate and aggressive behaviour. The rules and philosophy of law cannot be modified by the force of human arms, human aggressive conduct, insults, assaults, abuse, confiscation of each other's property, and by frustration of rules. We have to collect the similarity of rules, norms, provisions, and those principles that can be found within most regulations of civilisation of the world. These similarities have to be developed, extended, re-produced, re-stated, re-encouraged, and re-established in order to bring to light the ignorance or the delinquency of our existing law. Yet, this does not mean that the different enlightenments can abolish our beliefs; they can only help us improve our judgement of rules or provisions that are no longer practical and that have to be modified and readopted to the modern circumstances of the time.

In comparison, a reference can be made to European Union law. There are so many similarities between the basic intentions of European Union law and Islamic law that they cannot be ignored by any realistic lawyer. This means their terms and functions in many instances are interchangeable. In other words, when we burn the Islamic religious faith, we are, at the same time, burning European Union law. Serious objections may be made to this opinion regarding their similarities, philosophies, ethics, and the way in which they are implemented. For an understanding of both systems, it must be asserted that human rights principles are, in both systems, more or less the same, with the exception that one is directed by the power of religious mentality whilst the other is directed by the power of political attitude and interests. Furthermore, the European laws used to be not only brutal but also even in certain cases barbarous, much like Islamic practice. An offender under the European laws could not only be condemned to death but also tortured by the pouring of hot boiling oil down her/his throat. This has changed with the passage of the time and understanding and not by the burning or boiling. These changes and understanding should also come to those who follow the Islamic law, but not by insults, instead by love, education, and a law-making enlightenment.

In addition, both systems want the centralisation of power politics within one union and the distribution of wealth among all members of their unions. European Union members assist each other in case of armed conflict; the Islamic nations do the same. This means that burning one of these constitutions is the equivalent of burning both together. *We have to update both sides with the understanding of love for justice and love for the maintenance of purity and not cruelty. One can never spread a theory by the force of guns and one cannot use hate to create health.*

Yet, the question is whether the burning of the *Quran* or the European *Quran*—i.e. the European Constitution—is bad. Their burning may be good. The burning of the *Quran* brings the fact into recognition that it does not change any rules or provisions of the relevant law. If we burn the *Quranic* Union, we are proving at the same time our lack of knowledge, unawareness of political diplomacy, and ignorance of the rights of others. One of the serious problems of some Muslim societies is that they react very seriously to the burning of the book and sometimes handle the situation very aggressively.

It may be opportune if every Christian church, Islamic mosque, and even the European Union Court had an area to burn Constitutions, and this area could be used by anyone who wanted to burn a particular relevant statute. This could cause the area to be seldom used, and it would probably become a corner of peace for those who are looking for the similarity of the law and not divergences. The philosophy of pure theory of law is not and should not be the accusation of one another's nature, culture, religion, language, ethnic background, and social life. This philosophy also should not be either the burning of legislation or the flags of the United States, but it should be the way in which we understand one another's need for the expression of fairness, happiness, and justice by the norm and power of love.

References

Al-Hussein, Z. (2009). For love of country and international criminal law. *American University International Law Review, 24*(4), 647–664, 653.

Andersen, P. (2011). Klassisk og Kristen Naturret. In O. Hammerslev & H. P. Olsen (Eds.), *Restsfilosofi – ecntrale tekster og temaer* (pp. 71–96, 76–78). København: Hans Reitzels Forlag.

Bentham, J. (2002). Rights, representation, and reform: Nonsense upon stilts and other writings on the French revolution. In P. Schofield, C. Pease-Watkin, & C. Blamires (Eds.), *The collected works of Jeremy Bentham* (pp. 317–401). Oxford: Oxford University Press.

Cappelletti, M., Gordley, J., & Johnson, E. (1975). *Toward equal justice: A comparative study of legal aid in modern societies* (pp. 11–12). New York, NY: Oceana Publications.

Cohen, M. (1949). Moral aspects of the criminal law. *Yale Law Journal, 49*, 987–1026, 1025.

Cummings, S. L. (2011). Introduction: What good are lawyers? In S. L. Cummings (Ed.), *Paradox of professionalism lawyers and the possibility of justice* (p. 4). Cambridge: Cambridge University Press.

Devers, G., & Mendes-France, M. F. (2012). Presentation of the complaint filed before the international criminal court. In C. Meloni & G. Tognoni (Eds.), *Is there a court for Gaza? A test bench for international justice* (pp. 61–75, 71–72). The Hague: T.M. Asser Press, Springer.

di Beccaria, C. B. (1872). *An Essay on Crimes and Punishments* [1764] (De Voltaire, 1872), pp. 58–59.

Hallag, W. B. (2004). Can the Shari'a be restored? In Y. Yazbeck & B. F. Stowasser (Eds.), *Islamic law and the challenges of modernity* (pp. 21–53, 22). Altamira Press.

Harcourt, B. E. (2014). Beccaria's on crimes and punishments: A mirror on the history of the foundations of modern criminal law. In M. D. Dubber (Ed.), *Foundational texts in modern criminal law* (pp. 59–78, 43). Oxford: Oxford University Press.

Hart, H. L. A. (1982). *Essays on Benthan* (p. 79). Oxford: Clarendon Press.

Inger, G. (2011). *Svensk Rättshistoria* (pp. 308–309). Malmö: Liber AB.

Jazayery, M. A. (1973). Ahmad Kasravi and the Controversy over Persian poetry 1. Kasravi's analysis of Persian poetry. *International Journal of Middle East Studies, 4*(2), 190–203, 191–192.

Kelsen, H. (1957). *What is justice? Justice, law and politics in the mirror of science*. Oakland: University of California Press.

Kelsen, H. (1967). *Pure theory of law* (M. Knight, Trans.). Oakland: University of California Press.

Kennedy, R. F. (2016). *Why the Arabs don't want us in Syria: They don't hate 'our freedoms.' They hate that we've betrayed our ideals in their own countries—for oil*. Available at http://www.politico.eu/article/why-the-arabs-dont-want-us-in-syria-mideast-conflict-oil-intervention/. Accessed 4 March 2016.

Lehto, M. (2010). *Indirect responsibility for terrorist acts: Redefinition of the concept of terrorism, beyond violent act* (pp. 107–108). Leiden: Martinus Nijhoff Publisher.

Malekian, F. (1991). *International criminal law* (Vol. 2). Stockholm: Almqvist & Wiksell International.

Malekian, F. (2011). The laws governing crimes against women constituting obligatio Erga Omnes. In D. W. Pike (Ed.), *Crimes against women* (pp. 3–22). New York, BY: Nova Science Publishers.

Malekian, F. (2012). Judging international criminal justice in the occupied territories. *International Criminal Law Review, 12*, 827–869, 829.

Malekian, F. (2014). The international criminal law of children on war crimes. *Międzynarodowa odpowiedzialność karna za zbrodnie wojenne popełniane na dzieciach, 13*(25), 31–69, 48.

Mannheim, H. (1940). *War and crime* (pp. 19–20). London: Watts & Co.

Mayer, A. E. (2004). Internationalizing the convention on women's rights: Arab countries face the CEDAW committee. In Y. Yazbeck & B. F. Stowasser (Eds.), *Islamic law and the challenges of modernity* (pp. 133–160, 133). Altamira Press.

Mukerjee, M. (2011). *Churchill's secret war: The British empire and the ravaging of India during World War II*. New York, NY: Basic Books.

Nussbaum, M. C. (2013). *Political emotions: Why love matters for justice* (p. 15). Cambridge, MA: Harvard University Press.

Rejali, D. (2007). *Torture and democracy*. Princeton, NJ: Princeton University Press.

Schofield, P. (2003). Jeremy Bentham's 'Nonsense upon Stilts'. *Utilitas, 15*(1), 1–26.

Schwarzenberger, G. (1968). *International law: As applied by international courts and tribunals, Vol. II The law of armed conflict* (p. 469). London: Stevens & Sons Limited.

Sidney, A. (1698). *Discourses concerning government*. T. G. West (Ed.). London: MDCXCVIII. Available at http://oll.libertyfund.org/titles/sidney-discourses-concerning-government-1698-ed.

Wägenbaur, B. (2013). *Court of the European Union* (p. 12). C.H. Beck. Hart. Nomos.

Young, D. B. (1983). Cesare Beccaria: Utilitarian or Retributivist? *Journal of Criminal Justice, 11*, 317, 318.

Chapter 8
Maestro of the Norm of Love on the Morality of Criminal Law

8.1 Ensuring Morality

The concept of morality relates to a set of precepts, and rules about good, bad, evil, justice, injustice, right and wrong. It is based on a system of rules that relate to the reason for our conduct or our personal behaviour. This means the concept of morality is affected in several ways. This may be the morality in one's own family and the concept of morality in the culture. Although the concept of morality or personal reason varies from one person to another, the basic concept of morality is the same and cannot be changed because of personal will. According to Lysander Spooner, this basic concept of morality constitutes duties in *natural law* and is different from *honest morality* that forces man to carry out his duties towards the whole community as a whole. He explains that:

> Man, no doubt, owes many other moral duties to his fellow men; such as to feed the hungry, clothe the naked, shelter the homeless, care for the sick, protect the defenceless, assist the weak, and enlighten the ignorant. But these are simply moral duties, of which each man must be his own judge, in each particular case, as to whether, and how, and how far, he can, or will, perform them. But of his legal duty—that is, of his duty to live honestly towards his fellow men—his fellow men not only may judge, but, for their own protection, must judge. And, if need be, they may rightfully compel him to perform it. They may do this, acting singly, or in concert. They may do it on the instant, as the necessity arises, or deliberately and systematically, if they prefer to do so, and the exigency will admit of it.[1]

The concept of morality is also closely connected to the concept of humanity. Many of us have, more or less, a similar understanding of the principles of humanity. Even though we may have different opinions about certain matters, certain family interests, certain cultural practices, we are still aware that we should not, with the ethics of appropriate reason, protest against one another's liberty,

[1]Spooner (1882). Available at http://oll.libertyfund.org/titles/spooner-natural-law-or-the-science-of-justice-1882 (Accessed May 17, 2015).

F. Malekian, *Judgments of Love in Criminal Justice*,
DOI 10.1007/978-3-319-46900-3_8

freedom of choice, freedom of speech, and freedom of having our own interpretation of things. The concept of morality plays a significant role in regulating social relations and ensuring and maintaining social order. Some of these principles are our collective attitude towards having a good and healthy system of justice, not only in the corridors of national courts but also in international ones.

> The impact of morals on law is obvious and has many causes. Both have to do with people's behaviour in relation to each other, and they cover partly the same types of human activities. This makes for a continuous flow of ideas and conceptions from the one filed into the other. Similarities between the language of law and that of morals, e.g. the double connotation of words like 'right', 'wrong', 'duty' and 'obligation', give evidence of past interrelationship, and facilities the mutual influence. The fact that law is connected with force does not make it independent of moral support. Application of force has a tendency to be either inefficient or intolerable if it lacks foundation in moral convictions. . .Legal philosophy can in many cases be interpreted as a search for moral principles suitable to satisfy the need of justification. This tendency is particularly prominent in writings concerned with criminal law, where the element of force is most conspicuous.[2]

Law and morality have very interrelated relations, but each has its own realm of identity. Morality as a concept of philosophical reason is based on the intimate personal ethics of each individual in her/his behaviour in the given conduct. When a law is regulated, it is affected by the sense of our morality, such as the provisions of the Covenant on Civil and Political Rights. However, many claim that a law is almost a positive written document and does not contain the spirit of morality. Those who express such opinions are positivists. However, those who call themselves positivists are indeed not as numerous as the contemporary positions of international law. Those who believe in the existence of natural rights are naturalists. One of the serious problems of positivist views is that they ignore the fact that most of our laws are formulated upon a code of morality.

8.2 Abolishing the Code of Morality

A code of morality is the standard that we evaluate and consider necessary. A code of morality may, however, be divided into different groups. One is personal codes and family codes which may be different from one another. The second group is national and regional codes as, for example, the relations between the members of the European Union and the Union itself. The third group is international organisational codes compared with the universal human community code. By organisational we mean those rules of highly recognised international organisations such as the United Nations. By the universal human community code of morality we mean where the standard of morality of all these groups becomes one intention and solely one code. For example, none of us want to destroy the earth, massacre the United States population, commit genocide against the United Kingdom's

[2]Eckhoff (1963), p. 74.

inhabitants, eliminate the Spanish people, devastate French society, cause Denmark to disappear, annihilate the populations of China, Germany, Japan, Israel or Russia.

Although we are well aware of the fact that all these states have been engaged in the massacre or plundering of the population of our global neighbours at different historical times, the code of morality in the international community even goes against the drafting of such ideas. It guides us towards the principle of humanity that killing is not permitted, that revenge is abolished, that hate has to be replaced with the power of love, that humanity is not achieved by killing, that victims cannot be free from unpleasant historical evidence, and that justice does not mean killing. It is forgiveness. The reason is, we do not want to punish the children of the past generation, and nor do we want to punish the whole United States for the criminal acts of the presidents and election of all these governments by their past populations. *The reason is also that we want people to appreciate the appropriate connotation of each other's love for the creation of healthful co-existence on earth. An international lawyer who achieves the principles of humanity without the concept of morality and love is orchestrating a piece of music without sound.*[3]

For example, with different pieces of acts of legislation we have abolished slavery, capital punishment, and apartheid. When we abolish a law, the purpose is not solely the termination or repeal of the law. It does not just mean that we live in a modern time which does not accept and permit such conduct. But we want the very offensive concept of morality to become a legal norm, a customary norm, a moral norm, or a practice. When we use the term 'abolition,' it mostly expresses the character of a certain bad habit that was a norm. Thus, with the term we mean that it is high time to end immoral conduct against human dignity. This means that our moral norms or moral codes have been altered and we recognise immoral conduct as criminal conduct today.

It also means that we are applying a sense of human morality at a very high level of recognition and humanity. For instance, the international legal community, various bodies of the United Nations, and a considerable number of international entities condemn the Chinese regime for the violations of international human rights law, or the application of cruel penalties such as capital punishment, or torturing individuals for their democratic demands. Here, the world does not solely wish to implement the provisions of international human rights conventions but that they wish to make the leaders of criminal justice, criminal legislation, judges, prosecutors, and the high authorities of the relevant country, including its legislative organs, aware of the fact that engaging in the above conducts no longer implicates the application of punishment. They are instead a gross violation of norms of legality and morality.[4] *This is what I call the norm of love.*

---

[3]Cummings (2011), pp. 1–2.

[4]http://www.radioshahrvand.com/religious-rights/6279-judge-salvati.html (Accessed June 9, 2015).

It means a sophisticated degree of recognition of legal and moral norms for the implementation of human justice with love and a high level of forgiveness, not just by the order of law and time pressure but also with the power of human love for justice and law. As the international lawyer Martin Luther King expresses it, "have we not come to such an impasse in the modern world that we must love our enemies - or else? The chain reaction of evil - hate begetting hate, wars producing more wars - must be broken, or else we shall be plunged into the dark abyss of annihilation." Therefore, "I have decided to stick with love. Hate is too great a burden to bear."

Consequently, with the abolition of certain laws, we abolish our moral code of wrongful conduct—not only against the ethical or moral understanding of the law but also against the first principles of natural law, such as equality between all human beings, equality of race, equality of ethnicity, and equality of all men before the house of justice.

> When we look at modern man, we have to face the fact...that modern man suffers from a kind of poverty of the spirit, which stands in glaring contrast to his scientific and technological abundance; We've learned to fly the air like birds, we've learned to swim the seas like fish, and yet we haven't learned to walk the Earth as brothers and sisters...[5]

8.3 Departing from Morality

With most international conventions, international resolutions, or new international human rights legal norms, we terminate or amend the code of morality that we think has to be modified. The modification is not because we are seeking the modernisation of the legal system but re-modification of the code of morality or legality that is not equitable for the norms of love for human beings. A human rights mission is not supposed to win the minds but the hearts.[6] It means that the borderline of our love has increased and the borderline of our foolishness has decreased. Thus, most of the time, the intention of our amendment, legislation, adoption, termination, or approval is to change the direction of the law towards a better tolerance of its legal and moral norms. All these actions mean that the code of legality and the code of morality are affected by our high level of understanding, which can be termed the dignity of the code of love.[7]

Thus, the norm of love is a norm which is not directly referred to in positive, unwritten, or natural law. It has the function and the role of being the final norm of law that demands the expression of and enlightenment about wrongful human legal or moral conduct. This means that we attach ourselves to the concept of love in order to overcome the obscurity of wrongful behaviour, inhuman morality, irrational

---

[5]Martin Luther King.

[6]For instance, see a critical analysis of the Lisbon Treaty by Dougan (2008), p. 669.

[7]Martin Luther King. See also Vischer (2014), pp. 35–45.

legislation, imparted harm to human dignity, individualistic approaches to wealth, and incredibility of our conscience to mankind.

That is why, when you examine the legal and moral evolution of the system of international law, you will find that the law is changing all the time and adapting itself to the needs of human beings. I believe our generation lived imprudently, lacking proper judgement or was short of wisdom. This does not mean that human beings were stupid, the law was wrong, or morality was weak. *Rather, it means that all these were strong but not sufficient to understand that we cannot chase millions of people from one country to another country for the reason of trade, we cannot hunt people because they have a different skin colour, and we cannot kill people because they have different cultures, religions, beliefs, or languages. In addition, their children cannot be the food of our dogs and their brains the food on our plates. For example, the Spanish tore Indian children for their dogs and during the Thirty Years War in Europe, children's brains were cooked food.*

The evolution of international law does not necessarily mean that the view of our morality is changing; the borderline of our legality is shifting or the boundaries of our territory are stretching. On contrary to this, the evolution means that we are limiting our territory's borders, we are departing from colonisation, we are slowly realising that the terms of legality, morality, and various philosophies of law, religious ethical theories, and perceptions and enlightenments are not sufficient for the existence of justice between human beings. The Thirty Years War between different groups in Europe is a clear example of the fact that we were moving towards a norm that is the centre of the law, the end code of individual morality applying to collective conduct and the repeal of the monopolisation of the power of the law by religious mentality or any dictatorship. This was a move towards the concept of enlightenment as a whole. The theory of enlightenment went to the core of the issue of human value, including individual dignity. As we have mentioned, some well-known followers of this philosophy were Beccaria, Grotius, Kant, Montesquieu, Pufendorf, and Rousseau.

The various meetings and negotiations in the eighteenth and nineteenth centuries, the First World War, the League of Nations, and the establishment of the United Nations were small steps towards a norm that has to be stronger than any other norm. *This was the norm of understanding each other's individual and collective needs. It is a typical form of the norm of love but a very soft form of it because the love norm has to be influential, significant, leading, have a powerful character, and above all prohibit all types of killings.* However, these characteristics are not and cannot be seen in the Charter. This is because although this norm exists in the Charter, the norm of love is monopolised entirely to control the power of the Security Council. That is why I have mentioned in the above sections that there are different moral codes between groups, families, and nations.

8.4 Subdivision of Moral

One may divide moral groups into sub-groups. The most important facet of these classifications is that, although they are presenting different codes of morality and ethics, all have a green line that is more or less the same in their code of morality. Many codes of morality which can be found in the Christian, Catholic, Jewish, Muslim, European Union, Common Law, Chinese, Canadian, Russian, Australian, and United States constitutions are obviously the same, even though they are expressed in different terms. This understanding of the role of the moral code can also be seen in the structure of the laws. Obviously, most laws practised by most nations of the world have a number of similarities. Many Persian and French civil codes are the same, although the former also uses the Islamic legal system. Swedish codes followed many German codes, and most states of Europe are today abiding by the principles of the European Union governing the provisions of criminal law.

The civil law understanding of legal norms is the same among many European civil law systems. The basic difference between common law and civil law legal traditions relates to the sources of law. For instance, the common law systems mostly use statutes. Hence, judicial cases are the most significant source of law. The latter opens the hands of the judges to the development of rules. This includes the elements concerning proof of the crime of murder which can be found in case law rather than in statutes. The decisions of higher courts should therefore maintain consistency between various legal issues. In civil law systems, however, the provisions of the precise law restrict judges and they therefore have less possibility to develop the law.

In the common law systems, judges are arbitrators between parties whilst in civil law systems, the judges are investigators. Most countries in the world have civil law systems. The common law system is limited to countries which were English colonies and are, therefore, influenced by the Anglo-Saxon tradition. These include as Australia, Bangladesh, Canada, Hong Kong, Ireland, India, Pakistan (also Islamic), Uganda, and the United States. Yet, it is true that both common law and civil law systems are using the same methodologies. This means that, in a civil law system, a judge may or may not deliberately develop the law. In other words, the concept of murder is murder in any legal system, regardless of how we apply the law. Therefore, both systems not only rely on the code of legality but also on the code of morality. Therefore, both codes are developing the scope of the law and these developments cannot depart from the principles of international human rights laws, the provisions of which undoubtedly encourage the norm of love for true justice.

8.5 Differences Between Legality and Morality

Although we know that there are many similarities between the two concepts of morality and legality, there are also differences between these two significant elements of the theory of justice. Both are reasonably part of the theory of law but can sometimes interact closely and sometimes exhibit very distinctive characteristics of their own. One of the differences is that moral norms are not necessarily uniform, while legal norms are. Yet, quite a number of legal norms in international law and particularly in international criminal law cannot be separated from their moral codes of ethics.

The second difference concerns sanctions. Although both concepts of legal and moral norms are integrated into different laws, the force of legislation secures the rule of law. This is constrained by the state organs. Again, here, the situation is different in the international legal system. Since a law is combined of legal and moral norms, the sanctions for the enforcement of the law are also the sanctions for the enforcement of the moral code that is formulated into the law. For example, when we deal with the Convention on the Rights of the Child, we are applying three significant principles. These are the principles of legality, morality, and love. The relevant convention, like other international conventions, does not have any particular sanction for its enforceability. However, I am not dealing here specifically with the European courts and their measures concerning the fulfilment of the law by the state which violates it.

Yet other sanctions, such as reference to different regional or international courts, are symbolic and cannot be enforced by any international authority. The only remaining sanction or the remaining alternative for us has a moral nature. That means that when we sign and ratify an international convention, we have not only a legal but also a moral obligation to fulfil its requirements. The grave violations of the principles of certain international conventions may be a strong reason for collective actions against the violator state. This policy also depends on whether the state parties to the relevant international conventions are willing act.

Another difference is that rules of positive law may be altered, while the rule of morality is very difficult to change. Still, any change to the morality principle mostly concerns the *surface of the rules* of morality and not the substance of the principle. For instance, in recent decades, sexual relations between members of the same sex were not only seen as against the law but strongly against the principle of morality in most societies. This concept is now changing, while this change is solely of concern to the surface of the principle and not its substance. This means that the relevant relations do not have any effect on the substance of human morality. The new legislation evaluates the relations between human beings as a matter of individual choice and not a matter of collective decisions. Here, it is the individuals who have the highest natural value.

Clearly, the natural or positive law should not allow any individual to interfere with entirely private physical feelings of other individuals. This is also what can be called the principle of love for fairness which does not welcome legal or moral interference. Although such law and morality may exist amongst many nations, one has to look for the soul of the law and not solely its implementation. If the provisions of a law are harsh, its substance for fair justice must not follow the same tactic. The soul of all laws has to respect human beings. Still, many states may not permit sexual relations between members of the same gender and have criminalised such relations, even with the application of capital punishment or the like.

Evidently, judges of such legislation should bear in mind that justice is not fulfilled by the application of penalties but by the substance of good judgment accompanied by the principles of human rights laws.[8] Yet, one has to admit the theory that we still have far to go to realise that punishment of national or international criminals, and bringing the big powers into criminal jurisdiction does not help to any degree or level in preventing or decreasing criminality in the world; on the contrary, it may increase criminality. Plato, the founder of the Academy of Athens, asserts that "Good people do not need laws to tell them to act responsibly, while bad people will find a way around the laws."

This theory is based on the fact that when we rely on the mechanism of criminal justice, we also rely on the concept of criminality. That criminality of our nature is a fact and cannot be cured by means other than criminalisation of legislation, criminalisation of prosecution, and finally criminalisation of our judgment. In fact, criminalisation is employed as an easy solution, despite the well-settled principle that reference to criminal justice as a means of repressive control should only be used as the last alternative. This means we pay no attention to the fact that the nature of love in our legal system is ignored and is not sought with full love for justice and prevention of all crimes by the substance of our good nature.[9]

Almost no law has been enacted with the purpose that its subjects should violate its rules. We rely on the bad nature of man and ignore the fact that all individuals in the world have the same intention of living in peace, justice, and love. Therefore, the idea of punishment has to be abolished, and the idea of love for justice has to replace the concept of criminal jurisdiction. In other words, we have to establish courts that are persuading courts of love, their duties being from time to time to speak, and invite those who are experiencing conflicts or may create conflicts. They should come to the courts of love for humanity and justice and modify their position with such intentions.[10]

[8]Dan-Cohen (2014), pp. 116–118.

[9]Karnell (2011), p. 96.

[10]Examine section 9 *infra*.

8.6 Morality Effecting International Legal Personality

Another aspect of the principle of morality is that when the principles of law and morality contradict in certain significant matters, the principle of morality may prevail when the principle of legality does not function properly. Two clear examples are the priority of the principle of morality over legality after the end of the Second World War in 1944 and the official end of apartheid in 1990.

Yet the principle of morality may be a reason for the drafting, adoption, or re-modification of the law. Therefore, we may formulate new rules for the prevention of certain acts that are seen as being against the moral standard of the national or international community as a whole. As we have stated, norms of humanitarian law are codified to protect human suffering and protect the high value of human morality. The reason for their formulation is that the commission of certain acts has been considered to be against human morality, such as violent acts against civilians or those who are not combatants. The protection of the injured, sick women, children and other subjects has been seen as necessary for the daily life of civilians. These are all the effect of moral rules that are formulated into legal norms.

There is also the possibility that a legal norm be considered a moral norm because of its very high integrity. A clear example is the equality of the international legal personality of states which is a combination of politico-legal/moral standards. However, we do not deny the fact that classical international law recognises states under different categories. The non-recognition of the international legal personality of a state does not necessarily imply inequality of that state or nation in the world. An illustrative example is the full statehood of Palestine. We are also aware of the fact that states may not be equal in law and practice. Chapter VII of the Charter of the United Nations organisation points to this unfortunate fact.

From this perspective, the international legal personality today also constitutes the international moral personality of states, and it is almost against international community integrity to classify a state as not having an international legal personality. These international legal and moral personalities of states are in fact the pinnacle of understanding the norm of love for equality between nations. It is this international personality which also characterises the internationally criminally wrongful conduct of states. Likewise, there is also an international personality of love for the interests of justice and for the prevention of criminal conduct of states. The international legal personality also implies the end of suzerain states, colonial states, and wholly or half-dependent states. For instance, the occupation of the Gaza Strip is against the international legal or moral personality of the relevant state and above all the *international personality of the love norm of justice*.

One should also bear in mind that being a state is a fact which comes through recognition and is therefore not solely a question of law. This concept is developed from the fundamental premises known as the 'constitutive' theory of recognition. The theory maintains that a state is, and becomes, an international person only by the act or the declaration of recognition. This means political, moral, or humanitarian support of the population and territorial independence of the relevant state. The 'fact' principle could prevent any extension of the law concerning any other matter.[11] This also means that legal norms could not play any effective role for the purpose of recognition. Thus, two elements traditionally had a very decisive function for the purpose of recognition. These were, as we have mentioned above, political and moral elements. The political element encouraged and was a strong reason for the recognition of the relevant state by other states. The moral element demonstrated full sympathy with the population of the occupied territory. Both, and each one of them separately, demanded the establishment of the rights of the relevant state. It is a fact that naturalists and positivists had different opinions concerning recognition. Yet, there is a relationship between the theory of morality and the theory of justice. Accordingly,

> The relation between the theory of morality and justice is this: The latter is a component of the former, but exactly where the one ends the other begins is unclear. The most helpful way to make the distinction is to say that an account of justice is that part of the theory of morality that deals with the legitimate structure of institutions. The institutions of a just nation, for example, are designed to enforce some of people's obligations on the one hand and to protect people's freedom on the other. The theory of justice details the features of these institutions. It also details the features of international or global institutions enforcing obligations and protecting freedom.[12]

The basic principle of morality, as we have stated, varies from law to law and culture to culture. Yet, this disparity does not mean that morality should be violated. In addition, morality among different people may vary, but this variation does not refer to the code of morality that prevails among the members of the same society. A similar theory concerns the understanding of morality at the international level. The concept of morality is itself divided into the *descriptive* theory of morality and the *normative* theory of morality.

The first theory refers to the issue of how people understand different matters and their values and what is right or wrong. The second theory refers to the principle of how people ought to act and how they should understand the difference between right and wrong. The former covers our method of investigation and questions of values whilst the second covers the theoretical development of the idea. As Hobbes describes, "by manners I mean not here decency of behaviour, as how one man should salute another, or how a man should wash his mouth or pick his teeth before company, and such other points of small morals, but those qualities of mankind that concern their living together in peace and unity."[13] That means that men should love one another.[14]

[11]Crawford (1976), p. 95. Available at http://www.ilsa.org/jessup/jessup13/British%20Yearbook%20of%20International%20Law-1977-Crawford-93-182.pdf (Accessed February 14, 2015).

[12]Luper-Foy (Ed.) (1988a), pp. 3–4.

[13]Thomas Hobbes, *Leviathan*, Chapter XI, paragraph 1).

[14]de Vattel (1758, 1916), p. 117.

8.7 The Small System of International Criminal Law

If we could properly understand the significant function of the norm of love for justice and equality between man and man, villager and villager, and the educated or the uneducated, it would not be necessary for us to recognise a bulk of conventions on the system of international criminal law. By this, my intention is not to orient towards the views of the respectful international or national lawyers, judges, or any other law-abiding fellow man in my own poor interpretation of the law. However, I wish to convince the law, and particularly the system of international criminal law and justice, that its provisions do not necessarily need to be accepted by different populations, nations, regions, governments, or states. This is because a *small*, but virtually a substantive system of international criminal law and justice already exists within most civilizations of the world, and it has to be realised.

This small system of international criminal law and justice is called the motivation of the power of love, the canon of justice, or the canon of primary understanding of international criminal norms. In other words, nations do not necessarily need to understand what provisions of international criminal law and justice are. This is based on the fact that every civilisation already understands that rape is not permitted, murdering is prohibited, killing on a large scale is a massive killing and therefore indicates more violations of the people's integrity, their cultures, language, ethnic origin, religious beliefs, and any other social identity. This means that every nation benefits from the provisions of a small system of international criminal law. The system of cultural justice, which is located within the inner structure of each society, prohibits in accordance with the law of nature, by the law of man, by the law of the region, and by the law of love, any commission of criminal conduct. They are genocide, apartheid, discrimination, mass rape, and torture. Sir William Blackstone believed "crimes are more effectually prevented by the certainty than by the severity, of punishment."[15] As Beccaria articulates, this can be correct "if the relation between the object and the sensation is to remain constant"[16] in national or international criminal law. I shall modify slightly their statements by the fact that *it is not the large number of provisions of international criminal law or national criminal law which prevents criminal conduct but the expression of perpetual love to avoid criminal actions by the subjects of the law. Consequently, the intention should be to have preventive justice rather than punitive justice.*

The system of international criminal law does not need to be large but appropriate to the culture, understandable by all men, and able to prevent violations by the strength of love. On the one hand, speaking about the theory of the norm of love is simple since we are not requiring any extra tools or regulations to be adopted and integrated into the law of different nations or their cultures. They are already there. *This means that our small system of international criminal law has to be first*

[15]Blackstone (1765–1769), p. 17. Stern (2014), p. 73.

[16]Harcourt (2014), p. 58.

acknowledged by different cultures and the ICC before the concept of love can come to the main system of international criminal law. On the other hand, it is complicated for us because we are not used to talking about the norm of love in connection with law. We must therefore try to find a more elegant way to convince others of the significant function of the system of international criminal law. *However, we should remember that simplicity prevents complexity, and complexity rejects the simplicity of the theory that love is a norm and a faculty, the modesty, simplicity, and nakedness of which can be appreciated more easily by groups or nations than is the case for the complicated doctrine. This has to be lectured in our schools of law in order to prevent more violations and foster the unity of the laws by the norm of love.* Henry Corbin, the French philosopher, in describing the philosophy of a Persian philosopher, namely Mulla Sadra, concentrates on the significant effect of this unity of law in the soul of human beings and the holiness of humankind in order achieve to the valuable intelligence of a union of love. He points out that

> All the levels of the modes of being and perception are governed by the same law of unity, which at the level of the intelligible world is the unity of intellection, of the intelligizing subject, and of the Form intelligized — the same unity as that of love, lover and beloved. Within this perspective we can perceive what Sadra meant by the unitive union of the human soul, in the supreme awareness of its acts of knowledge, with the active Intelligence which is the Holy Spirit. It is never a question of an arithmetical unity, but of an intelligible unity permitting the reciprocity which allows us to understand that, in the soul which it metamorphoses, the Form—or Idea—intelligized by the active Intelligence is a Form which intelligizes itself, and that as a result the active Intelligence or Holy Spirit intelligizes itself in the soul's act of intellection. Reciprocally, the soul, as a Form intelligizing itself, intelligizes itself as a Form intelligized by the active Intelligence.[17]

The value of simplicity of the fact therefore denotes the purity of the norm of love. It may be relevant to explain here that by the term 'international human rights law' not only are we referring to the relevant law itself but also to other areas of the sciences of law, such as international criminal law or justice. Thus, referring to one type of law is as equal as referring to all three at the same time since they protect each other's legal province. Consequently, the simplicity of the fact is so great and logical for every human being, given that we become involved in a more complicated position with lawyers who want the law to be law, who struggle to extinguish the moral aspects of the law and who try to be totally positivist or Scandinavian realist.[18]

One should remember the fact that a norm of law is not, in the first stage, written for lawyers, nor is it written for judges, for prosecutors, or for any other relevant authorities. The law is at first glance obviously written for the layman. By the term 'layman' I mean anyone who is not directly involved with the questions of law. They are those who should understand the law and respect its merits. This is particularly obvious in the case of international crimes.

[17]Corbin (2014), pp. 343–344.

[18]Consult Holtermann (2006), pp. 37–44. See also Dalberg-Larsen (2006), pp. 11–13 and 90–91.

Predominantly, if the layman realises the small system of international criminal law—he will also realise the greater system of international criminal law, too. The substance of the love norm is to search for non-violation, which exists in our nature, which comes into action when there is a dynamic need for prevention of atrocities, and any man can understand this. Here, non-violation is or should be the pure theory of law. I suppose it is a principle within all legal systems that the pure theory of justice or pure theory of law or pure theory of humanity all concur with the non-violative principle. This principle of non-violation cannot properly be enforced so long as we do not understand the pure theory of the reason for non-violation of the law or non-violation of the given conventions. The pure theory of reason is itself here the pure theory of love for the respect of human integrity and common human will that can be found in our own homes, our institutions, and in our jurisdiction. This reason can also be translated into the common principle of humanity that is identical for every human being. We should remember that if a system becomes big, the problem also gets much bigger, but if a system becomes small, the problem also becomes smaller. This is due to the fact that the provisions of the international criminal law system are too complicated to be understood by most people, but there is no such condition on the norms of love for being understood by the same subjects of the law. This is what I call the small system of international criminal law with the love norm.

The theory is located in the reason that killing is against the love of humanity, a very simple logic that should be realised more easily than any other complicated theory of law. Furthermore, with the pure theory of love, we come across the fact that the reason for our laws is the fortification of our love or our more common interests. I mean, the language of love is the only language which is simple enough to be understood by all and does not necessitate education by law. *Love is the only entrance to the problems of violations which has to be understood not only by the faculties of laws and courts but also by our governments and the United Nations as a whole. If law exports and imports war, it will receive the same cargo, but if it exports and imports love as a basic reason for its formulation, it will bring and generate love in return for the theory of law. The norm of love therefore aims to secure the accuracy of this crucial and powerful component of jurisdiction which is called international criminal law and justice.*

8.8 Training Love for International Criminal Justice

It has hitherto been assumed that the law has always been a conflict between morality and legality, but it has rarely been said that the most serious conflict of law is the misunderstanding of its nature, mistreatment of its subjects, miscalculation by governments, misuse of its power by political parties, and misunderstanding of the intention of the law. This is to the benefit of its subjects. The law does not actually exist at all. It is and has always been an abstract idea which has, from time to time, been modified by us when we feel that the rules of the code of morality no longer function well. It is here that we have attempted to ascertain by different means the objects and the reason of the law. This is in order to extend our knowledge of the law and answer the question why the law does not prevent human suffering. It means there is a norm which is present or absent based on how we deal with the norm.

The question is whether we really need more evidence to prove that our international criminal law is not working properly. If murdering one million of our fellow humans in Rwanda is not enough to prove the case, if thirty million killings of individuals in the Soviet Socialist Republic are not sufficient, and if several thousand deaths of the Kurdish population was a joke, then we are completely with a completely mad theory of criminal law. Still, if the massive killing and destruction in Vietnam was a cold war game, if the killing of over one million individuals in the war between Iraq and Iran is not against human values, and if the killings of thousands and thousands Palestinian by the Zionist government is a tradition, then we are playing a productive sport. In addition, if the killing of several million innocent Jews was a school homework policy in Europe, and if the killing of one million pro-Pakistan Bengalis was only an accident, then we must realise that we are no longer lawyers in substance but solely in name.

> There is a whole range of behaviour, such as torture, murder of the innocent, and racism, that nearly all agree is wrong. A nation-state accused of torture does not respond by saying that a condemnation of torture is just a matter of subjective morality. The state's leaders do not respond by saying, 'We think torture is rights, but you do not.' Rather, the standard response is to deny that any torture took place. If the evidence of torture is too strong, a finger will be pointed either at the victim or at the morally outrage country. 'They do it, too.' In this case the guilt is spread to all. Even the Nazis denied that genocide took place. What is important is that no state relies there is nothing wrong with genocide or torture. Hence, the head of a multinational need have no fear of cultural imperialism when she or he takes a stand in favour of democracy and against torture and genocide.[19]

Do we really need more experience to be aware of the fact that our laws and legal systems are not working properly in national and regional conflicts? A new method of thought may therefore be necessary to give strength to the law in order to be acknowledged by our legal system and investigate the fact that the reasons of law are sometimes different from the principles of law. Here, we are looking for the elements of pure reason and not necessarily what constitutes the principles of the relevant law. By this, we are searching for the basic reasons that are the cause of the adoption of the law. For example, when a system accepts in its legislation that genocide constitutes a crime, this does not mean that the system is going to prevent the commission of genocide under its jurisdiction, but the system underlines the fact that genocide is against the legal spirit of love to human beings. In addition, it means wherever and whenever it is committed, the system will prosecute the relevant accused people if they are arrested under its jurisdiction. Here, the system applies the universality principle and manifests the fact that the principle encourages non-violation and that great violations of the system of international criminal justice are against the code of morality recognised by man.

---

[19]Norman Bowie, 'The Moral Obligations of Multinational Corporations' in Luper-Foy (1988b), p. 107.

8.9 Deliberation of Love in the Courtroom

Justice that is not honourable is not justice at all but a defeat of fairness. The ethic of love encompasses, in all its forms, a code of conduct. Love has no particular substance or characteristics that differentiate it from other codes of conduct. The norm of love is not the knowledge of mathematics nor is it the substance of chemical knowledge. The principle of love depends on the principle of truth and not only the truth but also the truth which does not give the right to choose. However, I am not speaking about different principles of codes of loves or moralities. These include personal codes, religious codes, and cultural codes. The concept of love must not be a false concept and should have a substance of understanding of the principles of empathy, truth, fairness, evidence, justice, and trust. This is particularly significant in the case of the code of conduct, which has an international character. It has to keep its impartiality and not violate the basic principles of the interests of justice and the truth.

An example is the Charles Taylor Trial and the possible falsification of evidence against the accused. This was asserted by the Senegalese judge, Justice El Hadji Malick Sow, who served as an alternate judge for Trial Chamber II of the Special Court of Sierra Leone that tried the former Liberian president, Charles Taylor. He had a dissenting view. According to him, *the three elementary principles of justice, i.e. legality, morality, and love, had disappeared from the Court decision because of the corruption of evidence and probably judges by Western money*. Although the Court reached a unanimous decision, he expressed his dissenting view because of information which came to him just before delivering the judgment. Of the three judges, one was intentionally absent. Sow's microphone was turned off before starting and Justice El Hadji Malick Sow was taken out of the Court by the use of physical force. He managed to state in the Court the following *brilliant declaration*:

> The only moment where a Judge can express his opinion is during the deliberations or in the courtroom, and pursuant to the Rules, when there are no serious deliberations, the only place left for me in the courtroom. I won't get — because I think we have been sitting for too long but for me I have my *dissenting opinion* and I disagree with the findings and conclusions of the other Judges, because for me under any mode of liability, under any accepted standard of proof the guilt of the accused from the evidence provided in this trial is not proved beyond reasonable doubt by the Prosecution. *And my only worry is that the whole system is not consistent with all the principles we know and love, and the system is not consistent with all the values of international criminal justice, and I'm afraid the whole system is under grave danger of just losing all credibility, and I'm afraid this whole thing is headed for failure.*[20]

According to the dissenting view, since the case was not proven beyond any reasonable doubt, it was against the principles of justice *and love*. Here, the reserving judge of the Court puts a powerful emphasis on the norm of love

---

[20]http://www.africalegalaid.com/IManager/MailingWeb/7332/yfPhhp5EuNMX/129684/2349472; http://www.ejiltalk.org/the-verdict-in-the-charles-taylor-case-and-the-alternate-judges-dissenting-opinion/ (Accessed December 12, 2014).

compared with any other principles. The question that remains is why the dissenter's microphone was cut off afterwards, why curtains of the public gallery were drawn, why the dissenting view was omitted from the official court record, and why he was subsequently sanctioned by a majority of the judges of both the Trial and Appeals Chambers of the Court for alleged "misconduct". Above all, why when the dissenter was delivering his opinion, did the other judges walk out of the courtroom? Sow clarifies that "what I said was that the prosecution did not prove beyond reasonable doubt the guilt of the accused. Also, it was a total surprise to me to hear that it was a unanimous decision because in each of the very few times we discussed anything, there were very different opinions. I was very surprised to see them coming up with this summary judgment talking about a unanimous decision."[21]

The basic requirement for liability for criminal punishment is proof beyond a reasonable doubt over all relevant elements. These are considered necessary for the commission of the crime under the Statute of the Special Court of Sierra Leone or any other criminal legislation. The significant function of this principle can be seen in the landmark statement delivered by *Justice William J. Brennan* in a case in the United States. Accordingly,

> The accused during a criminal prosecution has at stake interests of immense importance, both because of the possibility that he may lose his liberty upon conviction and because of the certainty that he would be stigmatized by the conviction. Accordingly, a society that values the good name and freedom of every individual should not condemn a man for commission of a crime when there is reasonable doubt about his guilt.[22]

In any event, there is particular doubt about the case and it may be reconsidered in the future. Regardless of the position of the judgment, it is evident that the case refers to the existence of certain aspects of morality that have to be kept in justice. Justice Saw insisted on the execution of this morality. In addition, Saw was not just a judge but also a judge with a highly positive reputation in his home state. A Senegalese professor of law associated with the merits of the case asserts:

> ...judge Sow is a judge of repute in Senegal. He is very well known in the Senegalese judiciary for his integrity, fierce honesty and scrupulous attachment to principles. He is known for a man of courage who will always stand up for what he believes is right, no matter what. As a Senegalese citizen I am proud that judge Sow showed abroad the same hardcore qualities for which is known and respected in his home country.[23]

---

[21]http://www.google.de/imgres?imgurl=http://www.africalegalaid.com/IManager/Image/474/21468/53980/322621/0/0/1/&imgrefurl=http://www.africalegalaid.com/news/justice-malick-sow-charles-taylor-trial-speaks&h=364&w=1029&tbnid=ITeZXD_vLjmovM:&zoom=1&tbnh=90&tbnw=254&usg=__8vHHz8YLwm1dWXJ5wsbPjeZBJLc=&docid=nDxbs7JJtOfAIM (Accessed May 25, 2015).

[22]The Supreme Court in *Winship*, 397 U.S. 358 (1970), Decided March 31, 1970.

[23]Professor Fatou Camara statement. See http://www.google.de/imgres?imgurl=http://3.bp.blogspot.com/-tZpcSA79PSM/T5s0vwdK2cI/AAAAAAAAAEs/DnrHzGRVamk/s1600/elhadjimalick.bmp&imgrefurl=http://www.intlawgrrls.com/2012/04/judge-sows-struck-statement-reflections.html&h=150&w=100&tbnid=udh-CEEja-DsEM:&zoom=1&tbnh=95&tbnw=63&usg=__mhl1Kk9x735LAyXFQ-98-SFxUyo=&docid=6vcUXgC0f9uAxM (Accessed May 25, 2015).

There were serious doubts about the legal validity of the evidence. *"If you don't see the truth, at least you must see the lies. I have seen too many lies, too many deceptions, and I haven't seen any proof of guilt of this accused."*[24] It is for this and several other reasons that it is firmly stated by many African States that the sole intention of the ICC and the SCSL is to punish African leaders.

Once upon a time, Alexander the Great captured one of the most infamous pirates and asked him, why are you plundering the high seas? The pirate turned the question back at him and asked Alexander the Great, why are you plundering the land? He said, I am the king. The pirate answered, if you are the king of the land, in that case, I am the king of the high seas. What is the difference? The business is the same for both of us. Obviously, Alexander presented the law and morality as independent personal norms of his own, and the pirate used the same code of conduct. Both loved the law but with the power of *a one-eyed justice*.

8.10 Persuading Leading Courts with Love

One may ask what the purpose of the ICC and its establishment is. The ICC was, first of all, established to bring accused persons under its jurisdiction and apply adequate punishment. These two are the main reasons for the creation of the Court. Thus, the ICC does not have, due to the power and the provisions of its Statute, any significant authority for the prevention of international crimes. This means that the Court is simultaneously very powerful and powerless. Its duties are mostly *prosecutive* and *punitive*. The Court has to hang around its corridors, corridors of member states, or the corridors of international politicians to see whether they are planning to bring certain international criminals under its jurisdiction. The best situation for it is when the permanent members hand over accused persons to its jurisdiction.

In addition, the Court has another serious task. This is to examine and prove that the accused persons are the real offenders. The reason is that no one can be recognised as an offender so long as her/his criminality is not proved without reasonable doubt before the jurisdiction of the Court, in particular in a written judgment. It means that the Court has the right to state that certain persons are suspected of committing certain international crimes, but it cannot describe them as criminals so long as they are not brought before and meet the end of the Court's

[24]http://newafricanmagazine.com/justice-sow-charles-taylor-should-have-walked-free/. See also Escrito por Findlay (2013). "The fact that Charles Taylor stands on trial for war crimes in Sierra Leone points to it partially, but often not realized are the roles that countries like Libya, Burkina Faso, Côte d'Ivoire, Ghana, and Nigeria played in initiating a truly multinational war. Recent revelations by the CIA — which have always been suspected — put the United States' role in the war at center stage, adding fuel to claims of outside intervention in Liberian politics, since its founding as a Western style nation-state, up until today." The CIA's Charles Taylor Revelation, available at http://africasacountry.com/2012/01/charles-taylor-cia/ (Accessed August 10, 2016).

jurisdiction. This is a basic recognised principle of criminal jurisdiction and not a matter of choice.

The question is more serious when one considers that the ICC is indeed powerless to prevent crimes which will be imminently committed. This means that the norms of legality and morality of the Statute of the ICC are solely workable and practicable when international crimes are committed. *I may compare its function with a person who digs a grave. In other words, the ICC is waiting in the courtrooms to calculate how many individuals have been killed and whether the crimes fall under its statutes. This means the ICC has a record of murders and it is the heavy coffin of this record which makes the function of the ICC imperative and, of course, establishing whether the principles of international criminal law have been violated. In practice, if the number of killings is low, the ICC has nothing to do with it, but if there are massive and provocative graves against the cultural morality of the population of the world, the ICC becomes active, becomes detective of the international jungle in order to hunt the wolves. Is this not a cowboy mentality?*

The reason for all these situations is that the policy of criminalisation of national or international crimes is only workable when violations have occurred and not for the prevention of the creation of victims.

All these situations mean that the function of the ICC and even the system of international criminal law, human rights law, and humanitarian law of armed conflict is non-practical from the view of prevention of crimes. This means we need to question the basic function of the system of international criminal law and justice and to find out whether our policy is correct and realistic. One should take into consideration that the ICC and other tribunals look for the statistics of the crime in order to decide whether the given conducts constitute international crimes. For example, the Nuremberg Tribunal would have never been established if the massive killing of the Jewish population of Europe had not occurred. This is because the great political powers of the time since the ratification of the Versailles Treaty were waiting to see how Germany would act concerning the very severe unequal conditions of the 1919 Treaty of Versailles.

The situation is more critical when we compare the establishment of the *ad hoc* tribunals such as the ICTY and ICTR and even the SCSL. These tribunals could only be created after the massive genocide, torture, school-table rapes, village rapes, and mass killings in Yugoslavia and Rwanda. Almost 60 million vaginas of Muslim women were not only raped but torn into pieces. The pain, humiliation, and systematic sexual terror inflicted by the offenders were not just to degrade their human personality as women but also to assault the entire community's cultural attitudes and the integrity of Muslims as a whole. Even in the age of *jus primae noctis* 'right of the first night', *droit du seigneur*, 'right of the lord', *droit de cuissage* 'right of the thigh' or *droit de jambage* 'right of the leg', such major insult would never be tolerated by the legal authorities.[25]

---

[25]Wettlaufer (2000), pp. 111–123.

Was European justice going to wait and see the effect of humanitarian law in practice and then later assist the victims? The Sierra Leone Court had the same problem. In other words, the Security Council of the United Nations, which is the basic international body for the creation of temporary international courts, did not create the Courts until it was sure that the crimes had been committed and sexual organs of women had been used as the most effective weapons of psychological destruction of the conflicting parties.

We have learned that, by the force of law and the force of morality of law, rule of the law has to be functional and fruitful. This means that the philosophy of the jurisdiction of a court and its responsibility, which rests on records of statistics of killings in order to function properly, may not be correct and may be painful for the structure of appropriate justice. A justice, which waits for killing or mass rape, is not justice but is obviously offensive and much stronger than rape. If our courts are going to function as the courts did several thousand years ago, but in a modern structure, their policy and theories must be wrong, and the commission of crimes will not only continue but also increase, as has been the case since the establishment of the Nuremberg Tribunal. It becomes obviously imperative that the ICC may search for other significant functions of its own. Such functions may be legally and morally much higher than its present functions. I call one of these functions of the ICC the fulfilment of *the principle of persuading*.

The function of the principle of persuading is to prevent the commission of crimes. In other words, there must be an organ to be created under the authority of the ICC. This organ has to consist of persuading judges and persuading prosecutors whose duties are to read reports of the provocation, political corruption, corruption over weapons, irritation, conflicts, and armaments between different groups in different parts of the world. The court should even have persuading advisers and lawyers who are specialised in wiping out differences and gathering similarities between different groups as much as possible based on the canon of love for justice. The persuading prosecutor, states' members, groups, individuals, or the Security Council should have rights to bring to the attention of the Court the aggravations or violations which are increasing or will imminently occur.

Likewise, the Court should call upon the leaders of the conflicting parties, with full respect for their personality, to come to the Court for consultation, negotiation, and other matters in order to prevent the commission of crimes which would otherwise imminently be committed by the parties. Clear examples are the conflicts between different groups in Rwanda and the former Yugoslavia. They should deliberate about the prevention of international crimes which are becoming reality. With all this retro-talk in this volume, I mean that the ICC, by the force of love for justice, has to prevent unlawful force, violations, murders, genocide, crimes against humanity, rapes, and tortures between different civilizations in the world before they are committed. As Martha Nussbaum correctly specifies:

> Disgust and envy, the desire to inflict shame upon others – all of these are present in all societies, and, very likely, in every individual human life. Unchecked, they can inflict great damage. The damage they do is particularly great when they are relied upon as guides in the

> process of lawmaking and social information (when, for example, the disgust that people feel for a group of other people is used as valid reason for treating those people in a discriminatory way). But even when a society has avoided falling into that trap, these forces lurk in society and need to be counteracted energetically by an education that cultivates the ability to see full and equal humanity in another person, perhaps one of humanity's most difficult and fragile achievement.[26]

Consequently, a *persuading leading court of love* is a court which has several functions for the identification of conflicts between different groups against one another. It is a court of love for justice to prevent the commission of crimes against the soul of justice. In addition, "real people are sometimes moved by the love of just principles presented just as such, abstractly."[27] Moreover, "the human mind is quirky and particularistic, more easily able to conceive a strong attachment if these high principles are connected to a particular set of perceptions, memories, and symbols that have deep roots in the personality and in people's sense of their own history."[28] All these significant characteristics of groups are undoubtedly interwoven with the code of love. The Court has to work with this principle which exists in all human bodies, minds, nature, and the *aquarium of humanity*.

Here, a *persuading leading court* is a court which brings, at the same time, violations, victims, witnesses, and accused persons before the jurisdiction of the ICC. This is with the difference that all parties may have the identity of all these subjects of criminal jurisdiction at the same time. They have also the possibility of avoiding criminal judgment through a peaceful method and love for human beings. This means again, *a persuading leading court of love is a court for the sake of security of the victims, the accused, and justice as well as the prevention of crimes against humanity and genocide at the same time. A persuading leading court of love calls upon the obligations, duties, and responsibilities of all individuals, groups, organisations, and states to refrain from all forms of use of force, including that which is permitted or rejected in* jus ad bellum - *the law of war - and* jus in bello - *international humanitarian law. It encourages them with the norm of love, which is an integral part of law, morality, legality, and justice, to solve their conflicts before coming to the ICC. The persuading leading court of love for justice points out to the conflicting parties the fact that the idea of legitimate or illegitimate war (and how to conduct themselves during an armed conflict) is indeed theoretical and that all acts will eventually end in violations of the system of international criminal law. It would therefore give rise to the concept of international criminal responsibility on the part of violators.*

---

[26] Nussbaum (2013), p. 3.

[27] *Id.*, p. 8.

[28] *Id.*

References

Blackstone, W. (1765–1769). *Commentaries on the Laws of England* (Vol. 4, p. 17).

Corbin, H. (2014). *History of Islamic Philosophy (Translated from French by Liadain Sherrard and Philip Sherrard)*. London, New York: Routledge.

Crawford, J. (1976). *The criteria for statehood in international law* (p. 95).

Cummings, S. L. (2011). Introduction: What good are lawyers? In S. L. Cummings (Ed.), *Paradox of professionalism lawyers and the possibility of justice*. Cambridge: Cambridge University Press.

Dalberg-Larsen, J. (2006). *Dansk retsfilosofi: Udviklingslinjer og portraetter*. Jurist- og Økonomforbunds forlag.

Dan-Cohen, M. (2014). Dignity, crime, and punishment: A Kantian perspective. In M. D. Dubber (Ed.), *Foundational texts in modern criminal law* (pp. 101–118). Oxford: Oxford University Press.

de Vattel, E. (1758, 1916). *Le Droit de Gens, ou Principes de la Loi Naturelle, appliquès à la Conduite er aux Affaires des Nations de de Souverains: The law of nations or the principles of natural law* (Vol. III the Classics of International Law, James Brown Scott, ed. (Book II, 11).

Dougan, M. (2008). The Treaty of Lisbon 2007: Winning minds, not hearts. *Common Market Law Review, 45*, 617–703.

Eckhoff, T. (1963). Justice and social utility. In *Legal essays to attribute to Frede Castberg on the occasion of his 70th birthday* (pp. 74–93). Universitetsforlaget.

Findlay, M. J. (2013). *International and comparative criminal justice: A critical introduction*. London: Routledge.

Harcourt, B. E. (2014). Beccaria's on crimes and punishments: A mirror on the history of the foundations of modern criminal law. In M. D. Dubber (Ed.), *Foundational texts in modern criminal law* (pp. 59–78). Oxford: Oxford University Press.

Holtermann, J. v. H. (2006). Ross og Erkendelsesteorien. In J. v. Holtermann & J. Ryberg (Eds.), *Alf Ross Kritiske Gensyn* (pp. 37–62). Jurist- og Økonomforbunds forlag.

Karnell, E. H. (2011). EU's anti-money Laundering Agenda: Built on risks? In C. Eckes & T. Kondtandinides (Eds.), *Crime within the area of freedom, security and justice* (p. 76). Cambridge: Cambridge University Press.

Luper-Foy, S. (Ed.). (1988a). Introduction global distributive justice. In *Problems of international justice* (pp. 1–24). London: Westview Press.

Luper-Foy, S. (Ed.). (1988b). Introduction global distributive justice. In *Problems of international justice* (pp. 97–113). London: Westview Press.

Nussbaum, M. C. (2013). *Political emotions: Why love matters for justice*. Harvard University Press.

Spooner, L. (1882). *Natural Law; or the Science of Justice: A treatise on natural law, natural justice, natural rights, natural liberty, and natural society; showing that all legislation whatsoever is an absurdity, a usurpation, and a crime. Part First.*

Stern, S. (2014). Blackston's criminal law: Common-law harmonization and legislative reform. In M. D. Dubber (Ed.), *Foundational texts in modern criminal law* (pp. 61–78). Oxford: Oxford University Press.

Vischer, R. K. (2014). *Martin Luther King Jr. and the morality of legal practice: Lessons in love and justice*. Cambridge: Cambridge University Press.

Wettlaufer, J. (2000). The *jus primae noctis* as a male power display: A review of historic sources with evolutionary interpretation. *Evolution and Human Behaviour, 21*(2), 111–123.

Chapter 9
Misleading the Rule of Love with Humanitarian Principles

9.1 Stagnate Concept of Legitimacy

Public international law governs the relations between states or international organizations. Its purpose is to achieve good international relations based on the rules of law and above all justice. One of the integral parts of public international law is the law of armed conflict constituting a significant part of international criminal law. Armed conflicts are generally of two types. One is *jus ad bellum* or regulations concerning the prohibition of used of armed force, which is also embodied in the Charter of the United Nations. The other concerns the legitimate use of force. Within customary and conventional international law, the concept of legitimate use of force consists of two categories. These are individual and collective self-defence. They are dealt with under the law of *jus in bello* or the law governing armed conflict. Regardless of the types of force which are used, the conflicting parties are obliged to follow the law of *jus in bello*. This law deals with humanitarian law of armed conflict.

As we will demonstrate, both these concepts—*jus ad bellum* and *jus in bello*—have lost their true validity under the principles of human rights law if the substance of the relevant law contains the proper rules of international justice and humanity. The theory of the principle of love is ultimately opposed to both legal categories and calls upon prohibition of all forms of use of force in international law. *Therefore, any claim that the provisions of Article 51 of the Charter of the United Nations permit the use of force for the purpose of self-defence has no legal validity under the new development of a system of international law which struggles to prohibit all forms of use of force in international relations of states. In other words, if the purpose of the United Nations Charter is peace, one should not defend this under the principle of war. If the philosophy of international human rights is equality of life and human justice, we cannot interpret it as permission to use armed force. If positive laws are laws of men and not laws of barbarity, we should not corrupt them by the rules of war*. This means the norm of love for justice, its positive obligations to create trust

F. Malekian, *Judgments of Love in Criminal Justice*,
DOI 10.1007/978-3-319-46900-3_9

for justice and transparency, has to be given priority over all norms that permit, by one means or another, legitimate or illegitimate use of force.

9.2 Primary or Secondary Rules

Any claim that the system of international humanitarian law of armed conflict is based on solely positivist views and not on the philosophy of morality is obviously far from the concept of law and ethics. Again, an allegation that international humanitarian law is a secondary form of rules and one may separate it from the primary rules is also a sad, idiosyncratic tactic. The law of the tribunals in Nuremberg and Tokyo relied heavily on customary and natural aspects of the law. The Charters of both tribunals had a solely psychological role rather than legal rule. It was a fact for both tribunals beyond any reasoning that arguments requiring prior statutory law were not valid. However, I am not here getting into the discussion concerning the whole theory of the Tokyo Tribunal which lost its validity, and all accused persons were released from their international criminal responsibility because of the deal between the United States and Japanese governments. The major issue is that there were not any primary rules in the system of international criminal law which could be applied to crimes against humanity or crimes against peace. The political power created them retrospectively.

One may conditionally apply the distinction between primary and secondary rules to certain important matters of law, especially criminal law. The most primitive concept of criminal law follows the concept of sanction or punishment, although there practically may not be any statutory law for the implementation of criminal norms. Even in the age of an eye for an eye which constituted the law, and in the age of the Hammurabi Code which constituted civil and criminal legislation, there absolutely was a form of statutory law that was not sanctioned by the law of the country but by the law of force or proportionality.[1] However, whether or not it could be used for reparation depended on the power of the victim.[2] In other words, each man had to implement his own statutory law.

The Hammurabi Code was applied by the supreme power of the country and based its method of implementation on severe punishment. The provisions of the Code denote the significant value of the rule of law for the maintenance of social justice or human rights law. It aimed at the prevention of oppression almost 2250 years B.C. and it particularly intended to help widows and orphans receive appropriate justice. Naturally, the Code not only contained primary rules but also secondary rules. This is because it was philosophically and legally impossible to separate these rules from one another. The civil and criminal law machinery of the

[1]Pradel (2010), p. 17.

[2]Andersen (2011), p. 71.

legal system were the same and emanated from the same source. We can still see the basic elements of this concept in the contemporary international legal systems.

Although we do not deny the rule of recognition to decide on how to identify a law due to the complex development of modern systems with different sources such as legislation, judicial precedents, and even the heavy body of the constitution, this does not necessarily guide us in determining the practical validity of the rule. For example, the rules regarding self-defence are today not only an integral part of primary and secondary rules of law but are even self-conducted in certain particular circumstances. This includes under national and international law. Although the validity of rules determines which rules should be recognised as laws and which rules should demand obligations for states within the international legal community, it has been, up until today, almost impossible to enforce international law on a statutory basis. This is because neither the ICJ nor the ICC has the authority to enforce the law if states do not permit its implementation.

Thus, the validity of international rules may not be measured by whether a rule is obeyed by states, but by whether the strength of a rule is recognised in the international relations of states. With the examination of a large body of legal conventions and materials, it seems that the entire legal system is without particular legal power if states do not politically interfere with the enforcement of the system. They may invoke control over the abolition of capital punishment, the prohibition of crimes against humanity, genocide, war crimes, torture, and rape, and the promotion of the rights of children and gender equality. All these have also been effective in the system of international humanitarian law of armed conflict. Thus, the enforcement of the law depends partly on the rule of the positive humanitarian law and partly on whether a conflicting party wants to respect the high merits of the law in its fighting.

9.3 The Conundrums of Humanitarian Law

If the purpose of international humanitarian law of armed conflict is supposed to be humane, it should not be a legalisation which permits criminal conduct by rules. If its purpose is to regulate killing, it is no longer law but the law of killing, the law of retaliation, the law of force, and the law of murder, yet according to the rules. It is also the law of destruction, the necessity of time, the law of barbarity, the urgent understanding of superiors, and also the law of terrorists in which there are no primary or secondary rules, that guides you to kill in order not to be killed. This means that the rules of the law violate three important basic principles of the same law. It also means the theory of Hart loses its positive philosophical function. This is because we promulgate the principle of love for justice by defending statutory law through killing.

The three norms are the *script* of the law or the legal norm, the *material* aim of the law or the moral norm, and the main *invisible* norm of the law or the norm of love. *What I am expressing here is that humanitarian law consists of three integral norms. The first two norms are interpretable—i.e. legal and moral norms—but the third norm is not, cannot, and should not be negotiated by the interpretation of the relevant law in order to kill. There is no such rule in international law or the whole body of law that respects the law and permits killing. This is what I call the norm of love, the power of love, the common interest of man, the similarities of interpretation, the parallelism of human cultural norms, and the connection between norms of legality and morality. This norm of love is also the relationship between hearts, the similarity in order to prevent unnecessary suffering, the illegality of legality, the disappearance of differences of language, the collective will to stop violence, the common requirement for humanity, and also the inner structure of our human conscience.* The ICJ commented on the Genocide Convention by asserting the important principle of the common interest of humanity and the integration of the principle of morality within this principle. It therefore concluded that:

> its object on the one hand is to safeguard the very existence of certain human groups and on the other to confirm and endorse the most elementary principles of morality. In such a convention the Contracting States do not have any interests of their own; they merely have, one and all, a common interest, namely the accomplishment of those higher purposes which are the *raison d'être* of the convention. ...The high ideals which inspired the Convention provide, by virtue of the common will of the parties, the foundation and measure of its provisions.[3]

With all this, we are aiming to arrive at the conclusion that no law is a legitimate law if its content is violating or permitting the violation of human integrity or of human natural substance. If humanitarian law permits killing, destruction, and annihilation of the enemy because the other side is being killed, this rule of law no longer respects fundamental principles of international human rights law and is against all principles of human civilisation. It should therefore be borne in mind that *human beings are not enemies of human beings at all, but friends of a lack of understanding of the fact that they are solely parts of the same substance of animality, which is called humanity. Otherwise, humanitarian law in that case should be called the regular law of retaliation, the polite way of killing, the Mohammedan interpretation of the necessity of war in order to achieve his own Islamic justice, and the criminal law of Hart with primary and secondary legal statutes in order to minimise or extend the value of legal order. This humanitarian with non-humanitarian content may also be supported by the rules of Kant to achieve justice with central enforcement of power politics or the rules of Immanuel Thomas Hobbes, Jeremy Bentham, John Austin,*[4] *and Hans Kelsen who permit war in certain situations. Obviously, when we permit war, we permit killing, and killing is itself subject to the rules of law and the rules of war as well as subject to legislation, and legislation is the way in which we witness the words of the law.*

I fully understand that the concept of self-defence is necessary and inevitable in certain situations, but when law prepares itself for a killing situation, it is no longer

---

[3]Reservations to the Convention on the Prevention and Punishment of the Crime of Genocide, ICJ Reports (1951), pp. 15, 23.

[4]Austin (1861).

a law but a way to encourage conflict and to ignore the norm of love for human beings. Even the entire theory of resorting to the institution of self-defence between states should be recognised as an illegitimate conduct when we encourage war with the industrialisation of weapons of all kinds and with a number of international conventions and protocols applicable to wartime. One can no longer refer to the legitimate theory of self-defence when the law incorporates the theory of war and constitutes a part of our own indirect criminal conduct. If law comprises true love for justice, there will not be any law of war and industrialisation of weapons.

9.4 Privatization of the Norm of Love

A body of law is, in general, selective written moral wills which have a tendency to be obligatory norms. All these imply the existence of certain chosen moral behaviour within the societies of the relevant states. These can be affirmative or negative. The moral norms are not separable from legal norms. The fact is that when we say that the German government acted wrongly, the Israeli government acts unjustly, the Iranian system violates the international standard of human rights principles, or the British government participated in the commission of crimes and destruction of Iraq in the Gulf crisis, we are not accusing their population by any means. However, it is a fact that each member of each society should take responsibility for the existence of certain rules called law or morality. The difference between rules of morality and rules of law is indeed very small. Almost all rules of law have moral virtue and *vice versa*. They impose obligations which are acceptable by a great majority of the relevant society and have binding effect.

This is more obvious in the case of international criminal law which has a particular position in the international legal and political community as a whole. Substantive norms cannot be considered norms if they are not accepted as an integral part of the social structure. Norms of law are not regulated for the purpose of regulation, but the intention is to bring certain needs of national, regional, or international society into recognition. This recognition means giving effect to those important patterns of social interests that are an integral part of the integrity of a given society. All these interpretations also imply the fact that the system of international humanitarian law of armed conflict is not and cannot be isolated from the moral standard of the international human community and ultimately from the norm of love for the same community interests.

By moral standard, we mean that the level at which the formulation of the law has been evaluated against other values. This means that, for the drafters of international humanitarian law of armed conflict, the respect for certain norms was not only reasonable but also necessary. The drafters were searching to find a certain standard of human behaviour that was without a doubt significant for all negotiating parties.[5] They were still limited by certain norms which certainly had a political nature for all participants in the negotiation process.

Yet one has to remember that the body of international humanitarian law of armed conflict was formed during three different evolutionary periods of international criminal law. One is the result of the nineteenth century and the other two parts are the consequence of the twentieth century. The difference is that the first part developed before the establishment of the League of Nations and the United Nations. This means the creation of slavery, when political morality of states was stronger than legal morality. In fact, the institution of slavery was seen as being an integral part of morality at least in Europe. By this, I am not rejecting other similar institutions in other parts of the world such as Islamic nations or the United States. My intention is to say that the standard of international morality and recognition of other nations were not as developed as they are today. I am not, however, discussing here the existence of "certain minimum standards of civilised behaviour" or humanitarian law of armed conflict in customary international law or natural law.[6]

The drafters of the humanitarian law of armed conflict did not care to any degree about respecting the rights of indigenous groups or other nations who were not parties to international negotiations concerning armed conflict. The morality or love for other nations was only *private business* between those who were powerful and had rights together around the political negotiation table. This morality was also limited to Europe and was not applicable in relation to nations or states, which were occupied by the European states themselves.

> European colonialism represented an oriental version of the Dark Ages. It negated all that the composite Indian civilization stood for. The European colonizers refused to apply to Asia and its princes what little international law they had developed in Europe. Indeed, they argued that the rules of international law applied only in Europe.... All wars throughout human history have violated the humanitarian law precepts. But colonialism was founded literally on the blood of Asians and Africans. Colonial history was replete with instances of wanton killings, plundering, looting, destruction and devastation, displaying unparalleled cruelty and impunity.[7]

All this means that the norms of law, morality, and love were served in order to save the European nations from attacks from one another and not from third nations. A Portuguese historian, rightly asserts that "It is true that there does exist a common right of all to navigate the seas and in Europe we recognize the rights which others hold against us; but the right does not extend beyond Europe and therefore the Portuguese as Lords of the Sea are justified in confiscating the goods of all those who navigate the seas without their permission."[8] This also means that the first principles of humanitarian law and international law, including the law of the see, were legislated to protect Europeans from other parts of the world.

---

[5]Walzer (2006).

[6]Schwarzenberger (1968), p. 717.

[7]Mani (2001), available at https://www.icrc.org/eng/resources/documents/misc/57jqzm.htm (Accessed June 13, 2015).

[8]Panikkar (1970), p. 35.

Yet, the key intention was to keep certain powerful states (according to their own conditions) from inhuman suffering. It was for these and several other reasons that norms of humanitarian law of armed conflict were restricted and the moral standards of the law limited to those states, and immorality was permitted in relation to other states or nations of the world. *By this, I mean that there was a norm of love, but a limited perspective of the norm, which was, as I have mentioned above, a private norm belonging exclusively to Europe, and it was not thought that it should be delivered to other nations or states, even all populations of Europe. For instance, one of the oldest populations of Europe—the Jews—was not a part of these humanitarian regulations. Behind the closed windows and doors of Europe, they had an inferior personality. It is for this reason that most active countries of Europe participated, directly or indirectly, in the murdering of this generation.*

Yet, to call the relevant rules in armed conflict "international humanitarian law" is to be very generous indeed with the rules of law and to humiliate the concept of humanity. This is because there is no such thing in international human rights law as being human when you are permitted to kill people under certain conditions.[9] *I shall repeat my intention again: no action of the people of the world can be humanitarian when it involves killing, crimes against humanity, genocide, or war crimes. We cannot have a law which is based on human rights law, or the moral norm and norms of love, but which permits murdering in accordance with a certain form of legality or morality. Thus, to call the rules of armed conflict humanitarian is indeed misleading. It has today become clear that most crimes committed under the theory of self-defence are aggressive and turn out to be crimes against humanity, war crimes, torture, or mass rape.*

The term 'humanitarian' came into existence to minimise the psychological effect of armed attacks. In other words, all of what is called international humanitarian law is nothing more than a legal body that regulates the rules of how to commit genocide at the time of armed activities between two or several nations or between a nation and a group. Many states will find themselves in a very dangerous situation of self-defence and engage in mass killing, reasoning that they would be subject to imminent mass killing by the opposite party. Although we do understand that these two terms, national and international armed conflicts, are employed interchangeably, they are seriously misleading the world and opening windows for official killing of civilians or non-civilians under the concept of humanitarian theory.[10] *The framework of humanitarian law of armed conflict may be compared to the Trojan horse of war, then a Trojan horse of love.*

[9]Unfortunately, most writers in international law still support the law of armed force. For instance, see De Wet (2004), pp. 369–386; and Chesterman (2003), pp. 234–236.

[10]Henckaerts and Doswald-Beck (2005), pp. xvii–xviii.

9.5 The Plea of *tu quoque*

Regarding international humanitarian law, the International Criminal Tribunal for the Former Yugoslavia (ICTY) has rejected the plea of *tu quoque*. One may argue this plea with similar argumentation in law. A *tu quoque* argument intention is to express that a legal disparagement or a juridical objection also relates to the party making it. This argument was put forth by several accused in the ICTY in order to justify their own criminal violations. The issue is entirely against the norm of love which aims to prevent inhuman suffering. In one of the cases before the ICTY, the defence argued that the attack on civilians in Ahmici was justified because Muslim military forces had attacked Croat civilians in other areas. Although the Trial Chamber believed that Muslims had probably carried out the attacks, it rejected the argument of *tu quoque*. Accordingly, the plea of *tu quoque* is against the body of international humanitarian law of armed conflict. This simply means that a conflicting party cannot excuse its own act by referring to similar acts by other conflicting parties in an armed conflict. Therefore, the Trial Chamber of the ICTY specified:

> the *tu quoque* defence as absolutely *fallacious and inapplicable*. The *tu quoque* defence can be defined as an argument based on the alleged reciprocal nature of the obligations under international humanitarian law which would entitle a party to violate its obligations under such law if they are being committed by the enemy... there existed no international precedent supporting this defence and that, in any case, such an argument misconstrued the nature of the rules of international humanitarian law. This body of law cannot be conceived as an aggregate of bilateral obligations, namely, as an exchange of rights and obligations. "Instead, the bulk of this body of law lays down absolute obligations, namely obligations that are unconditional or in other words not based on reciprocity." The Trial Chamber found that this is evidence of the progressive trend towards the so-called "humanisation" of international legal obligations. Humanitarian rules were designed primarily to benefit individuals *qua* human beings, not to protect State interests. They thus constitute obligations erga omnes, obligations towards the international community as a whole, not merely obligations of States vis-à-vis one another. In addition, most norms of international humanitarian law have attained the status of *jus cogens*, i.e. non-derogable and overriding rules.[11]

The theory of the Chamber is very simple. Parties to a conflict should not involve the principle of *tu quoque* in the case of international humanitarian law of armed conflict. Therefore, they are under obligation to respect all the provisions of the relevant law.[12] In other words, humanitarian law does not lay down reciprocal obligations such that if you do not respect, I will not respect either. The nature of the obligations is *erga omnes*, which calls upon the duties of individuals or states. It is "designed to safeguard fundamental human values and therefore must be complied

---

[11] secnet069.un.org/x/file/Legal%20Library/jud. . .e/kupreskic.htm.

[12] According to one writer "There are two widely held truisms. One is that one nation's terrorists are another nation's freedom fighters and heroes and vice versa. The other is that all is fair in war and love." This reasoning was argued by the accused persons for the defence of their criminal conduct during the 1990s former Yugoslavian war. Both were invalidated by the ICTY. Mojzes (2010), p. 221.

with regardless of the conduct of the other party or parties."[13] Thus, the ICTY entirely objected to the character of reciprocal obligations with due regard to humanitarian law defence and put a high legal value on obligations *erga omnes*.[14] These are treaty-based obligations in which all contracting parties have a similar legal interest.[15] The judgment of the Inter-American Court in the case of *La Cantuta, Alberto Fujimori*, the president of Peru, offered similar views. The Court referred to this issue, noting that:

> . . . States have the duty to investigate human rights violations and to prosecute and punish those responsible. In view of the nature and seriousness of the events, all the more since the context of this case is one of systematic violation of human rights, the need to eradicate impunity reveals itself to the international community as a duty of cooperation among states for such purpose. Access to justice constitutes a peremptory norm of International Law and, as such, it gives rise to the States' *erga omnes* obligation to adopt all such measures as are necessary to prevent such violations from going unpunished, whether exercising their judicial power to apply their domestic law and International Law to judge and eventually punish those responsible for such events, or collaborating with other States aiming in that direction. . .[16]

It is here that one needs to take into consideration the fact that the norms of the law of war cannot be imposed by the norms of humanity, morality, and love. I mean that no war is lawful, no human killing is just, no action on the use of armed force can be legal, and almost no massacre can be authorised by superiors. Based on the philosophy of law and theory of enlightenment of the principles of international human rights law, we should not bring any superior or subordinate before national courts for disobedience and violation of orders if she/he does not want to kill. The rules of such a court are evidently against the basic elements of human rights law as a whole. If killing is prohibited, it should be prohibited in all cases, even in wartime. Obedience of subordinates "to their officers can make wars of unjust aggression

[13]Zoran Kupreskic, Mirjan Kupreskic, Vlatko Kupreskic, Drago Josiprovic, Dragan Papoc, Vladimir Santic, also known as "VLADO", Decision on Evidence of the Good Character of the Accused and the Defence of Tu Quoque, 17 February 1999. The statement was made by the Chamber in its *Decision On Defence Motion to Summon Witness* of 3 February 1999.

[14]See the judgment of the Inter-American Court in the case of *La Cantuta*, Fujimori. 11 IACHR, Case *La Cantuta v. Peru*, judgment of 29 November 2006, Ser. C. No. 160, para. 160.

[15]The position is described in the following words: "The defence of *tu quoque* concerns the allegation that the opposing party to the conflict committed similar atrocities and, in the case in point, also included the allegation that that party was responsible for the commencement of the said conflict. Following its *Decision on Defence Motion to Summon Witness* of 3 February 1999 and its ruling at the hearing of 15 February 1999, the Trial Chamber held that evidence to prove such a defence is inadmissible because it does not tend to (dis)prove any of the allegations against the accused. In its Decision of 3 February 1999, the Trial Chamber had ruled that the principle of *tu quoque* does not apply to international humanitarian law since that body of law creates obligations erga omnes *(contractantes)* and not obligations based on reciprocity." Kupreskic et al. (IT-95-16-T), Decision on Evidence of the Good Character of the Accused and the Defence of Tu Quoque, 17 February 1999. Available at secnet069.un.org/x/file/Legal%20Library/jud. . ./supp2-e/kup.htm (Accessed June 4, 2015).

[16]11 IACHR, Case *La Cantuta v. Peru*, judgment of 29 November 2006, Ser. C. No. 160, para. 160.

possible."[17] This means, in order to respect the essential values of human rights law, no resistance against killing by a man should be specified as non-obedience to the rule of armed conflict. This is such if the fundamental merits of international conventions on human rights law are truly protecting the principles of the right to life, the hope for life, and the right to disobey unjust orders.

9.6 The Quest of Love for the Middle East

A clear example of prolonged antagonism is the useless conflict between the two neighbours in the Middle East, namely Israel and Palestine. The Israeli-Palestinian crisis can be solved solely by a proper understanding of the term "strength of love" and not just of "law". Grotius clearly indicates, "The debt of love and forbearance to our enemies is an obligation, which it is honourable to discharge." He further describes that:

> There are some who have neither ostensible reasons, nor just causes to plead for their hostilities, in which... they engage from the pure love of enterprise and danger. A disposition to which Aristotle gives the name of ferocity. And in the last book of his Nicomachian Ethics, he calls it a bloody cruelty to convert friends into enemies, whom you may slaughter.[18]

The military personnel of both sides and the members of the United Nations have to learn side-by-side from the lessons of international humanitarian law of armed conflict and international human rights law that to love one another is the first cornerstone of resorting to law as well as justice. Thereby, they should avoid violence and causing unnecessary human suffering. In fact, the canon of armed use of force must be replaced with the power of love, the power of understanding of the nature of human beings, and the power of brotherhood and unity. We have to take into recognition the obvious similarities between both systems of law.

If a superior order contains a command not to kill but to love, this upholds the pure philosophy of law for the security of humanity and provides the basis for peace. It also brings the governments of both sides face-to-face in a moral or legal obligation that the killing has to be prevented, that problems have to be solved, and that both nations are of the same human race. Although we know that a superior has a responsibility to obey orders and that our obedience to the law is a necessary condition of a legal system, one should not put aside the fact that any superior order to a subordinate to kill or destroy simultaneously constitutes in itself a use of force. This means violating the entire body of international human rights law.

If war is lawful, then peace is unlawful; if justice means killing, then all killing is just; if a law that does not contain the substance of love for human beings is judged

---

[17] Cohen (1949), p. 993.

[18] Grotius (1901), pp. 281, 267–268. Available at http://oll.libertyfund.org/titles/grotius-the-rights-of-war-and-peace-1901-ed (Accessed April 27, 2015).

to be acceptable, then let us announce that all laws in different civil societies are identical to human rights laws. Similarly, if the pure philosophy of Islamic and public international law or European Union law do not put any emphasis on the function of love in law, i.e. authentic justice for the protection of human dignity, let us declare that these laws are laws but without the first basic sense of humanity. Consequently, the word 'love' here means a mutual understanding of the fundamental rights of both sides, reciprocity denoting a relationship between both nations involving the historical exchange of favours, obligations, and allowing for similar requirements of daily life.

The concept of love should naturally require of both nations—Israel and Palestine—love for justice, love for human beings, and love of peace. These are surely not only the true cornerstones of Jewish norms but also the foundations of Islamic international law, European Union Law, and also the real meaning of public international law. One of the classical writers in international law correctly expresses the excellent inherent principle of Jewish law:

> The Jewish law indeed not only forbids the cherishing of hatred against a neighbour, that is, one of the same country and people, but requires certain common acts of kindness to be bestowed even upon enemies of that description. The Gospel therefore, comprehending all men under the appellation of neighbour, not only forbids us to hurt our enemies, but commands us to do them good; a commandment clearly stated in the Gospel of St. Matthew. Yet the law permitted the Jews to seek revenge for injuries of a more grievous kind, not with their own hands, but by appealing to the judge. But Christ does not give us the same permission, as appears from that opposition which he makes between the permissions of former times, and those of his own law. 'You have heard that it was said an eye for an eye—but I say unto you, love your enemies, etc.'[19]

All laws listed in the above paragraph surely have the status of being the highest legal and moral norms, which means that they no longer tolerate violence. Accordingly, "this highest-order norm is thought to be love, rather than obedience, in which case we must obey norms not because they have been commanded by God, but because they are positivizations of the most general, God given norm to love."[20] Here, we are obviously not looking for the inspiration of love with the inspiration of religious mentality but a norm of love that is practically significant to the existence of both nations. As Montesquieu puts:

> Admirable idea of the Chinese, who compare God's justice to a net so big that the fish that wander into it think they are free, but actually they are caught. Sinners, likewise, think they will not be punished by God; but they are in the net... Theologians are not pacified in one dispute except on behalf of a second one. They act like the cormorants that you send fishing: they come to bring you the fish that a ring has blocked in their gullets, but you put a gudgeoned in there.[21]

---

[19]Grotius (1901), p. 231 http://oll.libertyfund.org/titles/grotius-the-rights-of-war-and-peace-1901-ed (Accessed 27 April 2015).

[20]DeRoo (2013), p. 9.

[21]de Secondat and de Montesquieu (2012), translated by Henry C. Clark, available at http://oll.libertyfund.org/titles/2534#P828 (Accessed July 25, 2015), paras. 434 and 2176.

The point of justice is humanity and not development of religious attitude. This norm of love is based on the understanding that human rights norms are to be applied to situations of both nations with the power of love for justice, trust in justice, and in the nature of all Palestinian and Jewisch women/men.

9.7 The Pyramid of Love in Criminal Courts

A pyramid investigation is one of the best-known methods of investigation in criminal law and was created by the prosecutor's office of the ICTY in order to gather information and evidence about the crimes. It also refers to the selection of defendants. The method of questioning concerns all victims and is carried out between those persons who are, by one means or another, the victims of armed attack. These people are also those whose love for social justice has been ignored. This may also be called the pyramid of love for justice to be done, ruined cities to be built, installations to be restructured, hospitals, schools, houses, and life to be returned to the town. All these mean love with the essence of legality, morality, and justice in order that the social unity be re-established.[22]

Actually, the new ICTY method opens a bright way of finding those who have committed international crimes of concern to all states.[23] The investigation's division in the Office of the Prosecutor (OTP) became responsible for the collection of information and evidence which were then referred to whom for issuing charges against suspected persons. This method went to the source of the crime base and to collecting evidence, most of the time from refugee camps. Evidence related to all persons, even lower-ranking persons who actually ordered or committed the offences. All this was carried out in the interest of justice.[24]

> Investigations began in refugee centres throughout the world, where victims and witnesses were able to provide evidence implicating the persons who had physically committed the crimes, such as, for example, the persons in the camps where they were detained or the camp commanders. As the evidence grew, investigators began working up the pyramid to the persons who could be regarded as most responsible for the crimes . . . Indictments may be sealed or made public. Indictments were sealed when the Tribunal determined that this was in the interest of justice. This decreased the risk of the accused fleeing or hiding before arrest.[25]

The investigation and prosecution of large-scale crimes at the international level is not an easy task. One has to find a correct way to do it. The concept of love has different powerful voices. This has to be worked out in law, judgment, and justice

---

[22]Actually, there was a pyramid in the former Bosnia-Herzegovina which is called "pyramid lovet." The reason for the name is not clear to the author.

[23]http://www.icty.org/sid/97 (Accessed on April 24, 2015).

[24]*Id.*

[25]*Id.*

too in order to help the victims. The reasoning of the trial Chamber had to be effective in its efforts to lay the base of the pyramid for indictments against high-level leaders and not ignore the social love that had been damaged. A number of witnesses were prepared to come back to the Tribunal once again to testify against the offender in the Court. Therefore, the pyramid investigation was highly secured in the collection of evidence against the perpetrator. Obviously, all these witnesses or victims had strong feelings regarding love for justice to be carried out.

As I have demonstrated in this volume, love is a principle, the existence of which we have constantly ignored by the fact that we confuse it with the term 'morality' which is at first glance similar but is not the same as the norm of love. I have established that there are differences between the principle of morality and the principle of love. Many lawyers may object the existence of the principle of morality and more seriously to the principle of love. This was what the Scandinavian legal realists were doing for a long time. They almost ignored all theories of law in order to attest that the concept of legality is different from the province of morality. They became positivist and eventually rejected the existence of any idea of morality. According to one opinion, the school also consisted of seven cats (and a picture of these cats is painted on the wall of Uppsala museum). The cat's meow was that positivism is the king and the language of law. One of the leaders of this school received a seat within the European Commission and eventually in the Court, not with the pyramid of love but the pyramid of strict law.[26] As a matter of reflection of the school's theory, the Court had almost no cases. The situation caused the loss of the school's position and the judge was finally labelled with a lamentable caption in the corridors of the European Court as 'A court out of work'.[27] Naturally, if we do not carry out the pyramid of love in law, the courts will have a meteorological function of law rather than its purpose of unity. This means we will continue to have the "comedy of positivism....and ... utter lack of a sense of humour" that may create "chauvinism and racism" in the end.[28] In 2016, the Swedish government decided to pay eight million Swedish krona to researchers for efforts to lay the base of the pyramid for discrimination against foreigners in the country.

9.8 Gulf Replacement of Love with Cannons

As a matter of philosophical reasoning, no rule of law can be valid if it does not create justice. This is the theory of *lex injusta non est lex*. The force of guns and not love for justice may solely enforce its validity. Clear examples of are the resolutions of the Security Council concerning the Gulf Crisis. Certain permanent members of

[26]Sundberg (2010), p. 127.

[27]Id., pp. 127–128. For the theory of the relevant judge, examine Holtermann and Ryberg (2006).

[28]Nussbaum (2013), pp. 66, 68.

the Charter of the United Nations interpret them in such a way that the resolutions permitted the use of armed force. They could therefore intervene in the territories of Iraq in order to access the Iraqi oilfields.

The function of those resolutions started in 1991 with unlimited intensive armed attacks against the sovereign independence of Iraq, not only by the United States but also by the armed forces of the United Kingdom.[29] Both states seriously violated many principles of law, including but not limited to the principle of legality, the principle of morality, and the principle of love for true justice, which are clearly stated in the Charter of the United Nations. Article 1 of the Charter emphasises the duties of the Security Council. It reads that the aims of the organisation are to "maintain international peace and security, and to that end: to take effective collective measures for the prevention and removal of threats to the peace, and for the suppression of acts of aggression or other breaches of the peace." It goes even further and clarifies these aims of the organisation by asserting that the purpose is to "bring about by peaceful means, and in conformity with the principles of justice and international law, adjustment or settlement of international disputes or situations which might lead to a breach of the peace."

However, the actions of the permanent members proved that the resolutions of the United Nations were used in contrary effect to the jurisprudence of the law, human rights law, humanitarian law, and the principle of international legal personality of states. Obviously, none of the relevant resolutions of the Security Council and the criminal conduct of the permanent members could be interpreted as the fulfilment of the principles of the United Nations. Their actions were even theoretically wrong because the theory of justice does not permit killing in any situation, destruction, and occupation of an independent state. This is in particular significant when one considers that we are talking about those states which are considered the permanent members of the organisation for the purpose of promoting peace, equality, and justice. The Kuwait crisis was a game against the regime of Iraq, in order to involve the country in a war with Kuwait and then have a reason to initiate the Gulf wars against Iraq. These wars were also completed after the fate of September 11, 2001 and the murdering of Saddam.

Here, we cannot apply any reasonable philosophy of criminal justice which permits the big powers to kill and destroy everything for their interests. Again, here we may not have sufficient provisions to bring them to justice since the permanent International Criminal Court had not been established at the time. Even now, if the idea of implementation of such criminal sanctions against superpower politics were supported, it would be very difficult and scarcely possible. Even at present, we may not be able to apply the law because it may be claimed that the law is retroactive and therefore impossible to enforce. However, the reality is that it is no great dilemma for a court and that it existed for the Allied military powers or the German courts at that time.[30]

[29]Malekian (1994).

[30]See *infra* Chap. 10.

But if this justification is correct and ethical, then we do not need to think about whether the criminal actions of the permanent members were or are prosecutable or not. The practice of the German courts and the Nuremberg Tribunal demonstrated that such a justification was correct and possible from the view of philosophy of criminal law, regardless of the fact that the practice of the principle of *ex post facto* law does not permit it. However, the Tribunal statement is fully logical when it says: Many other authorities could be cited, but enough has been said to show that individuals can be punished for violations of international law. Men commit crimes against international law and not abstract entities, and only by punishing individuals who commit such crimes can the provisions of international law be enforced. Here, it was the norm of morality and "love of right" which were important and not other philosophical reasoning.[31] However, I am not now encouraging, to any degree, the implementation of *ex post facto* law. No system should permit the implementation of such law. The references are mostly *to have a hortatory* argumentation for the ethics of the law, for the justice of the law, and for the essence of the law rather than its actual implementation.

This in turn means that we do not necessarily need, at all times, to have a statute commanding or permitting us to do certain things. I am, however, aware of the fact that there are many basic principles in criminal law, such as *de lege lata*, *nullum crimen sine lege*, *nulla poena sine praevia lege*, and the principle of inviolability of the rights of individuals. However, these principles may not affect in any material way the prosecution of the great powers which do realise that the world's civilization is based on the harmony of the law and, particularly, that it is one of their duties to enforce the system of international law correctly. This is regardless of the fact that they may not subject themselves to the rules of the International Criminal Court—the ICC. Thus, one may find a lot of evidence regarding the duties of the permanent members to enforce the law and their responsibility for the violations of those laws. This is despite the fact that there is any statute for the evaluation of their criminal conduct. *Therefore, there is not any criterion in law for how the idea of proper justice can be measured. That is why, with the norm of love in law, we target the source of justice, which exists concretely for the positive application of justice and the prevention of diversity. This is because if justice's aims are not positive then it is not justice, but if the intention of justice is affirmative with purity then love is an integral part of that purity. Here, the norm of love means punctuality of justice and reliability for objectivity.*

[31] von Pufendorf (1931), p. 319. Available at http://oll.libertyfund.org/titles/2220 (Accessed March 29, 2015).

References

Andersen, P. (2011). Klassisk og Kristen Naturret. In O. Hammerslev & H. P. Olsen (Eds.), *Restsfilosofi – ecntrale tekster og temaer* (pp. 71–96). København: Hans Reitzels Forlag.

Austin, J. (1861). *The province of jurisprudence determined: Being the first of series of lectures on jurisprudence, or the philosophy of positive law* (1832) (2nd ed.).

Chesterman, S. (2003). *Just War or Just Peace? Humanitarian intervention and international law*. Oxford: Oxford University Press.

Cohen, M. (1949). Moral aspects of the criminal law. *Yale Law Journal, 49*, 987–1026.

de Secondat, C. L., & de Montesquieu, B. (2012). *My Thoughts (Mes Pensées)*.

De Wet, E. (2004). *The Chapter VII of Powers of the United Nations Security Council*. Oxford: Hart Publishing.

DeRoo, N. (2013). Culture regained? On the impossibility and meaninglessness of culture in (some) Calvinist thought. In G. Graham (Ed.), *Calvinism and culture*. Grand Rapids: Wm. B. Eerdmans Publishing.

Grotius, H. (1901). In A. C. Campbell (Ed.), *The rights of war and peace, 1625*.

Henckaerts, J.-M., & Doswald-Beck, L. (2005). *Customary international humanitarian law* (Vol. 1). Cambridge: Cambridge University Press.

Holtermann, J. v., & Ryberg, J. (2006). *Alf Ross Kritiske Gensyn*. Jurist- og Økonomforbunds forlag.

Malekian, F. (1994). *Condemning the use of force in the gulf crisis*. Stockholm: Almqvist & Wiksell International.

Mani, V. S. (2001). International humanitarian law: An Indo-Asian perspective. *International Review of the Red Cross, 841*.

Mojzes, P. (Ed.). (2010). *Balkan genocides: Holocaust and ethnic cleansing in the twentieth century*. Rowman and Littlefield.

Nussbaum, M. C. (2013). *Political emotions: Why love matters for justice*. Harvard University Press.

Panikkar, K. M. (1970). *Asia and Western Dominance: A Survey of the Vasco da Gama Epoch of Asian History 1498–1945*. London, 1959 (8th reprint 1970).

Pradel, J. (2010). *Droit Pénal Général* (18th ed.). Paris: Éditions Cujas.

Schwarzenberger, G. (1968). *International law: As applied by international courts and tribunals, Vol. II: The law of armed conflict*. London: Stevens & Sons Limited.

Sundberg, J. W. F. (2010). Human rights and traditional values. *Scandinavian Studies in Law, 55*, 125.

von Pufendorf, S. (1931). *Two books of the elements of universal jurisprudence* (1660) (W. Abbott, Oldfather, Trans.).

Walzer, M. (2006). *Just and unjust wars, a moral argument with historical illustrations* (4th ed.). New York: Basic Books.

Chapter 10
The Seat of Love in International Criminal Justice

10.1 Art of Love in International Criminal Courts

Our purpose in writing on international legal theory and practice is to provide a formal basis for the development of new rules of international law and to stipulate their procreative substantive legal validity. Consequently, paying due regard to the needs of individual human beings and humanity as a whole may depend, not only on the subjective appreciation of the authorities but also on their objectivity with respect to basic social values. It may be correct to assert that the truth or falsity of legal theories is almost impossible to define, since, while criticising other opinions or decisions, we may unintentionally compromise the spirit and intention of our own legal writings by not attributing value to other legal theories. This results in a one-eyed justice, which is manifest in the weighty scholarship of some prominent legal theorists and in the works of legislative authorities such as the Prosecutor and judges of the ICC.

This part stresses that the interpretation of legal texts is an art, rather than a science, the value of which does not rest on the quality or quantity of our output but on the extent to which we promote justice and recognise the primary role of love for the truth. The force of love commands us to raise justice to a higher level of purity by encouraging the principle of equality. The chapter, therefore, analyses the cornerstone of the Statute of the ICC, that is to say the principle of impartiality and its possible infringements in the practice of the Court or our writings.

10.2 Legal Criticism with the Canon of Love

Legal criticism is not an easy task.[1] It may be correct to assert that the truth or falsehood of legal theories is almost impossible to determine. What this view overlooks is that criticisms may be truly strong or weak, insofar as they are, or

[1]See the discussions in May and Hoskins (2010).

F. Malekian, *Judgments of Love in Criminal Justice*,
DOI 10.1007/978-3-319-46900-3_10

are not, valid interpretations of the essence of a legal theory.[2] It is a fact that people interpret the philosophy behind legal texts in different ways. When we formulate a theory about an international criminal court, international human rights law, or rules regarding the abolition of slavery and abolition of capital punishment, we are surely obliged to delve into the phenomena of these legal disciplines and evaluate their principles and foundations, including various international criminal cases concerning serious and egregious violations of international human rights law.[3] We may understand the legal terms but hesitate between different interpretations, reservations, understandings, and conclusions. Thus, we will most probably become conscious of our own legal theories by assessing how they do or would affect the terminologies of legal procedures, human rights norms, or the systems of international criminal tribunals.[4]

Yet, we may explain the logical structures of our own human rights theories and their usefulness in an international legal system with confidence. The reasons are very simple: we are normally bonded to various social phenomena, including cultural, political, ethnic, religious, minority or majority groups, and economic as well as linguistic demands.[5] This means that we may not only criticise other opinions, but we may also, without meaning to, compromise the spirit and intention of our own legal writings or interpretations by not acknowledging the value of other legal theories, human rights norms, rules, regulations, and jurisdictional mechanisms. Legal criticism becomes more complicated and problematic when one attempts to prove contrary views or clarify certain matters with the norm of love.

10.3 Learning the Norms of Love

Although, in their various interpretations and statements, international prosecutors deal with the content of international treaties, human rights law, legal cases, and the judgments of international criminal tribunals, it would be greatly beneficial if more of them also examined the legal norms of other nations and cultures. The prosecutors should also look at other nations' potential effect on the prevention and prosecution of war crimes, crimes against humanity, and on the humanitarian law of armed conflict.[6] These norms can include legal, moral, and love norms. Today one can scarcely deny the fact that the development of the humanitarian law of armed conflicts in the works of the classical writers of the European Law of Nations

[2]Rawls (1971).

[3]Silk (2014), p. 96.

[4]*Id.*, pp. 97–102.

[5]See Lord Lloyd of Hampstead (1979); Tamanaha (2001); Huntington (1942), pp. 359–387.

[6]Malekian (2015).

was not only influenced by Islamic law, but also by the established laws of other states, such as India.[7]

However, an awareness of the global jurisdiction of human rights law has too often been lacking. For example, many prosecutors—national, regional, and international—do not, so far as can be seen, acknowledge the necessity of prosecuting the leaders of major powers, who grievously violate human rights principles and yet persistently avoid international criminal prosecution, such as the authorities of China, the United States, the United Kingdom, and Israel.[8]

The Prosecutor of the ICC and the member states not only have a definite legal responsibility for implementing, on an equal footing, the consolidated norms of international law governing *jus cogens* but are also under very real obligations to fulfil the principle of *pacta sunt servanda*. Consequently, the fundamental principles of international human rights law should be enforced with a pure philosophy of love for justice and concern for the integrity of all individuals in the world.

> It is impossible for Nations to fully acquire themselves of their mutual duties if they do not love one another. Offices of humanity should proceed from that pure source, and they will thus retain the character and perfection of it. Then we shall see Nations aid one another with sincerity and true kindness, labour earnestly for their common happiness, and promote peace without jealously and without distrust.[9]

The events of the First and Second World Wars, as well as many other conflicts, demonstrate at the start of the twenty-first century that preventing a recurrence of the catastrophes associated with policies of serious discrimination between different ethnic groups requires that fundamental principles of human rights law governing criminal justice be imposed on the leaders of all guilty states.[10] This in turn means to have love for the implementation of justice and its legal constitution as it is legalised in the structure of the ICC.

10.4 Values of Justice with Love

The intention of this part is to reveal ourselves in the ink of justice and to show that legal interpretation and scholarship are works of art painted according to different rules, statutes, and legislations. Whether these argumentations or interpretations are known or unknown should in no way diminish the great value of other cultural attitudes to the concept of law, although this may be highly controversial within our own legal thinking.[11] At the same time, our discussion stresses that we must

[7]Bandyopadhyay (1920).

[8]See Malekian (2007a). Tieya (1990), pp. 195–370.

[9]de Vattel (1916), p. 116.

[10]This is particularly significant in the case of contemporary tensions in international political relations. These are the heavy aggressive attacks on the Gaza Strip in July 2014 and the killing of over 2000 civilians.

[11]Aubert (1963), 42–43.

interpret international criminal accountability in a way that is imputable to all individuals who have committed international crimes by means of the legal, political, and military power of their states.[12] It may be interesting here to examine the general picture of accountability in the following light:

> International and national prosecutions are not the only methods of accountability. There are other options that must be examined, though in the opinion of this writer, there exists a duty to prosecute, whether at the international or national level, for genocide, crimes against humanity, war crimes, and torture. Accountability measures fall into three categories: truth, justice, and redress. Accountability must be recognized as an indispensable component of peace and eventual reconciliation. Accountability measures which achieve justice range from the prosecution of all potential violators to the establishment of the truth. Accountability is the antithesis of impunity, which occurs either *de jure* through the granting of amnesties or *de facto* through the failure of a state to enforce legal norms.[13]

We have, therefore, the modest objective of examining various theories of law—cumulatively, rather than separately—on the substance of the relationship between our interpretations and the concept of justice itself. We argue that the value of interpretation in international law does not rest on the quality or quantity of our output or our decisions but the way in which we promote justice and understand the purity of love for justice and truth, even if we do so in a few words or actions. For instance, Florence Nightingale did so with the transparency of her love for the charitable practice of humanistic medicine. Mahatma Gandhi achieved this with the pureness of his love for the spirit of independence. Marx and Engels demanded this with the clarity of their love for practical social equality. Mohammed Mossadegh carried this out with the sincerity of his love for the establishment of international democracy. Martin Luther King motivated us with the honesty of his love for the enforcement of ethnic equality. Nelson Mandela directed us with the peacefulness of his struggle against the evil system of apartheid by the power of tolerance of love for justice. All these intelligent persons obviously fought for the gavel of love in justice.

One can also examine the significant value of the gavel of love for justice in connection with different international cases. The possibility of realising this goal was demonstrated by the Russell Tribunals in London, Stockholm, and Copenhagen, which prosecuted crimes committed during the Vietnam War, albeit only hypothetically because of their non-governmental character. Before the Russell Tribunal, we had the marvellous analysis of international lawyer—Martin Luther King—concerning the Vietnam War and its useless military costs:

> Money that should have been spent on Johnson's War on Poverty was being lost in Vietnam's killing fields ... A nation that continues year after year to spend more money on military defense than on programs of social uplift is approaching spiritual death ... We are taking the black young men who had been crippled by our society and sending them 8,000 miles away to guarantee liberties in South-East Asia which they had not found in South-West Georgia and East Harlem. So we have been repeatedly faced with the cruel

[12]Cassese (2008), pp. 33–35.

[13]Bassiouni (1996), p. 398.

> irony of watching Negro and white boys on TV screens as they kill and die together for a nation that has been unable to seat them together in the same schools.[14]

The Russell Tribunals put the theory of love for justice into practice in a way that we should all seek to emulate in our decisions and writings at all times. With the establishment of these non-governmental tribunals, Bertrand Russell assuredly did not intend the propagation of his theory for or against any state. However, he asked for an appropriate understanding of the virtue and spirit of international norms in order to actualise the principle of love for justice and love for the maintenance of international human rights law at every level and degree. As Robert Kennedy correctly put it before his assassination:

> We're killing children, we're killing women, we're killing innocent people, . . . Do we have the right here in the United States to say that we're going to kill tens of thousands, make millions of people, as we have. . . millions of people, refugees, kill women and children? As we have. . . I very seriously question whether we have that right. . . Now we're saying we're going to fight there so that we don't have to fight in Thailand, so that we don't have to fight on the West Coast of the United States, so that they won't move across the Rockies. But do we. . . our whole moral position, it seems to me, changes tremendously.[15]

Our discussion set out to show that we are all obliged by the spirit of justice to struggle for the equal application of the law to all states, weak or strong, and, therefore, for an equal interpretation of the term "justice" under international criminal law. To this end, our preceding deliberations as well as this chapter also analogically evaluate the cornerstone of the Statute of the ICC, that is the principle of the impartiality of the Prosecutor and judges of the ICC and whether the Prosecutor of the ICC has upheld this principle. According to the Statute, the Prosecutor is responsible for the initiation of an investigation into the commission of international crimes.[16] Therefore, if his responsibility is based on the principle of love for justice to be done, if it is promoting the dignity of humankind to its natural value, and if his responsibility is solely constitutional; then it is a superficial view of legal norms.

10.5 Contradictions on the Theory of Justice

Describing what the foundations of philosophy of law are is very complicated indeed.[17] Up until the seventeenth and eighteenth centuries, and even in the early nineteenth century, the most popular discussions in philosophy of law concerned

---

[14] John Blake, *The greatest MLK speeches you never heard* (January 20, 2014), available at http://edition.cnn.com/2014/01/19/us/king-speeches-never-heard/ (Accessed March 31, 2016). See *also* Sheppard (2014).

[15] http://www.pbs.org/wgbh/amex/rfk/filmmore/pt.html (Accessed October 23, 2015).

[16] Milanovic (2011).

[17] Ferencz (1995).

the questions of what is good and bad, just and unjust, or right and wrong.[18] Most questions of legal philosophy or legal ethics were connected to spiritual modes of thought, theological theories, and religious convictions.[19] In order not to come into conflict with popular opinion, writers on legal philosophy constructed and promulgated their views with reference to the law of God, and those who disagreed were not only severely criticised by their peers but also by other authorities who had law-making power.

Natural law theory states that there are laws that are spiritual and appeals to philosophical and metaphysical theories for a religious conceptualisation of law in which the divine is considered to be manifest in or encompassing the material world.[20] According to this theory, enacted laws should be in harmony with one another and should not ignore the divine law. Therefore, the doctrine of natural law asserted that any law which created unjust positions or inequality could not be considered a true law. However, all those who developed the natural law did not base the concept of natural law on religious theories but even had a demarcation from such theories. A good example of this comes from an American philosopher who expresses that:

> Natural law, natural justice, being a principle that is naturally applicable and adequate to the rightful settlement of every possible controversy that can arise among men; being, too, the only standard by which any controversy whatever, between man and man, can be rightfully settled; being a principle whose protection every man demands for himself, whether he is willing to accord it to others, or not; being also an immutable principle, one that is always and everywhere the same, in all ages and nations; being self-evidently necessary in all times and places; being so entirely impartial and equitable towards all; so indispensable to the peace of mankind everywhere; so vital to the safety and welfare of every human being; being, too, so easily learned, so generally known, and so easily maintained by such voluntary associations as all honest men can readily and rightfully form for that purpose.[21]

However, the dominance of natural law theories had begun to decline by the beginning of the twentieth century, when positivist views were taking priority over naturalist ones.[22] Positivists developed the idea that the law is the law and, as such, all men should respect the law. According to them, a dictatorship, monarchy, republic, or democratic government derive the legal power of law. They insisted on the obligations of man to his society to obey the rules and provisions of legislation. There was eventually a conflict between the theory of justice presented by naturalism and the method of justice demanded by positivism. The conflict was so deep and sometimes personal that it closed all possibilities for the seat of love in justice.

---

[18]Brownlie (1963).

[19]John Finnis (1998).

[20]See de Secondat and de Montesquieu (1989).

[21]Spooner (2015), p. 16.

[22]See George (1994).

10.6 Proximate Solution

Jeremy Bentham and John Austin are two of the well-known positivists.[23] According to them, law, is described by social practices and rules that concern certain norms of law, and the law constitutes the order of the sovereign power and is upheld by the implementation of punishment.[24] However, naturalist views that had originally developed from the natural rights of man continued to defend the idea that certain rights are an integral part of the rights of man and should not be restricted by the provisions of positive law which may be harsh and discriminative. These two theoretical schools—naturalism and positivism—discuss the philosophy of law in different contexts, although they may have overlapping elements.[25]

Both theories have struggled to defend justice but in different ways. However, the paradox is that the orientation of their views depended on the purpose of their interpreters. This means that there was, most often, a lack of moral purity and an insufficiently strong will or desire to maintain the equal application of justice. This caused conflicts, and the main intention of law—to uphold justice for every single individual—very often disappeared in the practice of states, and this eventually led to war. For this reason, positivism, naturalism, and even pluralism seek proximate solutions rather than absolute ones. Even Hart himself admitted that there is a strong reason to believe that positivism also relies on the final stage of examination of the strength of the concept of morality. He says:

> What surely is most needed in order to make men clear sighted in confronting the official abuse of power, is that they should preserve the sense that the certification of something as legally valid is not conclusive of the question of obedience, and that, however great the aura of majesty or authority which the official system may have, its demands must in the end be submitted to a moral scrutiny.[26]

This approach, from the beginning, failed to find constructive elements, and states searched for solutions that would allow them to achieve an equal system of justice. This quest resulted in the establishment of the ICC and a number of *ad hoc* tribunals. However, as we will see, the international court has not been successful and the problem of achieving justice with pure intentions and love for human beings has stagnated within the philosophy of law in the facet of the political, economic, and military power of many members of the United Nations.

---

[23]Binder (2014), pp. 79–99.

[24]*Id.*, p. 80.

[25]See Detmold (1984a); Malekian (2007b), pp. 1–31.

[26]Hart (1961), p. 206.

10.7 Variety of Argumentations

The term "philosophy of law" is a term of art rather than science.[27] There is not yet any generally accepted definition of it within the body of national or international legislation.[28] The philosophy of law is a branch of philosophy which deals with the basic questions relating to law, regulations, or legislations. It is, in fact, a broad legal term which addresses different relations and concepts of law and their aims, intentions, and perspectives.[29] *Inter alia*, it discusses what the law is. It also serves to underline the connection between law and morality as well as to determine what the criteria for legal validity are.

Yet, we also have the term 'moral philosophy' which refers to a sub-discipline of philosophy dealing with the application of human reason concerning what is right and what is wrong in human conduct with other persons in general. The ethical principles developed are applicable to all situations as tools for the laymen, religious believers, governments, lawyers, prosecutors, and judges. Thus, moral philosophy manifests the way in which we make our social, political, economic, or religious arguments. This is because our arguments always rely on our individual motivations. Thus, the sphere of moral obligations, from a philosophical perspective, is where reason has a dominant function and this has a close relationship to legal philosophy.[30]

Similarly, the term 'philosophy of law' refers to the description of social circumstances and to what is and is not possible or necessary. The scope of the term "philosophy of law" is thus subject to debate, there being broader or narrower definitions of its functions. Underpinning the term 'philosophy of law' is the foundational concept of legal philosophy. The theories of philosophy of law are cultivated, grown, and harvested in order to develop our legal reasoning and argumentation in law in this soil. Thus, the foundations of legal philosophy are very extensive and broad in themselves.

The term "foundations of legal philosophy" is also referred to using the terms "legal theory" or "jurisprudence." These denote the assimilation of the basic notions of legal thought and legal reasoning through the assessments and argumentations of a considerable number of doctrines which have been presented in different periods throughout the history of jurisprudence. They include contradictions between natural law theorists, positivists, normativists, realists, Marxists, feminists, and postmodernists. They include some major developments in legal philosophy, which have been effective in the drafting or formulation of various rules of law.

All of these categories of development are still the subject of differentiation and discussion between the legal systems of various countries. They are the

[27]See Raz (1979); Raz (1999); Phillips (1980); Detmold (1984b); MacCormack (1970a); MacCormack (1970b), p. 33; Olivecrona (1964), p. 794.

[28]*Id.*

[29]*Id.*

[30]Consult Stern (2012).

intellectual tools for argumentation on the subjects of legal orders and legal norms, and the practical reasoning and legal presentation of different theories. We may apply all these theories in international criminal justice in order to create equality between all men and to prevent impunity. In other words, there ought to be a strong will to bring all criminals under the jurisdiction of an impartial international court for the purpose of prosecution and punishment. The Statute of the ICC clearly states that:

> Affirming that the most serious crimes of concern to the international community as a whole must not go unpunished and that their effective prosecution must be ensured by taking measures at the national level and by enhancing international cooperation,
>
> Determined to put an end to impunity for the perpetrators of these crimes and thus to contribute to the prevention of such crimes.[31]

10.8 Connotation of Legal Philosophy

Legal philosophy refers not only to the principles of *de lege lata* but also to the whole jurisprudence of law, such as the legal history of civilizations, the rules of legislation, and the history of the evolution of the theories of law, including criminal law.[32] All of these together also constitute the basic elements of the foundation of legal philosophy.[33]

Hence, legal philosophy is not just the expression of theories but also the expression of theories of theories and their academic circulation. Legal philosophy also encompasses legislation, rules, provisions, norms, and principles of legal ethics. Legal philosophy may discuss the principle of understanding each other's obligations, rights, and duties on an equal footing. The purpose of legal philosophy should, therefore, in brief, be respect and love for humanity.

> Legal ethics is not the application of ordinary ethics in a particular context, rather, it is a *political* normative system that is informed primarily by the capacity of the law to enable people to treat one another as equal, live together, and cooperate, despite deep and persisting disagreement, about morality and other matters. The idea of political morality is a complex one, but the basic idea is that there may be properties of a political or legal system that gives us reasons to act in certain way with regard to that system. We may have reasons to respect, support or uphold ... that are designated for the purpose of sustaining our lives in communities, alongside other persons.[34]

Although "respect" may have different connotations because of its broad hypothetical content, it clearly denotes equality, reciprocity, the goals of freedom, liberty, common understanding, and the recognition of the foundation of equal

---

[31] The Preamble to the Statute of the International Criminal Court, UN Doc. A/CONF.183/9.

[32] See Gavison (1987); Hurd (1991), p. 1611; Hughes (1971), p. 695; Austin (1954); Dickson (2001); Hart (1961).

[33] *Id.*

[34] Wendel (2012), p. 18.

justice between men.[35] This means that the term "legal philosophy" not only encompasses the science of law and ethics and their development within our national, regional, and international civilizations but also the way in which we should *treat* human beings regardless of cultural, ethnic, religious, linguistic, social, or racial factors.

10.9 A One-Eyed Justice

Although the foundations of legal philosophy may vary from nation to nation, their basic function in humanising man's social conduct and their value in protecting human beings from wrongful behaviour must always be, more or less, the same: these are the minimal requirements for the maintenance of justice. Hence, when we discuss the foundations of legal philosophy, we are trying to formulate an appropriate interpretation of this phenomenon that constitutes the most effective method of regulating peaceful relations between human beings. Whatever theory of law is referred to, it has to function and apply to all its subjects equally. This applies to theories of natural law, positive law, Marxist law, Islamic law, Jewish law, European law, or the provisions of the permanent International Criminal Court. This also includes punishment for the purpose of prevention, rehabilitation, and stigmatisation. The Trial Chamber of the SCSL clarifies that one of the core purposes of a sentence implemented by an international court is "to influence the legal awareness of the accused, the surviving victims, their relatives, the witnesses and the general public in order to ensure them that the legal system is implemented and enforced. Accordingly the purpose of the sentencing is intended to convey the message that *globally accepted laws and rules have to be accepted by everyone*."[36]

The most interesting aspect of legal philosophy is that it not only applies to the present or future conduct of man but also tries, as much as possible, to create justice for those who were victims in the past.[37] By drawing upon this foundational principle of equality, legal philosophy may direct itself in the present to obtaining support from either legal positivism or legal naturalism to respond to the past.[38] This happened during and after the Second World War, when the military, political, and legal power of the victorious states enabled them to establish an international criminal tribunal to prosecute and punish those who were accused of committing crimes against humanity.[39]

[35]Cappelletti et al. (1975).

[36]SCSL-04-15-T-1251, p. 13, Para. 14. Available at http://www.rscsl.org/Documents/Decisions/RUF/1251/SCSL-04-15-T-1251.pdf (Accessed April 5, 2015).

[37]See above Ferencz (1994).

[38]George (1995).

[39]Robertson (2006).

The establishment of the Tribunal was clearly a necessary element in the implementation of the principles of justice. The war caused the killings and injuries of millions of civilians and large-scale devastation of their properties. In this light, using positivist legal philosophy to argue against establishing the Tribunal was both irresponsible and irrational, since the ethical and moral requirements of the case were unarguably compelling.[40] As a result, these requirements of the case implicitly overrode the necessity of legal reasoning for the establishment of the Tribunal.

Obviously, the world could not observe the murder of innocent Jews with a one-eyed justice and rely solely on positive international criminal law.[41] A one-eyed justice needed to be combined with other rules of social conduct, with the intention of fulfilling the basic requirements of a legal philosophy. This meant that the ethical and moral understanding of the case had to have priority over the positive circumstances of the legal philosophy, such as its body of legislation. We could not ignore the claims of the love of humanity, love of justice, and the duty of protecting the innocent. Although different juridical questions have arisen in my previous interpretations of the judgments of the Nuremberg Tribunal, the fact is that the future generation of human beings would have interpreted the non-establishment of the Tribunal as as a great insult to the foundations of both legal positivism and moral naturalism and as a grave dereliction of love for man.

It is of relevance here that one of the serious and deliberate failings of the major political powers was that they had not previously signed or ratified any international criminal conventions legitimating the establishment of an international criminal court, although they had the opportunity to do so before the outbreak of the Second World War. In 1937, there was already a Convention for the Creation of an International Criminal Court, dealing with the establishment of such a court.[42] Yet, because of the unwillingness of the major powers and international disagreement about the definition of the term "aggression," the great majority of states refused to ratify the convention. The outcome was that the Convention did not have treaty-making powers.

Interestingly, India alone ratified the agreement, but since there were not a sufficient number of signatories for ratifying the instrument, it never came into force.[43] Naturally, justice had not been seen as a necessary condition for the confirmation of the existing law but as a political process treating law as a means and not as an end to resolving injustices. This meant the imposition of a one-eyed justice, led to the neglect of the pure theory of love, and undermined the determination to implement the existing theories of international criminal law.

---

[40]Gross (2012), pp. 39 and 63.

[41]Malekian (1991).

[42]The Convention was opened for signature at Geneva in November 16, 1937. See 7 International Legislation 878 (Manley Ottmer Hudson ed., Washington, D.C. 1941).

[43]The 1937 Convention was signed by 24 states. There was also a Convention for the Prevention and Punishment of Terrorism containing a well-elaborated definition of terrorism. The Convention was signed by 20 states, but ratified solely by India.

10.10 Failure to Comply with Basic Norms

For human beings, laws are not in themselves the expressions of fact but are regulations, principles, rules, provisions, or norms, which approve a course of conduct and impose sanctions for failure to comply. Thus, any law contains certain criteria for the implementation of its purpose and, when we contemplate legal philosophy, we reflect on all aspects of its existence and all aspects of its relevance. This is because the term "legal philosophy" also refers to the "science of law" and the choice between these two terms is broadly a matter of terminology. Yet, regardless of which philosophy we choose, the norm love is integrated into its structure, depending on how we wish to see the interpretation of pure philosophy of love for justice.

In other words, "legal philosophy" refers to knowledge of law relating to what is fair and what is reasonable. The law-making authorities codify the prescriptive norms, while the science of law generally prepares the descriptive rules. A proper legal philosophy guides us in striving towards a science of the law and its proper implementation and urges us not to accept failure to uphold the primacy of purity of intention in the administration of justice.

A considerable number of legal philosophers have endeavoured to answer the fundamental questions concerning the nature of the law. They wish to find the reason why we refer to certain legal disciplines in our argumentation for ensuring compliance with the law. The term "compliance" describes the ability to act according to an order, set of rules, obligations, or provisions, the maintenance of which is necessary for the purity of the law and justice. Two examples of legal philosophers who have engaged in this process are John Austin and Hans Kelsen.

Austin's is the classical model of positive law. He attempted to define law and rejected the relationship between law and morality. He believed that God and man both create law and thus he made a distinction between the laws of God and the laws of man. The latter is the consequence of standards of social conduct determined by political "superiors."[44] He even divided the law into "figurative" law.[45] The concept of law and the science of legislation were, therefore, two different matters in the opinion of Austin. He concluded that:

> That department of the science of ethics, which is concerned especially with positive law as it ought to be, is styled the science of legislations: that department of the science of ethics, which is concerned especially with positive morality as it ought to be, has hardly gotten a name perfectly appropriate and distinctive. Now though the science of legislation or positive law as it ought to be is not the science of jurisprudence or of positive law as it is, still the sciences are connected by numerous and indissoluble ties.[46]

[44]Austin (1861), p. xiv.

[45]*Id.*, p. 136.

[46]*Id.*, at xiv.

Perhaps, it was for this reason that Kelsen mostly spoke about the science of law.[47] He created the idea of *pure theory of law* and tried to separate the science of law from politics.[48] He developed his arguments on the function of basic norms—*Grundnormen*—and their pure implementation. It was according to this theory that Kelsen developed the ethical theory of collective and individual criminal responsibility in international criminal law with regard to the punishment of war criminals.

Positivists are of the view that what civil or criminal courts enforce is positive law. This is because a law possesses a certain source or has a definite content. They believe that each law has certain reasons for its enforcement emanating from its sources. That means the sources of the relevant philosophy of one body of law may differ from other bodies of law. For instance, sources of Islamic law, Jewish law, English law, Canon law, European law, and international law are different from one another. English law relies on legislation, precedents, custom, and equity while American law relies on statutes, custom, precedents, opinions of experts, and equity. In fact, positive law is predominantly a response against that part of the natural law theory concerning law and morality. Positivists emphasise a division between human law—a law that has been accepted in human conduct—and moral law. However, as MacCormick specifies, there is still one serious problem with a pure positivist view:

> [at] the beginning of these lectures, it was represented as a paradox that those who argue for amoralism seem themselves committed to a moralistic line of argument. Even as of that time, one might have registered a little quibble as to "moralistic" there. That a case is grounded in moral reasons does not equate with its being a *moralistic* case in the precisely *nuance* sense noted a little while back. But, all quibbling apart, we certainly have shown at great and even painful length that there are moral grounds for each limb of the a moralist position, and that the position is sustainable only if the moral case for it is sound. 'Legal amoralism' cannot avoid being a moral position. What our revised version of the position makes perfectly clear is that it *is* a moral position, concerning both the question how we ought to determine legal validity and the question how far the law ought to replicate demands of morality.[49]

One of the serious problems of those who engaged in the development of basic norms is that they could not see the development of the positive effect of the rule of love in national or international law. They were engaged in argumentation relating to what does and what does not constitute a basic norm and its separation from the concept of morality.[50] Therefore, they mostly emphasise the significant effect of the legal norm whilst simultaneously rejecting the existence of other norms even though the concept of morality still exists in the inner structure of their argument. This unknowingly creates the circle of "moral dilemma of positivism."[51] They

---

[47]Kelsen (1941), p. 44.

[48]*Id.*

[49]MacCormick (1985), p. 37.

[50]Consult D'Amato (1985–1986), pp. 43–53.

[51]*Id.*, p. 2.

ignore the fact that a serious moral duty may constitute a serious legal duty and offer a sounder justification.[52] More curiously, they could not even see the new developments in the philosophy of law in combination with human rights law. This means that any discussions with them relating to the philosophy of the norm of love would have been an idealistic idea.[53] However, one should read today the excellent view of Nussbaum about why love matters for justice and respect of fundamental rights listed in human rights instruments.[54]

10.11 Ethical Requirements of Justice

The bulk of legal philosophy is a subdivision of ethics.[55] That is why one of the serious problems that the judges of a court face is a moral problem; a judge must decide and articulate the basic ethic behind his decision. Thus, although the realm of law binds the judge, he cannot easily deny the realm of moral philosophy or ethics. This is regardless of the fact that legal philosophy deals mostly with questions of justice rather than with questions of morality. Justice has itself to serve purity of intentions, love of equality, a commitment to truth and authentic evidence, and love and respect for both sides in a dispute in order not to harm the legal, social, and personal integrity of conflicting parties. The positive relationship between law, duties, morality, and love and their significant interconnection with the question of appropriate justice may be described as an unavoidable issue. We should, however confess that:

> a conceptual clarification rather than a precise and itemized practically applicable account of the duties which belong to the class of duties of justice as contradistinguished from duties of self-respect or of love, or matters of aspiration or supererogation. I think, however, that the conceptual clarification is perhaps that which most matters; for, if accepted, it rules out certain ways of arguing about law as abuses of the legal method. The thing to which anti-moralists have characteristically objected is legislative regulation of matters of aspiration (the good life, as distinct from the life of avoidance of wrongdoing), duties of self-respect (regulations of various forms of sexual and sensual indulgence) and duties of love or benevolence (trying to enforce the spirit or the motive of action, rather than concentrating on simple results). This they have thought of as the moralistic use of law, as distinct from the enforcement through law of duties of justice, where *what matters is the outcome and the impact (or non-impact) on others, not the spirit behind the outcome.*[56]

However, the question remains: what is the law really demanding? Does the law demand implementation in accordance with equal social norms of justice, or does it

---

[52]Neil MacCormick (1985).

[53]*Id.*, pp. 38–39.

[54]Nussbaum (2013), pp. 378–385.

[55]Finnis (1983).

[56]Neil MacCormick (1985), p. 36.

solely mean presentation and implementation? On what basis should we criticise it? Although we are aware that criticism of the basic principles of the legal order is ethical and permissible, this does not necessarily address all aspects of legal discipline. This is because the ethical evaluation of legal discipline may be based on other matters than the law itself. To understand that realm of ethics, which is pertinent to law, is solely to delineate the frame of ethically reasonable facts which contain substantive values. This theory is also worth examining in those writings which play an important part in the presentation of legal philosophy, ethical perception of the law, and our moral attitudes. When we judge, we should avoid personal judgement as much as possible.

Even though there are no written rules preventing us from forming personal opinions, the non-existence of such rules should not be interpreted as allowing us to disregard the basic principles of ethics, to close our eyes to other civilizations, and to discount different legal systems, with or without personal antagonism. Such a dismissive attitude can be seen in the writings of Oppenheim, one of the most prominent international jurists of the United Kingdom.[57] He divided the world into civilized and uncivilized nations. The European states were the civilized nations and the creators of the law of nations, while the other nations were barbarous and did not possess a law of nations. This division not only expressed his personal preferences in the rule of law but also completely subverted the appropriate foundations of legal philosophy, namely equality, justice, pure reciprocity, and the heart of justice.

By these foundations, we mean those necessary principles of humanity that, because of their significant function in the foundation of legal philosophy and their protection, should never be ignored, reduced, or broken within our writings or decisions. Almost all philosophies of law possess a form of norms or principles supporting human dignity and preventing any civilian from its violation. Oppenheim surely saw the system of international law and the foundation of legal philosophy through the gaze of a one-eyed justice and did not recognise, for example, the Chinese, Egyptian, Persian, Indian, or Turkish laws of nations.[58]

In doing so, he manifested his strong intention to claim international law for one continent and could not see that other nations of the world on other parts of the globe also had close relations with neighbouring countries. These relations, regardless of their nature, constituted a body of international law as they did in Europe. What was really missing in Oppenheim's theory was love for the expression of truth, trust in the purity of justice being done, and love and respect for the relations between other nations of the world. *Justice does not mean civilization, but a civilization may demand justice.*

[57]Oppenheim (1937 and 1950).

[58]Malekian (1987).

10.12 The Moral Obligations of Justice

Ethical questions of law may be presented in different ways. Of course, this does not necessarily mean that the substance of reasonable facts can be modified. Obviously, our knowledge of ethics and the real nature of human beings are very limited so that we cannot specifically say what constitutes the elements of good ethics for each individual of the international community. This limitation of our knowledge is not necessarily based on the fact that we cannot understand the language of all peoples but on the nature of the intervention of our personal judgement.

However, there are certain principles that impel us to assist, cooperate, understand, realise, and sympathise with one another, even though we do not speak the same language or share the same culture or the same elements of good ethics. Evidently, our interpretation or writing is the expression of our judgement, our judgement is the manifestation of how we think, our thoughts determine the way we understand legal discipline, legal discipline is an example of how we choose, and that choice is connected to the culture we are familiar with.

In any event, it is axiomatic that personal judgements must not be allowed to compromise some of the most fundamental principles of legal judgments. These include, *inter alia*, impartiality of writings, objectivity of thinking, neutrality of choice of materials, independence of juridical analysis, and proportionality of means to an end.[59] Furthermore, a judgement or an evaluation must not violate the rules of natural law, positive law or human rights law.[60] This is because all of these are interrelated and cannot be separated from one another, even though they may belong to different groups of thought.[61]

Two questions about our ideas of interpretation, judgment, human rights law, or writing which lack a clear answer are the followings: What is the limit or degree according to which we may legitimately exclude other philosophical or legal developments? How far we can go in not applying the law to certain persons to whom the law should in reality be applied, even superficially? An example of the former is the long philosophical development of the principles of Islamic international criminal law governing armed conflicts.[62] Here, I am not encouraging the development of Islamic law at all but asserting that we have to remember that the law has had a beneficial effect on the writing of classical writers of international law.[63] Included in the latter are the many alleged crimes committed by Tony Blair, the former British Prime Minister, and George W. Bush, the former President of the United States as well as Barack Obama.[64]

[59]Aubert (1963), pp. 41–63, at 44–45.

[60]On natural law, see Finnis (1980).

[61]*Id.*

[62]See Malekian (2015).

[63]Consult also Samuel (2013).

[64]Tony Blair is now facing many problems for the destruction of Iraq and murdering of thousands Iraqi.

Neither the legal papers of the Prosecutor of the ICC nor its judgments include any condemnation of the alleged crimes committed in Afghanistan by Barack Hussein Obama, the current President of the United States, or the crimes which were committed in Gaza in 2011 and in July 2014.[65] The excellent unbiased reports of the official reporters of the United Nations—such as Hans Blix from Sweden and Richard Goldstone, the head of the UN fact-finding mission on the Gaza war from South Africa[66]—also did not provide any grounds for the Court machinery to prevent political, economic, and legal impunity. This means love for justice and the truth was and is very divisive before the Court jurisdiction. If these principles were respected, the situation would be different today for both Israel and Palestine.

The Court and the prosecutor should have known that there is no inferior or superior crime under the code of love, or in other words, all individuals are equal and no impunity is permitted. The Inter-American Court of Human Rights formulates that "the right to effective judicial protection therefore requires that the judges direct the process in such a way that undue delays and hindrances do not lead to impunity, thus frustrating adequate and due protection of human rights."[67] The Prosecutor of the ICC and the Court should realise that the philosophical reflection and accountability based on *moral obligation* has a long record in human relations, and such responsibility constitutes an essential factor for the proper fulfilment of the provisions of international criminal justice. The concept of moral obligation here means that the Court should not keep itself neutral about powerful criminals and be active about weak criminals.

Almost 900 years ago, Dante Alighieri correctly asserted, "the hottest places in hell are reserved for those who, in times of great moral crisis, maintain their neutrality." Here, I must admit the fact that I am not at all referring to the concept of religious hell or paradise, but I am obviously promoting the fact that justice is a very incendiary concept, the ignorance of which creates hell for the victims and disregards countless judgements. Still, if we no longer recognise *the high value of the dignity of human unity as the basic factor and the enforcer of morality*, then the nature and the virtue of morality undergoes a serious modification. Evidently, without the concept of application of equal criminal obligations, we have significantly altered the concept of criminality in criminal law.[68] It is like saying that we categorise international crimes, but we do not have the legal body of international criminal law. It means there are no longer any trustable statutes of criminal law and

[65]Meloni and Tongnoni (2012), pp. 543–577.

[66]Although the Goldstone opinion has been modified, this modification cannot have any legal effect on his original report. The events of 2014 against Gaza also again indicate the fact that political opinion can have a strong effect on the contents of international reports, which should be based on love for justice.

[67]Bulacio Case, Judgment of September 18, 2003, Inter-Am. Ct. H.R., (Ser. C) No. 100 (2003), paras. 114 and 115. Available at http://www1.umn.edu/humanrts/iachr/C/100-ing.html (Accessed April 29, 2015).

[68]Tristram Engelhardt (2010), pp 317–340.

criminal courts, but a one-eyed justice. Clearly, the true essence of justice should be a decisive principle. In other words, the concept of treaties without moral obligations of judges and prosecutors are nothing but solely biased constructs.[69] The Court is not under obligation to love justice, but it is certainly under serious obligation to act for true international justice.[70]

If, by reason, we mean that international criminal justice is unable to bring all criminals under its jurisdiction because of their military and political powers, and is consequently unable to require accurate accountability by an inductive and efficient process of criminal justice, the Court will face many problems in the establishment of moral obligations. It will then follow that moral judgment is not a pressing act of the Statute of the Court, and therefore the true nature of its judgment remains short of morality. The fact is that morality of truth should be a faculty within the Court's jurisdiction, as it is within us for discovering of the truth, seeing the truth, and dealing with the truth. This is the substance of all morality. The Court should not separate its conclusions from the truth. If a single judgment of the Court is correct, this does not necessary mean that the moral policy of the Court is correct. This is what we may call the faculty of understanding of the truth in all relevant cases. It includes cases which are submitted to the Court and cases which are not submitted to the Court. The duties of this faculty are the notions from which we form solidarity, equality, equivalent accountability, receiving compensation, dealing with the substance of morality, and full understanding of the position of victims. A Court without the real power of accusation, its humanity with the principles of limitation, the Statute without equal, and understanding of the Prosecutor and judges without scarification of their positions is doing nothing more than encouraging violence. Obviously, I am not, at any degree or at any level, presenting and supporting the plea of *tu quoque* for the criminal conduct of criminals who have been brought before the jurisdiction of the Court. Their prosecutions and punishments have certainly been correct. But, I am asking why the Court itself is arguing with the ban principle of *tu quoque* when it comes to the establishment of the principle of ethical obligations of the Court?[71]

It seems that the abolition of truth and morality is the Court's greatest detriment. This is because, when truth and morality retreat from the main intention of the Court, such as non-impunity, fairness of justice decreases and violation becomes the last alternative for the victims in order to restore justice. There are still other types of inductive arguments, e.g. the philosophical reasoning that the moral obligation of the Court is not necessary for the delivery of a good judgment. This means that the Court accepts legal obligations about certain criminals and ignores the same obligations about other groups of criminals. Again, it means that not only the legal obligations of the Court are divided into two different categories, but also

[69]Cudworth (1678), pp, 891, 892, 894.

[70]Sankowski (1978), pp. 100–110.

[71]See Chap. 9 Sect. 9.5.

that its moral obligations have different concepts. In other words, the Court delivers judgments when it convicts the criminals. It also means a very strong totalitarian Court solely for the prosecution of certain criminals. As was practised after the Second World War.

Although the judgment of the Nuremberg Tribunal was a necessary requirement for the establishment of the rights of innocent victims, it obviously rejected the entire legal system of international criminal law or humanist moral obligation to bring the victorious states under its jurisdiction for the commission of serious international crimes. The Tribunal, customary social ethics, and almost no culture would disagree that we have a moral obligation to avoid committing murder. This does not need a law. It is the same concerning crimes against humanity, war crimes, and genocide. Evidently, there is a moral obligation for all states not to commit genocide; this is regardless of the requirements of the Convention on Genocide. *Consequently, the practice of the Tribunal proved that the Nuremberg Charter divided the concept of moral obligation into moral necessity and moral non-necessity. This means the concept of morality for the weak criminals as the German War Criminals, and the notion of morality for the strong criminals, as the victorious states themselves.* The philosophy of authentic criminal justice entirely rejects such division. Both reason and fact prohibit us from giving priority to the military, and the politico-moral strength of powerful states from controlling the basic ethic of recognition of criminality. In light of this philosophy, justice *becomes* itself a threat to peace, because justice can only be delivered by a court and the court cannot properly deliver it because of monopolisation of justice by superpower politics.[72]

The function of the ICC remains a *factotum* for the permanent members of the United Nations and their allies. "Injustice anywhere is a threat to justice everywhere."[73] The Court should not adjust itself to the military and economic conditions that will do away with justice from the table of the Court for the victims; however, the Court does so.

That is to say that in international political life, truth and morality are retreating, the real feature of justice is declining, and economic gains are competing with one another. This can be seen in the crippled function of the Court regarding the real criminals. The principle of love for justice to be done imposes upon international criminal courts—permanent or *ad hoc*—certain legal and moral obligations to not punish one individual and release another. As a result, the quintessence of the norm of law must not only be philosophically wise but also compatible and non-separable from the reasons of our judgement. We mean the principle of love for justice is an essential principle for the self-confidence of justice, self-discipline of justice, self-vocabulary of justice for fairness, and above all for determination of peace with talent and tolerance. The safest conclusion then seems to be that the perception of moral obligation is a crucial fact in the jurisprudence of justice if justice is going to

[72]Chartrand and Philpot (2014).

[73]Martin Luther king.

survive entirely. With morality here, we obviously mean, non-impunity of all criminals—weak and strong.[74]

10.13 Probating Justice with Love

The practices of thinking, writing, and lecturing about law, or preparing cases for international criminal courts, generally display different ways of presenting legal theories.[75] One person may just reflect other theories; one may intend to develop other theories; and another may not only present other theories but simultaneously aim to achieve certain objectives for the purpose of creating a common ground for the foundation of legal philosophy. All three methods, or any other alternative, may be good in their own way, and demand equal application of justice within the spirit of love, but may not be sufficient for the cultivation of justice and the creation of an appropriate international legal philosophy.[76]

Many prominent philosophers and writers of law or international law may be included here, whose philosophy others objected to after a critical evaluation of their published theories. The objections were not based only on their method of presentation but also on the fact that they simply could not reach the real heart of justice. For instance, the philosophy of Immanuel Kant in his essay *Zum Ewigen Frieden* (*Perpetual Peace*) was criticised by Georg Wilhelm Friedrich Hegel in the *Grundlinien der Philosophie des Rechts* (*Elements of the Philosophy of Right*), although it was developing in all of Europe. Swedish criminal law, for example, was under influence of German philosophers such as Immanuel Kant and Friedrich Hegel from 1809 to 1920.[77]

Likewise, there may be many objections to the decisions of the prosecutors or judges of international criminal courts. The reason is very simple: they see the violators of international criminal obligations through *a one-eyed justice*. One notes the many international lawyers who could not perceive the serious problems of the international criminal court and enthusiastically praised its establishment. They applauded its system because the time was ripe for punishing criminals, the violators of international criminal law, human rights law, and the humanitarian law of armed conflict, etc. They ignored the fact that the whole law and the whole machinery of justice was and has remained in the hands of strong political powers.

---

[74]In relation to the indictment of Milosevic, Justice Arbour has asserted that to love justice is fundamentally an essential norm for the continuation of the life of justice. Accordingly, "victims, and those everywhere who love justice, need to know that there will be no impunity for those who commit these heinous offenses. And we're committed to helping the Tribunal ensure that those responsible are held accountable." Available at http://emperors-clothes.com/docs/h-list.htm (Accessed March 7, 2016).

[75]Aubert (1963), p. 48.

[76]Also consult Mendus (1999), pp. 57–75.

[77]Inger (2011), pp. 288–289.

They also ignore the fact that, in the international forest, bringing rabbits into the court and prosecuting them for how many carrots they have eaten or damaged does not equate to bringing wolves into the court and asking them how many rabbits they have torn, eaten, and harmed and how many more they plan to pursue. In other words, demanding justice with the norm of love is reasonably different from bringing love into the power of a statute of justice. Malcolm X puts the theory in this way "If you're not careful, the newspapers will have you hating the people who are being oppressed, and loving the people who are doing the oppressing."

References

Aubert, V. (1963). The structure of legal thinking. In *Legal essays to attribute to Frede Castberg on the occasion of his 70th birthday* (pp. 41–63). Oslo: Universitetsforlaget.

Austin, J. (1861). *The province of jurisprudence determined: Being the first of series of lectures on jurisprudence, or the philosophy of positive law (1832)* (2nd ed., p. xiv). London: J. Murray.

Austin, J. (1954). *The province of jurisprudence determined and the uses of the study of jurisprudence*. New York, NY: Noonday Press.

Bandyopadhyay, P. (1920). *International law and custom in ancient India*. Calcutta: Calcutta University Press.

Bassiouni, M. C. (1996). Accountability for violations of international humanitarian law and other serious violations of human rights. *Law and Contemporary Problems Law and Contemporary Problems*, 398.

Binder, G. (2014). Foundations of the legislative Panoption: Benthan' principles of morals and legislation. In M. D. Dubber (Ed.), *Foundational texts in modern criminal law* (pp. 79–99). Oxford: Oxford University Press.

Brownlie, I. (1963). *International law and the use of force by states*. Oxford: Oxford University Press.

Cappelletti, M., Gordley, J., & Johnson, E. (1975). *Toward equal justice: A comparative study of legal aid in modern societies*. New York, NY: Oceana Publications.

Cassese, A. (2008). *International criminal law* (2nd ed., pp. 33–35). New York, NY: Oxford University Press.

Chartrand, S., & Philpot, J. (Eds.). (2014). *Justice belied: The unbalanced scales of international criminal justice*. Montreal: Baraka Books.

Cudworth, R. (1678). *True intellectual system of the universe* (pp. 891, 892, 894). London: Printed for Richard Royston.

D'Amato, A. (1985–1986). The moral dilemma of positivism. *Valparaiso University Law Review, 20*, 43–53.

de Secondat, C., & de Montesquieu, B. (1989). In A. M. Cohler, B. C. Miller, & H. S. Stone (Eds.), *The spirit of the laws. Cambridge texts in the history of political thought*. Cambridge: Cambridge University Press.

de Vattel, E. (1916). *Le Droit de Gens, ou Principes de la Loi Naturelle, appliquès à la Conduite er aux Affaires des Nations de de Souverains: The Law of Nations or the Principles of Natural Law* (Vol. III the Classics of International Law, James Brown Scott, ed., 1758, 1916), (Book II, 11), p. 117.

Detmold, M. J. (1984a). *The unity of law and morality: A refutation of legal positivism*. Law Book Co of Australasia.

Detmold, M. J. (1984b). *The unity of law and morality: A refutation of legal positivism*. Routledge and Kegan Paul.

Dickson, J. (2001). *Evaluation and legal theory*. Oxford: Hart Publishing.

Ferencz, B. (1995). *New legal foundation for global survival*. New York: Oceana Publications.
Ferencz, B. B. (1994). *New legal foundation for global survival*. New York: Oceana Publications.
Finnis, F. (1983). *Fundamentals of ethics*. Washington, DC: Georgetown University.
Finnis, J. (1980). *Natural law and natural rights*. Oxford: Oxford University Press.
Gavison, R. (1987). *Issues in contemporary legal philosophy: The influence of H.L.A. Hart*. Oxford: Clarendon Press.
George, R. P. (1994). *Natural law theory: Contemporary essays*. Oxford: Clarendon Press.
George, R. P. (1995). *The autonomy of law: Essays on legal positivism*. Oxford: Oxford University Press.
Gross, H. (2012). *Crime and punishment: A concise moral critique* (p. 23). New York, NY: Oxford University Press.
Hart, H. L. A. (1961). *The concept of law*. Oxford: Oxford University Press.
Hughes, G. (1971). Validity and the basic norm. *California Law Review, 59*, 695.
Huntington, C. (1942). Plato's theory of law. *Harvard Law Review, 56*, 359–387.
Hurd, H. (1991). Challenging authority. *Yale Law Journal, 100*, 1611.
Inger, G. (2011). *Svensk Rättshistoria* (pp. 288–289). Malmö: Liber AB.
John Finnis, A. (1998). *Moral, political and legal theory*. Oxford: Oxford University Press.
Kelsen, H. (1941). The pure theory of law and analytical jurisprudence. *Harvard Law Review, 55*, 44.
Lord Lloyd of Hampstead. (1979). *Introduction to Jurisprudence* (4th ed.). Arvada: Stevens and Sons.
MacCormack, G. (1970a). Scandinavian realism. *Juridical Review*, 33.
MacCormack, G. (1970b). Hägerström on rights and duties. *Juridical Review, 59*, 33.
MacCormick, N. (1985). A moralistic case for a-moralistic law? *Valparaiso University Law Review*, 37.
Malekian, F. (1987). *The system of international law: Formations, treaties, responsibility*. Uppsala: Uppsala University Reprocentralen HSC.
Malekian, F. (1991). *International criminal law* (Vol. 2). Stockholm: Almqvist & Wiksell International.
Malekian, F. (2007a). *Documents on the principles of international human rights*. Stockholm: Norstedts Juridik.
Malekian, F. (2007b). The functions of international criminal law and the problem of positivism and neutralism philosophy. *Contemporary Journal of International Criminal Law, 1*, 1–31.
Malekian, F. (2015). The canon of love against the use of force in Islamic and public international law: Part II: The anatomy of love against violations. *International Criminal Law Review*, 861–889, 889–892.
May, L., & Hoskins, Z. (Eds.). (2010). *International criminal law and philosophy*. Cambridge: Cambridge University Press.
Meloni, C., & Tongnoni, G. (Eds.). (2012). *Is there a court for Gaza: A test bench for international justice* (pp. 543–577). The Hague: Springer.
Mendus, S. (1999). The importance of love in Rawls's theory of justice. *British Journal of Political Science, 29*(1), 57–75.
Milanovic, M. (2011). Is the Rome Statute binding on individuals? (And Why We Should Care). *Journal of International Criminal Justice, 9*(1), 25–52. Oxford.
Nussbaum, M. C. (2013). *Political emotions: Why love matters for justice*. Cambridge, MA: Harvard University Press.
Olivecrona, K. (1964). The imperative element in law. *Rutgers Law Review, 18*, 794.
Oppenheim, L. (1937 and 1950). In H. Lauterpacht (Ed.), *International law*: *Peace* (Vol. I). London.
Phillips, P. (1980). *Marx and Engels on law and laws*. Barnes & Noble Imports.
Rawls, J. (1971). *A theory of justice*. Cambridge, MA: Harvard University Press.
Raz, J. (1979). *The authority of law: Essays on law and morality*. The Clarendon Press.
Raz, J. (1999). *Practical reason and norms*. Oxford: Oxford University Press.

Robertson, G. (2006). *Crimes against humanity: The struggle for global justice* (3rd ed.). London: Penguin.

Samuel, K. L. H. (2013). *The OIC, the UN, and counter-terrorism law-making: Conflicting or cooperative legal orders?* Oxford: Hart.

Sankowski, E. (1978). Love and moral obligation. *The Journal of Value Inquiry, 12*(2), 100–110.

Sheppard, R. (2014). *Why the U.S. Government assassinated Malcolm X and Martin Luther King, Jr.* Toronto: ReMarx Publishing.

Silk, J. J. (2014, Spring). International criminal justice and the protection of human rights: The rule of law or the Hubris of law? *The Yale Journal of International Law Online, 39*, 96.

Spooner, L. (2015). *Natural Law; or the Science of Justice: A Treatise on Natural Law, Natural Justice, Natural Rights, Natural Liberty, and Natural Society; showing that all Legislation whatsoever is an Absurdity, a Usurpation, and a Crime. Part First.* [1882] (p. 16). Available at http://oll.libertyfund.org/titles/spooner-natural-law-or-the-science-of-justice-1882. Accessed 17 May 2015.

Stern, R. (2012). *Understanding moral obligation: Kant, Hegel, Kierkegaard.* Cambridge: Cambridge University Press.

Tamanaha, B. (2001). *A general jurisprudence of law and society.* Oxford: Oxford University Press.

Tieya, W. (1990). International law in China: Historical and contemporary perspective. In E. McWhinney (Ed.), *Judicial settlement of disputes: Jurisdiction and justifiability.* Leiden: Martinus Nijhoff.

Tristram Engelhardt, H. (2010). Moral obligation after the death of god: Critical reflections on concerns from Immanuel Kant, G. W. F. Hegel and Elizabeth Anscombe. *Social Philosophy and Policy, 27*(2), 317–340.

Wendel, B. (2012). *Lawyers and fidelity to law* (p. 18). Princeton, NJ: Princeton University Press.

Chapter 11
The Gavel of Love in International Criminal Courts

11.1 Proportionate Mobility of Justice

The gavel of love for justice to be done has been the most significant tool for the respect of the dignity of man throughout the ages. In ancient Persian culture, tradition, and custom, justice was based on three significant elements: *good thoughts, good words*, and *good deeds*. This means that human beings have to orient themselves to the truth and not just present one side of the case or merely express themselves through *a one-eyed justice*. We can never escape from the conclusion that appropriate legal thinking is a link in the chain of cause and effect of many factors.[1] Therefore, legal thought should have strong contact with its objectives. This implies the fact that legal thinking cannot be based on what is just visible but also on what is invisible. It can be based neither solely on tangible material nor on intangible material. Legal thinking or legal interpretation is *like* the heart of justice: it is a human constitutional legal mechanism, which has to work and interact with different principles, great or small, and cannot rest at any time.

It is the task of justice to function appropriately. As with the heart of human beings, which functions as a pump for the proper distribution of blood throughout all the different organs of the body, the heart of justice is not permitted to give priority to one organ over another. They have all to operate continuously and receive sufficient attention from the heart. That is why the four chambers of the human heart cannot physically sleep. In fact, it is the nature of the heart of justice, as it is the nature of a physical heart, to maintain the melody and harmony of different organs under its control.

Thus, a correct legal judgment or interpretation cannot at the same time present the facts of justice with different conclusions and simultaneously reject or ignore other parts of justice, even unintentionally. The norm of love has to be present at all

[1]Aubert (1963), p. 49.

F. Malekian, *Judgments of Love in Criminal Justice*,
DOI 10.1007/978-3-319-46900-3_11

times. This is what we call it the legal requirement for the presence of justice with the rule of love. Every attempt to ethically maintain that legal thinking should not have any connection with the different social phenomena of human beings, or to maintain that there is no ethical obligation to treat all criminal actions with the same degree of justice, necessarily leads to absurdities and also to great legal, juridical, and moral contradictions. We therefore have here the dividing line between interpretation by a prosecutor when making a decision, interpretation for carrying out our duties, and interpretation or writing for the purpose of the pure theory of justice *proportionate to the needs of the human beings of all civilizations*.

11.2 Chambers of Law

Chambers of international criminal law and justice, international criminal courts and proceedings, international human rights courts and presentation of evidence, and regional human rights courts and judgments cannot be entirely healthy if the gavel of the court is not combined with the essence of love for justice and the truth. We should not forget that, at present, the machinery of the legal systems of the world and the binding force of international criminal law, international humanitarian law, and international human rights law are in reality only an idea in our writing, since their enforceability largely depends on who or what they are aiming at.[2] In other words, the implementation of the system of international criminal law and its relevant branches are heavily influenced by the military and political strength of states rather than by the value of the relevant law. If this were not the case, the system would apply to all individuals who, in one way or another, seriously violated its basic intentions.

Looking at the serious problems of international criminal law or the mechanism of the ICC and considering that the system is incapable of enforcing the law on all of those who are accused of committing war crimes, crimes against humanity, genocide and so forth, we are forced to turn to the pure theory of justice. This also means turning to the basic principles of humanity recognised in natural law or formulated in positive law to orient our legal interpretation, thinking, or writing, so that it should not assist the real criminals or create impunity.[3] This is in order that we may enter the chambers of the heart of justice with purity, love, and respect with the appropriate gavel of justice.[4]

But, what *is* the heart of justice? It is a significant question. As we have just described, at first glance the body of law is not a human body with a physical heart serving many other organs. Much ink would be needed to express that, although the

[2]See Osiel (2009a, b).

[3]*Id*. See also Osiel (2002).

[4]For an excellent analysis of torture and its negative effect in the process of social justice, see Rejali (2007).

framework of law does not have a physical heart, it does have a metaphorical heart that should be called "justice." It consists, like the physical heart, of four chambers: the first is for rules; the second deals with the subject of law; the third is our interpretation or judgment/writing; and chamber four contains the truth, which can also be interpreted as the chamber of love.

The difficulty of finding the proper heart of the law has caused many philosophers of law, in particular those who deal with the foundation of legal reasoning, to appeal to justice, for example, Aristotle, Austin, Avicenna, Bentham, Grotius, Hamidullah, Hegel, Kant, Kelsen, Montesquieu, Plato, Rawls, Schwarzenberger, and Socrates. Thus, if we would like to frame a definition of the heart of "justice," we are surely obliged to examine the phenomena of legal philosophy with which the concept of justice is usually associated. One great advantage of this approach is that it acts as a kind of guideline for the development of our philosophy and may be helpful in discovering the essence of international justice and how it is interpreted by politicians, prosecutors, judges, lawyers, writers, or laymen.

This attitude may be identified in the writing of legal philosophers like Austin or Kelsen. The former seeks to define law and justice as "properly so-called." Thus, he was known for his clear intention to separate moral law from positive law, and he concluded that the law is the command of the sovereign and that the phenomenon of justice is the state of being bound by rules of the sovereign that are habitually obeyed by individuals. The latter aimed to detect the essential logical and ethical formation of a legal system according to the *pure theory of law* and to find a way for the consolidation of municipal or international justice.

The ideas of both philosophers have been criticised. The problem is that under the system of international criminal law and its machinery of jurisdiction—the ICC, ICTY, ICTR and others—none of these courts has been successful. Although one cannot deny the fact that positivists have achieved their aims, the implementation of the positivists' view has not helped the structure of justice. The legacies of the propagation of positivist or naturalist views have been the impunity of real criminals, and great harm has been caused to their victims because of a very weak international society. Regrettably, the corridors of international criminal jurisdiction have still not faced the attributability and accountability of the biggest criminals with real love for justice.

11.3 The Resolution of Accurate Thinking

The works of many writers have uncovered and discovered the struggles for the presentation of a correct conception of the philosophy of justice. The earliest theorists emphasise the concept of social relationships, morality, and personal duties in various forms. For example, Plato compared democratic equality with proportional equality in law: according to him, reasonableness varies quantitatively with a given claimant's value. Plato teaches us about the reality of things, rights, and justice and also to circumvent all things that cause misunderstandings in our minds.[5]

Avicenna, a philosopher and the father of classical medicine, and the author of the *Book of Healing* and the *Canon of Medicine*, among others, did not just believe in the actual effect of medicine on our physical body but also in the therapeutic curing of our natural body. *The Book of Healing does not actually deal with the substance of medical treatments but with the essence of our spirit and understanding the dignity of humankind. Avicenna tried to heal the ignorance of the soul or our vision of various social matters through our cognition. It was in this way that he tried to find the truth and realise the real need of the human mind. Although he was not in any sense an international human rights law lawyer or, indeed, a lawyer at all, he developed the idea of the philosophical recognition of the integrity of human beings owing to their physical nature.*

In the first place, the precise legal consequences of these theories elucidate a valuable point about the development and reconstruction of the philosophy of law. In the second place, legal philosophers help us to realise that justice may not only be worked out with legal reasoning but also with an effective understanding of the function of legal norms. This can be examined in the work of Rawls. He refers to the fact that the concept of justice as objectivity is part of the tradition of a democracy. It is, therefore, justified as 'acceptable' or the presentation of reasonable issues.[6] There is, thus, nothing in the nature of legal knowledge to justify a limited application of the principle of justice: on the contrary, there are many reasons and underlying principles which call for a wider interpretation of the law and its scope of applicability to all individuals. Nussbaum goes even further and says, "If love is needed even in Rawls's well-ordered society – and I believe it is – it is needed all the more urgently in real, imperfect societies that aspire to justice."[7]

In our case, this means that legal thinking must not be limited and should support a method by which a just deduction of rules may be obtained and applied to achieve justice. For instance, the system of international criminal law should not only apply to the criminal activities which are carried out by the individuals of one state against another but also to the criminal activities of all individuals who hide themselves behind the legal, military, and political power of their own states.[8]

In other words, legal thinking should not be controlled by a one-eyed justice that is represented by the political diplomacy of the superpowers under the monopolized rules of Chapter VII of the Charter of the United Nations.[9] This is why the world has continually faced many unjust decisions taken under the authority of the Security Council. Most recently, this can be seen in the comedy of dictatorial changes in the Gulf Crisis in Iraq, solely for the purpose of securing access to oil

[5]Tarrant (2006), pp. 9–16.

[6]Rawls (1971).

[7]Nussbaum (2013).

[8]Schwarzenberger (1950), pp. 263–296.

[9]See Nincic (1970).

resources.[10] Other examples are the commission of 26,000 air terror attacks in Libya by the US and the UK air forces under the auspices of NATO for the control of oil supplies; and the propaganda mechanism of building two atomic bombs in Iran to stand against the 20,000 remaining in the world.[11] Apparently, "this is the bloody history that modern interventionists like George W. Bush, Ted Cruz and Marco Rubio miss when they recite their narcissistic trope that Mideast nationalists 'hate us for our freedoms.' For the most part they don't; instead they hate us for the way we betrayed those freedoms — our own ideals — within their borders."[12] This malicious philosophy of big political powers continues all the time for the possession of oil and bringing down its price.

11.4 Purity with Love

We are not trying to say here that a one-eyed justice is the clear mark of the monopolization of law, policies, and politics.[13] *On the contrary, we are aiming to emphasise that, if United Nations law, the system of international criminal law, human rights law, the humanitarian law of armed conflict, the application of capital punishment, and the body of international criminal courts are monopolized in certain sensitive, serious, and necessary situations, our interpretation or writing should not blindly tolerate these sicknesses. In other words, where political power corrupts justice, our interpretation of law should still be strong enough to tell the truth, to hear the truth, to fight for the truth, and live with the truth. This means purity: to reach for the pure theory of justice. It also implies the strong position of truth with love. This means one cannot demonstrate the truth properly if love for justice does not exist.*

This concerns everybody, including the Prosecutor and the judges of the ICC. For instance, with reference to grave violations of the system of international criminal law, it is indeed very difficult to accept why the Prosecutor of the ICC has not enquired into the many serious crimes committed directly and indirectly by the British, United States, and Israeli governments after the establishment of the Court. Should we understand the position as being that the norm of love for justice does not apply in the above matters? Or, should we say that the Court shows, full love for justice with its action, but it applies its laws solely to African criminals?

Although we recognise that the Prosecutor of the ICC understands these issues, he should have nevertheless dealt with certain issues of the monopolization of the

---

[10]Malekian (1994).

[11]Falk (2011a). The issue finally ended by the ratification of a treaty between the United States, Iran, and some European states (Accessed March 12, 2016).

[12]Robert F. Kennedy, *Why the Arabs don't want us in Syria: They don't hate 'our freedoms.' They hate that we've betrayed our ideals in their own countries—for oil* in http://www.politico.eu/article/why-the-arabs-dont-want-us-in-syria-mideast-conflict-oil-intervention/ (Accessed 4 March 2016).

[13]Malekian (1995).

International Criminal Court much more explicitly in his statements.[14] If he had taken up this subject in his interviews and meetings, it might have sent a much stronger signal to the major powers of the United Nations and, consequently, it may have had a preventative effect on their criminal activities. For instance, the Prosecutor's correct engagement could have had a positive effect on the prevention of crimes in the Gaza Strip, Afghanistan, and Chechnya, or even on the serious violations of human rights law in China. This is what one could call "a one-eyed policy." It must be clear in this chapter that with the term "prosecutor" I not only mean the person who was in charge but also the person who is in charge and the person who will be in charge. The prosecutors and the judges must learn the real meaning of the code of love for justice and for the substance of the truth.

Here again the norm of love is not, as I have repeatedly said, a visible tool in the body of international criminal law or the court but a norm which can be seen in the final inspiration of judgment of mankind, the strength of love for justice, and the ultimate spirit of legal and moral norms. The norm love is the will or the tool by which we move together towards an altogether much more acceptable justice system. This justice invites us to reveal all secrets that prevent human happiness and morality as a whole. It can be called revolution for justice in the Court, improvement of human morality by the Court, the integration of European States and other parts of the world into one unity by the Court, or the strong will of the Court to create an international united form of justice which is theoretically fighting against justice without love. This implies the fact that love for universal justice has to exist in the nature of the Court and its respectful judges and prosecutors. By the word justice in this respect, I do not mean its confusing traditional definition, function, rules, or enforcement. Rather, the term 'justice' is used in its real or correct construction in the literature of the language. Thus, the term here means a common will and interest to stop violations that are no longer acceptable in human conduct and in the mind of the Court.

11.5 The Link Between Justice and the Prosecutor

Under no circumstances should a prosecutor, a conscientious writer of international criminal law and others ever abandon their struggle against any kind of monopolization of law and justice. Reference should be made here to the works of one of the most profound voices speaking out for human rights justice, Richard Falk. Any fair-minded human rights lawyer can scarcely deny the brilliancy of his achievement in comprehending the heart of justice.

The situation he describes involves the method of understanding the facts and the real function of the provisions of the Statute of the ICC. Does justice come through the commentary on the provisions of the Statute by the Prosecutor? How far

[14] *Id.*

and for how long does the commentary on the Statute help in the true implementation of its provisions? As we will see in the remainder of this analysis, the cornerstone of the Statute is the maintenance of the impartiality of the Prosecutor and judges of the Court and, naturally, this should be a basic principle in the actual practice of the law. With this in mind, we will also see whether the foundations of legal philosophy have unknowingly been violated.

As a whole, the ICC is responsible, in various ways, for dealing with international criminal violations that fall under the provisions of its Statute. The core aim of the ICC is to bring the perpetrators of international crimes under its jurisdiction for the appropriate implementation of prosecution and punishment. The requirement for the investigation of the commission of crimes may be suggested by its Prosecutor, a member or non-member state, the Security Council, or any national or international body which supposes that the provisions of the Statute have been violated. It is evident that none of these bodies or individuals alone is permitted to violate the law of the Statute and bring an inappropriate accusation before the Court. The intention is to develop the principle of legality and protect the foundations of legal philosophy for the maintenance of justice.

More obviously, the principle of legality in the Statute has not been formulated in order to create injustice but rather justice. This requires the purity of jurisdiction, transparency on the part of the Prosecutor of the Court, and the strong determination to establish justice for the victims collectively and individually. All of these requirements reflect the strong will of humanity with a wholehearted love for justice and implementation of international criminal responsibility. Therefore, the Prosecutor is personally responsible for investigating each case brought before the ICC in order to be sure that justice is carried out to the highest degree and for all, as well as ensuring that impunity is not permitted.

It is, in fact, one of the duties of the Prosecutor to examine the scope of evidence and to remain impartial about the merits of any case submitted for investigation by a member or non-member state. Neither the Prosecutor nor any bodies of the Court are permitted to act against the principle of impartiality, and this policy of impartiality has to be the main strategy of the ICC.[15] This principle would also seem to be a basic requirement for all other national, regional, or international decisions or judgments. For example, the principle of impartiality constitutes an integral part of the Code of Judicial Ethics in Russia. This is regardless of the deep corruption in the Russian legal system. It states that:

> The judicial defense of human rights and freedoms may be ensured only by competent and independent justice effectuated on the principles of justness and impartiality. Such justice assumes compliance by each judge with the rules of professional ethics, honest and good-faith performance of his duties, manifesting due concern for the preservation of his personal honour and dignity, and the dignity and authority of judicial power.[16]

[15] For different theories of impartiality in judgment, see Ofstad (1963), pp. 135–152.

[16] Butler (2013), p. 447.

Article 2 of the Statute of the European Court of Justice also implies this important fact. It reads that "before taking up his duties each Judge shall, before the Court of Justice sitting in open Court, take an oath to perform his duties impartially and conscientiously and to preserve the secrecy of the deliberations of the Court."

In general, the merit of the principle of impartiality is not only significant for the ICC and its staff, but it should also be highly respected in our writings. This is because the Statute shows the way in which we should make our judgments and how we should cultivate the seed of justice for the protection of humanity from unjustified behaviour and to prevent criminals from fleeing appropriate prosecution. *The principle of the impartiality of the Prosecutor unambiguously means serving justice with pure motive and love for the purity of the gavel of justice in order to uphold human dignity with an impartial attitude.*

11.6 Scope of Impartiality

An appropriate maintenance and application of the principle of impartiality in the practice of investigators, prosecutors, judges, witnesses, victims, and the Court may be interpreted as the appearance of full justice for love. It may be very difficult to search for the full implementation of the principle of impartiality by witnesses and victims during the proceedings of a case because of their very involvement as the subjects and objects of the offense. However, it should not be so difficult to demand the upholding of the principle by the Prosecutor or the judges of the Court. This is because the accomplishment of the principle constitutes an established conventional obligation of the relevant authorities.

There are several ways to understand the principle of impartiality. However, the question is who should decide what suffices to prevent any form of personal or organisational misinterpretation of the principle of impartiality, and how can we reach a peaceful and undisputed answer which does not diminish the concept of justice. The answer is, hypothetically, very simple: any action or decision indicating a lack of proportionality between the means and the end should be considered biased and therefore as breaking the theory of impartiality. Thus, for instance, the obvious non-impartiality of the Prosecutor of the ICC or the Court between one accused and another of the same degree should be sufficient to ascertain that the Court has not kept its objectivity or has been influenced by the political conditions of a case.

This non-impartiality is most obvious when one examines instances where the Court has taken action concerning the criminal acts of one accused but had no policy of investigation regarding a case which was much more harmful than the previous one. A clear example of this discrepancy can be seen in the recent responses to crises in Libya and Gaza. The Prosecutor, Luis Moreno-Ocampo, of the Court responded correctly to the criminal activities of the Government of Libya and investigated the commission of crimes against humanity and grave violations of international human rights law by the relevant individuals of the Libyan government, in particular, the command responsibility of the head of the state. However, at the same time, one may *query the silent policy of the ICC* and the Prosecutor of the same Court regarding crimes against humanity, war crimes, grave violations of humanitarian law of armed conflict and genocidal attacks against children in the Gaza Strip in 2011 and 2014.[17] What is really wrong here? Is it the rules of justice themselves or is it the lack of love required in order to maintain the pure theory of justice by prosecuting the individuals responsible?

One may note other cases concerning this inconsistent application of policy by the ICC. Falk has correctly evaluated the position of the ICC regarding the Libyan case[18]:

> The selectivity is made more objectionable by the impunity accorded to European, American, and Israeli leaders. Double standards so pervasively evident in this behaviour undermine the authority of law, especially in relation to a subject as pressing as war and peace. Unless equals are treated equally most of the time, what is called 'law' is more accurately treated as 'geopolitics.'[19]

Largely, the legal position of the principle of impartiality in its traditional form has been seen as a consequence of the doctrine of fair and reasonable justice. The Statute of the ICC has emphasised, in many subsections of its articles, the important position of the principle of impartiality in the procedures of justice. The principle can in fact be considered one of the core principles of the ICC mechanism and a vital tool for the proper application of the provisions of the Statute.

The term "impartiality" has sometimes also been accompanied by terms like "independence," "objectivity," "impartiality," "honourably," or "faithfully." All of these terms express the importance of the maintenance of impartial justice, objective judgment, and neutral action. For instance, Article 17 of the Statute deals with the issue of admissibility. It provides that the Court should determine that a case is inadmissible where the "proceedings were not or are not being conducted independently or impartially, and they were or are being conducted in a manner which, in the circumstances, is inconsistent with an intent to bring the person concerned to justice."[20] Here the Statute clearly clarifies that an accused may be brought before the jurisdiction of the Court according to the principle of *complementarity* if the state in question, which has jurisdiction over the accused, has acted in a manner that that has been in contradiction of the principle of appropriate prosecution.[21] The principle of complementarity should, however, be seen from the perspective of the principles of complexity and complicity, too.[22]

---

[17]Darcy (2011), p. 23.

[18]Falk (2011b), available at www.transnational.org/SAJT/tff/people/r_falk.html (Accessed July 20, 2015).

[19]*Id.*

[20]Article 17 (2) (c).

[21]The Statute also provides similar provisions relating to the principle of *ne bis in idem*. Article 22 (3) (b).

[22]Consult Clapham (2003), pp. 30–67.

11.7 Elements of Impartiality of Justice

The principle of impartiality intends to establish fair and acceptable proceedings and procedures for judgment and to minimise the possibility of damning criticisms of, and reputational damage to, the legal personality of the Court. This is because all judgments of the Court are written and all writings present the judgments of the Court. The policy encourages us to write for justice and the truth, the whole truth, and nothing but the truth.

It is on this basis that the principle of impartiality denotes the application of several other parallel principles which have significant value for the jurisdiction of the Court and the creation of international trust in the personality of the Court. Consequently, the application of the principle of impartiality also implies the implementation of the following principles: *a)* the principle of fairness; *b)* the principle of independence; *c)* the principle of qualified justice; *d)* the principle of the objectivity of the Court; *e)* the principle of the objectivity of judgement; and *f)* the principle of proportionality. All of them have to be based on the principle of love for justice, including a love for the victims, love for the accused, and love for the witness.

Without doubt, all of these principles follow from each other and amount to the same thing: a statement of the value of impartial justice. This should be acknowledged as the highest quality of the Court and the legal guarantee of its international integrity. In fact, it is one of the consolidated principles of international criminal jurisdiction that the states' members to the Court should give sufficient attention to the independence and impartiality of the Court. In principle, the essence of impartiality of the Court should not be susceptible to breaches by different organs of the Court. This means that we have to maintain the customary and legal position of the principles of good faith, good judgment, and good outcomes.[23]

What this means in short is that the Court should not, in any circumstances, practice the policy of a one-eyed justice. Naturally, the foundation of legal philosophy should be brought within the structure of its judgments. *The Court should not and cannot choose two different methods for writing its judgments. All of its judgments must demonstrate fairness and justice*. Our own writings and judgments should also follow similar criteria.[24] For instance, suppose that the Court chooses to be guided by the theory of Marxist-Leninism, United States criminal law, or Islamic criminal law, the Court is obliged to use the relevant moral limits of the criminal sanction concerning all criminal cases occurring in the world. It should not give priority to one case and disregard international criminal violations concerning another case. The philosophy of justice has to be the same, with the same method, to the same degree, and with the same criminal provisions.

The moral philosophy of law does not allow us to appeal to two different philosophies when applying sanctions in the same forum. Hypothetically speaking, the permanent International Criminal Court has to follow the same law for the same

[23]See Malekian (2010), pp. 41–65.

[24]Consult *also* the sentiments of our judgment in Smith (2004), pp. 54–59.

crimes and criminals. This is regardless of whether it is the regulation of an ecclesiastical court, Christian court, the Ottoman court, Stalin's trials or the Court of the Red Tsar, Mussolini's court, a court of the Third Reich, the International Criminal Tribunal in Nuremberg, the International Criminal Tribunals in Yugoslavia, Rwanda, or Sierra Leone. *Any discrimination between different criminals is naturally against the basic philosophy of moral law and against the rule of love for justice.*

In other words, the principle of impartiality has to be upheld, not only in the case of the application of the same philosophy of justice but also in the case of all procedures and the individual objectivity of prosecutors and judges. It means the respect for pure philosophy of love with the gavel of love for justice. These mean we should not close our eyes and apply injust rules in our criminal courts and procedures. Clearly, this is not the case in the case of the Statute of the ICC, but its practice may soon irritate the entire school of justice in the world and be a model for impunity under the national legal systems of different nations.

11.8 Keeping Impartiality of the Prosecutor

Reasoning by analogy to the legal function of the Prosecutor, which exists under the regulations of the office of the Prosecutor of the ICC, it is possible to suggest that the Prosecutor has a recognised legal duty to maintain her/his impartiality regarding all cases brought to her/his office.[25] In some cases, the evidence presented by the Prosecutor initiates a case before the jurisdiction of the Court. The Prosecutor has a recognised and consolidated responsibility before the chambers of the Court not to provide inauthentic information. Similarly, the Prosecutor is also responsible for not initiating a case when she/he has been involved in the events of the case and its development. The principle of the impartiality of the Prosecutor, like the principle of the impartiality of a judge, plays an important part in the proceedings of a case. Comparatively, the European Union Court also requires the application of the principle of impartiality.[26]

[25]The ICC has been involved in 20 situations around the world including Colombia, Georgia, Afghanistan, and Korea. They have some of the current situations under preliminary examination. Four state parties referred their own situations to the Court: Uganda, Democratic Republic of the Congo, Central African Republic, and Mali. Ivory Coast accepted the Court's jurisdiction, and the Court independently opened investigations in Kenya. The prosecution decided not to open investigations into Iraq and Venezuela and dismissed a request by Palestine for failure to meet the preconditions for jurisdiction. Office of the Prosecutor, Report on Preliminary Examination Activities, INT'L CRIMINAL COURT (Nov. 2012), available at http://www.icc-cpi.int/NR/rdonlyres/C433C462-7C4E-4358-8A72-8D99FD00E8CD/285209/OTP2012ReportonPreliminaryExaminations22Nov2012.pdf.

[26]Wägenbaur (2013), p. 12.

Whilst the Statute of the ICC has been very clear about the principle of the impartiality of the Prosecutor, it is not easy to describe the precise scope of such impartiality when such a question arises because of the political nature of a case. According to the regulations of the Statute, the office of the Prosecutor constitutes an independent organ of the Court. The core responsibility of the office is to receive any evidence under the framework of the Statute that crimes have been committed. In particular, the Prosecutor is responsible for examining the evidence and conducting investigations for prosecutions before the Court whenever the evidence is deemed juridically adequate.

The Statute especially emphasises that "a member of the office shall not seek or act on instructions from any external source." The Statute's purpose is not necessarily to emphasise the important character of the independence of the office of the Prosecutor but to create a clear line between what may be called a direct or indirect order or influence by an external source. The purpose is to prevent the Prosecutor from being subject to pressure from outside instruction which may invalidate the impartiality principle. *Our aim is clearly to prevent the influence of a one-eyed justice upon the system of written judgments and not misuse the gavel of love for justice in criminal law.*

11.9 Impartial Morality of the Prosecutor

The moral dimension of legal philosophy is based on ethical understanding and requires fairness.[27] Although the concept of morality does not necessarily denote the existence of impartiality, it points to the fact that we are obliged not to base our statements upon personal emotions and cultural influences.[28] A close reading of the Statute of the ICC also reveals this: "[the] Prosecutor and the Deputy Prosecutors shall be persons of high moral character."[29]

What this means is that the Prosecutor should not undermine justice and should be a person of excellent reputation, who has not, and will not, breach the elements of justice, either in practice or in writing. It also means that the Prosecutor and the deputy Prosecutor will maintain fairness and neutrality in each case in the pursuit of justice. Furthermore, the Prosecutor, with his excellent legal knowledge and ability, will understand that he should not only investigate the cases of those who have politically or juridically lost national or international support and are weak but also of those who are strong and have committed international crimes but are protected under the jurisdiction of their own states.

Essentially, all individuals have to be treated equally and may be accused by others, including the Prosecutor. This also implies the fact that the Prosecutor

[27] Fuller (1969).

[28] Hacker and Raz (1977).

[29] Article 42 (3).

should be politically and ideologically independent and his opinion should not form the initiation of a case. This is particularly obvious in the case of the Prosecutor of the ICC who has, because of her/his high moral character, a great responsibility before the international legal community. It is, therefore, always an open question how the "high moral character" of an international Prosecutor can remain uninfluenced by the distribution of international political power.

For instance, up until today, it seems that the Prosecutor of the ICC has not found any compelling evidence demonstrating violations of the law of the Statute by the permanent members of the Security Council and their allies. The serious violations in the Gaza strip and the Goldstone report did not convince the Prosecutor to initiate a case against persons accused of infringing international criminal law.[30] In 2014, this question was not even discussed when the children of the Occupied Territories were suffering because of the murderous and illegal activities of the military commanders of the Government of Israel. The only new change is the recognition of the Palestinian state as a member of the ICC and its statehood in the United Nations.

Although the United Nations has chosen a new reporter for further crimes committed in 2014, it is very doubtful that the Court will bring the accused persons under its jurisdiction for prosecution and punishment. The serious violations of human rights law and armed conflict in Iraq and Afghanistan did not, and will not, give any legal grounds for the prosecution of the heads of state of the permanent member states.[31] *Noticeably, many writers on international criminal law do not always follow the same policy as the Prosecutor of the ICC. However, the question we must ask is why they fail to seriously question such significant cases in their books on international criminal courts and tribunals. They honestly discuss many of the cases brought by states before the jurisdiction of international criminal tribunals but not those concerning the major powers. What is really wrong?*

11.10 What Is the High Moral Character of the Prosecutor?

What is the actual definition of the phrase "high moral character," for a Prosecutor or for those writing about a Prosecutor's character? Does the phrase solely mean the Prosecutor's national, regional, or international reputation, or does it actually mean the way in which we intentionally or unintentionally express the will of the strongest political actors? A simple question is: how can the Prosecutor of the ICC witness the existence of evidence necessary for the initiation of a case against certain members of the Libyan government or any other such accused but not see any reason for the initiation of a case against other governments? Should politico-

[30] Blumenthal (2002), p. 593.

[31] Malekian (2005), pp. 673–723.

legal monopolization, strength, or motivation in the United Nations Charter be much stronger than juridical indications within our important duties or work in human rights law, international criminal law, or the judiciary? Or, is it sufficient to deal with these important questions only in our inaugural meetings, lectures, or conferences as the prosecutor of the ICC does?

Since the legal status of the Prosecutor's office itself does not provide a clue, it is not so easy to argue that the arguments presented in the Libyan or Omer Hassan Al-Bashir case by the Prosecutor were obviously a correct decision.[32] Al-Bashir has definitely committed international crimes, but international accountability must be applicable to all those who commit international crimes and one should not select criminals. Ironically, it seems that the prosecutor of the non-governmental Bertrand Russell War Crimes Tribunal held in London, Stockholm, and Copenhagen had violated his political boundaries when he initiated the Vietnam Case against the United States government.[33] In the Taylor Case, it is easy to see this shortcoming of the system of justice even today.[34]

One of the valuable principles of this little-known Bertrand Russell War Crimes Tribunal was that it recognised the political monopolization of the Charter of the United Nations very early and clearly. It discussed simply justice and asked why, if the rules of International Military Tribunals at Nuremberg and Tokyo could manifest the language of justice in 1945, why the Bertrand Russell War Crimes Tribunal could not do the same? The Tribunal was surely not against the foundations of the legal philosophy of the Nuremberg Tribunal. *This means that the chief question of the Russell Tribunal was not which philosophy of law or criteria of morality was employed in the Nuremberg Tribunal, but why the relevant theory was not applicable against the criminal activities in the Vietnam War.*

The matter is more complex because the actions or reactions of the Prosecutor of the ICC did not condemn the unlawful use of force by the United Kingdom and the United States in the territories of Iraq.[35] It also does not analyse the real feature of those who are the cause of the creation of the ISIS and international terror. It is more critical when such a significant office of international criminal justice does not seriously question the accumulation of massive nuclear weapons by the major powers and classify it as a precursor to the commission of international crimes. Although we understand that the production of weapons has been manufactured under the provisions of treaties, and that the Prosecutor of the ICC is not responsible for dealing with those issues, would it not be better to deal with these questions and the prohibition of such weapons for the sake of humanity?

---

[32]Some writers suggest that, in order for the ICC be successful, certain Islamic provisions should be adopted into the Statute of the Court. For instance, see Roach (2006), pp. 143–144.

[33]Consult *also* Kennedy (2004).

[34]See Chap. 8, Sect. 8.8.

[35]Malekian (1993).

Whether or not the Prosecutor acknowledges these shortcomings of the office is a very serious question. In addition, the purpose of the doctrines within the system of international criminal law is not primarily to make propositions or commentaries about the structure of the system, its development, and particular functions. Instead, however, it is to bring the truth into justice and justice into peace. Such was in the show tribunal for the prosecution of the Iraqi dictator[36] or "the lie that Saddam Hussein in Iraq had 'weapons of mass destruction.'"[37] Other similar examples are the facts of 9/11, the political killing of Muammar Muhammad Abu Minyar Gaddafi under the supervision of the CIA,[38] "lies told about Libya,"[39] the facts concerning the establishment of the Islamic State groups, and various accusations of occupation and use of chemical weapons by different states.[40]

All of these and a considerable number of cases concerning African states, which have been brought before the ICC's jurisdiction, demonstrate the fact that the ICC has, a long time ago, lost its impartiality, love for justice, and truth and that it works with a policy of one-eyed justice. The referrals and deferrals of the Security Council of the United Nations to the ICC confirm also the policy of give and take between both international legal bodies, whether intentionally or unintentionally. The international legal or political community cannot therefore ignore the explicit and implicit dependency of the Court.

11.11 Honesty in Justice

The substance of impartiality helps to bring into focus the significant function of legal philosophy in our judgements. The Statute of the Court has even foreseen the situation under which a judgment of the Court may not have the effect of a binding decision. This is when the Court discovers that the integrity of the element of impartiality, i.e. the basis of legal philosophy, is under question. One may examine the qualification of prosecutors and judges in connection with the legal position of the principle of impartiality and its critical value for the theory of judgment. As a rule of national, regional, or international jurisdiction, a judge must be completely objective regarding a case and should not take part in a case in which her/his

---

[36] *Id.*, pp. 673–723.

[37] See the excellent article by Dr. Paul Craig Roberts, '*Washington's Secret Agendas—Truth is Being Disguised to Suit*'. Available at http://www.oneworldofnations.com/2014/09/washingtons-secret-agendas-truth-is.html (Accessed January 15, 2016).

[38] Ron Paul, former Republican Party top politician, has admitted that the CIA killed Gaddafi. www.godlikeproductions.com/forum1/. . ./pg1—(Accessed 20 July 2015).

[39] Robert F. Kennedy, *Why the Arabs don't want us in Syria: They don't hate 'our freedoms.' They hate that we've betrayed our ideals in their own countries—for oil* in http://www.politico.eu/article/why-the-arabs-dont-want-us-in-syria-mideast-conflict-oil-intervention/ (Accessed 4 March 2016).

[40] *Id.*

involvement, in one way or another, may violate the principle of impartiality. The principle here applies to any matter of interest which concerns the judge.

The provisions of Article 41 of the Statute assess the value of this significant principle of justice and of writing the rules of justice with a correct attitude. This prevents the participation of a judge whose neutrality is in doubt on any grounds. Likewise, the language of the article is emphatic and clear regarding the principle of impartiality: any judge of the Court who is not impartial should immediately be dismissed, and the Prosecutor may submit the request for her/his disqualification or any other person concerned with the case.

It seems indisputable that there exists a clear rule on the matter of impartiality, and this rule is established in the provisions of other international courts that do not have a permanent character, the *ad hoc* tribunals. The Statute disqualifies a judge for having an interest in a case. The disqualification should not, however, be interpreted as a condemnation of the judge but as the way in which the integrity of the victims, jurisdiction, justice, and fairness is protected by the ICC. This protection obviously benefits the international human community as a whole.

The Statute aims to ensure that the judgment of the Court is sound and unbiased. This is regardless of whether the judge violates the principle of impartiality knowingly or unknowingly. Obviously, the intention of the legislators of the ICC is not to offend the judges but to defend those involved against a one-eyed justice and to avoid an *insult* to the foundations of legal philosophy and justice. This impartiality also requires objectivity in bringing the accused into the jurisdiction of the Court in the first place.

11.12 Procreative Substantive Legal Validity

By writing texts on international legal theory, we wish to provide the formal basis for the development of the new rules of international law and to emphasise their procreative substantive legal validity in the international community of states as a whole. Most of these texts are, therefore, in one way or another, orientated towards not only giving advice to the governments of states, politicians, judges, prosecutors, and lawyers but also to positively or negatively affecting the lives of human beings.

By "positive" or "negative" we do not necessarily refer to their definitions as usually understood by the layman but to the way in which one may see the legal interpretation as for or against oneself. For example, dictatorial governments frequently consider the interpretation of human rights law as directed against their own position and do not want to submit themselves to a correct definition of human rights principles. Consequently, thoughtfulness of the needs of human beings, humanity, and justice may depend on the subjective appreciation of a prosecutor, but more objectively, it may concern the basic values of humankind that are already protected by the norms of international human rights law or legal positivism. In other words, cultural, social, economic, religious, and ethnic origin, aboriginality, language, and other individual backgrounds may play an important role in the interpretation, selection, presentation, and analysis of legal rules.

Thus, we may unknowingly fight within our own presentations against any rule that is not welcome to our personal values, although we are aware that ignoring the basic principles of human rights law is not acceptable and may be a matter of discrimination or segregation, too. This means we may not have the intention to diminish the value of justice but we may in actual circumstances end up doing so.[41]

Observably, this argument here should not diminish the legal value of the office of the Prosecutor of the ICC to any degree. The fact is that, even when the Prosecutor has a great desire to respect all opinions, rules, or legislations, it is not easy to do this satisfactorily, since we expect the Prosecutor of the ICC to be personally responsible for sustaining the pillars of international justice and peace. Her/his legal baggage is expected to produce justice. Criticisms of the works and decisions of the Prosecutors are thus also criticisms of our own writings as legal scholars, which have not led to the prevention of war and have witnessed the justified and unjustified killing of millions of human beings, even after the establishment of the United Nations Organization. This means that the Prosecutor of the ICC or lawyers in any other court, including ourselves, have to keep the word "justice," its application, interpretation, and results with the strength of love for justice and humanity. This is in order not to violate the realm of justice by punishing some individuals while encouraging others by acquiescing in their impunity.[42]

References

Aubert, V. (1963). The structure of legal thinking. In *Legal essays to attribute to Frede Castberg on the occasion of his 70th birthday* (pp. 41–63). Universitetsforlaget.

Bass, G. (2000). *Stay the hand of vengeance: The politics of war crimes tribunals.*

Blumenthal, D. A. (2002). The politics of justice: Why Israel signed the international criminal court statute and what the signature means. *Georgia Journal of International and Comparative Law, 30*, 593.

Butler, W. E. (2013). *Russian public law* (3rd ed.). London: Wildy, Simmonds & Hill Publishers.

Clapham, A. (2003). Issues of complexity, complicity and complementarity: From the Nuremberg Trials to the dawn of the New International Criminal Court. In P. Sands (Ed.), *From Nuremberg to The Hague: The future of international criminal justice*. Cambridge: Cambridge University Press.

Darcy, S. (2011). Prosecuting the war crime of collective punishment: Is it time to amend the Rome statute? *Journal of International Criminal Justice.*

Falk, R. (2011a). *Criminalizing diplomacy: Fanning the flames of the Iran War Option.* Available at www.transnational.org/SAJT/tff/people/r_falk.html

Falk, R. (2011b). *The international criminal law plays politics? The Qaddafi Arrest Warrants.*

Fuller, L. L. (1969). *The morality of law* (2nd ed.). New Haven: Yale University Press.

[41] Bass (2000).

[42] See Malekian (2014).

Hacker, P. M. S., & Raz, J. (Eds.). (1977). *Law, morality and society: Essays in honour of H.L.A. Hart*. Clarendon Press.

Kennedy, R. F. (2004). *Crimes against nature: How George W. Bush and his Corporate Pals are plundering the country and hijacking our democracy*. Harper, New title edition.

Malekian, F. (1993). *Condemning the use of force in the gulf crisis*. Almqvist & Wiksell International.

Malekian, F. (1994). *Condemning the use of force in the gulf crisis* (2nd ed.). Stockholm: Almqvist & Wiksell International.

Malekian, F. (1995). *The monopolization of international criminal law in the United Nations, a jurisprudential approach* (2nd ed.). Stockholm: Almqvist & Wiksell International.

Malekian, F. (2005). Emasculating the philosophy of international criminal justice in the Iraqi special tribunal. *Cornell International Law Journal, 38*(3), 673–723.

Malekian, F. (2010). The principle of good faith within the sources of international criminal law. *Retfaerd, Nordisk Juridisk Tidsskrift*, 131 nr.4 –årgang 33, 41–65.

Malekian, F. (2014). *Jurisprudence of international criminal court*. Cambridge: Cambridge Scholars Publishing.

Nincic, D. (1970). *The problem of sovereignty in the Charter and in the practice of the United Nations*. Martinus Nijhoff.

Nussbaum, M. C. (2013). *Political emotions: Why love matters for justice*. Harvard University Press.

Ofstad, H. (1963). Impartiality. In *Legal essays to attribute to Frede Castberg on the occasion of his 70th birthday*. Universitetsforlaget.

Osiel, M. (2002). *Mass atrocity, ordinary evil, and Hannah Arendt: Criminal consciousness in Argentina's dirty war*. New Haven: Yale University Press.

Osiel, M. (2009a). *Making sense of mass atrocity*. Cambridge: Cambridge University Press.

Osiel, M. (2009b). *The end of reciprocity: Terror, torture & the law of war*. Cambridge: Cambridge University Press.

Rawls, J. (1971). *A theory of justice*. Oxford, London, New York: Oxford University Press.

Rejali, D. (2007). *Torture and democracy*. Princeton: Princeton University Press.

Roach, S. C. (2006). *Politicizing the international criminal court: The convergence of politics, ethic, and the law*. New York: Rowman & Littlefield Publishers.

Schwarzenberger, G. (1950). The problem of an international criminal law. *Current Legal Problems, 3*, 263–296.

Smith, A. (2004). *Selected philosophical writings* (edited and introduce by James R. Otteson). Exeter: Imprint Academic.

Tarrant, H. (2006). Platonic interpretation and eclectic theory. In H. Tarrant & D. Baltzly (Eds.), *Reading Plato in Antiquity*. London: Duckworth.

Wägenbaur, B. (2013). *Court of the European Union*. C.H.Beck. Hart. Nomos.

Chapter 12
A Lecture with the Confidence to be Cultivated by the Future Carriers of Love for Justice

"There comes a time when nothing is meaningful except surrendering to love."[1] This means "my great peace woman has only a single name: she is called universal justice, humaneness, active reason ... Her function, in accordance with her name and her nature, is to inculcate dispositions of peace."[2] National, regional, and international justice will never come to peace if there is not charity to justice's nature and construction.[3] A rational and the pure democratic government does not come from Kantian unity, Mohammedan spirituality, Nelson Mandela's tolerance, the Gandhian theory of independence, Martin Luther King's dream, or Leninism's division of wealth. However, it springs from the fact that our intentions and efforts have achieved the highest level of respect for human beings—not by the dead words of human rights law but by bearing in mind the consequences of our own actions and decisions:

> When love for true justice does not exist, justice will never come. When justice is the product of a political deal, love for justice will never be achieved. When the killing of millions of people, the destruction of their countries, and the devastation of their homes are sanctioned repeatedly by the resolutions of the Security Council, love for justice will even be confused between the inhabitants of the victim nations and their neighbours. If the ICC is going to deliver a genuine love for justice, it has to be based on a true love for justice, proper love for prevention of impunity, and a love that prioritizes quality over quantity.[4]

Although an interpretation of law, an implementation of the same law, and proceedings under the same law may be very wise, comprehensive, and realistic, it still has to operate with the norm of love for justice, which is free of any personal interference. Here, I mean love as a norm of reality, as a norm against humiliation,

[1]Jalāl ad-Dīn Muhammad Rūmī (1207–12073). Persian-Afghan lawyer and philosopher.

[2]Johann Gottfried Herder, *Letters for the Advancement of Humanity* (1793–7). See also Forster (2002), pp. 403–404.

[3]Herder (2002), pp. 3–30.

[4]Malekian (2017), pp. 10–44, at 36.

F. Malekian, *Judgments of Love in Criminal Justice*,
DOI 10.1007/978-3-319-46900-3_12

as a norm of equality with substance, and also as a norm in which we trust and which is going to be performed by any judge, prosecutor, or court, even if the court is manipulated to condemn the accused.[5] "The ability to love justice can only come from a good character."[6]

The complex issue is not the matter of humiliation but the irresponsibility of those who call themselves the prosecutors of Scandinavian laws, German courts, Commonwealth law courts, Austrian courts, the Netherlands Grotius holders of justice, United States courts, Islamic courts, the international criminal jurisdictions in The Hague, and French Cour de Cassation, and so forth. The Cour was established for the determination of miscarriages of justice in the *Palais de Justice* in Paris.

Are our courts delivering justice or is injustice delivering them? If it is the latter, no questions would remain for us and we could end our lecturing of this basal philosophy of justice here as well the writing of this distressing, traumatic, and annoying volume. If the answer is that they are delivering justice because of injustice, then the question arises why justice is delivered solely at home. Is the function of justice to be silent on the matter of grave violations of international criminal law? Does the concept of justice just apply by international courts against African criminals? And, is justice the power of reasons of love for justice or the power of justice to control the love norm?

Whatever the answer is and is given by the relevant courts in the above or other regional or international courts, it is axiomatic that justice has to be accurate and that justice has to maintain the excellence of the proportionality principle. Justice does not maintain the measures of the principle of proportionality when it does not react against grave criminal violations by reasoning that it is not within its capacity to do so. Naturally, one may argue that our courts are not authorised to work with international cases, and that judges are not empowered to speak out about international violations for the reason of going beyond their remit or going against the politics of their state.

Here, we are not talking about the universal principle of justice. We also have not spoken about the responsibility of one court for the conduct of another court in another country. However, we are referring to the reason why we have chosen to be the forum of justice, the forum of international legality and morality, the forum of international human rights law, the representatives of human integrity, freedom, and liberation, and the forum of love for justice as well as independence of our international legal personality. Let me put it this way, if states and organisations have established international legal personality, which is a crucial facet of their independence in the international legal community, the system of international criminal law and the system of international criminal justice must also arrive at the platform of successful independent international legal personality without ties. Justice should not rise from the

---

[5]A very clear example is the hanging of Saddam Hussein by the Iraqi Tribunal.

[6]Abū Ḥāmid Muḥammad ibn Muḥammad al-Ghazālī (1058–1111). Persian lawyer and philosopher.

traditional values of political orientation as it exists today but from transparency and transparency alone united with the canon of love.[7]

If we formulate hundreds of international treaties exclusively dealing with the highest questions of humanity, justice, and morality, they will still not be successful, so long as their leadership rests on lies, injustice, and the power of guns. However, if you formulate hundreds of the same international treaties with the leadership of the norm of love for equal humanity, truth, justice, and understanding of the poverty of men, including the value of the substance of human nature, this should be much more imperative, pioneering, and successful. Those who think that they will arrive at the pinnacle of justice with the provisions of the permanent international criminal court or the attribution of certain punishments are obviously mistaken.

We must realise the fact that the height of justice, of generosity, of happiness of all nations, of honour of human integrity, and of the gift of equality are not achieved by the implementation of human rights laws of the Court and by the dead words of different regional or international political organisations. These are the Arab, the Latin American, the European Union, or the North Atlantic Treaty Organization (NATO). As Boethius, the Italian philosopher of the early sixth century indicates, "*A man content to go to heaven alone will never go to heaven.*" We have to walk together into the depths of injustice or into the elevation of justice. Our choice should not be to treat criminals compared with criminals and innocents compared with innocents in isolated tactics.[8] "Equality is the soul of liberty; there is, in fact, no liberty without it."[9] That is the means and the end for humanity. We are to be identical. The question that arises at the closing stage of this treatise is, are we educated with the knowledge of the law to be the guardians of law or are we educated to shelter justice with love for the implementation of the substance of reasons of human nature for equal justice?

Whereas we all are familiar with the forum of love, its magnificent power, and its positive devoted soul in the service of men, we did not really study the nature of the norm of love in this discourse. Such deliberation is located in every single human heart. Consequently, our reflection was the appraisal of the virtue of the norm of love in the rule of law. If such genuine "study does not always inspire the love of virtue, it is because it sometimes, and even too often, unhappily meets with an incorrigibly vicious heart"[10] of many individuals. They not only include lawyers,

[7]Bentham (1789, 1907). See *also* Bentham (2016).

[8]For instance, see some critical views concerning the policy of the Special Tribunal for Lebanon. The Tribunal even violates the basic principles of fair prosecution of the accused. It applies sanctions in absentia. Alamuddin et al. (2014); Jacobs (2014), pp. 111–133.

[9]Frances Wright (1795–1852), the lecturer of equality.

[10]"To instruct the nation is not sufficient: in order to conduct it to happiness, it is still more necessary to inspire the people with the love of virtue, and the abhorrence of vice. Those who are deeply versed in the study of morality, are convinced that virtue is the true and only path that leads to happiness; so that its maxims are but the art of living happily; and he must be very ignorant of politics, 'who does not perceive how much more capable a virtuous nation will be, than any other, of forming a state that shall be at once happy, tranquil, flourishing, solid, respected by its neighbours, and formidable to its enemies." Vattel (1844), pp. 48 and 50.

government workers, politicians, and highly acknowledged military officers but also those authorities who love to use the victims' statute for the promotion of their own policies, positions, and theories in order benefit from economic gains.

I shall share here at the end of my book the conclusion of one of our classical fathers—Vattel in his book Le Droit de Gens, ou Principes de la Loi Naturelle, appliquès à la Conduite et aux Affaires des Nations de Souverains (1758). It clarifies love with love and love as the first norm of national, regional, and international relations:

> At length, I have reached the end of work that I undertook accomplish. I do not flatter myself that I have given a complete and detailed treatise on the Law of Nations (the norm of love). That was not my purpose; and it would have been presuming too much on my abilities to have attempted such as work on a subject of so extensive and varied a character. I shall be satisfied if the principles I have set forth prove to be clear, sound, and sufficiently comprehensive to enable persons of intelligence to solve questions of detail by applying the principles to the specific cases. Happy shall I be *if my work may be of service to those in power who have a love for humankind and a respect for justice*. If it furnishes them with a weapon for the defense of a just cause, and a means of compelling unjust rules to observe at least some limits and to keep within the bounds of propriety.[11]

References

Alamuddin, A., Jurdi, N. N., & Tolbert, D. (2014). *The special tribunal for Lebanon: Law and practice*. Oxford: Oxford University Press.

Bentham, J. (1789, 1907). *An introduction to the principles of morals and legislation*. Oxford: Clarendon Press.

Bentham, J. (2016). *An introduction to the principles of morals and legislation* (p. 62). Available at www.earlymoderntexts.com. Accessed 18 January 2016.

de Vattel, E. (1758, 1916). *Le Droit de Gens, ou Principes de la Loi Naturelle, appliquès à la Conduite er aux Affaires des Nations de de Souverains: The Law of Nations or the Principles of Natural Law* (Vol. III the Classics of International Law, James Brown Scott, ed.), (Book II, 11), p. 117.

Forster, M. N. (2002). *Herder philosophical writing* (pp. 403–404). Cambridge: Cambridge University Press.

Herder, J. G. (2002). How philosophy can become more universal and useful for the benefit of the people (1765). In *Herder: Philosophical writings* (pp. 3–30) (Edited and translated by M. N. Forster). Cambridge University Press.

Jacobs, D. (2014). The unique rules of the procedures of the STL. In A. Alamuddin, N. N. Jurdi, & D. Tolbert (Eds.), *The special tribunal for Lebanon: Law and practice* (pp. 111–133). Oxford: Oxford University Press.

Malekian, F. (2017). Comparative substantive international criminal justice. In R. Slye (Ed.), *The nuremberg principles in non-western societies: A reflection on their universality, legitimacy and application*.

Vattel, M. (1844). *The law of nations or the principles of the law of nations applied to the conduct and affair of nations and sovereign* (6th American Addition, A new edition by Joseph Chitty, para. 231, p. 108). Available at http://www.loc.gov/rr/frd/Military_Law/Lieber_Collection/pdf/DeVattel_LawOfNations.pdf. Accessed 16 December 2016.

[11]de Vattel (1758, 1916), p. 398.

Bibliography

Alamuddin, A., Jurdi, N. N., & Tolbert, D. (2014). *The special tribunal for Lebanon: Law and practice*. Oxford: Oxford University Press.

Alexis, R. (2002). *A theory of constitutional rights* (Trans.). OUP.

Alexius, K. (1997). Politisk Yttrandefrihet: *En Studie i Lagstiftning och Praxis under Demkratins Genombrottstid*. Lund.

Al-Hussein, Z. (2009). For love of country and international criminal law. *American University International Law Review, 24*(4), 647–664.

Allen, W. B. (Ed.). (1988). George Washington, *George Washington: A collection*.

Andenaes, J. (1965). *The general part of criminal law of Norway*. London: Sweet & Maxwell Limited.

Andernaes, J. (1974). *Alminnelig Strafferett*. Oslo: Universitertsforlaget.

Andersen, P. (2011). Klassisk og Kristen Naturret. In O. Hammerslev & H. P. Olsen (Eds.), *Restsfilosofi – ecntrale tekster og temaer* (pp. 71–96). København: Hans Reitzels Forlag.

Andreopoulos, A. (2014). Exchange of life: The Love of God in the Orthodox Christian tradition. In S.T. Hidden (Ed.), *Jewish, Christian, and Islamic mystical perspectives on the Love of God* (pp. 57–71). Springer.

Arnold, T. W. (1961). *The preaching of Islam: A history of the propagation of the Muslim faith* (pp. 115–119). Lahore, Pakistan: Muhammad Ashraf Publications.

Ashton, C., & Finch, V. (2002). *Human rights & Scots law* (pp. 51–54). Edinburgh: W. Green/ Sweet & Maxwell.

Ashworth, A. (2006). Four threats to presumption of innocence. *South African Journal*, 63–97.

Ashworth, A. (2008). Criminal procedure, human rights and 'balance': Towards the dark night sea? In *Ikke Kun Straf: Festskrift til Vagen Greve* (pp. 11–20). Jurist- og Økonomforbunds forlag.

Ashworth, A. (2013). *Positive obligations in criminal law*. Oxford: Hart Publishing.

Atwell, B. L. (2008). The jurisprudence of love. *University of Detroit Mercy Law Review, 85*, 495.

Aubert, V. (1963). The structure of legal thinking. In *Legal essays to attribute to Frede Castberg on the occasion of his 70th birthday* (pp. 41–63). Oslo: Universitetsforlaget.

Austin, J. (1861). *The province of jurisprudence determined: Being the first of series of lectures on jurisprudence, or the philosophy of positive law (1832)* (2nd ed., p. xiv). London: J. Murray.

Austin, J. (1954). *The province of jurisprudence determined and the uses of the study of jurisprudence*. New York, NY: Noonday Press.

Awadallah, I.Z. (2005). Islam, civil and political rights and the universal declaration of human rights. Florida International University. http://digitalcommons.fiu.edu/etd/1347. Accessed 11 Sept 2016.

Badar, M. E. (2015). *The concept of Mens Rea in International Criminal Law*. Oxford: Hart Publishing.

F. Malekian, *Judgments of Love in Criminal Justice*,
DOI 10.1007/978-3-319-46900-3

Bandyopadhyay, P. (1920). *International law and custom in ancient India*. Calcutta: Calcutta University Press.

Barnes, M. (2014). Between task and gift: Jews, Christians, Muslims, and a spirituality of dialogue. In S.T. Hidden (Ed.), *Jewish, Christian, and Islamic mystical perspectives on the Love of God* (pp. 11–42). Springer.

Bass, G. (2000). *Stay the hand of vengeance: The politics of war crimes tribunals*.

Bassiouni, M. C. (1996). Accountability for violations of international humanitarian law and other serious violations of human rights. *Law and Contemporary Problems Law and Contemporary Problems*, 398.

Bassiouni, M. C. (1999). *International criminal law: Crimes* (2nd ed.). New York: Transnational Publishers, Inc. Ardsley.

Bassiouni, M. C. (2014). *The Shari'a and Islamic Criminal Justice in time of war and peace*. Cambridge: Cambridge University Press.

Bederman, D. J. (2002). *The spirit of international law*. The University of Georgia Press.

Bentham, J. (1789, 1907). *An introduction to the principles of morals and legislation*. Oxford: Clarendon Press.

Bentham, J. (2002). Rights, representation, and reform: Nonsense upon stilts and other writings on the French revolution. In P. Schofield, C. Pease-Watkin, & C. Blamires (Eds.), *The collected works of Jeremy Bentham* (pp. 317–401). Oxford: Oxford University Press.

Bentham, J. (2016). *An introduction to the principles of morals and legislation* (p. 62). Available at www.earlymoderntexts.com. Accessed 18 January 2016.

Bentzon, A. W., & Agersnap, T. (2005). Retssikkerhed, Legitimitet og Tillid i et Aendringssmfund med Kulturelfoldighet. In C. Damgaard, C. Henrichsen, & H. Peterson (Eds.), *Ret & Usikkerhed* (pp. 5–20). Jurist- og Økonomforbunds forlag.

Berman, M. (1982). *All that is solid melts into air: The experience of modernity*. New York: Simon and Schuster.

Bernstein, R. J. (2002). *Radical evil: A philosophical interrogation*. Cambridge: Blackwell Publishing.

Binder, G. (2014). Foundations of the legislative Panoption: Benthan' principles of morals and legislation. In M. D. Dubber (Ed.), *Foundational texts in modern criminal law* (pp. 79–99). Oxford: Oxford University Press.

Blackstone, W. (1765–1769). *Commentaries on the Laws of England* (Vol. 4, p. 17).

Blanke, H.-J., & Mangiameli, S. (2006). *Governing Europe under a constitution: a hard road from the European treatise to a European constitutional treaty* (pp. 169–184). Erfurt: Springer.

Blumenthal, D. A. (2002). The politics of justice: Why Israel signed the international criminal court statute and what the signature means. *Georgia Journal of International and Comparative Law, 30*, 593.

Bohlander, M., & Birkett, D. (2014). *The codification of criminal law* (p. xxiii). Ashgate.

Bondeson, U. V. (2006). Theory of law and morality. In U. V. Bondeson (Ed.), *Law and morality* (pp. 3–16). Forlaget Thomson.

Boot, M. (2002). *Genocide, crimes against humanity, war crimes: Nullum Crimen Sine Lege and the subject matter jurisdiction of the International Criminal Court*. Cambridge: Intersentia nv.

Boyle, A. (2002). In A. Boyle, C. H. Worth, A. Loux, & H. M. Queen (Eds.), *Human rights and Scots law: Introduction* (p. 1). Oxford: Hart Publishing.

Bozbayindir, A. E. (2013). *Turkey and the international criminal court: A substantive criminal law analysis in the context of the principle of complementarity*. Baden-Baden, Germany: Nomos Verlagsgeseells.

Branlard, J.-P. (2014). *Master Droit Pénal: Droit pénal general & Procédure pénale*. Paris: Editions Eska.

Brierly, J. L. (1948). Suárez's vision of a world community. *An address delivered before the University of Granada*.

Brownlie, I. (1963). *International law and the use of force by states*. Oxford: Oxford University Press.

Butler, W. E. (2013). *Russian public law* (3rd ed.). London: Wildy, Simmonds & Hill Publishers.

Cappelletti, M., Gordley, J., & Johnson, E. (1975a). *Toward equal justice: A comparative study of legal aid in modern societies*. New York: Oceana Publications.

Cappelletti, M., Gordley, J., & Johnson, E. (1975). *Toward equal justice: A comparative study of legal aid in modern societies* (pp. 11–12). New York, NY: Oceana Publications.

Carty, A. (1986). *The decay of international law?* Manchester University Press.

Cassese, A. (2008). *International criminal law* (2nd ed., pp. 33–35). New York, NY: Oxford University Press.

Cassese, A., Eser, A., Gaja, G., & Conor, R. E. (1980). *Justice at Nuremberg*. New York: Harper & Row.

Charlesworth, H., & Chinkin, C. (2000). *The boundaries of international law: A feminist analysis*. Manchester: Manchester University Press, Melland Schill Studies in International Law.

Chartrand, S., & Philpot, J. (Eds.). (2014). *Justice belied: The unbalanced scales of international criminal justice*. Montreal: Baraka Books.

Chayes, A., & Chayes, A. H. (1995). *The new sovereignty: Compliance with international regulatory*. Cambridge: Harvard University Press.

Chesterman, S. (2003). *Just War or Just Peace? Humanitarian intervention and international law*. Oxford: Oxford University Press.

Chittick, W.C. (2014). Themes of Love in Islamic Mystical theology. In S.T. Hidden (Ed.), *Jewish, Christian, and Islamic mystical perspectives on the Love of God* (pp. 155–180). Springer.

Clapham, A. (2003). Issues of complexity, complicity and complementarity: From the Nuremberg Trials to the dawn of the New International Criminal Court. In P. Sands (Ed.), *From Nuremberg to The Hague: The future of international criminal justice*. Cambridge: Cambridge University Press.

Clough, J., & Mulhern, C. (2004). *Criminal law* (2nd ed.). Australia: LexisNexis Butterworth.

Coffey, G. (2010). *Criminal law*. Round Hall: Thomson Reuters.

Cohen, M. (1949). Moral aspects of the criminal law. *Yale Law Journal, 49*, 987–1026.

Comprés, T. (2009). Labour of love: Using international labour law to achieve human rights for women sex workers in the Dominican Republic. *Georgetown Journal of International Law, 40*, 1027.

Conley, R. W., Luckasson, R., & Bouthilet, G. N. (1992). *The criminal justice system and mental retardation*. Baltimore: Paul H. Books Publishing Co.

Cookerly, J. (2001). *Recovering love: Co-dependency to co-recovery*.

Corbin, H. (2014). *History of Islamic Philosophy (Translated from French by Liadain Sherrard and Philip Sherrard)*. London, New York: Routledge.

Crawford, J. (1976). *The criteria for statehood in international law* (p. 95).

Cryer, R. (2009). A message from elsewhere: Witnesses before International Criminal Tribunals. In P. Roberts & M. Redmayne (Eds.), *Innovations in evidence and proof*. Oxford: Hart Publishing.

Cryer, R., Friman, H., Robinson, D., & Wilmshurst, E. (2010). *An introduction to international criminal law and procedure* (2nd ed.). Cambridge: Cambridge University Press.

Cudworth, R. (1678). *True intellectual system of the universe*. London: Printed for Richard Royston.

Cummings, S. L. (2011). Introduction: What good are lawyers? In S. L. Cummings (Ed.), *Paradox of professionalism lawyers and the possibility of justice*. Cambridge: Cambridge University Press.

Czarnetzky, J. M., & Rychlak, R. J. (2003). An empire of law: Legalism and the international criminal court. *Notre Dame Law review, 79*, 55–126.

D'Amato, A. (1985–1986). The moral dilemma of positivism. *Valparaiso University Law Review, 20*, 43–53.

Dalberg-Larsen, J. (2006). *Dansk retsfilosofi: Udviklingslinjer og portraetter*. Jurist- og Økonomforbunds forlag.

Dan-Cohen, M. (2014). Dignity, crime, and punishment: A Kantian perspective. In M. D. Dubber (Ed.), *Foundational texts in modern criminal law*. Oxford: Oxford University Press.

Daniele, M. (2015). Evidence gathering in the realm of the European investigation order from nations rules to global principles. *New Journal of European Criminal Law, 6*(2), 179–194.

Darcy, S. (2011). Prosecuting the war crime of collective punishment: Is it time to amend the Rome statute? *Journal of International Criminal Justice*.

Darcy, S., & Powderly, J. (2010). *Judicial creativity at the international criminal tribunals*. Oxford: Oxford University Press.

de Secondat, C., & de Montesquieu, B. (1989) In A. M. Cohler, B. C. Miller, & H. S. Stone (Eds.), *The spirit of the law. Cambridge texts in the history of political thought*. Cambridge: Cambridge University Press.

de Secondat, C. L., & de Montesquieu, B. (2012). *My Thoughts (Mes Pensées)*.

de Vattel, E. (1758, 1916). *Le Droit de Gens, ou Principes de la Loi Naturelle, appliquès à la Conduite er aux Affaires des Nations de de Souverains: The law of nations or the principles of natural law* (Vol. III the Classics of International Law, James Brown Scott, ed.), (Book II, 11).

De Wet, E. (2004). *The Chapter VII of Powers of the United Nations Security Council*. Oxford: Hart Publishing.

DeRoo, N. (2013). Culture regained? On the impossibility and meaninglessness of culture in (some) Calvinist thought. In G. Graham (Ed.), *Calvinism and culture*. Grand Rapids: Wm. B. Eerdmans Publishing.

Derrett, J. D. M. (1968). *An introduction to legal system*.

Detmold, M. J. (1984a). *The unity of law and morality: A refutation of legal positivism*. Law Book Co of Australasia.

Detmold, M. J. (1984b) *The unity of law and morality: A refutation of legal positivism*. London: Routledge and Kegan Paul.

DeValve, M. J. (2014). *A different justice: Love and the future of criminal justice practice in America*. Carolina Academic Press.

Devers, G., & Mendes-France, M. F. (2012). Presentation of the complaint filed before the international criminal court. In C. Meloni & G. Tognoni (Eds.), *Is there a court for Gaza? A test bench for international justice* (pp. 61–75, 71–72). The Hague: T.M. Asser Press, Springer.

di Beccaria, C. B. (1872). *An essay on crimes and punishments* [1764]. De Voltaire.

Dickens, C. (1859). *A tale of two cities a story of the French revolution*.

Dickson, J. (2001). *Evaluation and legal theory*. Oxford: Hart Publishing.

Dougan, M. (2008). The Treaty of Lisbon 2007: Winning minds, not hearts. *Common Market Law Review, 45*, 617–703.

Drapkin, I. (1989). *Crime and punishment in the ancient world*. Toronto: Lexington Books.

Duncan, J., & Derrett, M. (1968). *An introduction to legal system* (pp. 177–179). London: Sweet & Maxwell.

Dworkin, R. (1996). *Taking rights seriously* (8th ed.). Duckworth.

Earl, J. (2009). *The Nuremberg SS-Einsatzgruppen Trial, 1945–1958*. Cambridge: Cambridge University Press.

Eastwood, M. (2011). *The Nuremberg Trial of Julius Streicher: The crime of "Incitement to Genocide"*. Lewiston: The Edwin Mellan Press.

Eckes, C., & Kondtandinides, T. (2011). *Crime within the area of freedom, security and justice*. Cambridge: Cambridge University Press.

Eckhoff, T. (1963). Justice and social utility. In *Legal essays to attribute to Frede Castberg on the occasion of his 70th birthday* (pp. 74–93). Universitetsforlaget.

Elior, R. (2014). The Love of God in the Jewish mystical tradition: Mysticism of freedom and commemoration versus mysticism of hope and redemption. In S.T. Hidden (Ed.), *Jewish, Christian, and Islamic mystical perspectives on the Love of God* (pp. 103–134). Springer.

Elshtain, J. B. (2006). Concrete levels of being and their political implications. In D. Browning (Ed.), *Universalism vs. Relativism: Making moral judgments in a changing, pluralistic, and threatening world*. England: Rowman and Littlefield Publishers.

Engelhardt, H. T., & Spicker, S. F. (Eds.), (1976). *Mental health: Philosophical perspectives* (pp. VII and XIII. xv). Dordrecht: D. Reidel Publishing Company.

Erich, F. (1956). *The art of loving*. Harper & Row.

Erich, F. (2006). *The art of loving*. Harper & Row.

Eser, A. (2007). The nature and rationale of punishment. *Cardozo Law Review, 28*, 2427–2436.

Eser, A. (2008). Article 31: 'Grounds for Excluding Criminal Responsibility'. In O. Triffterer (Ed.), *Commentary on the Rome Statute of the International Criminal Court. Observers' Notes Article by Article* (2nd ed.). C.H. Beck, München et al.

Eser, A. (2009). Human rights guarantees for criminal law and procedure in the EU-Charter of Fundamental Rights. *Ritsumeikan Law Review, 26*, 163–190.
Eser, A. (2011a). Procedural structure and features of international criminal justice: Lessons from the ICTY. In B. Swart, A. Zahar, & G. Sluiter (Eds.), *The legacy of the international criminal tribunal for the former Yugoslavia* (1st ed., pp. 108–148). Oxford University Press.
Eser, A. (2011b). *Transnationales Strafrecht/Transnational Criminal Law*. Ausgewählte Beiträge/Collected Publications. Compiled and edited by G. Heine, B. Burkhardt, W. Gropp. Berliner Wissenschaftsverlag.
Eser, A. (2012). Transnational measures against the impunity of international crimes. *Journal of International Criminal Justice, 10*(3), 621–663 (Oxford University Press).
Eser, A., & Rettenmaier, F. (2009). Criminality of organizations: Lessons from domestic law – A comparative perspective. In A. Noellkaemper & H. van der Wilt (Eds.), *System criminality in international law*. Cambridge: Cambridge University Press.
Eskeland, S. (2000). *Strafferett*. Oslo: Cappelen Akademisk Forlag.
Falk, R. (1981). *Human rights and state sovereignty*. New York: Holmes & Meier Publishers.
Falk, R. (2011a). *Criminalizing diplomacy: Fanning the flames of the Iran War Option*. Available at www.transnational.org/SAJT/tff/people/r_falk.html.
Falk, R. (2011b). *The international criminal law plays politics? The Qaddafi Arrest Warrants*.
Fashing, I. A., & Gottschalk, P. (2008). *Kriminelle Organisasjoner: Hvordan forstp organisert kiminalitet*. Fagbokforlaget.
Fedorova, M. (2012). *The principles of equality of arms in international criminal proceedings*. Cambridge: Intersentia.
Ferencz, B. B. (1994). *New legal foundation for global survival*. New York: Oceana Publications.
Ferencz, B. (1995). *New legal foundation for global survival*. New York: Oceana Publications.
Fichtelberg, A. (2015). *Hybrid tribunals, a comparative examination*. Heidelberg: Springer.
Findlay, M. J. (2013). *International and comparative criminal justice: A critical introduction*. London: Routledge.
Finnis, J. (1980). *Natural law and natural rights*. Oxford: Oxford University Press.
Finnis, F. (1983). *Fundamentals of ethics*. Washington, DC: Georgetown University.
Fischer, M. (1998). The human rights implications of a cultural defense. *Southern California Interdisciplinary Law Journal, 6*, 663–702.
Fitzgerald, P. J. (1962). *Criminal law and punishment* (p. 10). Oxford: At the Clarendon Press.
Forster, M. N. (2002). *Herder philosophical writing* (pp. 403–404). Cambridge: Cambridge University Press.
Fouladvand, S. (2012). *Complementarity and cultural sensitivity: Decision-making by the International Criminal Court (ICC) Prosecutor in Relation to the Situations in the Darfur Region of the Sudan and the Democratic Republic of Congo (DRC)*. Sussex.
Fournet, C. (2014). The human body: Victim, witness and evidence of mass violence. In E. Anstett & J.-M. Dreyfus (Eds.), *Human remains and mass violence: Methodological approaches* (pp. 56–80). Manchester: Manchester University Press.
Fournet, C. (2015). The *Actus Reus* of genocide in the Croatia v. Serbia Judgment: Between legality and acceptability. *Leiden Journal of International Law, 28*(4), 915–921.
Franck, T. M. (1995). *Fairness in international law and institutions*. Oxford: Oxford University Press.
Fromm, E. (1956). *The art of loving*. Harper & Row.
Fromm, E. (1956, 2006). *The art of loving: En enquiry into the nature of love*. New York: Harper.
Fuller, L. L. (1969). *The morality of law* (2nd ed.). New Haven: Yale University Press.
Gaeta, P. (1999). Defence of superior orders: The statute of the international criminal court versus customary international law. *European Journal of International Law, 72*, 188–191.
Gandhi, M. K. (2001). *Non-violent resistance (Satyagraha)*. Ahmedabad: Jitendra T. Desai.
Gandhi, M. K. (2015). *The story of my experiments with truth*. Ahmedabad: Jitendra T. Desai.
Gans, J. (2012). *Modern criminal law of Australia*. Cambridge: Cambridge University Press.
Gavison, R. (1987). *Issues in contemporary legal philosophy: The influence of H.L.A. Hart*. Oxford: Clarendon Press.
George, R. P. (1994). *Natural law theory: Contemporary essays*. Oxford: Clarendon Press.

George, R. P. (1995). *The autonomy of law: Essays on legal positivism*. Oxford: Oxford University Press.

Gilligan, J. (1996–1997). *Violence: Reflections on a national epidemic*. New York: Putnam.

Gilmore, W. C. (2011). *Dirty money: The evolution of international measures to counter money laundering and the financing of terrorism* (4th ed.). Strasburg: Council of Europe Publishing.

Ginsburgs, G., & Kudriavtsev V. N. (Eds.). (1990). *The Nuremberg trial and international law*. Leiden: Martinus Nijhoff Publishers.

Goldsmith, J. L., & Posner, E. A. (2007). *The limits of international law*. Oxford: Oxford University Press.

Goodale, M., & Merry, S. E. (Eds.). (2007). *The practice of human rights tracking law between the global and the local*. Cambridge: Cambridge University Press.

Goodrich, P. (2006). *Law in the courts of love: Literature and other minor jurisprudences*. The Politics of Language.

Gorsky, J. (2014). Maimonides spirituality: Intellectual mysticism and the Love of God. In S.T. Hidden (Ed.), *Jewish, Christian, and Islamic mystical perspectives on the Love of God* (pp. 43–55). Springer.

Gray, M.A. (1995). The International Crime of Ecocide. *California Western International Journal, 26*(2), 215–271. http://scholarlycommons.law.cwsl.edu/cgi/viewcontent.cgi?article=1335&context=cwilj. Accessed 25 Aug 2016.

Graybill, R. V. Courts of love: Challenge to feudalism. In *Essays in Medieval Studies* (Vol. 5).

Greve, V. (2005). Sheep or wolves. *European Journal of Crime, Criminal Law and Criminal Justice, 4*, 515–532.

Gross, H. (2012). *Crime and punishment: A concise moral critique*. New York: Oxford University Press.

Grotius, H. (1625). *The rights of war and peace* (A.C. Campbell, ed. 1901).

Grotius, H. (1901). In A. C. Campbell (Ed.), *The rights of war and peace, 1625*.

Grotius, H. *Commentary on the Law of Prize and Booty*.

Guild, E. (Ed.). (2008). *Security versus justice? Police and judicial cooperation in the European Union*. Hampshire: Ashgate.

Gur-Arye, M., & Jessberger, F. (2011). The protection of human dignity in interrogations: May interrogative torture ever be tolerated? Reflections in light of recent German and Israeli experiences. *Israel Law Review, 44*, 229–263.

Hacker, P. M. S., & Raz, J. (Eds.). (1977). *Law, morality and society: Essays in honour of H.L.A. Hart*. Clarendon Press.

Hallag, W. B. (2004). Can the Shari'a be restored? In Y. Yazbeck & B. F. Stowasser (Eds.), *Islamic law and the challenges of modernity* (pp. 21–53, 22). Altamira Press.

Hanly, C. (2006). *An introduction to Irish criminal law* (2nd ed.). Dublin: Gill & Macmillan Ltd.

Hannikainen, L. (1988). *Peremptory Norms (Jus Cogens) in International Law*. Helsinki.

Harcourt, B. E. (2014). Beccaria's on crimes and punishments: A mirror on the history of the foundations of modern criminal law. In M. D. Dubber (Ed.), *Foundational texts in modern criminal law* (pp. 59–78). Oxford: Oxford University Press.

Hart, H. L. A. (1961). *The concept of law*. Oxford: Oxford University Press.

Hart, H. L. A. (1982). *Essays on Benthan* (p. 79). Oxford: Clarendon Press.

Hart, H. L. A. (2008). *Punishment and responsibility: Assays in the philosophy of law* (2nd ed.). Oxford: Oxford University Press.

Haveman, R., Kavran, O., & Nicholls, J. (2013). *Supranational criminal law: A system sui generis*. Intersentia.

Hazan, P. (2004). *Justice in a time of war: The true story behind the International Criminal Tribunal for the former Yugoslavia*. College Station: Texas A & M University Press.

Henckaerts, J.-M., & Doswald-Beck, L. (2005). *Customary international humanitarian law* (Vol. 1). Cambridge: Cambridge University Press.

Herder, J. G. (2002). How philosophy can become more universal and useful for the benefit of the people (1765). In *Herder: Philosophical writings* (pp. 3–30) (Edited and translated by M. N. Forster). Cambridge University Press.

Hinarejos, A. (2009). *Judicial control in the European Union: Reforming jurisdiction in the intergovernmental pillars*. Oxford: Oxford University Press.

Hirst, M. (2003). *Jurisdiction and the ambit of the criminal law*. Oxford: Oxford University Press.

Hoffman, R. L. (1980). *More than a trial: A struggle over Captain Dreyfus* (pp. 94–95). New York: Free Press

Holtermann, J. v. H. (2006). Ross og Erkendelsesteorien. In J. v. Holtermann & J. Ryberg (Eds.), *Alf Ross Kritiske Gensyn* (pp. 37–62). Jurist- og Økonomforbunds forlag.

Holtermann, J. v., & Ryberg, J. (2006). *Alf Ross Kritiske Gensyn*. Jurist- og Økonomforbunds forlag.

Hora, T. (1986). *Beyond the dream: A wakening to reality*. The Crossroad Publishing Co. 1996.

Hughes, G. (1971). Validity and the basic norm. *California Law Review, 59*, 695.

Huntington, C. (1942). Plato's theory of law. *Harvard Law Review, 56*, 359–387.

Hurd, H. (1991). Challenging authority. *Yale Law Journal, 100*, 1611.

Inger, G. (2011). *Svensk Rättshistoria*. Malmö: Liber AB.

Ingraham, B. L. (1979). *Political crime in Europe: A comparative study of France, Germany and England*. London: University of California Press.

Jackson, R. H. (1946–1947). Forward the Nuremberg trial becomes a historical precedent. *TEMPLE L Q, 20*.

Jackson, T. P. (2009). *The priority of love: Christian charity and social justice* (p. 7). Princeton: Princeton University Press.

Jacobs, D. (2014). The unique rules of the procedures of the STL. In A. Alamuddin, N. N. Jurdi, & D. Tolbert (Eds.), *The special tribunal for Lebanon: Law and practice* (pp. 111–133). Oxford: Oxford University Press.

Jareborg, N., Friberg, S., & Asp, P. (1995). *Svensk Internationell Straffprocessrätt*. Uppsala: Iustus Förlag.

Jazayery, M. A. (1973). Ahmad Kasravi and the Controversy over Persian poetry 1. Kasravi's analysis of Persian poetry. *International Journal of Middle East Studies, 4*(2), 190–203, 191–192.

John Finnis, A. (1998). *Moral, political and legal theory*. Oxford: Oxford University Press.

Kamal, M.H.M. (2014). International legal personality of Prophet Muhammad International Islamic University Malaysia. http://www.ocis.org.au/files/pdf/full-papers/ocis14final00103.pdf. Accessed 6 Aug 2016.

Kant, I. (1793). *Religion within the Limits of Bare Reason*.

Kant, I. (1948). *Moral law: Groundwork of the metaphysics of morals* (H. J. Paton, Trans., p. 71). New York, NY: Routledge.

Kant, I. (1996). In M. Gregor (Ed.), *The metaphysics of morals (1797)* (p. 209). Cambridge: CUP.

Kant, I. (2014). *The critique of pure reason* (J. M. D. Meiklejohn, Trans.). An Electronic Classical Series Publication.

Karimsky, S., & Simoncelli, T. (2012). *Genetic justice: DNA data banks, criminal investigations and civil liberties*. New York, NY: Columbia University Press.

Karnell, E. H. (2011). EU's anti-money Laundering Agenda: Built on risks? In C. Eckes & T. Kondtandinides (Eds.), *Crime within the area of freedom, security and justice* (p. 76). Cambridge: Cambridge University Press.

Katouzian, N. (2003). The quality of justice in judgment. *The Journal of Faculty of Law and Political Science* (Persian language), *62*, 361.

Kelsen, H. (1967). *Pure theory of law* (M. Knight, Trans.). Oakland: University of California Press.

Kelsen, H. (2016). *The reason for the validity of a normative order: The basic norm*. http://www.philosophy.hku.hk/courses/law/KelsenNormValidity.htm. Accessed 18 March 2016.

Kelsen, H. (1941). The pure theory of law and analytical jurisprudence. *Harvard Law Review, 55* (1), 44–70.

Kelsen, H. (1957). *What is justice? Justice, law and politics in the mirror of science*. Oakland: University of California Press.

Kennedy, R. F. (2004). *Crimes against nature: How George W. Bush and his Corporate Pals are plundering the country and hijacking our democracy*. Harper, New title edition.

Kennedy, R. F. (2016). *Why the Arabs don't want us in Syria: They don't hate 'our freedoms.' They hate that we've betrayed our ideals in their own countries—for oil*. Available at http://www.politico.eu/article/why-the-arabs-dont-want-us-in-syria-mideast-conflict-oil-intervention/. Accessed 4 March 2016.

King, Jr., M. L. (2008). A time to break the silence. In D. A. Hicks & M. R. Valeri (Eds.), *Global neighbours: Christian faith and moral obligation in today's economy* (p. 31). Eerdmans Publishing.

Knoops, G.-J. (2008). *Defenses in contemporary international criminal law* (2nd ed., p. 251). Leiden: Martinus Nijhoff Publisher.

Koskenniemi, M. (2001). Human rights, politics and love. *Mennesker & Rettigheder*, *4*, 33–45.

Koskenniemi, M. (2005). *From apology to Utopia*. Cambridge: Cambridge University Press.

Krarup, O. (2006). Justice and legal seismology. In U. V. Bondeson (Ed.), *Law and morality*. Forlaget Thomson.

Kruse, K. R. (2010). Lawyers in character and lawyers in role. *Nevada Law Review*, *10*, 393.

Kymlicka, W., Lernestedt, C., & Matravers, M. (2014). Introduction: Criminal law and cultural diversity. In W. Kymlicka, C. Lernestedt, & M. Matravers (Eds.), *Criminal law and cultural diversity* (pp. 1–14). Oxford: Oxford University Press.

Ladd, J. (1991). The idea of collective violence. In N. Graver (Ed.), *Justice, law and violence*. Philadelphia: The Temple University Press.

Lagerwall, A. (2014). The duty not to recognize unlawful situations and the European court of human rights. In C. Binder & K. Lachmayer (Eds.), *The European court of human rights and public international law: Fragmentation or unity* (p. 11). Nomos.

Langsted, L. B., Greve, V., & Garde, P. (2011). *Criminal law in Denmark*. London: Kluwer Law International.

Lee, H., Macbeth, A., Pagani, J., & Young, W. R. (2009). Oxytocin: The great facilitator of life. *Progress in Neurobiology*, *88*, 127–151.

Lehto, M. (2010). *Indirect responsibility for terrorist acts: Redefinition of the concept of terrorism, beyond violent act* (pp. 107–108). Leiden: Martinus Nijhoff Publisher.

Lewis, T., Amini, F., & Lannon, R. (2000). *A general theory of love*. Random House.

Lewis, T., Amini, F., & Lannon, R. (2001). *A general theory of love*. Vintage Books.

Lewis, T., Amini, F., & Lannon, R. (2007). *A general theory of love*. Vintage Books.

Lindell, B., Eklundo, H., Asp, P., & Andersson, T. (2005). *Straffprocessen*. Justus Förlag.

Lloyd, D. (1963). Legal and ideal justice. In *Legal essays to attribute to Frede Castberg on the occasion of his 70th birthday* (pp. 111–124). Universitetsforlaget.

Locke, J. (1689a). *The two treatises of civil government (Thomas Hollis (ed.), Of the State of Nature*, Chap. XVII, section 5, Book II, 1689).

Locke, J. (1689b). *The two treatises of civil government (Thomas Hollis (ed.),* Of Tyranny, Chap. XVIII, section 202, Book II, 1689).

Lord Lloyd of Hampstead. (1979). *Introduction to Jurisprudence* (4th ed.). Arvada: Stevens and Sons.

Lumbard, J.E.B. (2016). *Ahmad Al-Ghazali, remembrance, and the metaphysics of Love* (Sunny Series in Islam). State University of New York Press.

Luper-Foy, S. (Ed.). (1988). Introduction global distributive justice. In *Problems of international justice* (pp. 1–24 at 3–4). London: Westview Press.

Luther King, M., Jr. (1963). *Strength to love*. United States: Fortress Press.

Luther King, M., Jr. (1967). *Where do we go from here: Chaos or community?*

MacCormack, G. (1970a). Scandinavian realism. *Juridical Review*, 33.

MacCormack, G. (1970b). Hägerström on rights and duties. *Juridical Review*, *59*, 33.

MacCormick, N. (1985). A moralistic case for a-moralistic law? *Valparaiso University Law Review*, 37.

Maeland, H. J. (2013). *Norsk Alminnelig Strafferett*. Bergen: Grafisk Formidling AS.

Magon, N., & Kalra, S. (2011). *Indian Journal of Endocrinology and Metabolism, 15*(Suppl. 3), S156–S161. doi:10.4103/2230-8210.84851. http://www.ncbi.nlm.nih.gov/pmc/articles/PMC3183515/.

Malekian, F. (1985). *International criminal responsibility of states*. Stockholm: Almqvist & Wiksell International.
Malekian, F. (1987). *The system of international law: Formations, treaties, responsibility*. Uppsala: Uppsala University Reprocentralen HSC.
Malekian, F. (1991). *International criminal law* (Vol. 2). Stockholm: Almqvist & Wiksell International.
Malekian, F. (1994). *Condemning the use of force in the gulf crisis* (2nd ed.). Stockholm: Almqvist & Wiksell International.
Malekian, F. (1995). *The monopolization of international criminal law in the United Nations, a jurisprudential approach* (2nd ed.). Stockholm: Almqvist & Wiksell International.
Malekian, F. (1999). International criminal responsibility. In M. C. Bassiouni (Ed.), *International criminal law: Crimes* (2nd ed.). New York: Transnational Publishers, Inc. Ardsley.
Malekian, F. (2005). Emasculating the philosophy of international criminal justice in the Iraqi special tribunal. *Cornell International Law Journal, 38*(3), 673–723.
Malekian, F. (2007a). *Documents on the principles of international human rights*. Stockholm: Norstedts Juridik.
Malekian, F. (2007b). The functions of international criminal law and the problem of positivism and neutralism philosophy. *Contemporary Journal of International Criminal Law, 1*, 1–31.
Malekian, F. (2009a). The miserable wedding of naturalism into positivism. *ID EST Journal*, 139–215.
Malekian, F. (2009b). The homogeneity of International Criminal Court with Islamic Jurisprudence. *International Criminal Law Review, 9*, 595–621.
Malekian, F. (2010). The principle of good faith within the sources of international criminal law. *Retfaerd, Nordisk Juridisk Tidsskrift*, 131 nr.4 –årgang 33, 41–65.
Malekian, F. (2011). The laws governing crimes against women constituting obligatio Erga Omnes. In D. W. Pike (Ed.), *Crimes against women* (pp. 3–22). New York, BY: Nova Science Publishers.
Malekian, F. (2012). Judging international criminal justice in the occupied territories. *International Criminal Law Review, 12*, 827–869, 829.
Malekian, F. (2013). Islamic criminal justice systems. In J. S. Albanese (Ed.), *The encyclopaedia of criminology & criminal justice* (5 volumes, Vol. III). Wiley-Blackwell.
Malekian, F. (2014a). *Jurisprudence of international criminal court*. Cambridge: Cambridge Scholars Publishing.
Malekian, F. (2014b). The international criminal law of children on war crimes. *Prawa Dziecka i Ich Ochrona, Horyzonty Wychowania, 13*(25), 31–69.
Malekian, F. (2015a). The Canon of love against the use of force in Islamic and public international law: Part I: The chamber of love within legal discipline. *International Criminal Law Review, 15*(4), 591–628.
Malekian, F. (2015b). The Canon of love against the use of force in Islamic and Public International Law: Part II: The anatomy of love against violations. *International Criminal Law Review, 15*, 861–895.
Malekian, F., & Nordlöf, K. (2012a). *The sovereignty of children in law* (pp. 1–3).
Malekian, F., & Nordlöf, K. (2012b). *Confessing the international rights of children* (pp. 1–5).
Mani, V. S. (2001). International humanitarian law: An Indo-Asian perspective. *International Review of the Red Cross, 841*.
Mann, K., & Roberts, R. (1991). *Law in Colonial Africa*. Heinemann Educational Books.
Mannheim, H. (1940). *War and crime* (pp. 19–20). London: Watts & Co.
Marcin, R. B. (1984). Justice and love. *Catholic University Law Review, 33*(2), 363–391.
Marks, S. (2000). *The riddle of all constitutions: International law, democracy, and the critique of ideology*. Oxford: Oxford University Press.
Mastellone, S. (2001). *Thought upon democracy in Europe*. Florence: Cntro Editoriale Toscano.
May, L., & Hoskins, Z. (Eds.). (2010). *International criminal law and philosophy*. Cambridge: Cambridge University Press.

Mayer, A. E. (2004). Internationalizing the convention on women's rights: Arab countries face the CEDAW committee. In Y. Yazbeck & B. F. Stowasser (Eds.), *Islamic law and the challenges of modernity* (pp. 133–160, 133). Altamira Press.
McAuley, F., & McCutcheon, J. P. (2000). *Criminal liability*. Round Hall, Seet & Maxwell.
McIntyre, T. J. McMullan, S., & Togohda, S. O. (2012). *Criminal law*. Round Hall, Thomson Reuters.
Meloni, C., & Tongnoni, G. (Eds.). (2012). *Is there a court for Gaza: A test bench for international justice* (pp. 543–577). The Hague: Springer.
Mendus, S. (1999). The importance of love in Rawls's theory of justice. *British Journal of Political Science, 29*(1), 57–75.
Meron, T. (2006). *The humanization of international law*. Netherland: Martinus Nijhoff Publishers.
Meyer, P. (1963). Justice in politics. In *Legal essays to attribute to Frede Castberg on the Occasion of his 70th Birthday*. Universitetsforlaget.
Milanovic, M. (2011). Is the Rome Statute binding on individuals? (And Why We Should Care). *Journal of International Criminal Justice*, *9*(1), 25–52. Oxford.
Mill, J. S. (1863). *Utilitarianism: What unitarianism is?*
Mitsilegas, V. (2003). *Money laundering counter-measures in the European Union: A new paradigm of security governance versus fundamental legal principles*. The Hague: Kluwer Law International.
Mojzes, P. (Ed.). (2010). *Balkan genocides: Holocaust and ethnic cleansing in the twentieth century*. Rowman and Littlefield.
Montgomery Watt, W. (1972). *The infiuence of Islam on Medieval Europe* (pp. 72–84). Edinburgh: The University Press.
Montgomery Watt, W. (1976). The significance of the theory of Jihād. In *Akten des VII. Kongresses für Arabistik und Islamwissenschaft, eds. Herausgegeben Von and Albert Dietrich* (p. 390). Göttingen: Vandenhoeck and Ruprecht.
Morris, C. (Ed.). (1959). *The great legal philosophers: Selected readings in jurisprudence*. Philadelphia: University of Pennsylvania Press.
Morrow, A. (2002). *Killing in the name of love: Genocide of a nation*. Rising Sun Publications.
Mo-Tse. (1929). *The ethical and political works of Motse*. London: Arthur Probsthain.
Mukerjee, M. (2011). *Churchill's secret war: The British empire and the ravaging of India during World War II*. New York, NY: Basic Books.
Murdoch, R. R. J. (2011). *Human rights in Scotland* (pp. 1–7). West Sussex: Bloomsbury Professional Ltd.
Nincic, D. (1970). *The problem of sovereignty in the Charter and in the practice of the United Nations*. Martinus Nijhoff.
Novak, A. (2014). *The global decline of the mandatory death penalty: Constitutional jurisprudence and legislative reform in Africa, Asia and the Caribbean*. Surrey: Ashgate.
Nussbaum, M. C. (2013). *Political emotions: Why love matters for justice*. Cambridge, MA: Harvard University Press.
O'Shea, A. (2002). *Amnesty for crime in international law and practice*. Hague/London/New York: Kluwer Law International.
Ofstad, H. (1963). Impartiality. In *Legal essays to attribute to Frede Castberg on the occasion of his 70th birthday*. Universitetsforlaget.
Olivecrona, K. (1964). The imperative element in law. *Rutgers Law Review, 18*, 794.
Olmstead, A. T. (1948). *History of Persian Empire*. Chicago: University of Chicago Press.
Opar, A. (2008). Search for potential autism treatments turns to 'trust hormone'. *Nature Medicine, 14*, 353.
Oppenheim, L. (1937 and 1950). In H. Lauterpacht (Ed.), *International law: Peace* (Vol. I). London.
Osiel, M. (2002). *Mass atrocity, ordinary evil, and Hannah Arendt: Criminal consciousness in Argentina's dirty war*. New Haven: Yale University Press.

Osiel, M. (2009a). *Making sense of mass atrocity*. Cambridge: Cambridge University Press.

Osiel, M. (2009b). *The end of reciprocity: Terror, torture & the law of war*. Cambridge: Cambridge University Press.

Ossowska, M. *Moral and legal norms, the journal of philosophy*. University of Warsaw.

Panikkar, K. M. (1970). *Asia and Western Dominance: A Survey of the Vasco da Gama Epoch of Asian History 1498–1945*. London, 1959 (8th reprint 1970).

Pearce, R. (2002). Model Rule 1.0: lawyers are morally –accountable. *Fordham Law Review, 70*, 1805.

Pepper, S. L. (1986). The lawyer's amoral ethical role: A defence, a problem, and some possibilities. *American Bar Foundation Research Journal*, 613.

Phillips, P. (1980). *Marx and Engels on law and laws*. Barnes & Noble Imports.

Pinto, C., & Jardine, M. (1997). *East Timor's unfinished struggle: Inside the Timorese Resistance*. USA: South End Press Collective.

Pour-Golafshan, F. (2012). *Love of Jesus and Mary in Islam: An enlightening course for all, including Islamists and Islamophobists*. Independent Publishing Platform.

Power, J. (2007). *Conundrums of humanity: The quest for global justice*. The Hague: Martinus Nijhoff Publisher.

Pradel, J. (2010). *Droit Pénal Général* (18th ed.). Paris: Éditions Cujas.

Pufendorf, B. (1717). *Of the law of nature and nations*. Eight books (translated by Basil Kennet).

Ramcharan, G. B. (1985). *The right to life in international law*. Dordrecht: Martinus Nijhoff Publishers.

Ramcharan, B. G. (Ed.). (2006). *Human rights protection in the field*. Leiden: Martinus Nijhoff.

Raoult, S. (2011). *La theorisation de l'évolution pénale*. Presses Universitaires D'Aix-Marseille.

Ratner, S. R., & Jason A. S. (Eds.). (2001). *Accountability for human rights atrocities in international law: Beyond the Nuremberg Legacy*. Oxford: Oxford University Press.

Rawls, J. (1999). *A theory of justice* (revised ed., p. 3). Oxford: Oxford University Press.

Rawls, J. (1971a). *A theory of justice*. Cambridge, MA: Harvard University Press.

Rawls, J. (1971b). *A theory of justice*. Oxford, London, New York: Oxford University Press.

Raz, J. (1979). *The authority of law: Essays on law and morality*. The Clarendon Press.

Raz, J. (1994). *Ethics in the public domain: Essays in the morality of law and politics* (p. 11). Oxford: Oxford University Press.

Raz, J. (1999). *Practical reason and norms*. Oxford: Oxford University Press.

Rejali, D. (2007). *Torture and democracy*. Princeton, NJ: Princeton University Press.

Richards, D. A. J. (2016). *Why love leads to justice: Love across the boundaries*. New York: Cambridge University Press.

Riesman, W. M. (2008). Learning to deal with rejection: The International Criminal Court and the United States. In M. S. Elis & R. J. Goldstone (Eds.), *The International Criminal Court: Challenges to achieving justice and accountability in the 21st century*. New York: International Debate Education Association.

Rinceanu, J. (2011a). Extraterritorial jurisdiction – The applicability of domestic criminal law to activities committed abroad in Romania. In U. Sieber, S. Forster, & K. Jarvers (Eds.), *National criminal law in a comparative legal context*. Volume 2(1): *Max-Planck-Institute für ausländisches und internationals Strafrecht* (pp. 281–296). Berlin: Duncker & Humblot.

Rinceanu, J. (2011b). Objective aspects of the offense in Romania. In U. Sieber, S. Forster, & K. Jarvers (Eds.), *National criminal law in a comparative legal context*. Volume 3(1): *Max-Planck-Institute für ausländisches und internationals Strafrecht* (pp. 227–238). Berlin: Duncker & Humblot.

Rinceanu, J. (2011c). The principle of legality (Nullum crimen sine lege) in Romania. In U. Sieber, S. Forster, & K. Jarvers (Eds.), *National criminal law in a comparative legal context*. Volume 2 (1): *Max-Planck-Institute für ausländisches und internationals Strafrecht* (pp. 89–101). Berlin: Duncker & Humblot.

Rinceanu, J. (2011d). Concept and systematization of the criminal offense in Romania. In U. Sieber, S. Forster, & K. Jarvers (Eds.), *National criminal law in a comparative legal context*.

Volume 3(1): *Max-Planck-Institute für ausländisches und internationals Strafrecht* (pp. 73–85). Berlin: Duncker & Humblot.

Rinceanu, J. (2016). *Criminal liability of legal persons in Romania in Riccardo Borsari, Responsabilità da reato deli enti* (pp. 407–418). Padova: Padova University Press.

Rinpoche, S. (2002). *The Tibetan Book of Living and Dying: A spiritual classic from one of the foremost interpreters of Tibetan Buddhism to the West*. CPI Cox and Wyman, Reading, RG1 8EX.

Roach, S. C. (2006). *Politicizing the international criminal court: The convergence of politics, ethic, and the law*. New York: Rowman & Littlefield Publishers.

Roback, M. J. (2001). *Love & economics: Why the Laissez Faire family doesn't work*.

Roberts, P. (2009). Why international criminal evidence. In P. Roberts & M. Redmayne (Eds.), *Innovations in evidence and proof*. Oxford: Hart Publishing.

Roberts, P. (2014). Theorising procedural tradition: Subjects and values in criminal adjudication. In P. Roberts (Ed.), *Theoretical foundations of criminal trial procedure* (pp. 129–156). Farnham: Ashgate.

Roberts, P., & Redmayne, M. (2009). Introduction: Teaching evidence scholarship. In P. Roberts & M. Redmayne (Eds.), *Innovations in evidence and proof*. Oxford: Hart Publishing.

Robertson, G. (2006). *Crimes against humanity: The struggle for global justice* (3rd ed.). London: Penguin.

Rollins, H. E. (Ed.). (1985). *The Letters of John Keasts, 1814–1821* (Vol. 1).

Römer, J. (Ed.). (2010). *Killing in a gray area between humanitarian law and human rights: How can the National Police of Colombia Overcome the Uncertainty of Which Branch of International Law to Apply?* Heidelberg: Springer.

Ross, A. (1946). *Towards a realistic jurisprudence: A criticism of the dualism in law*. Copenhagen: Einar Munksgaard.

Ross, A. (1952). Retsfilosofiens Problem. 7-9 Svensk Juristtidning 1952, 701–732.

Ross, A. (1958). *On law and justice*. London: Stevens & Sons Limited.

Ross, A. (1959). *On law and justice* (pp. 274–275). Berkeley and Los Angeles: University of California Press.

Ross, A. (1975). *On guilt, responsibility and punishment*. London: Stevens & Sons Limited.

Ross, W. D. (1930). *The right and the good*. Oxford: Clarendon.

Ross, W. D. (1939). *Foundations of ethics*. Oxford: Clarendon.

Rousseau, J.-J. (1761). *The social contract and discourses* (1761) (G. D. H. Cole, Trans., London & Toronto: J.M. Dent § Sons LTP § in New York, E.P Dutton & Co, 1923).

Rydenfelt, S., & Larsson, J. (1966). *Säkerhets Polisen Hemliga Register: Om Åsiktfrihet och Åsiktförföljelse*. Uddevalla: Zindermans förlag.

Samuel, K. L. H. (2013). *The OIC, the UN, and counter-terrorism law-making: Conflicting or cooperative legal orders?* Oxford: Hart.

Sankowski, E. (1978). Love and moral obligation. *The Journal of Value Inquiry, 12*(2), 100–110.

Schabas, W. A. (2002). *The abolition of the death penalty in international law* (3rd ed.). Cambridge: Cambridge University Press.

Scheffer, D. (2009). Tenth annual Grotius lecture response – For love of country and international criminal law, further reflections. *American University International Law Review, 24*(4), 665–78.

Schmid, A. P. (2014). Austria's reformed law on Islam – A model for Europe? Available at http://icct.nl/publication/austrias-reformed-law-on-islam-a-model-for-europe/?dm_i=1ADT,3FCGN,76AWD2,C9CO7,1. Accessed 1 June 2014.

Schofield, P. (2003). Jeremy Bentham's 'Nonsense upon Stilts'. *Utilitas, 15*(1), 1–26.

Schwarzenberger, G. (1950). The problem of an international criminal law. *Current Legal Problems, 3*, 263–296.

Schwarzenberger, G. (1968). *International law: As applied by international courts and tribunals, Vol. II: The law of armed conflict*. London: Stevens & Sons Limited.

Seagrave, S., & Seagrave, P. (2003). *Gold warriors: America's secret recovery of Yamashita's gold*. Verso.
Shaffer, T. L. (1997). The legal ethics of radical individualism. *Texas Law Review, 65*.
Shah-Kazemi, R. (2014). The metaphysics of oneness and sanctifying love in Islamic mysticism. In S.T. Hidden (Ed.), *Jewish, Christian, and Islamic mystical perspectives on the Love of God* (pp. 73–101). Springer.
Shay, J. (1994). *Achilles in Vietnam: Combat trauma and the undoing of character*. New York: Scribner.
Sheldon, G. (1946). *The Nuremberg trial and aggressive war*. New York: Alfred A Knopf.
Shelton, D. L. (2014). *Advanced introduction to International Human Rights Law*. USA: Edward Elgar Publishing.
Sheppard, R. (2014). *Why the U.S. Government assassinated Malcolm X and Martin Luther King, Jr*. Toronto: ReMarx Publishing
Sidney, A. (1698). *Discourses concerning government*. T. G. West (Ed.). London: MDCXCVIII. Available at http://oll.libertyfund.org/titles/sidney-discourses-concerning-government-1698-ed.
Silk, J. J. (2014, Spring). International criminal justice and the protection of human rights: The rule of law or the Hubris of law? *The Yale Journal of International Law Online, 39*, 96.
Simon, W. H. (1998). *The practice of justice: A theory of lawyers' ethics*. United States: Harvard University Press.
Skeie, J. (1937). *Den Norske Strafferett*. Oslo: Olaf Norlis Forlag.
Smith, A. (2004). *Selected philosophical writings* (edited and introduce by James R. Otteson). Exeter: Imprint Academic.
Sohm, R. (1935). *A textbook of the history and system of Roman private law* (J. C. Ledlie, Trans.). Oxford: Oxford University Press.
Souryal, S. S. (2015). *Ethics in criminal justice: In search of the truth* (6th ed.). New York: Routledge.
Spooner, L. (1882). *Natural law; or the science of justice: A treatise on natural law, natural justice, natural rights, natural liberty, and natural society; showing that all legislation whatsoever is an absurdity, a usurpation, and a crime. Part First* [1882]. Available at http://oll.libertyfund.org/titles/spooner-natural-law-or-the-science-of-justice-1882. Accessed 18 May 2015.
Starr, C. G. (1965). *A history of the ancient world*. Oxford: University Press.
Stern, R. (2012). *Understanding moral obligation: Kant, Hegel, Kierkegaard*. Cambridge: Cambridge University Press.
Stern, S. (2014). Blackston's criminal law: Common-law harmonization and legislative reform. In M. D. Dubber (Ed.), *Foundational texts in modern criminal law* (pp. 61–78). Oxford: Oxford University Press.
Sundberg, J. W. F. (2010). Human rights and traditional values. *Scandinavian Studies in Law, 55*, 125.
Sundin, J. (1992). För Gud, Staten, Folket: *Brott och Rättskipning I Sverige*. Lund.
Sunstein, C. R. (2001). *Designing democracy: What constitutions do*. Oxford: Oxford University Press.
Swanson, J. (2010). *God, science and the universe: The integration of religion and science*. Eloquent Books.
Tamanaha, B. (2001). *A general jurisprudence of law and society*. Oxford: Oxford University Press.
Tarrant, H. (2006). Platonic interpretation and eclectic theory. In H. Tarrant & D. Baltzly (Eds.), *Reading Plato in Antiquity*. London: Duckworth.
Taylor, R. (1970). *Good and evil* (p. xii). New York, NY: Macmillan.
Thornton, B. (2011). *The Book of Ancient Bastards: 101 of the Worst Miscreants and Misdeeds from the Ancient Sumer to the English Tenement*. USA: Adams Media.

Tieya, W. (1990). International law in China: Historical and contemporary perspective. In E. McWhinney (Ed.), *Judicial settlement of disputes: Jurisdiction and justifiability*. Leiden: Martinus Nijhoff.

Tomuschat, C., & Thouvenin, J.-M. (Eds.). (2006). *The fundamental rules of the international legal order: Jus Cogens and Obligations Erga Omnes*. Leiden: Brill.

Trechsel, S. (1997). Why must trials be fair. *Israel Law Review, 31*, 94–119, at 100.

Trechsel, S. (1997b). Why must trials be fair. *Israel Law Review, 31*, 94–119.

Tristram Engelhardt, H. (2010). Moral obligation after the death of god: Critical reflections on concerns from Immanuel Kant, G. W. F. Hegel and Elizabeth Anscombe. *Social Philosophy and Policy, 27*(2), 317–340.

Turner, D. (2014). The uniting wisdom of Love: The story of a late Medieval controversy. In S.T. Hidden (Ed.), *Jewish, Christian, and Islamic mystical perspectives on the Love of God* (pp. 135–153). Springer.

Vattel, M. (1844). *The law of nations or the principles of the law of nations applied to the conduct and affair of nations and sovereign* (6th American Addition, A new edition by Joseph Chitty, para. 231, p. 108). Available at http://www.loc.gov/rr/frd/Military_Law/Lieber_Collection/pdf/DeVattel_LawOfNations.pdf. Accessed 16 December 2016.

Venturi, F. (1972). *Italy and enlightenment: Studies in a cosmopolitan century*. New York: New York University Press.

Vischer, R. K. (2014). *Martin Luther King Jr. and the morality of legal practice: Lessons in love and justice*. Cambridge: Cambridge University Press.

Voegelin, E., & Franz, M. (2000). *Order and history* (Vol. 4). University of Missouri Press.

von Lockey, B. C. (2006). *Law and Empire in English Renaissance Literature*. Cambridge: Cambridge Publications.

von Pufendorf, S. (1931). *Two books of the elements of universal jurisprudence* (1660) (W. Abbott, Oldfather, Trans.).

von Rovira, M. G.-S. *The project of positivism in international law*. Oxford: Oxford University Press.

Wägenbaur, B. (2013). *Court of the European Union*. C.H.Beck. Hart. Nomos.

Walsh, M. (2006). *Criminal law*. Dublin: Thomson, Round Hall.

Walton, W. S. (2008). *The Demos at Dawn*. US: Author House.

Walzer, M. (2006). *Just and unjust wars, a moral argument with historical illustrations* (4th ed.). New York: Basic Books.

Ward, I. (2001). Universal jurisprudence and the case for legal humanism. *ALTA Law Review, 38*, 941.

Weiler, J. H. H. (1999). *The Constitution of Europe: "Do the New Clothes have an Emperor?" and other Essays on European Integration*. Cambridge; New York: Cambridge University Press.

Weiler, J. H. H., & Wind, M. (2003). *European Union law consult European constitutionalism beyond the state*. Cambridge, UK; New York, NY: Cambridge University Press.

Wendel, B. (2012). *Lawyers and fidelity to law*. Princeton, NJ: Princeton University Press.

Wettlaufer, J. (2000). The *jus primae noctis* as a male power display: A review of historic sources with evolutionary interpretation. *Evolution and Human Behaviour, 21*(2), 111–123.

White, R. M., & Willock, I. D. (2007). *The Scottish legal system* (4th ed.). Glasgow: Tottel Publishing.

Young, D. B. (1983). Cesare Beccaria: Utilitarian or Retributivist? *Journal of Criminal Justice, 11*, 317, 318.

Young, L. (2009). Being human: Love: Neuroscience reveals all. *Nature, 457*, 148.

Zahle, H. (2005). *Praktisk restfilosofi*. Christian Ejlers' Forlag.

Zak, P., Stanton, A., & Ahmadi, S. (2007). Oxytocin increases generosity in humans. *PLoS One, 2*, e1128.

Zawati, H. M. (2001). *Is Jihad a just war? War, peace, and human rights under Islamic and Public International Law*. Lewinston: The Edwin Mellen Press.

Index

F. Malekian, *Judgments of Love in Criminal Justice*,
DOI 10.1007/978-3-319-46900-3

T

Printed in the United States
By Bookmasters